DATE DUE

DEMCO 38-297

RECORDS MANAGEMENT

4ed.

Mina M. Johnson
Professor of Business Emeritus
San Francisco State University

Norman F. Kallaus
Professor of Business Administration
The University of Iowa
Iowa City, Iowa

Published by
K69 SOUTH-WESTERN PUBLISHING CO.

CINCINNATI   WEST CHICAGO, IL   DALLAS   LIVERMORE, CA

ISBN: 0-538-11690-0

Library of Congress Catalog Number: 86-61042

2 3 4 5 6 7 8 D 3 2 1 0 9 8 7

Printed in the United States of America

PREFACE

RECORDS MANAGEMENT, Fourth Edition, continues the strong tradition of serving as a basic introduction to the increasingly comprehensive field of records management. As such, the Fourth Edition emphasizes principles and practices of effective records management for all types of records systems. This approach offers practical information to students as well as to professionals at managerial, supervisory, and operative levels.

The experiences and basic philosophies of the authors are clearly presented in this latest revision. Emphasis is given to the need to understand the cycle within which information functions in the office as well as the systems that are developed for managing and using information. Even though increasing attention is also given to automation in today's offices, the authors stress the overall importance of understanding how paper records systems function before undertaking the more complex task of studying automated records systems.

As a text for students in postsecondary institutions, RECORDS MANAGEMENT, Fourth Edition, may be used for: (1) short courses or seminars emphasizing either broad views of records management or filing systems, or (2) longer courses, such as quarter or semester plans. Basic information systems concepts and new storage methods are offered within a management context built upon a framework of planning, organizing, leading, and controlling records systems, both manual and automated.

As a reference book, this latest edition of RECORDS MANAGEMENT serves several purposes. It presents sound principles of records management that include the entire range of records—paper, microrecords, and magnetic media used in automated systems. It also includes expanded coverage of management principles and practices and of job opportunities and career paths in records management. Professionals who direct the operation of records systems will find the Fourth Edition to be especially valuable since it includes new simplified filing rules plus a discussion of the latest information technology and its impact on records systems.

The text consists of five parts and 15 chapters. Part I is an introduction to the field of records management and to the broad management programs available for solving records problems. The information cycle and the systems that are created to process information are highlighted here. Part 2 centers on alphabetic storage and retrieval systems using filing rules that are in compliance with the filing rules of the Association for Records Managers and Administrators, Inc. Part 3 presents a detailed description of adaptations of the alphabetic storage and retrieval method; namely, subject, numeric, and geographic storage methods.

Part 4 covers special records storage and retrieval and includes updated material on card records systems. It also presents a thorough update of microrecords systems and the emerging technology that integrates micrographics and the computer. Chapter 14 is a completely new chapter explaining the principles of mechanized and automated records systems with emphasis on computer and word processing systems. This chapter also stresses the continuing need to understand basic records management principles before delving into the complexities of automated systems. To complete the textbook from a systems perspective, Part 5 offers a comprehensive view of the role of control in records systems. In addition, it reviews many practical procedures for controlling paperwork problems in both large and small offices.

Learning objectives are included at the beginning of each chapter in the new Fourth Edition. Important terms are printed in bold type throughout each chapter and are listed at the end of each chapter for easy review. New questions for review and discussion are provided. Decision-Making Opportunities (DMO), new tools for developing management thinking, are provided at the end of each chapter. Two new Comprehensive Cases, each of which provides broad coverage of major sections of the textbook, are included in this Fourth Edition.

The filing practice set that accompanies RECORDS MANAGEMENT, entitled RECORDS MANAGEMENT PROJECTS, Fourth Edition, is completely new. This set of practical learning materials consists of 13 manual filing jobs. Students will practice card filing and correspondence filing in alphabetic, subject, consecutive numeric, terminal digit numeric, and geographic filing systems. In addition, students will practice requisition/charge-out and transfer procedures. The learning materials in the text and the set of projects used together give practice in storage and retrieval problem solving under conditions similar to those in the office.

The testing package that accompanies RECORDS MANAGEMENT, Fourth Edition, includes a Placement Test, four Achievement Tests, and a Final Examination.

The Instructor's Manual that accompanies RECORDS MANAGEMENT, Fourth Edition, provides instructors with suggested methods of instruction, teaching aids, suggested readings, a listing of professional associations, and time schedules that apply to different teaching situations. Teaching suggestions are also provided for each chapter as well as the answers to the review and discussion questions, solutions to the DMOs, the Comprehensive Cases, and the Checking Your Knowledge of the Rules activities that appear in Chapters 5 and 6. Detailed solutions for all of the practice set jobs are also included in the Instructor's

Manual, in addition to finding tests to be used with the practice set. Answers to the Placement, Achievement, and Final tests are provided. An important new feature in the Manual for this Fourth Edition is the inclusion of 15 transparency masters. These transparency masters will provide additional teaching tools for classroom use.

The authors are grateful to many firms and individuals who assisted in completing this extensive revision of RECORDS MANAGEMENT. We appreciate the filing equipment and supply manufacturers and vendors who gave time and information to the authors in their efforts to update this edition effectively. Special thanks are given to Lois M. Garrett, Southwest Missouri State University; Carolyn E. Karnes, Macomb Community College; Lillian Lenhoff, Hillsborough Community College; Jack L. Nelson, Ferris State College; and Rita Jane Van Pevenage, Everett Community College, whose critical reviews provided helpful guidance to the authors. In addition, special appreciation is extended to our families, friends, and each other, as well as to the editorial staff of the publisher, whose encouragement and direction have been invaluable in completing this revision. The result, we believe, is an easily readable, instructive, up-to-date, and comprehensive introduction to the field of records management.

Mina M. Johnson
Norman F. Kallaus

ACKNOWLEDGEMENTS   (Chapter 4):

Color Illustration A   Jeter Systems Corporation

Color Illustration B   Photos courtesy of The Smead Manufacturing
                            Company

Color Illustration C   Photos courtesy of KARDEX Systems, Inc.

Color Illustration D   The Shaw-Walker Company

CONTENTS

1 – The Nature of Records Management

Part 1 introduces you to the field of records management and the growing career opportunities available. In this first Part, the nature and purpose of records are explored, and the development of management programs to solve records problems is discussed. A highlight of the Part is the presentation of a set of principles for managing records at all stages in the life cycle of a record.

1 AN OVERVIEW OF RECORDS MANAGEMENT

Objectives

After you have completed this chapter, you will be able to:

1. Describe the role of information in the modern organization.
2. List the steps in the information cycle.
3. Define the terms *record* and *records management*.
4. Classify records found in an office.
5. List the steps in the record cycle.
6. Identify problems involved in the use of records.
7. Summarize the main features of early and modern records management programs.
8. Discuss systems concepts used in managing a records program.
9. Describe various levels of records management positions and qualifications needed to attain a position at each level.
10. Understand the continuing role of paper records in organizations with computer facilities and equipment.

The present time is often called the Age of Information. The management of all types and sizes of organizations, including those of business, government, education, and health care, have come to realize that their success depends totally upon having the right information to make the decisions needed to manage their firms.

Generally, information is placed on records of various types; and, in turn, records are organized into complex systems. This chapter introduces important concepts of information and records management and discusses the growing opportunities for careers in this important field.

THE ROLE OF INFORMATION

The office is an information-production factory. From the earliest days to the present time, offices have taken raw material (**data**) and changed or processed it into **information**. In the earlier offices, all of this work was done by hand. Today, by contrast, an increasing amount of office work is done by machine, especially the computer. In either case, however, information is the office product that is stored on records, as discussed in this chapter.

The Information Cycle

The lives of people as well as organizations follow a set of steps that are repeated on a regular basis. When combined into a sequence, these steps are called a **cycle**. Examples are the economic cycle, the human life cycle, the production cycle in an automotive firm, or the registration-through-graduation cycle in your school. In a similar way, there is such a cycle for processing information in the office.

An **information cycle** consists of the following general steps:

1. *Collecting* the information needed for management decision making.
2. *Retaining* the information needed for future use. All other collected information is discarded.
3. *Storing* the information for later use.
4. *Retrieving* the information from storage when such information is needed.
5. *Transporting* the retrieved information to the requesting person for use.
6. *Using* the information.
7. *Returning* the information to storage. (In automated systems, this step is not required, as explained in Chapter 14.)
8. *Destroying* the information when it is no longer of any value.

Managing Information

Because information has value, it must be managed. To handle this important responsibility, a growing number of information specialists are needed. In large firms, data and word processing departments require managers to supervise computer and computer-related systems; telecommunication departments need managers to supervise the linkage of the computer and the telephone; and controlling the firm's records requires a records management specialist. In small offices, the managing of information may be centered in the office manager, the owner, or the senior person in charge.

All such managers, to be effective, must be skilled problem solvers and must be able to make decisions about business operations based on a clear understanding of not only the *costs* but the *benefits* to be realized from such decisions. In turn, such decisions must be based on reliable information.

THE NATURE AND PURPOSE OF RECORDS

As you begin a study of records management, several basic concepts need to be understood. These include definitions of key terms, classifications of records, the record cycle, and an understanding of important records problems.

The Nature of Records

A **record** is written or oral evidence of information that has been collected for use by people or machines. The most common records, such as correspondence, forms, and books, are written and appear on paper. Oral records capture the human voice and appear on cassettes and other magnetic media. Less obvious to the human eye are records that appear on film, such as movies, photographs, and microfilm. Even less obvious are the records produced by the computer, which are discussed in Chapter 14.

All resources used by the firm must be managed; and records as information resources are no exception. Thus, the term **records management** refers to the process of planning, organizing, staffing, directing, and controlling all the steps involved in the life of a record, from the time a record is created until its final destruction or permanent storage.

To manage records effectively, a clear understanding of the composition of the record is necessary. Prior to the time of computers, office managers thought of records as paper documents on which information was placed with little or no thought given to the organization of the information on the records. However, since computer systems require a far deeper study of records as they are processed and used throughout an entire firm, computer specialists studied the basic nature of all records, looking for features common to all of them. From their studies, a set of basic characteristics found in all records has been identified.

All records are composed of fundamental units that are organized into a structure called a *hierarchy*. Figure 1-1 (beginning at the bottom and continuing to the top) shows the place of a record in the information hierarchy. The most basic unit is the *character*, the alphabetic, numeric, and related symbols ($, %, and #, for example) used in business communications. The combination of characters into words or numbers results in a higher level of the hierarchy called the *field*. In the human resource department, for example, the name of an employee would be entered into a name field on the form, a field that is made up of many characters.

A group of related fields constitutes a **record**. (Note that this definition in the hierarchy does not contradict the more general definition given earlier in this section but rather describes an additional characteristic of a record—its place in the total organization or structure of information.) Thus, the name field, the address field, the sex of employee field, and the date of employment field on one form are defined as a record. And a collection of related records, in turn, is called a **file**. All of the human resource employment forms relating to one employee could be grouped together in one folder and the contents of that folder would represent the file. A collection of files—the highest level in the hierarchy—is known as the **library** (or **database** in automated systems, or in everyday language in the office, the *files*). This last category is usually

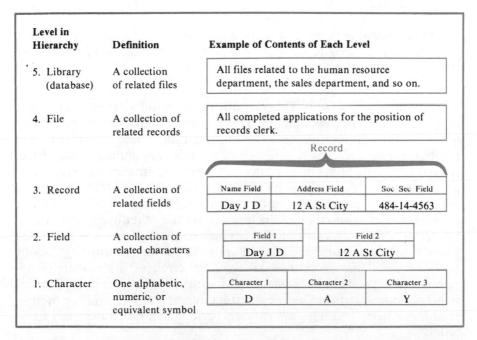

FIGURE 1-1 — The Role of a Record in the Information Hierarchy

what is found in the contents of file cabinets or in an equivalent form in automated systems.

Purposes of Records

Records serve as the "memory" of a business. They "remember" the information needed for operating the firm from day to day, month to month, and year to year. For example, policies are developed and recorded in order to furnish broad guidelines for operation. Each department (finance, marketing, accounting, and human resources) bases its entire mode of operations upon records. In addition, records have widespread legal value and must be retained as specified by law. Tax records are a prominent example of this type of record. Many records, too, have historical value which increases with the passage of time. Original copies of the Declaration of Independence and the Gettysburg Address are well-known examples, as is the original drawing of Ford's first Model T automobile.

Classification of Records

Records can be classified in two basic ways: (1) according to their *use*; and (2) according to the principal *place or destination of use*. These two classifications are discussed in this section.

Classification by Use.   This classification includes transaction documents and reference documents. **Transaction documents** are paper records of day-to-day operations of an organization. These documents, the most common and largest category of records maintained in an office, consist primarily of business forms. Examples are invoices, requisitions, purchase and sales orders, bank checks, statements, contracts, shipping documents, and personnel records such as employment applications and attendance reports. **Reference documents**, on the other hand, contain information needed to carry on the operations of the firm over extended periods of time. Such records are referenced for information about previous decisions, quotations on items to purchase, statements of administrative policy, and plans for running the organization. Typical reference documents are business letters, reports, and interoffice memorandums. Other examples are catalogs, price lists, brochures, and pamphlets.

Classification by Destination.   This classification is divided into external and internal records. An **external record** is created for use outside the firm. Examples of such records are letters sent to a customer or client, to an organization's suppliers, or to the various branches of the government. The largest group of records classified by their destination is that of internal records. An **internal record** contains information needed to operate the organization and may be created inside or outside the organization. Examples are communications between the organization and its employees (payroll records, bulletins, and government regulations) and communications among an organization's departments (inventory control records, interoffice memorandums, purchase requisitions, and reports). Critically important internal records are maintained by the accounting department regarding the presence and use of assets and debts owed and local, state, and federal taxing information.

The Record Cycle

The life span of a record from creation to final disposition (or from "birth" to "death") is called the **record cycle**, as shown in Figure 1-2. All types of records follow these steps.

A brief explanation of the terms used in Figure 1-2 should be of help at this point in understanding the record cycle. Whenever a letter is typed,

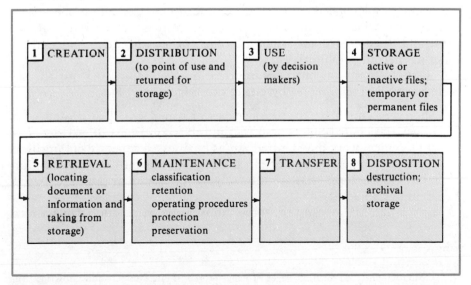

FIGURE 1-2 — The Record Cycle

a form filled out, a cassette tape dictated, or a pamphlet printed, a record is *created*. This record is then *distributed* to the person responsible for its use. Then, when a decision is made to keep the record for use at a later date, the record must be *stored* (filed). After it is stored, a request is made to *retrieve* (find and remove) the record from storage for use. During the record cycle, a series of *maintenance* or service steps is required for preparing materials and placing and preserving them in storage, for updating stored information, and for purging or throwing away obsolete records that are no longer useful or that have been replaced by more current ones.

After a predetermined period of time has elapsed, records to be kept are *transferred* to less expensive storage sites within the organization or to an external storage center. At the end of a stated number of years, the record is *disposed of*, either by destruction or by being put into a final storage place, the **archives**, to be kept permanently.

The record cycle is an important concept and must be understood, for it serves as a basis for the management programs that control an organization's records.

Records Problems

Without an overall program to control all phases of the record cycle, serious problems, such as those outlined in Figure 1-3, may occur. Solving these problems becomes critical to the smooth, effective operations of any firm when information vital to the firm is not available at the time and place needed and when the costs of operating such information systems become prohibitive.

One authority on business information systems points out the severe nature of the problem by citing these facts:

1. There are currently 21 trillion pages of paper stored in file drawers across the United States, and this number continues to grow.
2. On a typical work day, United States businesses generate 600 million pages of computer output, 235 million photocopies, and 76 million letters, documents that are multiplying at an annual rate of between 20 and 22 percent.
3. At this rate the amount of stored information could double every four years.[1]

---

[1]"Micrographics: 21 Trillion Pages of Paper Stored in File Drawers and Growing," *Infosystems* (April, 1984), p. 13.

Problem	Symptoms of Problem	For Discussion, See
1. Lack of policy	• No overall program for managing records	Chapters 1, 2
	• Failure to consider the need for automating the records function	Chapter 14
2. Human difficulties	• Lack of management concern about the importance of records	Chapters 1, 2
	• Hoarding of records	Chapter 2
	• Lack of training in records management operations	Chapters 1, 2
	• Assuming that people know how to operate the files	Chapter 2
3. Poor filing systems and procedures	• Overloaded and poorly labeled drawers and folders	Chapter 4
	• Failure to protect records	Chapter 2
	• Misfiles resulting in lost records or slow retrieval	Chapters 4, 7
4. Lack of control	• Records taken from and put into files without proper authorization	Chapters 4, 7
	• No standards for evaluating workers	Chapter 15
	• Little attention given to costs	Chapters 3, 15
5. Poor use of equipment	• No equipment standards	Chapter 15
	• No use of fire-resistant equipment	Chapters 2, 13, 14
	• Wrong type of cabinets for records being stored	Chapter 3
	• Inadequate use of automated systems	Chapter 14
6. Inefficient use of space	• Crowded working conditions	Chapter 2
	• Poor layout of records storage area	Chapter 2
	• Inadequate use, or absence, of microfilmed records	Chapter 13
7. No plans for records retention and disposition	• Too many duplicate records	Chapters 2, 15
	• No plan for what records are to be kept for what time periods	Chapter 2
	• No permanent records storage plan	Chapter 2

FIGURE 1-3 — Principal Records Problems

The records management programs discussed in the next section have been developed to ensure that solutions will be found for these serious problems; or better still, that such problems will not occur in the first place.

THE DEVELOPMENT OF RECORDS MANAGEMENT PROGRAMS

Carvings on the walls of caves tell us much about the lives of prehistoric peoples and how they conducted their business affairs. In our own age, computerized records provide similar information about our population and the way our organizations operate. During this long period, attitudes toward records have changed as this section briefly shows.

Early Records Management

Most of the business records of early days were based upon primitive transactions and provided evidence of moneys received and spent, lists of articles bought and sold, and simple contracts. Such records were created by hand until the printing press and the typewriter were invented, machines that increased the speed by which records could be made.

Until the 1950s, when computers were first used in business, records were almost exclusively paper documents. The most important emphasis during this stage in history was getting the records properly placed in the files so that they could be quickly found when requested.

Historically, management has directed its attention toward the factory or plant. Usually the plant work force was large compared to the office staff, and it was believed that the factory, rather than the office, produced the tangible products from which profits came and expenses were generated.

In such an environment, management placed less importance on office functions and, therefore, assumed that records were the sole responsibility of the clerical staff. This narrow, limited view of the records function resulted in the attitude that "records are necessary evils," and that the office cannot get along without them. Accordingly, few workers considered records maintenance activities important and few really liked to process records. The broad view—*that all aspects of records are important and must be carefully managed because they contain valuable information*—was not widely held. Thus, little importance or status was granted to the records function in early business organizations.

Modern Records Management

World War II caused many changes in society and in the economies of the world. A highly productive industrial system operating under an increase in government regulations required huge numbers of records. The federal government recognized the need for controlling the volume of records created in the war period and in the post-war environment. Thus, in 1946, acting under the powers granted by the Lodge-Brown Act, President Truman appointed the first Hoover Commission to study the policies and needs of broad areas of government. The Commission's work was responsible for establishing the General Services Administration (GSA) to improve practices and controls in records management, as provided by the Federal Property and Administrative Services Act of 1949. Another law, the Federal Records Act of 1950, provided guidelines for improving the procedures for creating records under the supervision of the GSA.

A second Hoover Commission was appointed under the provisions of the Brown-Ferguson Act of 1953. This Commission appointed a task force to study government records and found that many reports required of business and industry were already available in other government agencies. Also, great numbers of records were submitted to government by industry but never used.

The second Hoover Commission concluded that there was a critical, continuing need for the management of governmental records. Thus, a government-wide records management program was implemented under the direction of the General Services Administration. Under this program, each government agency appointed its own official who was made responsible for reducing the volume of paperwork in that agency.

This pioneer work by the federal government in records management studies was widely acknowledged and provided the example needed by business and industry as well as by state and municipal governments. In each of these organizations, programs similar to those created at the federal level were developed for the purpose of studying the nature and application of records and for setting up programs that would cover all phases of the record cycle.

Systems Concepts in Records Management

As a direct result of using computers, records managers and other information specialists now have a much broader view of the organization and how its parts work together. Early in the history of computer usage, it became clear that the computer's awesome potential for processing, storing, retrieving, and distributing information could be applied to all functions in an organization, and not just to payroll and billing operations, the first application areas. Top-level managers who formerly fixed their attention on one or two divisions of their firms soon saw that the computer had potential for use in the total organization. The term "seeing the whole picture" stems from this expanded view of company-wide operations made possible by the computer. A new way of thinking about problem solving, often called the **systems approach**, was born. Fundamental systems concepts as tools of the problem solver who uses this approach are summarized in this section.[2]

Figure 1-4 defines several basic systems concepts that are highly important for the study of records management, since records managers use all of the systems elements to provide records services. First, all systems must organize the **elements** (sometimes called economic resources) necessary to perform the required work. These elements are discussed in detail in Chapter 2. In each department where records are produced, **inputs**, **processes**, **outputs**, **feedback**, and **controls** are used in their production. These terms refer to phases or stages (from start to finish) in the operations of the **system** with the input phase usually considered as starting the systems cycle. All of these elements and phases in the system operate within a changing **environment** that determines the rules by which the system functions. Thus, it is appropriate to consider the records area in the modern organization as the **records system**.

By studying each of the concepts in Figure 1-4, you can analyze, from a systems point of view, the steps that are required to create by hand a new record, such as a bank check:

1. The *output* or goal is a completely legible, accurate check recorded on the proper check form. (This step is listed first, for if you understand the goal, the remaining phases in the system's operations will have more meaning.)
2. The *input* necessary to produce such output requires:
   a. Complete, accurate data on payee name, amount, date check is written, and reason for writing.
   b. An acceptable blank check form.
   c. The human skill (labor) necessary to fill out the check form.
   d. The pen, typewriter, or printer necessary to fill out the form.
   e. An approved signature.

---

[2]For more thorough coverage of systems, consult Norman F. Kallaus and B. Lewis Keeling, *Administrative Office Management*, 9th ed. (Cincinnati: South-Western Publishing Co., 1987), Chapters 20 and 21.

Systems Concepts	Definitions	Examples
System	A set of related elements that are combined to achieve a planned objective or goal.	Educational system, economic system, data processing system, human system.
Elements	Systems resources (people, space, equipment, forms and related records, and data to be processed) that work together to achieve the system's goal.	Typewriters, clerks, office space, sales order forms, and data obtained from surveys.
Systems phases:	Sequential steps by which a system achieves its goal.	
1. Input	Data, energy (from labor and other sources), space, and money that are brought into a system to be used to achieve the system's goals.	Employees, machines, procedures, customer orders.
2. Process	Human and machine methods for changing the inputs into the desired product or service (the output).	Sorting, calculating, thinking, summarizing, and typing activities.
3. Output	The goal of the system that results when raw material or data are changed into a finished product.	A business letter, a report, a retail sale, a satisfied employee.
4. Feedback	That phase of the system in which the output of the system is compared against the expected standards. From the feedback, corrections in the system are made.	Reports on sales for the last year, on employee attitudes toward a new policy, on customer satisfaction with a new product.
5. Control	That function of the system that regulates the behavior of all other phases of the system in line with the desired outcomes.	Policies, plans, procedures, programs, and standards of performance and human behavior.
6. Environment	The conditions surrounding the system that influence the system's operations.	Laws, government regulations, ethics, the economy, and other systems in the firm.

FIGURE 1-4 — Basic Systems Concepts

3. The *process(es)* required include:
    a. Selecting the necessary data to enter on the form.
    b. Performing the actual physical steps of filling out the form.
4. The *feedback* step results in proofreading to be sure the check is properly filled out. It includes comparing the amount written on the check with the amount that should have been written. If there is an error, a new check must be written.
5. The *control* step refers to having the correct type of check form, ensuring accurate input data, making sure that handwriting is legible in the processing stage, and so on.
6. The *environment* within which this system operates includes the rules of the banking system for writing checks; similar rules of the legal system; the procedures for dispensing funds within the business; the attitudes and morale of the firm's employees; and the like.

The systems approach to problem solving considers each of these phases of a system as interdependent, and all the elements of the system discussed earlier are also interrelated and thus interdependent. The operation of a system thus depends on the proper "meshing" of all these factors. Consequently, actually solving the problems that arise in finding records when workers are to be assigned to tasks in the human resources department, or when writing a computer program makes it necessary for the records manager to consider all of these phases and elements and how well they work together to achieve the final result.

The entire records management program may, under these circumstances, be considered as the total records system and is composed of all the *interrelated* elements mentioned in Figure 1-4. Further, each of the individual phases in such a program (or the steps in the record cycle) has its own inputs, processes, outputs, feedback, and controls as well as an operating environment. Thus, each is considered to be a system. For this reason, this text makes repeated use of these concepts in discussing the phases of the records program, such as storage systems, retrieval systems, micrographic systems, and automated (computer) systems. The more you understand such basic systems concepts, the better you will be able to know and solve records management problems.

Trends in Records Management

Various forms of information technology continue to make inroads in business and industry. Microfilm use is increasing in offices throughout the world; and computers are being used increasingly in all settings including the home, office, and factory. From the constant barrage of publicity about the so-called "computer takeover," however, it could be inferred that paper records—along with file cabinets, folders, and other aspects of traditional records systems and procedures—are obsolete. This "takeover," however, is far more fiction than fact.

What is true, on the other hand, is that noncomputer records (largely paper records) are increasing at an enormous rate. A recent study by Frost and Sullivan, a New York-based market research firm, shows that the use of office filing equipment to house paper and computer-paper records will rise by 51 percent with the use of micrographics equipment which is expected to jump by 65 percent in the next few years.[3] These figures project a continuing growth in the volume of paper records.

The computer at this point is not capable of automating all typing, sorting, storing, and retrieving functions. In fact, it is estimated that nearly two-thirds of all business information used in the nation's offices cannot be read by the computer. This type of information is handwritten on typed forms, or on microfilm; it remains on desks, in storage cabinets, and behind vault doors.[4]

For these reasons, the paper record system is the place to begin a study of records management. The tangible nature of such records, the fact that paper records are familiar to every student of records management, and that such records can be easily located make the study of paper records the logical introduction to the records management field.

CAREER OPPORTUNITIES IN RECORDS MANAGEMENT

Opportunities to work with records exist in every type and size of office. In the smallest office with one secretary and an owner/manager, working with records occupies much of the time of both people. In this setting, opportunities for records work are unlimited. The classified ads section of all daily newspapers regularly lists many positions of this type. In larger offices where more specialization of staff is found, firms often employ records supervisors who direct the work of several records clerks. And in major corporations or other large administrative headquarters, such as the City Hall in major cities, there are three levels of persons working with records.

---

[3]"Memo: Still in the Files," *Office Administration and Automation* (New York, July, 1983), p. 22.

[4]"Blend of Technologies Seen as Key to Automating 'Office of Tomorrow,'" *The Secretary* (Kansas City: August/September, 1983), p. 18.

At the top or *managerial level* is the records manager who is responsible for directing the entire program. Forms managers and reports managers are sometimes included also. Reporting to the records manager are several specialists at the *supervisory level* who are responsible for all forms and records systems including records retention, records storage, and micrographics. At the *operating level* are (1) technicians who analyze forms and records and (2) forms and records clerks and other types of technicians who deal with computer records. With the passage of time, all information service areas including records management and computer systems are slowly combining their operations under a Vice-President of Information Services. This new type of administrator is, therefore, responsible for manual as well as automated records systems and for developing newer types of positions and position titles as needed.[5]

General Records Management Opportunities

Figure 1-5 outlines the positions most commonly found in large records departments. In addition, it indicates key duties typically assigned to each position and qualifications required for attaining that position. The path leading up the career ladder to records manager is also shown. As a rule, both a college degree and considerable work experience in records systems are required for the top position; however, highly motivated persons often move up through the "experience" ranks to such a position without the degree. Positions at the supervisory level usually require some college training; and at the operating level, a high school education should be considered essential. A more detailed description of the various positions needed to staff a records management program is provided in Chapter 2.

Information on this rapidly growing profession is regularly published by the various professional associations specializing in administrative systems. For example, the Association of Records Managers and Administrators, Inc. (ARMA) is the most important professional group interested in improving educational programs in schools and industry and on-the-job knowledge in records management. Through ARMA's leadership, the Institute of Certified Records Managers (ICRM) was founded in 1975 to provide educational programs designed to certify the qualifications of capable persons for managerial work in records man-

---

[5]For more information on job description guidelines, see *ARMA Standards Program—Job Description Guidelines*, published by the Association of Records Managers and Administrators, Inc., 4200 Somerset, Suite 215, Prairie Village, KS 66208.

Job Level	Typical Job Titles	Key Duties	Qualifications	Career Path
Managerial	Records Manager	Develops and implements all records management policies and practices	Education Required: Bachelor's Degree or extensive education in business adminis-tration, MBA preferred Experience Required: 3-5 years as supervisor in records management program	Promotion to Manager of Administrative Services or Vice President, Information Services
Supervisory	Records Center Supervisor	Operates records center; selects, trains, and evaluates center staff; advises departments on records protection, storage, and disposal	Education Required: 2 years college in business or office education Experience Required: 3-5 years in Records Center operations	Promotion to Records Manager
	Forms Supervisor; Reports Supervisor	Plans and implements forms, directs reports control program; assists all departments with design, use, and procurement of forms/reports	Education Required: 2 years college Experience Required: 5 years as forms analyst	Promotion to Records Manager
	Micrographics Services Supervisor	Operates micrographics machines; develops micrographic applications; trains micrographics technicians	Education Required: high school and added training in micrographics Experience Required: 3 years as micrographics technician	Promotion to Records Center Supervisor

FIGURE 1-5 — Typical Job Levels, Titles, and Career Paths in Records Management (Continued on pg. 18)

agement. To be certified, a candidate must have a minimum of three years of full-time documented professional experience in three or more categories of records management and a baccalaureate degree from an accredited institution. (Work experience can be substituted for education at the discretion of the ICRM Board.) In addition, the candidate must pass the Certified Records Manager (CRM) examination that is comprised of the following parts: management principles and the records management program; records creation and use; records systems, storage, and retrieval; records appraisal, retention, protection, and disposition; equipment, supplies, and technology; and case studies. By meeting

Job Level	Typical Job Titles	Key Duties	Qualifications	Career Path
Operating	Forms Analyst	Analyzes forms requirements; designs and revises existing forms; maintains records to control all company forms	Education Required: 2 years college Experience Required: 5 years in records and general office work	Promotion to Forms Supervisor
	Records Analyst	Analyzes records and works with departments to solve records problems	Education Required: 2 years college Experience Required: 5 years in records and general office work	Promotion to Records Center Supervisor
	Micrographics Technician	Operates various types of cameras and microfilm preparation equipment	Education Required: high school plus technical training in microfilming Experience Required: Records experience helpful but not necessary	Promotion to Micrographics Services Supervisor
	Records Center Clerk or Records Clerk	Assists in reference, retrieving, and disposal of records; assists with vital records; searches, sorts, and stores records	Education Required: high school with some training in office procedures Experience Required: previous records experience desirable; speed and accuracy required	Promotion to Records Center Supervisor

FIGURE 1-5 — Continued from pg. 17

these educational, experience, and test requirements, the candidate is given the designation Certified Records Manager, which indicates a high degree of professional competence in records management.

Information on career opportunities can be regularly found in ARMA's publication, the *ARMA Records Management Quarterly*, in the *Dictionary of Occupational Titles*, and in the *Occupational Outlook Handbook*. Other professional associations, such as the Administrative Management Society (AMS), the Association of Information and Image Management (AIIM), and the American Medical Records Association (AMRA), publish valuable periodicals that contain information about career trends in records management. Copies of such publications are commonly found in college, university, and city libraries.

Specialized Records Management Opportunities

The preceding discussion of records management careers applies generally to positions in business, industry, and government. In addition to these areas of employment, there are other highly specialized fields offering extensive opportunities for careers in records management. Two of the most important are highlighted here.

Large law firms employ records personnel at the three levels (managerial, supervisory, and operating) to manage records. All three levels require an understanding of general records management principles and practices. Further, such staff members must have specialized knowledge of how attorneys think and work and of the unique characteristics of storing legal records.

The medical and health care field also makes extensive use of records which must be carefully managed. Basic patient charts are used not only for histories, diagnoses, treatment, and research, but also as information needed for bill collection purposes. Other typical records include discharge summaries, operative and pathology reports, X-ray information, and correspondence. To promote a high degree of competence in the medical records profession, the American Medical Records Association sponsors two certification programs. Upon completion of specialized courses or AMRA's correspondence study and a qualifying examination, the individual becomes an Accredited Record Technician (ART). Students with management of medical records as a goal may consider completing a medical records administrator (MRA) degree, a four-year baccalaureate program available at a small number of colleges.

A person passing AMRA's accrediting examination at this level is designated a Registered Records Administrator (RRA).[6]

IMPORTANT TERMS AND CONCEPTS

archives	data
controls	database
cycle	elements

---

[6]Information on educational programs, certification examinations, and career opportunities in medical records management is available from the American Medical Records Association, 875 North Michigan Avenue, Suite 1850, Chicago, IL 60611. Similar information on careers in the library records field can be obtained from the American Library Association, 50 East Huron Street, Chicago, IL 60611.

environment
external record
feedback
file
information
information cycle
inputs
internal record
library
outputs

processes
record
record cycle
records management
records system
reference documents
system
systems approach
transaction documents

REVIEW AND DISCUSSION

1. List ten examples of the main uses of information in organizations in your community, such as your school or the business in which you are employed. How critical is this information to the life of the firm? (Obj. 1)

2. Identify the steps in the information cycle. Which of these steps did you follow in getting information about, and in registering for, the course you are now taking? (Obj. 2)

3. Is filing a simpler, more down-to-earth term for records management? Explain. Is a record a file? Explain. Discuss the relationship between these two questions. (Obj. 3)

4. What are the main classifications for records? What types of records are commonly found in each classification? (Obj. 4)

5. List the steps in the record cycle. In what ways do these steps differ from the steps found in the information cycle? (Obj. 5)

6. Which type of record problem discussed in this chapter is probably the most difficult to solve? Why? (Obj. 6)

7. Identify at least three differences between early and modern records management. (Obj. 7)

8. What is a system? Can your definition be used to describe people and business firms as well as records? Explain. (Obj. 8)

9. Identify various levels of positions found in records management programs. What qualifications are required for each? What professional help is available to assist persons in meeting these qualifications? (Obj. 9)

10. Why, with increasing use of automation and computers, is the paper record so commonly created, used, and stored in offices? (Obj. 10)

DECISION-MAKING OPPORTUNITIES (DMO)

DMO 1-1: Developing Systems Thinking

To understand the records management field and to solve problems in this course, you need to develop skills for using the systems approach. At this time you are asked to think about your records management class as a systems analyst would; and in so doing, you will develop the systems approach to problem solving. Begin this development process by making some decisions about the following questions; then compile a brief report, as instructed, in which you answer each of these questions. (Obj. 8)

1. From a systems point of view (that is, using systems language), what is your class called?
2. What are the systems elements of your class?
3. How do the viewpoints of your instructor compare with the viewpoints of the students regarding the nature of your class system?
4. Identify each of the phases of your class system. What are the inputs, processes, outputs, feedback, and control? What is the nature of the environment in which your class system operates? Why are these phases important for you to know?

DMO 1-2: Investigating Career Opportunities in Records Management

From your full-time summer jobs or part-time jobs during the school term in various offices over the past three years, you have developed an interest in office work. And from television and newspaper ads you notice a growing opportunity for careers in automated offices. Most recently your new course in records management has provided information on this specialized field. The result of all this information is a gradually increasing serious interest in investigating career opportunities in records management. But the problem facing you is: *how to go about it?*

Using the systems knowledge developed during your introduction to this course, investigate reliable sources of information for solving your problem, which involves finding answers to the following questions:

1. What information would a beginning records management student need to know about this field? How will you evaluate the reliability of such information?
2. Where can such information be obtained?
3. How much will such information cost?
4. What other basic questions should be asked?

Based on your research, carefully outline a plan to educate yourself about the career opportunities in records management. Share this information with other members of your class as directed by your instructor. (Obj. 9)

2 ESTABLISHING A RECORDS MANAGEMENT PROGRAM

Objectives

After you have completed this chapter, you will be able to:

1. Explain the main causes of paperwork problems in offices.
2. Compare the work simplification approach to problem solving with the input-output approach to problem solving.
3. Identify significant government legislation that directly relates to records.
4. List the basic management principles to be applied in establishing a records management program.
5. Classify the principal staff levels in the records management program and the typical positions found at each level.
6. Describe the typical responsibilities involved in directing the records management program.
7. Outline the objectives that must be achieved in order to have an effective records management program.
8. Cite the most important requirements for managing each of the phases in the record cycle, from creation through disposition.
9. Explain the main advantages and disadvantages of an in-house records center and a commercial offsite records center.
10. Discuss the principal methods used to manage records in the small office.

The vital need for information stored on records has captured the attention of top executives and has resulted in establishing many company-wide programs to administer all phases of the records cycle. The records function is thus elevated to management status, which contrasts sharply with the clerical-support idea of efficient records filing that prevailed earlier.

This chapter identifies basic management principles upon which records management programs are built. In addition, it discusses, from

the management point of view, the steps followed in establishing a records management program. Attention is given to both large and small
size offices.

PAPERWORK: THE ROOT OF RECORDS PROBLEMS

Organized human activity relies almost completely on records. If
you consider the medical, legal, religious, educational, governmental, and
financial requirements of the typical citizen/employee, you will rapidly
see the role played by records. Most records at the present time either
exist on paper in manual systems or are ultimately printed out as **hard
copy** (e.g., in paper form) by computer systems. The end result remains
the same: an increasing burden of paperwork that must be managed in
order that it can serve the organization properly.

Causes of Paperwork Problems

The growth of paperwork has many causes, all related to the lack
of proper management. A leading cause of additional paperwork is the
convenient methods available for making copies of records which allow
office personnel to produce unnecessary numbers of records on such machines as the copier and the computer (with unlimited capability for
printing forms and reports). Another reason for paperwork growth is the
attitude of many managers who are often uncertain about the future information needs of their firms. They demand more records "just in case
they are needed," without paying enough attention to the cost of records
creation, use, and storage.

Today the public makes greater use of services provided by automation. More extensive buying on credit, increased use of banking and
medical facilities, and the growing availability and acceptance of communication systems have brought about a tremendous growth of service
industries—all heavy users of records. At the same time, state and federal laws require the creation and retention of more records. A garage
mechanic operating a small business spends approximately 270 hours
each year filling out 548 government-required forms, costing several
thousand dollars in time alone. Large firms, such as major oil companies,
must file over 400 reports to 47 federal agencies and an equal number
of additional reports to 228 state offices on an annual basis. These requirements result in a fast-growing type of administration in which the

records can get out of control unless someone is assigned to manage them properly.

Solving Paperwork Problems

By reviewing Figure 1-4 (page 13) on basic systems concepts, you can see that output represents the end result of any system. Whenever the *actual output* of the system is less than the *desired output*, a problem exists. For example, a problem exists when a salesperson does not meet the quota of selling five suits each half day; or when a word processing specialist does not meet the average expected production rate of four two-page letters each hour; or an employment interviewer completes only three interviews each half hour, rather than the required five. In each case a problem arises that is detected at the feedback stage of the system: the amount of work completed (the output) is less than the amount desired. Some controls in the system have failed.

Paperwork problems can be explained in the same way. However, the causes of these problems are not so easily determined. Some causes stem from the poor attitudes of managers toward the need for controlling records. Often work is distributed unequally. Lack of attention to basic management techniques can also result in problems, whether it be poor space usage, inefficient procedures, or poor time management. While the overall problem-solving process involves points too complex and lengthy to be discussed in this textbook, two problem-solving methods are briefly described—both useful at all levels in the records management program.

Work Simplification Approach to Problem Solving.   The effective manager uses common sense, intuition, and good judgment to solve problems. The logical combination of these traits when applied to solving problems is called the **work simplification approach** to problem solving. To use this approach, the effective records manager gathers information by asking the following questions:

1. WHAT is the real problem, and what resources (human, information, equipment, space, etc.) cause or contribute to the problem?
2. WHERE did the problem occur, and why did it occur there?
3. WHEN did the problem occur, and why did it occur at that time?
4. HOW did the problem occur, and why did it occur in that way?
5. WHO is involved with, or responsible for, the problem, and why?

By asking these basic questions, the records manager can gather information about *any* paperwork problem. Such information is then analyzed and used to develop a workable solution to the problem.

The Input-Output Approach to Problem Solving.   Because of the widespread use of the systems approach to problem solving, records managers examine each of the elements in the system as well as each of the systems phases (starting with input and continuing through output) in an attempt to solve information-related problems (See Figure 1-4). The term **input-output approach** has been coined to explain this method of problem solving.

Briefly, this approach involves viewing a problem, such as slow retrieval of records, in systems terms. In so doing, the problem solver gathers information by asking a set of questions related to each of the phases in the system. Examples of records retrieval questions related to each phase in the system are as follows:

1. Input

What employees work with the records?

What equipment is used to retrieve records?

How much time is expected for satisfactory retrieval?

2. Process

How does the records clerk use the filing system to retrieve records?

How specific is the request for the desired record?

Is the system computerized or are operations performed by hand?

3. Output

How often are records found (or not found) as requested?

4. Feedback

What standards are used to evaluate records retrieval?

How is the standards information used to evaluate the retrieval operations?

5. Controls

What manuals of operation, time limitations, written procedures, and rules for storing and retrieving records are available?

Are they consistently used?

6. Environment

What is the overall working atmosphere within which the people in the records department work?

Is there a democratic climate so that reasonable freedom is provided the workers?

By examining the essentials of both problem-solving approaches, you will note that each has the same purpose—that is, to collect the most complete information possible for solving the problem. Both methods can be useful for solving any of the problems discussed in this book.

Government Legislation of Records

In addition to the early legislation on records discussed in Chapter 1, a number of significant laws have since been passed that deal with modern records problems. Here is a list of the federal legislation on records that has had the most impact on business organizations:

1. **Freedom of Information Act of 1966 with Amendments:** This act gave citizens the right of access to information collected and maintained by government agencies. The amendments were designed to expedite the administration of the act, especially the handling of requests for information.
2. **Family Educational Rights and Privacy Act of 1974** (better known as the Buckley Amendment): This act permitted individuals access to personal information collected and maintained by federal agencies for nonroutine uses. The act also provided a series of safeguards to prevent the misuse of personal information by the federal agencies. The act also gave individuals the right to access information about themselves, the right to exclude others from gaining access to their personal information without consent, and the right to know who has had access to their records. In 1977 the provisions of the Privacy Act were extended from Federal agencies to the private sector.
3. **Federal Records Management Amendments of 1976** that updated the Federal Records Act of 1950: The amendments defined records management to include the entire record life cycle and established a new program aimed at reducing paperwork in federal agencies.
4. **Paperwork Reduction Act of 1980:** This act called for federal agencies to consider information as an organizational resource to be managed and included in their budgets. Also, the act sought to minimize the federal paperwork burden on individuals, small businesses, and state and local governments.

Today records are used as a substitute for face-to-face contact and include information of a personal nature about credit ratings, insurance, medical care, employment, education, and social services. To create records for these areas requires individuals to divulge information about themselves to various organizations. When such information is required, individuals have little choice but to submit to an organization's demands.

In addition to the personal privacy problem, other regulatory decisions have been made regarding records. For example, under the direction of the Association of Records Managers and Administrators, Inc. (ARMA), a nationwide campaign was waged to eliminate the use of legal-size files (that is, those files using 8 1/2 by 14-inch paper and correspondingly larger file cabinets). This effort was labeled **Project ELF** (Eliminate Legal-Size Files) and resulted in the adoption of the standard letter-size paper rather than the longer legal size by the Judicial Conference of the United States. By such action, this paper standard is now recommended for use by the legal profession as well as for thousands of other offices that traditionally used both the regular letter-size and legal-size papers. This development should help to standardize paper size and filing equipment and thus result in many cost savings to records management programs.

BASIC PRINCIPLES OF MANAGING RECORDS

The person heading a records program must apply sound business management principles, which involve the responsibility for supervising these five managerial functions: (1) careful planning, (2) proper organization of all resources necessary for following the approved plan, (3) thoughtful selection and maintenance of an effective staff, (4) efficient direction of operating procedures in well-designed office space, and (5) sound control of the program's operations.

Planning a Records Management Program

Planning is the basic managerial function for determining a course of action—*the plan*—that will enable the program to meet its stated goals. The result of such planning is a set of objectives or "blueprints" for achieving the goals. Examples of records management objectives may be found in Figure 2-1.

The objectives set the stage for putting the other management functions into motion; and in turn, the objectives, both short- and long-term, serve as yardsticks against which the day-to-day operations of the program may be checked.

The objectives of the records management program at the XYZ Company are to:

1. Provide accurate, timely information whenever and wherever it is needed.
2. Provide information at the lowest possible cost.
3. Provide the most efficient records systems, including space, equipment, and procedures for creating, storing, retrieving, retaining, transferring, and disposing of records.
4. Protect information by designing and implementing effective measures for records control.
5. Determine methods for evaluating all phases of the records management program.
6. Train company personnel in the most effective methods of controlling and using records.

FIGURE 2-1 — Objectives of a Records Management Program

Organizing a Records Management Program

Organizing refers to the process of bringing together all economic resources (the tasks to be performed, the workplace, the information, and the staff) to form a workable unit so as to achieve the objectives mentioned earlier. To achieve such objectives—whether the office is large or small—the following basic organizational principles must be applied:

1. Lines of authority and responsibility are made clear so that all employees understand to whom they are accountable and who is accountable to them.
2. No member of the organization reports to more than one supervisor.
3. Work is fairly distributed among the workers in keeping with the goals of the records management department and worker qualifications and interests.
4. Personnel who are assigned the responsibility for tasks are given sufficient authority to perform those tasks.
5. The number of persons reporting to a supervisor or manager is small enough to permit good coordination. (This is called the **span of control**.)
6. Good managers develop and control policy problems of special importance rather than give constant attention to routine actions within their group. (This is known as **management by exception**.)

7. Policies and operating procedures of the unit (department) are written and distributed to the entire staff. (In a records management program, such material appears in the records manual.)

8. Adequate orientation to their job and training to do assigned work
is provided for all levels of personnel.

9. Work areas provide for efficient movement, comfort of personnel,
and convenience to workers and customers alike. In the records program this involves efficient layout of storage containers, proper
equipment and supplies, good lighting and noise control, good traffic
flow, and a clean and attractive work area.

10. Periodic follow-up studies are made to evaluate the effectiveness of
a department, to take steps to correct problems, and to make plans
for future operations of the department.

Centralized and Decentralized Organization. One basic question
that must be answered before any records management program is set
up is: *How will the program be organized;* that is, will the records be
centralized (physically located and controlled in one area), or *decentralized* (with the physical location of storage in departments where records are created and used)? Some variation of these two forms of organization is often found, depending on the needs of the individual firm.

Centralized control of records as pictured in Figure 2-2 simplifies
assigning responsibility for records since all of them are handled in one
records center. Also, centralization speeds up most methods for controlling forms, especially spotting unauthorized or poorly designed forms
used by several departments. Duplication of personnel, equipment, supplies, and the needed space is reduced since one central unit performs
this type of work. A centralized unit has specialized staff with more
expert talent available, which permits a higher quality of work and broader
distribution of new ideas throughout the firm.

Decentralized control is recommended when the physical distance
between a department and the records center prevents fast service and
does not provide quick access to the information needed. The main advantages of decentralized *and* centralized systems are realized in a modified system in which files are physically decentralized in various departments but over which centralized control is maintained.

The development of computerized files, with records available on
video display terminals, has had a direct effect on how files are organized. This type of storage and retrieval system, as discussed in Chapter
14, physically stores information in computer files operating under the
central control of data processing and records management personnel.

FIGURE 2-2 — A Centralized Records Center
White Power Files, Inc.

The main computer equipment and record controls are centralized, but the viewing equipment is decentralized by being located in each department. Information can then be distributed quickly and simultaneously to many different locations. The growing use of microcomputers permits even greater decentralization and control of computer files within departments.

Organizational Placement of Records Management.   Since the records manager serves as an organization-wide advisor to *all* departments on how to solve their records problems, the records management program should not be placed within any one department that it serves (accounting, sales, or data processing, for example). Such an arrangement could bias its operating effectiveness. Instead, the records management program is most frequently located on the organization chart as one of the specialized areas of administrative services (sometimes called information services) along with other service departments dealing mainly with information processing and administration. Such an administrative services division, headed by a vice president, represents a move up the organization ladder from earlier days when the office had more limited responsibilities and was headed by a middle-level office manager (See Figure 2-3).

Staffing the Records Management Program

The success of records management programs depends on the selection, training, and continuous development of a full-time staff (if the size and financial standing of the firm permit) to handle all the records responsibilities. Small offices assign these duties as the part-time responsibility of a qualified person, usually the office manager or an assistant.

As discussed in Chapter 1, usually such a full-time staff operates on three levels: managerial, supervisory, and operating. The positions most commonly found on these levels, shown in Figure 1-5, page 17, are discussed in this section.

Managerial Staff.   The top position in the program is that of the **records manager** who is responsible for developing policies and setting objectives for the firm's records systems. This position also includes such management duties as organizing resources, staff procurement and development, establishing effective operating procedures, and evaluating the administration of the program. Technical areas that are included in

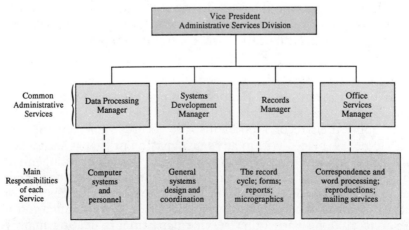

FIGURE 2-3 — Records Management on the Organization Chart

the records manager's responsibilities include micrographics (the micro-records systems), forms control, records protection and preservation, and the growing field of automated records storage and retrieval.

An even more important responsibility relates to the management of the staff. Thus, for the records manager's position, basic skills are required for motivating and evaluating all levels of the staff and for selling and coordinating the program among all divisions of the organization. Many of these skills are administrative in nature, such as setting objectives, budgeting, and cost control, and are developed in college degree programs. Technical skills needed, such as forms and records analysis, are also developed through short courses offered by forms and machines suppliers or through intensive workshops in community colleges and professional records management groups, such as ARMA. Wherever such knowledge is obtained, the records manager must possess a broad understanding of the total record cycle, systems, and manual and automated information-handling processes.

Other managerial staff members include the **forms manager** and **reports manager** who work directly with individual departments to develop forms and reports control programs. When the need for a new form arises or when an old form needs revision, the forms manager analyzes its use and cost and provides the skill needed to design the form. Similar assistance on the proper use of all types of business reports is furnished by a reports manager. Two-year college degrees in business administration and experience in forms analysis and reports analysis are recommended for promotion to the forms manager and reports manager positions, respectively.

Supervisory Staff.   At this level, three positions are most commonly found. One important administrator is the **records center supervisor**, found in large offices. The person holding the position of records center supervisor is responsible for people-related tasks, such as planning what work is to be done, assigning such work in a fair manner, and then coordinating and evaluating how well the work is performed. Usually the supervisor is not directly involved in salary or promotion decisions or in hiring and firing. These duties usually fall to the records manager. Because previous work experience in records operations is an important qualification for the records center supervisor, one of the best sources of candidates is the records analyst or capable records clerk who has the technical knowledge of the firm's records operations and has shown the ability to work well with others. As further applications of automation come to the records field, new career paths are appearing for records center supervisors.

Large records systems usually provide the services of a **forms supervisor** and one or more **reports supervisors** who coordinate the work of the forms and reports analysts and work directly with all departments in providing technical advice on forms and reports. A more technical level of supervisor is represented by the **micrographics services supervisor**. Such a position requires technical knowledge and experience in various microfilming applications as well as the ability to train micrographics technicians.

Operating Staff. As Figure 1-5, page 18, shows, two sublevels of workers are found among the operating staff. At the analyst level there are forms analysts and records analysts whose work is not supervisory but broader and more technical than the work of the records clerk. A **forms analyst** is a type of "trouble-shooter" who studies systems for creating, processing, and distributing forms throughout the firm to make the forms more efficient and less expensive. The principal qualifications for the analyst position are shown in Figure 1-5, as found in larger firms; but in small firms, forms design and control duties are handled by the office manager.   .

The **records analyst** position is on a similar level. A records analyst is responsible for the creation, maintenance, and disposition of active and inactive records. The one who occupies such a position also needs considerable knowledge of the systems in which the records are used.

A **micrographics technician** must have good mechanical ability in order to operate the various types of cameras, film processors, and microfilm preparation equipment. Maintaining quality control and production standards of developed film as well as analyzing problems are also the technician's responsibilities. Records experience, although helpful, is not necessary. Technical training in microfilming is required.

The **records clerk** is primarily responsible for daily records processing in the records unit. Other names for this position are *file clerk, general clerk, files operator,* or *filer*. The records clerk may be assigned to active or inactive records centers. The typical responsibilities of this position include receiving records, preliminary sorting, filing and finding, occasional microfilming, and related reference services. In an automated records setting, other duties may be added, such as responsibility for the library of programs in a computer installation and responsibility for the documentation work (the "backup" records for the computer programs). These positions are found more often in large firms, such as banks, insurance companies, and public utilities. Sometimes, too, related administrative support functions, such as printing, copying, and mailing services, are added to the duties of the records clerk. These activities give more variety to the work assignments and enable the administrative support staff to be utilized more completely. Of the qualifications required for this operating-level position, as outlined in Figure 1-5, an interest in records work is most important since it affects both the speed and accuracy with which the work is performed.

Directing the Records Management Program

The heart of any management program is directing its day-to-day operations. To the records manager, this means making decisions about all phases of the records management program in order to make it as efficient as possible. The chief decisions affect the development and maintenance of sound operating procedures and the wise management of space allocated to records. These topics are discussed in the following paragraphs.

Maintaining Effective Operating Procedures. Basically, good operating procedures answer the question, *"Who* does *what* in *what manner* at *what time* and in *what order?"* Such procedures are actually instructions for completing the tasks assigned and specifying who is responsible for doing the work. Examples of operating procedures in records management are how to: index and store correspondence; retrieve and control outgoing records; design forms; purchase equipment and supplies; and hire, orient, train, and evaluate employees. These procedures must be efficient in order to reduce the amount of paperwork and reduce the costs of the records system. At the same time the effectiveness of the management in the firm is increased by using the information stored in the firm's records.

Managing Records Space. Guidelines for the best use of office space apply to records departments as well as to other office operations. Records storage areas need to be as attractive, well lighted, and climate controlled as are other office areas. The records need to be located for convenience to all users. Such a plan saves storage time and the travel time of filers who will spend less time moving back and forth to the files and devote more time to their other assigned duties. Tasks on which the most mental concentration is required need to be located away from noisy areas and frequent movement of workers. Confidential records need to be controlled by highly reliable persons and not be allowed to circulate freely in the office. Computer terminals need to be placed on the desks of people authorized to enter information into and retrieve information from the computer files. Frequently file cabinets are arranged to provide privacy for workers without interfering with the open-space effect of the office.

Typical techniques for saving space in records management are using open-shelf files that occupy approximately 50 percent of the space required by regular file cabinets; five-drawer cabinets instead of four, resulting in a 25 percent increase in storage space in the same square footage; and microfilming documents or using commercial (offsite) records centers.

Controlling the Records Management Program

The managerial function of **control** involves the process of evaluating how well the program is meeting its goals. Periodically managers must determine answers to the following control-related questions:

1. Has the department met its objectives?
2. How well have the supervisors and their employees met the quotas or goals assigned to them?
3. Has the department operated within its budget?
4. How many units of product or service are being produced compared with the number expected?
5. How often are employees absent from work?

With the facts provided by such an evaluation, the manager can take steps to correct any problems uncovered.

DEVELOPING AN EFFECTIVE RECORDS MANAGEMENT PROGRAM

The need to manage *all* phases of the record cycle becomes more important as the percentage of the national payroll devoted to office workers grows larger. According to one estimate, 66 percent of the work force is composed of office workers whose paperwork accounts for 84.4 percent of the cost of business.[1]

Records management programs are based on a careful application of the management and organization principles and of the program objectives discussed in the previous section of this chapter. Each principle is

---

[1]Kay F. Gow and Betty R. Ricks, "Records Administration is a Management Priority," *The Office* (April, 1984), p. 136.

also equally important to the management of the various phases in the record cycle.

Selling the Records Management Program

The records manager must be constantly alerted to the need for keeping track of company records problems, their costs, and methods of eliminating such problems. With current information about these problems, the records manager can forcefully tell the records management "story"—that is, show top management and department managers how a well-managed program of records control can prevent many information problems from occurring and can make a big contribution toward increasing the productivity of the firm. To justify such a program, its benefits must exceed its costs.

Once management approval is given, the various stages in such a program—the so-called record cycle as outlined in Figure 1-2, page 7—can be organized. Two of these phases—step 2 on distribution and step 3 on use—are frequently controlled by sources outside the records department and hence are not typically included in a discussion of records management programs.

Managing the Creation of Records

The creation of unnecessary or excessive numbers of records occurs in all offices. Copiers and computers generate unnecessary copies of reports, correspondence, and business forms, because no one in authority has set clear standards for records creation, reproduction, and storage. The lines of people waiting at the copiers and the alarming increase in the use of file cabinets and shelves to house both regular records and the hard copy output of computer systems show that this creation phase needs to be much better managed.

One effective way of studying the records creation problem uses the work simplification formula discussed earlier in this chapter. This approach involves determining:

1. *What* records are created? (The most important records must be identified.)
2. *Who* creates records? (The typical answer to this question is that all employees do.) What is the prevailing attitude toward the creation of records? (That records costs are low and relatively insignificant compared to other operating costs.)

3. *Where* are records created? (In all areas of the company—factory and office.)
4. *When* are records created? (Whenever employees feel the need for a record and often without getting a superior's approval.)
5. *How* are records created? (By hand or by machine—copiers, word processors, and computers.)
6. *Why* are records created? (To store and relay information from one person, department, or business to another and to serve as a source of information vital to the business.)

To manage this universal office problem calls for careful planning, organizing, and control measures by office personnel. Usually, records control starts with the records manager's showing that the control of records is the responsibility of *every* department manager. Every manager must, in turn, educate each member of the department staff to the need for justifying each new record created. Some of the successful ways of ensuring that only necessary records will be created are as follows:

1. Requiring that each department submit all requests for new records— or revisions to existing records—to a records manager or to a departmental supervisor for approval. In addition, the request for records needs to be explained in writing.
2. Stressing the cost of creating new records. Studies show that creating new forms is a costly process since spending $1 for forms paper and printing results in $25 or more in processing and filing costs after the form is created.

   In the same way, creating correspondence adds to the costs of keeping records. Taking into consideration that a standard letter-size file drawer holds from 3,500 to 5,000 sheets of correspondence (30 percent of which are usually copies of original correspondence) together with file folders and guides, one can see that much cost is incurred through creating correspondence alone. Therefore, in a five-drawer file containing 4,000 copies of outgoing correspondence in each drawer, 20,000 copies of correspondence would be filed. If the cost of creating the original of the copy filed were $7, a total of $140,000 in correspondence production expense would be involved.
3. Making sure that each record serves a valid purpose and also by determining whether one copy can be circulated so as to be shared by several persons. Often a single copy of a record can be posted on a centrally located bulletin board. Many "information only" copies, for which no action is required or for which the reader has no direct responsibility, can be eliminated.

4. Asking office employees to prepare a list by subject matter of the records they receive regularly and to indicate whether they need such records. In addition, department managers may ask for a list of the files and records that each employee normally maintains. By comparing the two lists, the manager may find that several employees are saving the same records and that some are not using such records at all.
5. Finding alternatives to creating the record. Even for very short letters that may cost from $4 to $5 to produce, a more economical method of communication might be a short telephone call. Responding to questions through marginal notations on the letters received and returning the original letter to the sender saves time and paper. If needed, a copy of the letter with the answer noted in the margin can be quickly produced on a copier.

Managing the Storage and Retrieval of Records

This phase of the records management program offers an excellent opportunity for emphasizing an important relationship—between *filing* (storage) and records management. The *task-oriented records clerk* discussed earlier follows a set of efficient steps for storing records and for finding them when they are needed later. On the other hand, the *systems-oriented records manager* considers storage and retrieval as *two* important phases in the overall program of records management. Each level of employee brings a different point of view toward the management of records.

The storage of records for later retrieval in manual (paper record) systems represents a basic framework for this book. Even in automated systems, the basic methods of indexing, coding, sorting, and storing of information are built on the methods used in manual systems. Thus, Parts 2 and 3 as well as a portion of Part 4 in this textbook are devoted to detailed procedures for managing manual storage and retrieval systems. An introduction to records management requires that students master these concepts and be able to apply the principles in the many exercises that are provided for users of the text.

Managing the Maintenance of Records

Records maintenance is the set of service activities needed to operate the main storage and retrieval systems. These activities include classifying records, developing efficient procedures for operating the records systems, updating and purging the files, and procedures for preserving and protecting the records.

To be efficient, records systems need to make full use of equipment. Drawer and shelf files need to be carefully checked to avoid overcrowding. Record folders and drawers also need to be properly labeled and dividers used to make retrieval easy.

By maintaining indexes, the process of locating records in the files is speeded up. Regularly the files need to be purged of records that are no longer needed and efficient procedures developed for indexing, coding, storing, retrieving, and charging out documents from the files. In automated systems, such procedures are built into the computer or word processing systems.

Retaining Records.   Before a records manager can decide what records to keep and for how long, an inventory of records must be made. Then, from an analysis of the information collected during the inventory, a records retention plan can be developed.

Records Inventory.   A **records inventory** is a survey used to find the types and volume of records on file as well as their location and frequency of use. Without this information, the records program cannot be properly managed. Important goals of such a survey include locating duplications in records, determining how long to keep records, deciding when to transfer records to less expensive storage, and deciding when to destroy them.

The person conducting the records inventory asks each department to furnish the following information about each of the records that are vital to the operation of the department:

1. Name and number of the record.
2. Purpose of each copy of the record.
3. Volume and frequency of use of the record.
4. Nature of each copy of the record: original, carbon, photocopy, and copy color.
5. Suggested time period for retaining the record with explanation.
6. Method of storing the record (by customer name, by order number, and so on).
7. Distribution and filing location of each copy of the record.
8. Quantity in cubic feet, number of file drawers, or lineal inches of records stored. (This information is useful for paper records, for records in microform, and for tape and disk records used in computer and word processing systems.)

9. Name of the person and department responsible for controlling the record.

A simple form that combines inventory and records retention information is shown in Figure 2-4. Merging these two types of information is convenient because the inventory will often uncover duplicate files and records no longer used—information needed to develop the remaining phases of the records management program.

Information collected during the records inventory helps the records staff to place a value on each record; and on the basis of this evaluation, a sound retention program can be developed. Usually records will have one or more of the following values to the organization:[2]

1. *Administrative value*, in that they perform assigned operations within the organization. Examples of these records include policy and procedures manuals and handbooks, organization charts, and major contracts.
2. *Fiscal value*, as they document operating funds or serve audit purposes. Examples of these records include tax returns, records of financial transactions such as purchase and sales orders as well as common financial statements. Apart from the Internal Revenue Service,

RECORD TITLE *Attendance Records*					
INVENTORY			RETENTION		
DEPARTMENT *Personnel*			APPROVALS		YEARS
RECORD COPY ☒	DUPLICATE COPY ☐		RECOMMENDED (SPECIFY SOURCE) *May 1978 article in "Modern Office Procedures"*		7
VOLUME			ADMINISTRATIVE		
INCLUSIVE DATES	LOCATION	QUANTITY	BY *Betty Cozin* DATE *8-12-87*		6
1980–1985	OFFICE	*150 cu. ft.*	LEGAL COUNSEL BY *Paula Payne* DATE *8-30-87*		7
1975–1979	STORAGE	*180 cu. ft.*	EXECUTIVE BY *Karl J. King* DATE *9-15-87*		7
REMARKS *Redesign of attendance form to small size will reduce amount of space required for storing this inventory of records*			FINALIZED SCHEDULE		
			IN OFFICE *1 year*	IN STORAGE *6 years*	DESTROY *after 7 years*
			BY *Gloria Diaz* DATE *10-22-87*		
			SPECIAL INSTRUCTIONS		
COUNTED BY *Jason Barnes*	DATE *3-30-85*				
FORM 1606		RECORDS INVENTORY AND RETENTION CONTROL CARD	BB BANKERS BOX *Records storage systems Division of Fellowes Manufacturing Company*		

FIGURE 2-4 — A Records Inventory/Retention Control Card
Courtesy of Bankers Box/Records Storage Systems Division of Fellowes Manufacturing Company

---

[2]For more comprehensive coverage on the training of records personnel, see Betty R. Ricks and Kay F. Gow, *Information Resource Management* (Cincinnati: South-Western Publishing Co.), 1984, p. 48.

no government regulation requires the retention of computer records; rather, they are treated as is any other copy of a record.[3]

3. *Legal value*, since they provide documentation of business transactions. Examples of such records include contracts, financial agreements, deeds, and other legal documents.

4. *Historical value*, inasmuch as they document the organizational process, operations, and major shifts of direction in the firm. Minutes of meetings, the corporate charter, public relations documents, and information on corporate officials all fall into this records category.

Records Retention Schedule.   With the value of each record determined, the records manager must then determine how long records are to be kept (retained). The resulting **records retention schedule** lists each general records category with the length of time each category is to be retained.

For making retention decisions, one useful classification system divides records into four categories: (1) *records that are not worth keeping*, such as bulk mail announcements, simple acknowledgments, bulletin board announcements, and the like; (2) *records for short-term storage* of up to three years, used mainly for active files of business letters and interoffice memorandums, business reports, and bank statements; (3) *records for long-term storage* of, say, seven to ten years for retaining more important financial and sales data, credit histories, and statistical records; and (4) *records for permanent storage*, such as student transcripts, customer profile records, and business ownership records, which have lasting value.

A portion of a retention schedule showing the various types of records and the recommended periods for keeping each record is shown in Figure 2-5. Information needed to create and keep up-to-date such a list can be obtained at little or no cost from various sources. The U. S. Government annually publishes the *Guide to Records Retention Requirements*, which is available from the Superintendent of Documents, U. S. Government Printing Office. Each of the 50 states has developed statutes of limitations that specify the time after which legal rights cannot be enforced by civil action in the courts. Once a record reaches an age beyond which the statute of limitations applies, the record has no value as evidence in a court of law.

---

[3]Joseph L. Kish, Jr., "Establishing Retention Periods for Magnetic Tape-Based Records," *Information and Records Management* (July, 1981), p. 46.

Type of Record	Retention Period in Years	Type of Record	Retention Period in Years
Accounting/Fiscal		Corporate	
Accounts receivable	10	Annual reports	P
Balance sheets	P*	Contract, employee	P
Budget work sheets	2	Stockholders' minutes	P
Cash books	P		
Cash sales slips	3	Insurance	
Checks, payroll	7	Accident reports	P
General journal	P	Claims, automobile	10
Uncollected accounts	7		
		Legal	
Administrative		Mortgages	P
Correspondence, accounting	5		
Correspondence, general	3	Personnel	
		Applications	P
Correspondence, purchase	5	Attendance records	7
Correspondence, tax	P	Disability and benefits records	6
Requisitions	3	Workmen's compensation reports	10
*Permanently filed			

FIGURE 2-5 — A Portion of a Suggested Retention Schedule for Business Records

Adapted from a retention schedule appearing in Records Control and Storage Handbook with Retention Schedules *(8th Edition), Bankers Box Records and Storage Systems (Itasca, IL, 1977), pp. 24–25*

Preserving and Protecting Records. When highly important records are lost or their confidentiality has been violated, many times the firm fails to survive. Thus, important records must be given special attention so that their condition is properly preserved and protected. In particular, records must be protected against two main hazards: (1) physical hazards, such as fires, floods, earthquakes, dust, insects, rodents, excessive temperatures, and too much humidity that causes mildew; and (2) human-created hazards that include theft, explosions and bombings, record misplacement, and unauthorized access to records.

The selection of appropriate methods for protection of records is not a simple one. Associations and agencies specializing in this type of activity (such as the Safe Manufacturers Association, National Fire Protection Association, the Office of Civil Defense, and the Atomic Energy Commission) should be consulted by records managers interested in improving the protection of their records.

Some of the protection methods available are: (1) using existing file storage but making duplicate copies of records to be stored in another location; (2) sending an extra copy of an active record to a vital records storage area; and (3) using a fireproof area, usually a safe or vault, for maximum protection.

Fires are perhaps the most common physical disaster and the most damaging. According to the National Fire Protection Association, 65 percent of those businesses suffering major fire damage fail to reopen.[4] To prevent such disasters, alarm systems and water sprinkler and foam systems are available for extinguishing fires. Also, no-smoking areas are set up so that records personnel do not subject the records to undue fire hazards. However, records may be damaged if sprinkler and foam systems are activated by mistake. Halon (hydro-carbon) gas is available to extinguish fires; unlike dry chemicals or water, halon will not damage the record.

To control the environment in which records are stored, a temperature between 70° and 75° with a relative humidity between 48 and 52 percent needs to be maintained. Special records, such as those in magnetic form, cannot withstand as much heat as paper and thus must be managed under strict environmental conditions. Even the 5 1/4 inch diskette commonly used in microcomputer systems must be carefully protected from improper filing and handling to prevent fingerprints, dust, and scratches.

A greater security threat to information is created by people. For example, new products are stolen off the drawing board when blueprints fall into the wrong hands. In one such case, a large distribution company in Chicago had its entire customer list lifted from a trash dumpster. Many other instances are found in which unauthorized personnel gain access to stored information.[5]

---

[4]Richard C. Donaldson, "Protecting the Business from Disaster," *ARMA Records Management Quarterly* (January, 1983), p. 34.

[5]For an interesting description of systems to control the entry of people to records centers, see Belden Menkus, "Access Control Systems for Security," *Office Administration and Automation* (April, 1984), pp. 57, 58, 60.

To restrict access to storage areas, firms maintain close controls over keys issued to unlock file cabinets and file centers. Access may also be controlled by photographic identification cards or badges or by magneti cally encoded cards used in devices that permit access through certain doors at certain times. An automatic computer printout provides a record of what door was entered at what time by means of what card number. Other controls over access include internal alarm systems, motion detectors that spot movement in the storage area during certain time periods, and round-the-clock guard service.

Managing the Transfer of Records

In the record cycle, **records transfer** refers to the physical movement of active records from the office to semiactive or inactive storage areas. The basis for making the decision to transfer records is the activity (frequency of use) of the record.

Records analysts define three degrees of records activity:

Active records:	Records that are used three or more times a month and stored in very accessible equipment in the active storage file in the office.
Semiactive records:	Records that are used about twice a month and stored in the less accessible cabinets or shelves in the active storage area in the office.
Inactive records:	Records that are referred to less than 15 times a year and stored in a less expensive storage area outside the office.

As a rule, the following alternatives are available to a records manager in making decisions regarding transfer or retention of records:

1. Keep the record in active (more expensive) storage permanently.
2. Keep the record in active or semiactive storage and transfer it to inactive (less expensive) storage at a later time.
3. Transfer the record to inactive storage and destroy it within a stipulated period of time according to the records retention schedule.
4. Transfer the record to inactive storage and retain it permanently.
5. Destroy the record immediately.

In most cases, the current year's records plus those of the past year are all that are needed in the active files. However, several other factors must be considered when making transfer decisions.

First of all, transfer helps to reduce equipment costs, since transferred records may be stored in cardboard containers that are less expensive than the steel cabinets used for storage of active materials. Second, the cabinets or shelves formerly used by the transferred files provide additional space for the active files. Finally, efficiency of storage and retrieval is improved because crowding of files has been eliminated; and, as a result, the work space in drawers, cabinets, or shelves has been increased.

Setting Up an In-House Inactive Records Center.   Before records can be physically transferred to inactive storage, the records manager must set up the records center. If internal storage is too costly or is not available, the inactive records may be moved to an external or commercial records center. Storage of the files sent to either location is specified by the records retention schedule.

From the standpoint of good management, an inactive records center provides the following:

1. A location offering reliable protection from physical and human hazards discussed earlier in this chapter. In small offices, in-house storage may be located in the basement of the office or safely housed in an adjacent warehouse.
2. Storage space that is low in cost but provides proper utilization of floor space with provision for aisles wide enough to maintain an efficient traffic pattern and that can accommodate the stresses of heavy file cartons or cabinets.
3. Proper environmental controls including humidity and temperature regulation (from 70° to 75° F.), lighting and plumbing facilities, and general receiving and dispatching space for the distribution of records.
4. Proper equipment and supplies (cabinets, boxes, and cartons) that are inexpensive along with appropriate shelving, as shown in Figure 2-6. Other equipment to be provided includes work tables for sorting, staplers, and moving equipment such as dollies.
5. An efficient system for filing and finding inactive records with provisions for cross-referencing and charge-out. Also, a records inventory needs to be conducted that includes a request for all the information on the records inventory discussed earlier.
6. A security system that restricts the records center to authorized personnel only.

FIGURE 2-6 — Inactive Records Storage in an In-House Records Center

Using a Commercial Offsite Records Center. Several reasons account for the growth of commercial records centers that specialize in the storage of other firms' records. Such centers provide low-cost storage, estimated to be as low as 1/10 of onsite storage costs; yet these centers provide the efficiency of specialization which means fast retrieval. In some cases, a telephone call will retrieve information that is then delivered by messenger. All reputable records centers furnish reliable protection and security, often in underground vaults, that eliminate the need for such costly services in the firm itself. Some commercial centers also furnish technical assistance in developing retention schedules, in setting up total records management programs, and in selecting the equipment required to operate them.

Managing the Disposition of Records

The final phase in the record cycle is called **records disposition**. Usually this term means destroying records that have no further value. Too often, obsolete records are discarded in the wastebasket, which is an example of a lack of good records management practice. For important records, this method is not recommended, for there is no evidence concerning what information has been destroyed. Rather, the systematic, effective approach to records disposition calls for keeping the records in a transfer file in the records center until receipt of authorization that the records no longer have any value and are to be destroyed. Such an authorization form, shown in Figure 2-7, bears the signature of the department manager, which releases the records manager from the responsibility for any mistakes made in destroying records.

RECORDS DISPOSAL AUTHORIZATION

TO: Department Manager   LOC. CODE: 00-1612 BLDG. 28A

FROM: Corporate Records Center

RECORDS DUE FOR DISPOSAL

Box Number	Description and/or Retention Number	Remarks	Disposal Due Date	Disposal Code*
081079	Trade Show Correspondence		11/87	C
081080	Employment Applications		11/87	C
081081	Travel Itineraries		11/87	A
087322	News Releases		11/87	A
087323	Division Financial Statements		11/87	B

DISPOSAL APPROVED _____ *Susan Miller* _____   DATE: 9/10/--
(Department Manager or Designated Records Representative)

DISPOSAL CARRIED OUT: _____ *a.k. Montoya* _____   DATE: 9/12/--
(Records Center Operator)

*DISPOSAL CODE

A. Recycle or deposit in dumpster for nonsensitive material
B. Bury at city dump for sensitive material (CONFIDENTIAL)
C. Onsite destruction for sensitive material (PRIVATE or SECRET)
  (shred or equivalent)

Form 40 (85)

FIGURE 2-7 — Form for Authorizing the Destruction of Records

Records disposition is no longer a simple matter of burning confidential papers and throwing useless records in the wastebasket. Rather, the process has become more complex because of the greater number of confidential records, greater volumes of records in general, and the increased use of nonpaper records (microfilm, plastic cards, magnetic tape, and other related media) that require new methods of records disposal. Some of the most confidential records need special attention. Examples are sales reports, customer mailing lists, new product proposals, confidential correspondence, cost estimates, and bank statements.

Several of the most common disposal methods are as follows:

1. Shredding: The most popular method for destruction of records. A shredder cuts into confetti-like strips all kinds of paper as well as offset aluminum and zinc duplicating plates and plastic credit cards; it can even destroy paper clips, staples, and fasteners along with the records fed into the machine.
2. Disintegrating: Many types of records that cannot be handled by shredders are destroyed in disintegrators. Disintegrators pound the material to be destroyed against a screen until it becomes pulpy. Disintegrators are commonly used to dispose of paper, microfilm, motion picture film, video tape, or magnetic tape as well as three-ring binders and heavy bound computer records with metal binding shafts.
3. Recycling: Obsolete records are recycled or converted into roofing paper, cardboard, and poster paper. Recycling plants arrange to pick up records from businesses for recycling. In the local telephone directory such plants can be found under "Recycling Centers," "Scrap Metals," or "Wastepaper."
4. Incinerating: With stricter laws governing the environment, burning of records has become less popular.

MANAGING RECORDS IN THE SMALL OFFICE

Full-fledged programs to manage records, as discussed in this chapter, originated in large organizations, such as the government and major business firms. And it is in these firms that such programs are expanding. However, in the thousands of small offices throughout the country (the local insurance, bank, legal, and medical offices, for example), there are also enormous numbers of records to be managed. In this type of setting, specialization cannot be provided. Thus, there is no full-time records manager, records center supervisor, forms analyst, or records clerk.

The person managing the office is solely responsible for the records along with many other duties; and if someone to assist the office manager is available, the records management functions may be delegated to that assistant.

Even in the small office, however, the same record cycle is found and the same *principles* of management must be applied even though the amount of time available and the knowledge about records management will be more limited. However, the *effective* manager of a small office recognizes the importance of information and how essential records are for providing needed information. Under such conditions, the right climate exists for creating an informal records management program in which the following principles and practices are applied:

1. The responsibility for managing records needs to be assigned to one or two persons who have the greatest knowledge of the firm's information needs as well as the best aptitude (accuracy, patience, and knowledge of filing procedures) for this type of work. Others in the office are to be discouraged from direct use of the files.

2. All records created need to be approved by a designated person who can analyze the need for such records. Assistance on records design, production, and storage can be obtained from printing firms and business forms sales representatives. Usually this service is provided without a charge.

3. A copy of all records and a list of records management practices need to be centrally stored by the office manager. Frequently a three-ring notebook is used to house such a control set of records. The need for a time-consuming survey is, therefore, eliminated; but continuous follow-up is necessary. A special section of this notebook needs to be devoted to a chronologic listing of records by time periods showing when they can be destroyed, or where such records are permanently stored.

4. The small-office manager needs to be aware of the need to classify records on the basis of (a) the frequency of their use and (b) legal and government requirements for retaining them. At least once a year during a slack work period, the office staff should work its way through the files in an effort to remove all unneeded records.

5. Disposal of records, while handled informally, needs to be done with caution so that all records destroyed have been so authorized and a list kept of the records and the date on which they were destroyed.

6. Since so many small offices now use microcomputers, control measures are required to make sure that only authorized personnel use the computer files.

7. Small-office filers need to be encouraged to participate in professional programs (such as those provided by the Professional Secretaries International and the Association of Records Managers and Administrators, Inc.) so as to increase their understanding of modern storage and retrieval systems.

By following these guidelines, office managers in small offices will be assured that their records systems are managed in an effective, economical manner. In addition, the application of the principles of management discussed in this chapter is essential to the operation of the systems discussed in each of the remaining chapters.

IMPORTANT TERMS AND CONCEPTS

active records
control
Family Educational Rights and Privacy Act of 1974
Federal Records Management Amendments of 1976
forms analyst
forms manager
forms supervisor
Freedom of Information Act of 1966 with Amendments
hard copy
inactive records
input-output approach
management by exception
micrographics services supervisor
micrographics technician
organizing

Paperwork Reduction Act of 1980
planning
Project ELF
records analyst
records center supervisor
records clerk
records disposition
records inventory
records maintenance
records manager
records retention schedule
records transfer
reports manager
reports supervisors
semiactive records
span of control
work simplification approach

REVIEW AND DISCUSSION

1. What basic problem accounts for much of the uncontrolled growth of paperwork in offices? Explain how business and human practices have intensified this big problem. (Obj. 1)

2. List the steps found in the work simplification approach to problem solving. By knowing these steps, can the records staff be assured of solving problems satisfactorily? Explain. (Obj. 2)

3. How does the input-output approach to problem solving differ from the work simplification approach? (Obj. 2)

4. Summarize the key records legislation since 1966. How does its coverage compare with that found in earlier legislation as discussed in Chapter 1? (Obj. 3)

5. Are management *functions* and management *principles* the same? If not, why not? Explain. (Obj. 4)

6. Identify the main areas of responsibility in the three levels of a records management staff. As a rule, what education and work experience are required for each level? (Obj. 5)

7. Define the term *directing* as it is used in a records management program. How is directing related to staffing? (Obj. 6)

8. Review the steps in the record cycle. What objectives need to be developed for each step in order to ensure an effective records management program? (Obj. 7)

9. Identify several key problems common to managing each phase in the record cycle. Suggest sensible solutions for solving each of these problems. (Obj. 8)

10. Assume you must provide the management of your firm with some guidelines for deciding whether to store inactive records in-house or to purchase the services of an offsite commercial records center. What will your guidelines list include? (Obj. 9)

11. Outline several of the main similarities and differences between managing records in large and small offices. (Obj. 10)

DECISION-MAKING OPPORTUNITIES (DMO)

DMO 2-1: Developing a Management Orientation Toward Records Systems

Six months before the beginning of the present school year, you began working in the county treasurer's office as a general office clerk. By working afternoons you are able to finance your college education which, this term, includes the records management course. In this five-person office the following problems have caught your eye week after week:

1. Personnel records for employees are kept in the treasurer's private office and are not made available to employees when a request is made.
2. Confidential tax records of county residents are shown "on the sly" to other persons upon request.
3. Legal-size paper is used in standard letter-size files since, in the words of the office manager, "It saves paper."
4. There are no locks on storage cabinets.
5. Materials to be stored accumulate in a basket labeled "To Be Filed" until one of the five employees decides it's time to get the records "out of sight."

From your study of records management thus far, you are able to detect many such problems and hope for the right opportunity to help correct them. Also, your management and systems thinking tells you that you need a sound base or framework for recommending changes; and special care must be given to the seniority of the staff (all are over 45 years of age with job tenure ranging from 13 to 35 years).

Develop a report in which you provide the following information:

1. A managerial orientation to records systems (scope, objectives, and basic systems thinking to be followed) that seems to be needed in this small office.
2. A task orientation that involves work efficiency, record cycle controls, and cost considerations.
3. Your suggestions for successfully introducing your "young" ideas to a staff of oldtimers. (Objs. 4, 6, 7, 8, and 10)

DMO 2-2: Evaluating the Need for New Records

For the second straight summer, four of your close friends have been working almost full time in a rock band playing throughout your state. As the popularity of the band has increased, your friends have noticed that their responsibilities for record keeping also have increased. Up to the present time they have kept few records. Consequently, several serious misunderstandings and lost bookings have resulted from faulty memory and lost notes.

The leader of the group, Mark Tanner, has asked you for advice on what records are needed and how to organize the records needed by the band. Use either the work simplification or the input-output approach to problem solving in order to provide support for your advice to Mark. (Obj. 2)

COMPREHENSIVE CASE 1

Applying Management Principles to Student Organization Records

Assume that your class has been asked to set up a large committee called Basic Records Services (BRS). The purpose of this committee is to provide advice to other student organizations in the management of their records.

At the outset, one student needs to be appointed or elected to serve as manager of BRS so that someone is immediately responsible for getting your group organized. After that task has been accomplished, it is important to develop ideas for helping other student organizations in solving their records problems.

Decisions must be made on the following topics:

1. What BRS needs to do as a group to organize its members to achieve their goals.
2. What general plans to make regarding contacts with other student groups. Consider publicity, administrative matters such as equipment, supplies, machines, and so on, needed for BRS projects.
3. What specific records to create in order for your group to start functioning.

Using the management principles discussed in Chapter 2 as well as ideas obtained from other related chapters, develop a set of materials in outline form that shows a sound organizational plan for BRS. Also, develop written guidelines that can be used to explain the fundamental principles and practices for managing records to student club groups. Oral reports may also be used. Note that you do not need to develop a records management program for each student club. Rather, you are expected to apply your knowledge of management principles in drafting an organizational plan for such a club. Comply with this request as directed by your instructor. (Obj. 4)

2 – Alphabetic Storage and Retrieval

Part 2 first presents an overview of the equipment, supplies, and methods for storing paper records. Considerable emphasis is then placed on the alphabetic rules for storing records. Principles and procedures for retrieval and transfer of paper records conclude this Part.

3 RECORDS STORAGE EQUIPMENT, SUPPLIES, AND METHODS

Objectives

After you have completed this chapter, you will be able to:

1. Explain terms used in records storage systems.
2. Identify the basic types of storage equipment for paper records.
3. Identify four kinds of storage supplies commonly used.
4. Illustrate the meaning of "cut" and "position" as these terms relate to folder tabs.
5. Identify five records storage methods.
6. List similarities and differences among the five records storage methods.
7. Explain how the alphabetic storage method is used in other records storage methods.
8. Explain the difference between a storage system and a storage method.

The same management concepts that you have studied in the previous two chapters apply to the storage of records. The storage function must be planned, organized, properly directed, and controlled. In this chapter, you will be learning about equipment and supplies used in the proper storage of records. Also, you will be introduced to the methods used for storing records. Emphasis will be placed on the manual storage of paper records although you will see in later chapters how the principles studied here will apply to nonpaper records, such as microrecords and disks, and to storing information contained within computers and word processors.

Reference to the records cycle in Figure 1-2, page 7, will remind you that storage is only one step in the records cycle. Records are stored because the information contained in them helps in making decisions, assists departments in communicating with each other and the outside world, provides a record of the past, and supplies data useful for legal purposes.

Placing records into storage can be easy if no thought is given to the need to find them again! Storing records without using specific procedures and without consistency means much time is wasted in searching for information. Tempers become frayed and control over stored records is minimal. Records must be stored with consistency so that they can be found (retrieved) immediately when needed.

To understand records storage methods and systems, one needs to know the terminology that is used. The definitions given in the following paragraphs will help your understanding.

BASIC TERMINOLOGY OF RECORDS STORAGE

As you learned in Chapter 2, a records system can be manual or automated. To store and retrieve records effectively in either system requires a knowledge and understanding of storage terms.

1. *System.* System as used in records storage means any storage plan devised by a storage equipment manufacturer. System has a broader meaning in management, however (See Figure 1-4, page 13).
2. *Storage.* **Storage** is the actual placement of materials into a folder, on a section of a magnetic disk, or on a shelf, according to a plan. The term *filing* may be used to mean storage, but filing is usually associated with paper records only.
3. *Storage Method.* A **storage method** is a systematic way of storing records according to one of the following arrangements: alphabetic, subject, numeric, geographic, or chronologic.
4. *Storage Procedures.* **Storage procedures** are a series of steps for the orderly arrangement of records as required by a specific storage method.
5. *Indexing (Classifying).* Mentally determining the name, subject, or number by which a specific record is to be stored is called **indexing** or **classifying**. For example, if a letter is written by someone in the First National Bank to Marriott Gregory about his or her account, determining that the storage of that letter would be by the name *Marriott Gregory* is called indexing.
6. *Coding.* Marking a record to indicate by what name, number, or subject the record is to be stored is called **coding**. Coding is the physical act of underlining, numbering, checking, circling, or marking the record in some other way. In the example shown in term 5, above, the name could be coded by underlining: Marriott Gregory.

7. *Unit.* Each name, initial, or other word used in determining the alphabetic order of records to be stored is called a **unit**. The name *Marriott Gregory* has two units.

These are basic terms; other terms will be defined as you encounter them in the text.

BASIC STORAGE EQUIPMENT AND SUPPLIES

In the control of records storage, the records manager or person in charge of procuring equipment and supplies needs specific information to ensure wise selection. Equipment and supplies mentioned in this chapter are indicative of a wide variety available. Each year improvements are made and innovative items appear.

Storage Equipment

Types of storage equipment most commonly used for paper records are: (1) vertical file cabinets, (2) lateral file cabinets, (3) shelf files, and (4) computer printout files. A brief discussion of each of these types of equipment will help to better understand records storage. Other types of storage equipment and their special uses will be discussed in later chapters.

Vertical File Cabinets. **Vertical file cabinets** are the conventional storage cabinets in one- to five-drawer sizes. The popular three-drawer vertical file cabinet is shown in Figure 3-1. Several three-drawer cabinets are often placed together with a countertop across all of them to provide additional office work space. The type and volume of records to be stored will determine the width, depth, number, and size of drawers. The most common sizes of vertical file cabinet drawers are for cards, letters, and legal records. However, many other sizes and combinations are available for storing larger or smaller materials such as combinations of card- and letter-size drawers; blueprint cabinets; invoice files; and jumbo drawers to house large items such as X rays, artwork, or engineering and architectural plans.

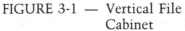

FIGURE 3-1 — Vertical File   FIGURE 3-2 — Lateral File
               Cabinet   Cabinet

All-Steel, Inc.

Lateral File Cabinets.   **Lateral file cabinets** have drawers that open
from the long side and look like a chest of drawers or bookshelves with
doors. Figure 3-2 shows a three-drawer lateral file cabinet with roll-back
drawer fronts.

Because the long (narrow) side opens, lateral file cabinets are particularly well suited to narrow spaces. They are available in a variety of
shapes and sizes, depending on the number and depth of the drawers.

Shelf Files.   **Shelf files** are simply shelves arranged horizontally and
used for storing records. Shelf files may be the open style or have roll-
back or roll-down fronts. Shelves may be arranged as a stationary book-
shelf (See Figure 3-3), in rotary form (See Figure 3-4), or be mobile with
shelves that move as needed for storage and retrieval (See Figure 3-5).
There is further discussion of mobile shelving in Chapter 14.

Computer Printout Files.   **Computer printout files** are available as
cabinets on wheels or as open-shelf files. Either style is designed to hold
binders containing the printouts (See Chapter 14).

Storage Supplies

Efficient storage and retrieval requires the use of not only the right
equipment but also the right supplies. The principal supplies used in
manual storage of paper records are discussed briefly below.

FIGURE 3-3 — Open-Shelf File

FIGURE 3-4 — Rotary Shelf File

FIGURE 3-5 — Mobile Shelf File
Acme Visible Records

Folders.   **Folders** are containers used to hold stored records in an orderly manner and ordinarily are made of heavy material, usually manilla, Kraft, plastic, or pressboard. Folders are creased approximately in half; the back is higher than the front. A folder may be reinforced across the top of the back edge since that is the place receiving the greatest wear, as it is usually grasped by that edge. Folders are available with a straight edge or with tabs in various positions. A **tab** is a portion of a folder that extends above the regular height or beyond the regular width of the folder. If the folder has a tab extending across its complete width, it is said to be *straight cut* (See Figure 3-6). One-third-cut tabs extend only one third the width of a folder and may be in any of three positions (See Figure 3-6). **Position** refers to the location of the tab at the top of the folder as seen from left to right. *First position* means the tab is at the left; *second position* means the tab is second from the left; and so on. Folders may have all tabs in one position, known as *straight-line position*. If the tabs on the folders are in a series of several different positions from left to right according to a set pattern (as are the one-fifth-cut folders pictured in Figure 3-6), this is known as *staggered position*. Straight-line position is increasing in usage because of ease in reading; the eye travels faster

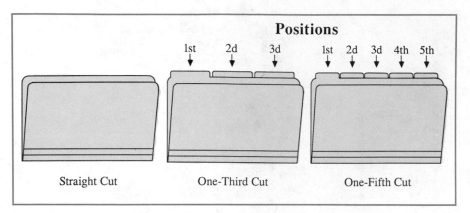

FIGURE 3-6 — Commonly Used Folder Cuts and Positions

in a straight line than it does when it jumps back and forth from left to right. Folders for open-shelf equipment have their tabs on the side edge (See Figure 3-7) in various positions according to the manufacturer's system or the customer's preference.

Other types of folders often used in offices include (1) the **suspension** or **hanging folder** which hangs from parallel bars on the sides of the storage equipment (Figure 3-8 left), (2) **bellows (expansion) folder** used when the volume of stored records is small (Figure 3-8 middle), and (3) **pocket folder**—a folder with a great deal more expansion at the bottom than that of the ordinary folder (Figure 3-8 right). More specialized folders will be described later in the text.

Guides. **Guides** are rigid dividers that, as their name implies, guide the eye or point the way to the location of the folder being sought. Guides

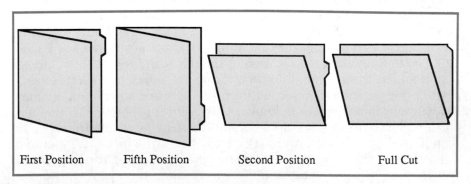

FIGURE 3-7 — Open-Shelf File Folders

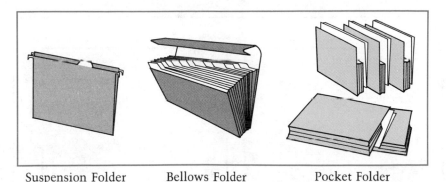

Suspension Folder   Bellows Folder   Pocket Folder

FIGURE 3-8 — Special Folders Used to Store Paper Records

are made of heavier material than are folders; pressboard, plastic, or lightweight metal guides are available. Some guides have reinforced tabs of metal or acetate to give added strength for longer wear.

Guides protect folders from extensive wear since the hand passes quickly and frequently from guide to guide, without touching the folder tops. Guides, like folders, are available with a straight top edge or with tabs of various cuts and in various positions. Guides are available in many sizes and colors and may be blank or preprinted with alphabetic divisions, with days (numbered 1 to 31), with combinations of dates (such as Jan-June and July-Dec; bimonthly; monthly; semimonthly), and with numbers.

Guides for open-shelf equipment are similar to the guides used for drawer filing except that their tabs are at the side (See Figure 3-9). Since materials stored in open-shelf equipment are visible at one edge instead of across the top (as is true in drawer files), the alphabetic or other divisions must extend from the side of the guide so that they can be seen easily. The printing on these side-guide tabs may be read from either side. Special guides and their uses will be discussed later in the text.

Labels.   The tab on a folder is usually covered with a piece of gummed paper called a **label** that identifies the contents of the folder. Labels are available in many varieties to meet the needs of particular filing systems. Labels may be plain or colored, printed or blank, lined or color-striped (with narrow or wide bands and with single or double stripes). Colored or striped labels are especially helpful for locating stored materials quickly. Labels may be gummed on the back, requiring moistening and pressure, or they may have adhesive backs to be peeled from a

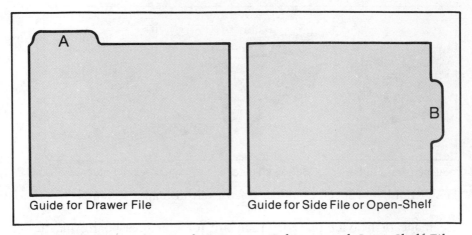

Guide for Drawer File   Guide for Side File or Open-Shelf

FIGURE 3-9 — Guides Used in Drawer Cabinets and Open-Shelf Files

protective sheet and pressed on the tabs. Figure 3-10 shows folder labels in the process of being typed.

Labels or captions are also used for identification on the front of a file cabinet drawer or a file box to show the range of contents within, at the ends of the aisles of open-shelf files to indicate the section of storage encompassed, on the spines of binders to show their contents, and sometimes on the shelving edges of rotary files to act as guides to retrieval.

Sorters.   A **sorter** is used to hold temporarily records to be stored later. The records are organized in a roughly alphabetic order or by number

FIGURE 3-10 — Labels

(depending on the method or system in use) so that they may be stored quickly when time is available for the storage function. The type of sorter to be used in any office depends on the volume of records to be stored.

One sorter that will accommodate records with one dimension as large as ten inches (such as checks, sales slips, time cards, correspondence, and ledger sheets) is shown in Figure 3-11.

Other specialized supplies will be discussed in later chapters of the text, as their use becomes necessary. The supplies just explained and illustrated are basic ones.

Selection of Storage Equipment and Supplies

Efficiency, increased productivity, and overall savings result when the right type, size, number, and quality of storage equipment and supplies are used. Records managers should welcome information furnished by manufacturers and keep themselves up-to-date on new and improved products by reading business periodicals, trade magazines, and catalogs; by attending business shows; and by participating in professional records management association meetings.

Because every organization has its own kinds of records to be stored and used, control over them is an individual matter. The selection of storage equipment and supplies requires that each of the following interrelated factors be taken into consideration:

1. *Type and volume of records to be stored and retrieved.* An inventory of what is to be stored may reveal papers, cards, books, disks, microrecords, architectural drawings, computer printouts, etc. Such an inventory will also show the current volume of records already stored.

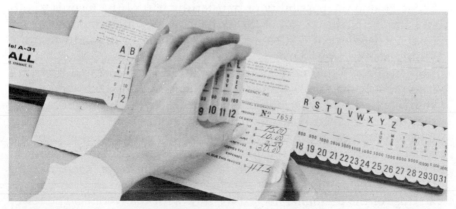

FIGURE 3-11 — General-Purpose Sorter
Boorum & Pease Co.

Future volume must be forecast as well as any anticipated changes in method of storage, such as the possibility of microfilming records. If that were done, there would be a decrease in paper records stored and an increase in microfilm to be stored. Also, personal computers may be introduced, with the storage of diskettes, then, an item to be considered. Records that are called for daily need to be located close to the point of request; those that are accessed weekly, monthly, or yearly may be stored much farther away.

2. *Degree of required protection of records.* Confidential or classified records may require equipment with locks; irreplaceable records will need fireproof or fire-resistant storage equipment; legal documents may be duplicated, one copy then being stored within the organization and the other copy at an offsite location.

3. *Efficiency and ease of use of equipment and systems.* The ease with which records can be found is another consideration—can they be stored so that they are found by going directly to them or is there an intermediate step necessary (such as looking in a card index to determine a number for which to search)? The simpler the system is to understand, the easier it is to use. Also, less training of new employees is needed when the system is a simple one. Time saved by personnel who store and retrieve records means dollars saved. Efficiency of usage also is affected by the location of the equipment, either within departments or in a central place. Movable versus stationary equipment should also be considered. The ease of expansion or modification of a system or of the addition to it of compatible equipment will be important in meeting the changing needs of an organization.

4. *Space Considerations.* Floor-weight restrictions, usage of space to the ceiling or the advisability of counter-type equipment or something in between, and the possibility of transferring part of the records to offsite storage facilities—all of these affect space which, in an office, is costly. The effect of new equipment on present layout and workflow should also be considered.

5. *Cost.* After all other criteria have been examined, cost and the company budget may be the final determinants as to which equipment and supplies may be acquired. The astute records manager realizes that the least expensive equipment and supplies may not provide the most economical records storage. Quality in construction and in materials is important; inferior materials or lightweight stock may need frequent and costly replacement. In determining costs, keep in mind the following points:

   a. Cost of the personnel needed to work with the records. The fewer the people who work with records, the better; fewer records will be misplaced or lost and, therefore, less cost is incurred.

b. Compatibility of supplies and equipment. Folders used in shelf storage differ from those used in drawer cabinets, for example. Standardization of brands and models of equipment may make discounts possible as well as improve the appearance of the office. Standard forms and sizes of supplies are less costly than those that must be ordered specially or be secured from only one vendor.

c. Advisability of using local vendors rather than purchasing from out-of-town vendors. Company policy may be the determining factor here, however.

d. Possibility of discounts for quantity purchases.

e. Feasibility of choosing used rather than new equipment.

f. Volume of records that can be stored within the equipment. Lateral, shelf, or rotary equipment can house more square feet of records than can conventional drawer file cabinets in the same square footage of floor space.

Other factors may need to be added to your list of considerations because of the special needs of your organization. Also, it will be helpful to consult with users of the same equipment that you are now considering acquiring.

BASIC METHODS OF RECORDS STORAGE

Records management professionals do not agree on the number of methods of records storage. Some say there are just two: alphabetic and numeric. Others add a third: alphanumeric. Still others add a fourth: chronologic. To make storage systems easy for you to understand, we will consider five storage methods: alphabetic, subject, numeric, geographic, and chronologic. With the exception of chronologic storage, each of these methods uses alphabetic concepts in its operation. A quick look at each method follows.

Alphabetic Storage Method

With the **alphabetic storage method**, all material is stored in dictionary order, A through Z. If the first letters of the first units in a name or subject are alike, the second, third, fourth, and succeeding units are used to arrange alphabetic sequence. You will find many examples of names arranged alphabetically as you read Chapters 5 and 6. A detailed study of the alphabetic storage method begins in Chapter 4.

A very simple alphabetic arrangement is illustrated in Figure 3-12. The contents of the drawer are divided into a number of alphabetic sections with a guide for each section (See circled 1 in Figure 3-12). For every guide there is a corresponding **general** or **miscellaneous folder** (See circled 2 in Figure 3-12) that contains records for which no other folder has been prepared. The general folder bears the same caption as the guide and is the last item in the section designated by the guide. It is preceded by **individual folders** (See circled 3 in Figure 3-12) that contain records that have accumulated for the designated individuals. All the individual folders fit into the alphabetic range indicated by the label on the guide tab. The labels on the tabs may be letters only or a combination of letters and numbers.

Subject Storage Method

Basically, the **subject storage method** is the alphabetic arrangement of records according to their subjects. Folder tabs bear the subject names.

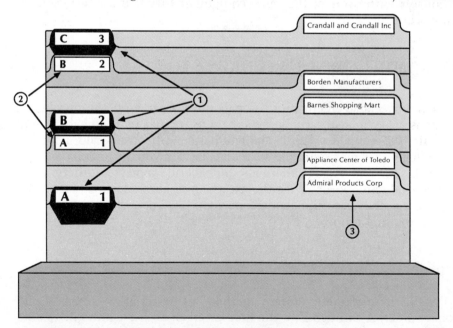

FIGURE 3-12 — A Portion of an Alphabetic Arrangement

(See Landscape Contractors, Language Schools, Laundries, Machine Shops, and so on, in Figure 3-13.) Within each subject folder, records are arranged alphabetically by correspondents' names. The subject method is used when the content of the records is more important than are the names of the individuals or organizations whose records are being stored.

Only a person who is familiar with the records to be handled and who knows the firm's operations thoroughly can use the subject method efficiently. Selecting the subject titles to be used as captions and maintaining an up-to-date index of them, which must be easily accessible and understandable since it will be constantly referred to, are important duties of the one who uses the subject method. Chapter 8 contains further discussion and detailed illustrations of the subject method.

Numeric Storage Method

In the **numeric storage method**, records are assigned numbers and then stored in numeric sequence. This method of storage lends itself especially well to storing invoices and purchase orders that have preprinted numbers. Correspondence may be stored in this manner when

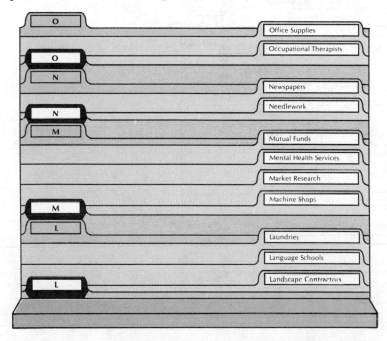

FIGURE 3-13 — A Portion of a Subject Arrangement

it is preferable to use numbers instead of the names of the correspondents on folder tabs (See Figure 3-14). This method is very useful in offices where customers' names are kept in confidence or where many people have access to the stored records and the chances of misfiling are great. Since numbers are more easily arranged in sequence than are letters of the alphabet, people store and retrieve more easily and quickly by number. Detailed procedures for the numeric storage method, with explanations of variations of the method and specialized numeric systems, are discussed in Chapter 9.

Geographic Storage Method

The **geographic storage method** is an alphabetic ordering based on the locations or addresses of the correspondents instead of on their names.

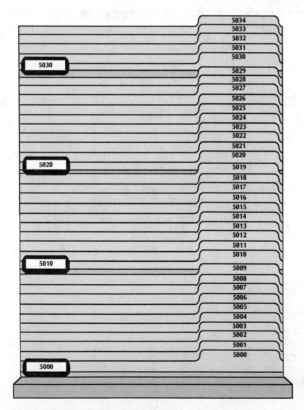

FIGURE 3-14 — A Portion of a Numeric Arrangement

Records are stored alphabetically by the geographic areas indicated on the labels placed on the guides and folders (See circled 1 and 2 in Figure 3-15). Within the general folder for each city (See circled 3 in Figure 3-15), records are stored alphabetically by names of the correspondents. Individual folders are used for correspondents who have or will have a sufficient number of records to warrant a separate folder—stored by location first, however (See circled 4 in Figure 3-15). Records in individual folders are stored chronologically.

Geographic storage is often used in utility companies and real estate offices where reference is made first to *place* instead of to a name. Details of the geographic storage method are given in Chapter 10.

Chronologic Storage Method

As its name implies, the **chronologic storage method** consists of storing by calendar date. Exact chronologic storage is not well suited to correspondence because of the need for keeping together all records of communications from, to, and about one individual or organization. Chronologic storage is often used for daily reports, deposit tickets, freight bills, statements, and order sheets, which may best be stored by date.

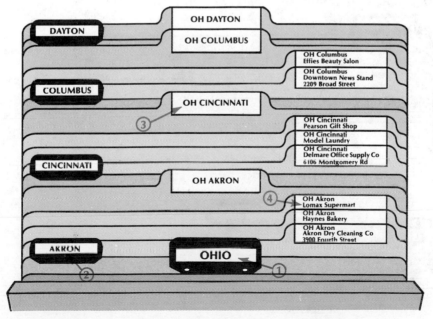

FIGURE 3-15 — A Portion of a Geographic Arrangement

The chronologic principle is followed in all methods of storage
as records are placed in their folders. The top of each record is
at the left of the folder, and the record with the most recent
date is on top.

Some offices keep a chronologic arrangement called a **reading file**,
that consists of copies of all daily correspondence arranged by date, the
most recent date being on top. This reading file may be circulated so
that all executives have an opportunity to read the previous day's correspondence. A secretary or administrative assistant may keep a reading
file for easy access to an extra copy of correspondence written within
the past few days.

A reading file Another form of chronologic storage is a **tickler file**, which is always
arranged by date. As the name suggests, it "tickles" the memory by serving as a reminder that a specific action must be taken on a specific date.
Chapter 7 contains an additional explanation of the tickler file.

A chronologic arrangement may be needed within an alphabetic
storage arrangement when a folder becomes too full. The contents of the
overcrowded folder may be removed and divided into folders with monthly
labels. (See the Kaine Paper Co. section in Figure 3-16.)

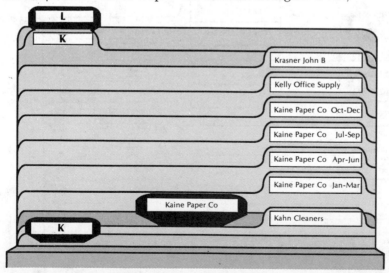

FIGURE 3-16 — Chronologic Arrangement Within an Alphabetic Arrangement

This chapter has stressed the storage of paper records because this knowledge is basic to retrieval of *any* record. Information is also stored on disks, in computer memories, on magnetic media, and on microfilm—stored by subject, by name, by number, by location. Further discussion of this type of storage will be found in Parts 4 and 5. In the remaining chapters of Part 2, alphabetic storage will be presented in detail.

IMPORTANT TERMS AND CONCEPTS

alphabetic storage method
bellows (expansion) folder
chronologic storage method
coding
computer printout files
folders
general (miscellaneous) folder
geographic storage method
guides
indexing (classifying)
individual folders
labels
lateral file cabinets
numeric storage method

pocket folder
position
reading file
shelf files
sorter
storage
storage method
storage procedures
subject storage method
suspension (hanging) folder
tab
tickler file
unit
vertical file cabinets

REVIEW AND DISCUSSION

1. What is a reading file? How is it used? (Obj. 1)

2. Why is the straight-line arrangement of tabs on folders and guides easier to use than the staggered arrangement? (Obj. 1)

3. What are the four kinds of commonly used storage equipment for paper records? (Obj. 2)

4. What are four important supplies used in records storage? (Obj. 3)

5. What do "cut" and "position" mean with regard to folder tabs? (Obj. 4)

6. What are the five methods of records storage? (Obj. 5)

7. What are the similarities between alphabetic and subject storage methods? (Objs. 5, 6)

8. What is the fundamental difference between alphabetic and geographic storage methods? (Objs. 5, 6)

9. Explain what is meant by: "The chronologic principle is followed in all storage methods." (Obj. 6)

10. Why is numeric storing usually faster than alphabetic storing? (Obj. 6)

11. Which storage method does not also use the alphabetic storage method? (Obj. 7)

12. What is the difference between a storage system and a storage method? (Obj. 8)

DECISION-MAKING OPPORTUNITIES (DMO)

DMO 3-1: Evaluating Storage Methods

You work in a doctor's office where patients' records are stored in vertical file cabinets in the waiting room. Presently the folders are labeled with the names of the patients and the alphabetic storage method is used. You refer to the file folders many times during the day while patients are waiting to see the doctor; each time you open a drawer, the names of patients are visible to several people. This situation bothers you because you believe patients' names should be confidential.

What can you do to preserve the confidentiality of patients' names? What other method of storage might be better? Is new equipment necessary? Why? (Objs. 6 and 7)

DMO 3-2: Changing Storage Equipment

Assume that you work in an office where correspondence is stored alphabetically in traditional five-drawer vertical file cabinets. Everyone in the office has access to the file cabinets. You usually must retrieve 10 to 20 stored records daily, one paper at a time. You believe open-shelf files would be better. Why do you think so? What factors would contribute to your decision? Whom would you consult to help you assemble the facts needed to approach your supervisor with a suggestion for change? List the facts you believe would help you to present your suggestion for change. (Objs. 2, 3, and 4)

4 ALPHABETIC RECORDS STORAGE

Objectives

After you have completed this chapter, you will be able to:

1. List the kinds of alphabetic arrangements that you encounter in your everyday life.
2. Explain the different kinds of labels and captions used in alphabetic records storage and explain their use.
3. Identify the different types of guides and folders used in alphabetic records storage and explain their use.
4. List the advantages and disadvantages of the alphabetic method of records storage.
5. Explain the necessity for careful selection and design of an alphabetic records storage system.
6. Describe the six steps that must be followed in order to store a record properly according to the alphabetic method.

In almost every office, alphabetic storage in one form or another can be found. Many of these offices use various alphabetic systems that have been developed by filing equipment and supplies manufacturers to make alphabetic storage easy. Several of these systems will be illustrated in this chapter.

You are already familiar with many alphabetic arrangements in your everyday life: library card files and magazine lists, telephone directories, dictionaries, city directories, your address book, student records—the list could go on and on! In this chapter you will study the alphabetic storage method—the arrangement of records using the letters of the alphabet to determine order.

You will need to know the composition of an alphabetic storage arrangement and the systematic procedures involved in storing records alphabetically because this arrangement is basic to other storage methods. The business world refers to people and organizations by name in most instances, even though we are sometimes also identified by number (social security, checking account, etc.). These numbers, however, each relate to a name. Subject storage, too, uses the alphabetic method—whether the records are contained in file folders or stored in a computer—because the subjects are arranged in alphabetic order. One way the alphabetic method is used in geographic storage is to arrange the named geographic locations in alphabetic order. All of these storage methods will be explained in detail in later chapters.

Although the information in this chapter will pertain to paper records primarily, the principles you learn will also be used in mechanized and automated records storage. In this chapter, you will first study the components of an efficient alphabetic arrangement and look at some illustrative systems. Then the procedures for storing records alphabetically will be explained in detail. Knowledge of these procedures is necessary so that you can analyze, store, retrieve, and protect records entrusted to your care as well as explain your alphabetic storage method to others who may work with you.

ALPHABETIC STORAGE ARRANGEMENT

An alphabetic arrangement has many small sections, each representing one alphabetic division. An alphabetic division does not necessarily mean a letter of the alphabet, however, as you will see later. A simple illustration of part of an alphabetic arrangement in a drawer is shown in Figure 4-1. You will need to refer to Figure 4-1 regularly. First, read the discussion; then, turn to the figure and locate the component being discussed. You will understand the material much more easily if you continue to read and study this figure carefully.

Labels and Captions

An alphabetic arrangement may be used in drawers, on open shelves, in card files, in lateral files, or on card strips in a visible file. No matter what kind of equipment is used, however, there must be a caption or label to identify what section of the alphabet is contained in that special piece of equipment.

Container Captions or Labels.   The terms caption and label are used interchangeably. The labels on drawers, shelf files, or other storage containers should be as briefly worded and as clear as possible. The caption on the drawer illustrated in Figure 4-1 reads A-B, indicating that the records of the correspondents whose names are within the A and B sections of the alphabet are stored in that drawer. Labels indicating the alphabetic range of contents may be one of three types:

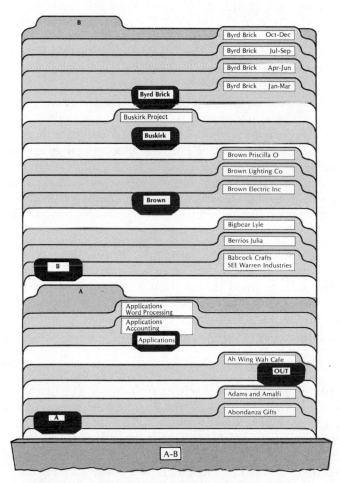

FIGURE 4-1 — One Section of an Alphabetic Arrangement

1. **Open notation** shows only the beginning letter of the alphabetic section contained.
2. **Closed notation** shows both the beginning and end of the alphabetic section contained.
3. **Multiple-closed notation** shows not only the alphabetic range of the material contained but also the most frequent combinations within that range. (The range is from A to Be, with Al and Ba frequent combinations within the A to Be range.)

| A | A - Be | A - Be
(Al - Ba) |

Open notations (sometimes called *single notations*) are easily read. However, there is no indication of the letter of the alphabet where the contents end. If the label reads A, the filer does not know what that container includes until the second container label is read—and it might be E. This would mean that records from A through D are stored in the first container.

Closed notations (often called *double notations*) indicate at once the entire alphabetic range of the stored contents. One need not look at the label on the next container to see with which letter its contents begin.

Multiple-closed notations indicate the entire alphabetic range of the stored contents in the same manner as do closed notations. In addition, however, multiple-closed notations also show important subsections within that alphabetic range. These subsections are the letter combinations shown in parentheses on the label.

Guide Labels. Labels on guides consist of words, letters, or numbers (or some combination of these items). In Figure 4-1, the guides shown have window tabs into which typed information has been inserted (A, Applications, B, Brown, Buskirk, Byrd Brick). If the **primary guides** (A, B) have numbers as well as letters on their captions, as is sometimes the case, the **special guides** (Applications, Brown, Buskirk, Byrd Brick) also should have corresponding numbers.

Folder Labels. A folder is best labeled with gummed or pressure sensitive paper strips placed on the tab. In Figure 4-1, all of the individual folders at the right, the special folders in the middle (Applications Accounting; Applications Word Processing; Buskirk Project), and the general folders A and B at the left have been labeled with typed, gummed strips. A number code may be used in addition to the name on a primary guide tab, appearing on the label of every folder in the section behind the guide. The combination of letters and numbers, and sometimes the color of the label on which the caption is printed, help to avoid mistakes in storage. For example, the filer should almost unconsciously note the appearance of a blue-tabbed folder in an otherwise tan section; the filer should note, too, a folder with the number 10 in a section with folders numbered 50, for example.

Rolls of labels in boxes, continuous folded strips, separate strips, or pressure-sensitive adhesive labels are only four of the various ways in which labels are packaged. The use of pastel-colored labels is preferable to deeper colored ones because the typing on the pastel labels can be read easily. Sometimes a colored stripe across the top is used on a white or buff-colored label, for the same reason.

Satisfactory labels have the following characteristics:

1. For pressure-sensitive labels, good quality paper that will not tear when it is removed from its backing and that is coated with a gummed substance that will adhere firmly to all types of folder tabs (paper, plastic, or metal).
2. For fold-over labels, good quality paper that will not break when folded over the top of a tab and perforations that tear easily but are strong enough to hold the labels together while information is being typed on them.
3. For both pressure-sensitive and fold-over labels, a light background so that typing can be easily read.

The typing format on the label is a matter of office preference. Handwritten labels are a source of trouble because of illegibility. Hand-printed labels, too, are not advisable because of the lack of uniformity between individual printing styles. Uniform typing ensures neat-looking files and makes storage and retrieval easier. Several acceptable practices for typing on labels are listed below:

1. All typing should begin the same distance from the left edge of the label (usually 2 or 3 typewriter spaces) and the same distance from the top of the label (usually the top typing line is left blank).
2. If the label has a ridge that divides the label in half, the caption is typed on the lower half. The ridge is the fold line, with the blank half of the label being on the back side of the folder tab.
3. The captions may appear in **indexing order** (personal names are reversed and business names are in the order written). Captions also may appear in the **as-written** or **straight order** in which all names, including personal names, are printed as they are written. A comparison of the two lists of identical names below shows how much easier it is to check the alphabetic arrangement of the list on the left.

Indexing Order	As-Written Order
Navarro Luisa	Luisa Navarro
Nichols H A	H A Nichols
Nieves Charles P	Charles P Nieves
Nilson-Nisbett Co	Nilson-Nisbett Co
Nishimura Jane L Mrs	Mrs Jane L Nishimura
Noel Nyberg and Daughter	Noel Nyberg and Daughter

4. The caption may consist of:

   a. the name only.

   b. the name on the first line and the city and state on the second line.

   c. the name on the first line, the city and state on the second line, and the street address on succeeding lines.

Adams Arno F Dr

ADAMS Arno F Dr
Lawrence KS

ADAMS ARNO F DR
Lawrence KS
17471 Tam OShanter Drive

Choice of the style to be used in the office is the responsibility of the records manager, supervisor, or office manager.

5. Although previous practice has been to type captions with punctuation and parentheses, the trend today is to type personal names in transposed order without punctuation. Business and other names are typed in as-written order without punctuation. Symbols such as &, #, $, %, ¢, are typed in spelled-out form, and no parentheses are used (See 4a, b, and c). You will find this style used throughout this textbook and in *Records Management Projects*, 4th ed., that accompanies it.

6. The name on the label may be typed with all capital letters, but it is then somewhat difficult to read (See 4c); the name may be typed with capitalization of only the first letter of each important word (See 4a), or with all capitals for the first unit and capitals and lower case letters for the other units (See 4b).

7. Block style (all lines starting at the left margin) is preferred to conserve space. If the wording is too long for the label, however, the continuation of the wording is indented on the second line.

8. Labels should be affixed to all folders at the same place on the tabs. Uniform placement can be achieved as follows: When a new box of folders is opened, remove all the folders, keep them tightly together, and stand them upright on a flat surface. Place a ruler or stiff card over the tab edges at the spot where all the labels are to be attached (See Figure 4-2). Make a pencil mark across the top edge of all the tabs. A very small pencil mark will show on each of the tabs at the same place and will serve as a guide for attaching all the labels.

9. When new folders are prepared, care should be taken to make sure the placement of the labels and the typing format are the same as those on other folders. New folders may be needed because:

   a. A new group of names is to be added to the file.

   b. Older folders have become full and additional ones must be added to take care of the overload.

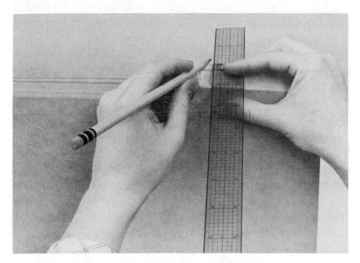

FIGURE 4-2 — Marking Folders for Uniform Label Attachment

c. Enough records have accumulated for certain correspondents so that their records can be removed from the general folders and put into individual folders.
d. Folders have worn out from heavy use and must be replaced.
e. The regular time of the year has arrived for replacing folders and transferring infrequently used folders to semiactive or inactive storage.

Guides

Guides are rigid dividers placed between alphabetic sections to guide the eye from section to section. The proper placement of guides eliminates the need to spend time searching through similar names to find the part of the alphabet needed. Guides are usually very sturdy since they are expected to last many years. The same set of guides may be used year after year with no change, or they may be added to or changed as the quantity of records expands. Because of their thickness and sturdy construction, guides serve also to keep the contents of a container upright. When contents stand upright, neatness and efficiency of storage and retrieval result.

If too few guides are used, unnecessary time is spent looking for the correct place to store or to find a record. Using too many guides and an uneven distribution of them throughout the files can also slow storage and retrieval, because the eye must look at so many tabs to find the right storage section. Several filing authorities recommend using about 20 guides for each drawer in a file cabinet or for each 28 inches of stored records.

Guides for the alphabetic method are of two types: One shows the letters of the various sections of the alphabet; the other shows names or subjects that are frequently referred to or have many similarly named folders behind them. Both types are explained here.

Primary Guides.   A **primary guide** always precedes all other materials in a section. In Figure 4-1, the A and B guides, in first position, are primary guides. If the volume of stored correspondence with many individuals or firms is comparatively small, only primary guides need to be used to indicate the alphabetic sections. In systems that use color extensively, only primary guides with the letters of the alphabet may be used. (You will see illustrations of color usage later in this chapter.)

Guide sets that divide the alphabet into many different segments are available from manufacturers of filing supplies. The simplest set is a 23- or 25-division set, the latter having a tab for each letter from A to W, a tab labeled Mc, and a last tab with the combination XYZ. A more complex set of guides, with the alphabet subdivided into 40, 80, 120, and 160 sections may be necessary if the volume of stored records is great. Suppose, for example, you have hundreds of folders for names beginning with A. Instead of just one A guide, you might need a sequence of guides that would have tabs reading Aa, Ah, Am, An, Ar, and At. An 80-division and a 120-division breakdown of guides printed by manufacturers is shown in Figure 4-3. Up to 10,000 alphabetic divisions are available for A to Z.

As you study the columns in Figure 4-3, you will note that some parts of the alphabet have more subdivisions than do others; notably, B, C, H, M, S, and W. Subdivisions within those letters are necessary because there are more names that begin with those letters than with other letters in the alphabet. Similarly, names beginning with I, O, Q, U, V, X, Y, and Z occur far less frequently and, therefore, no subdivisions of those letters are usually needed.

The number of guides furnished by different manufacturers may vary even though each one may divide the alphabet into 40 subdivisions. Manufacturers may elect to omit Mc, subdivide letters differently, or combine different letters. Before a set of guides is purchased, the records manager needs to get a list of the subdivisions of the alphabet from the manufacturer to see if they fit specific office requirements.

Some guides may be purchased with preprinted tabs. Others have tabs with slotted holders into which can be inserted labels showing

80 Div. A to Z				120 Div. A to Z					
A	1	L	41	A	1	Gr	41	Pe	81
An	2	Le	42	Al	2	H	42	Pi	82
B	3	Li	43	An	3	Han	43	Pl	83
Be	4	Lo	44	As	4	Has	44	Pr	84
Bi	5	M	45	B	5	He	45	Pu	85
Bo	6	Map	46	Bar	6	Hen	46	Q	86
Br	7	McA	47	Bas	7	Hi	47	R	87
Bro	8	McH	48	Be	8	Ho	48	Re	88
Bu	9	McN	49	Ber	9	Hon	49	Ri	89
C	10	Me	50	Bl	10	Hu	50	Ro	90
Ce	11	Mi	51	Bo	11	I	51	Rog	91
Co	12	Mo	52	Br	12	J	52	Ru	92
Coo	13	N	53	Bre	13	Jo	53	S	93
Cr	14	O	54	Bro	14	K	54	Sch	94
D	15	P	55	Bu	15	Ke	55	Scho	95
De	16	Pl	56	C	16	Ki	56	Se	96
Do	17	Q	57	Car	17	Kl	57	Sh	97
Dr	18	R	58	Ce	18	Kr	58	Shi	98
E	19	Re	59	Ci	19	L	59	Si	99
En	20	Ro	60	Co	20	Lar	60	Sm	100
F	21	S	61	Com	21	Le	61	Sn	101
Fi	22	Sch	62	Cop	22	Len	62	Sp	102
Fo	23	Se	63	Cr	23	Li	63	St	103
G	24	Sh	64	Cu	24	Lo	64	Sti	104
Ge	25	Si	65	D	25	M	65	Su	105
Gi	26	Sm	66	De	26	Map	66	T	106
Gr	27	St	67	Di	27	McA	67	Th	107
H	28	Sti	68	Do	28	McD	68	Tr	108
Har	29	Su	69	Du	29	McH	69	U	109
Has	30	T	70	E	30	McN	70	V	110
He	31	To	71	El	31	Me	71	W	111
Her	32	U	72	Er	32	Mi	72	Wam	112
Hi	33	V	73	F	33	Mo	73	We	113
Ho	34	W	74	Fi	34	Mu	74	Wh	114
Hu	35	We	75	Fo	35	N	75	Wi	115
I	36	Wh	76	Fr	36	Ne	76	Wil	116
J	37	Wi	77	G	37	No	77	Wim	117
K	38	Wo	78	Ge	38	O	78	Wo	118
Ki	39	X-Y	79	Gi	39	On	79	X-Y	119
Kr	40	Z	80	Go	40	P	80	Z	120

FIGURE 4-3 — Comparison of Guide Sets for A to Z Indexes
Esselte Pendaflex Corporation

whatever sections of the alphabet are needed. (The guides in Figure 4-1 are of this kind.)

Special Guides.   To lead the eye more quickly to a specific place in the file, a **special** or **auxiliary guide** may be used. This guide may:

1. Indicate the location of the folder of an individual or a company with which there is a large amount of correspondence. In Figure 4-1, the guides labeled Brown, Buskirk, and Byrd Brick are special (auxiliary)

name guides. In some organizations, a complete file drawer may be needed for one such correspondent.

2. Introduce a special section of subjects, such as one pertaining to Applications (See Figure 4-1), Bids, Conferences, Exhibits, Projects, or Speeches, that may be found in an alphabetic name arrangement. The special subject section is necessary to bring together in one place all the correspondence relating to one subject rather than to have it dispersed throughout the file by the names of the different correspondents. Figure 4-1 shows a special subject guide, Applications, placed in alphabetic order in the A section. All correspondence concerning applications for positions in accounting and word processing is stored behind Applications, in properly labeled folders.

3. Introduce a section reserved for names that have the same first indexing unit. In Figure 4-1, the Brown auxiliary guide leads the eye to the section with numerous folders labeled with Brown as the first indexing unit.

Folders

Behind every guide are folders that are used to keep like records together. The proper grade and weight of folders have much to do with the efficiency of the storage system. A folder that is too lightweight will not withstand wear; one that is too heavy wastes needed space in storage. A folder that is frequently used should have a double- or triple-thick top to provide protection from wear. The rest of the folder can be of lighter weight material, saving cost and storage space.

Types of Folders.   The three main types of folders used in alphabetic storage are general folders, individual folders, and special folders.

General Folders.   Every primary guide has a correspondingly labeled folder, called a general folder, bearing the same caption as that on the guide. In Figure 4-1, the A folder is a general folder in first position and is the last folder in that section.

Records stored in a general folder are those to and from correspondents with volume so limited that an individual folder is not necessary. Within the general folder, records are arranged first alphabetically by the correspondents' names. Then, within each correspondent's records, the arrangement is by date with the most recent date on top (See Figure 4-4).

FIGURE 4-4 — Paper Arrangement in a General Folder

Individual Folders.   Individual folders are used to store the records of individual correspondents. Within an individual folder, records are arranged chronologically, with the most recently dated record on top. In Figure 4-1, all folders that are third cut, third position are individual folders.

When records pertaining to one correspondent accumulate to a predetermined number in the general folder, they are removed and placed in an individual folder. Individual folders are usually placed in alphabetic order between the primary guide and its general folder.

Office policy determines whether five pieces, eight pieces, or some other number of records shall accumulate in the general folder before an individual folder is prepared for them. In special cases, when correspondence is received from an important customer, an individual folder may be prepared for the first piece of correspondence. When correspondence with one firm is very heavy and so actively used that all of it must be kept in the active files, the correspondence may be placed in several folders with the months indicated on the folder tabs. The four folders for Byrd Brick in Figure 4-1 are examples of these individual folders, sometimes called **period folders.**

Special Folders.   **Special folders** follow auxiliary guides in an alphabetic arrangement. In Figure 4-1 three special folders are shown: two behind Applications and one behind Buskirk. Within the Applications Accounting folder, all records pertaining to accounting positions are arranged first by the names of the correspondents who applied. If a correspondent has more than one record in the folder, those records are arranged by date with the most recent date on top. Within the Buskirk Project folder, records are arranged by date, the most recent one on top.

Care of Folders.   Proper care of folders is necessary so that records that have been stored will be readily accessible. Three sources of storage difficulty relate directly to the care of folders:

1. Overloading the folders.
2. Overcrowding the file drawers.
3. Failing to use proper means to hold drawer contents upright.

When records start to "ride up" in any folder, it is *overloaded*— there are too many papers. The number of records that will fit into one folder obviously depends on the thickness of the papers. Records should never protrude from the folder edges and should always be inserted with their tops to the left. The most useful and most often recommended folders have **score marks** (indented or raised lines or series of marks) along the bottom edge to allow for expansion of the folder. As it becomes filled, the folder is refolded along a score mark and expanded to give it a flat base on which to rest. Most folders can be expanded from 3/4 to 1 inch. If folders are refolded at the score marks (See Figure 4-5), the danger of folders bending and sliding under others is reduced, papers do not curl readily, and a neater looking file results.

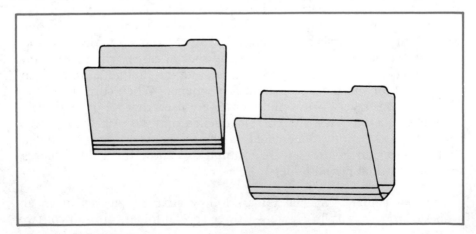

FIGURE 4-5 — Flat Folder and Expanded Folder

Jeter Top Coder Color - Coded System
and Supplies

Jeter Systems Corporation

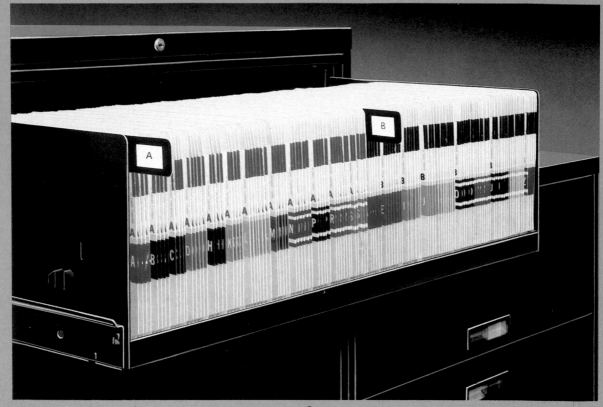

ALPHA - Z® SYSTEM
The Smead Manufacturing Company

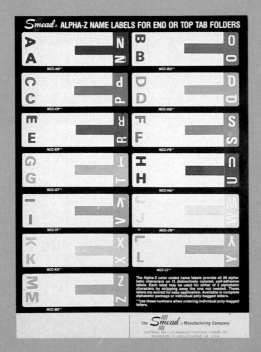

Alpha - Z color-coded name labels

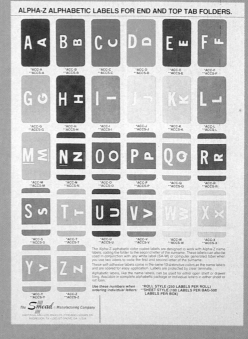

Alpha - Z color-coded alphabetic labels

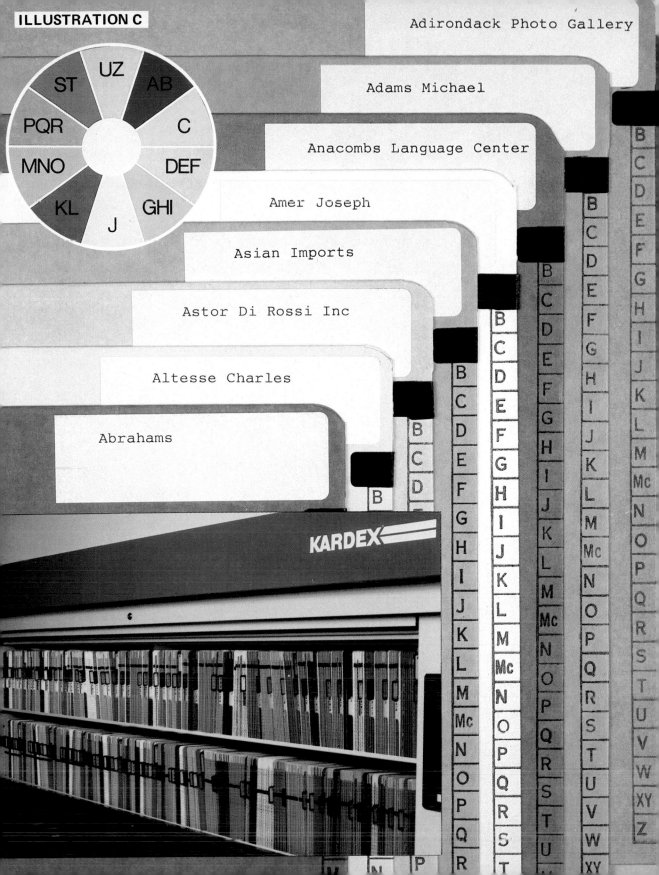

ILLUSTRATION C

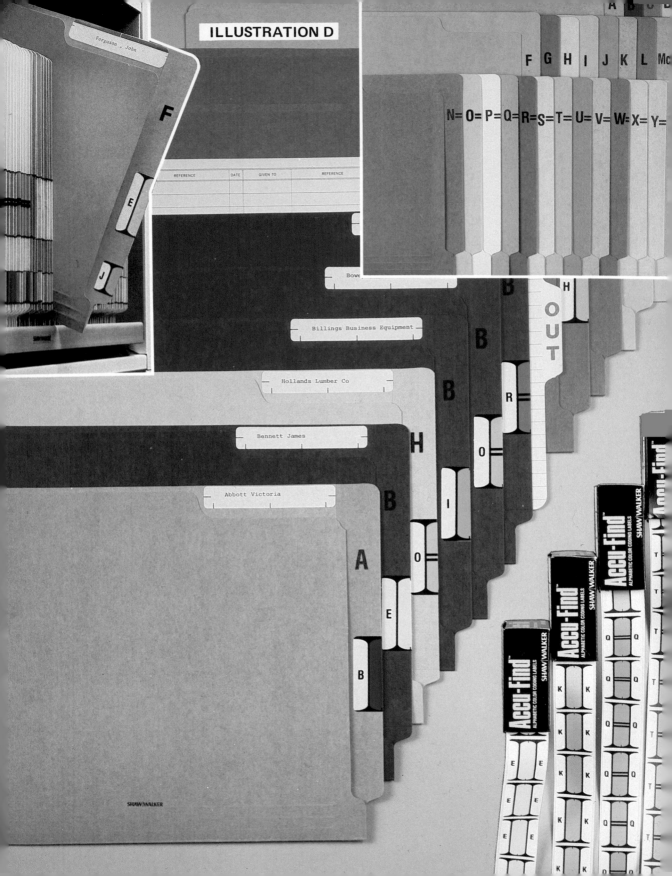

ILLUSTRATION D

A folder lasts longer and is easier to use if it is not stuffed beyond its capacity. If too many papers are contained in an individual folder, it is time to make a second folder for that correspondent. The folders may then be labeled to show that the records are arranged chronologically in them (See the four Byrd Brick folders in Figure 4-1). Sometimes the papers are redistributed in folders by subjects instead of by dates, as is the case with Applications in Figure 4-1.

If overloading occurs in a general folder, the records should be reviewed to determine the advisability of making individual folders for some of the correspondents. New primary guides and general folders can be inserted to provide more subdivisions within the alphabet, and records in the general folders can be redistributed. For example, if the divisions of the alphabet are A, B, C, D, etc., it might be wise to use Aa-Am, An-Az, Ba-Bm, Bn-Bz, and so on. In this way, the volume of correspondence formerly in the general A folder would be separated into two groups: Aa to Am correspondence would go into the general Aa-Am folder, and An to Az correspondence would go into the general An-Az folder.

Another way to alleviate congestion in general folders is to set up special subject guides and corresponding folders to take care of records that could better be housed by subjects rather than by correspondents' names. At times, older records in any folder may be transferred to inactive storage to relieve overloading. Further explanation of transfer is contained in Chapter 7.

When file drawers become stuffed tightly with guides and folders, removal of folders may be difficult but reinsertion of them is even more difficult. And getting a single piece of paper into or out of the files is almost impossible. If a careless person attempts to jam a folder into an overcrowded file, the edges may be bent, the tab may be crushed, or the folder being inserted may inadvertently be crushed into another folder instead of being placed ahead of or behind it. When great pressure is exerted to force a folder downward between two others, the entire folder may bend.

If a check of the folder contents reveals that all of the records are necessary and that no materials can be disposed of, and if all file drawers are filled to capacity, the solution to this *overcrowded* condition is to add more drawers. To do this, all folders and guides should be removed from the last few file drawers and carefully moved, in order, to another set of file drawers. Space should be left in the back of each drawer for expansion, and folders and guides should be moved methodically from each drawer. When all of the moving has been done, the drawers should be relabeled to show the range of the contents within them. When space for expansion has been left at the back of each drawer, the file folders can be inserted and removed easily with no fear of damage.

Follower Blocks or Compressors

Failing to use proper means to hold drawer contents upright causes folders to bend and slide under one another. Folders are kept upright by using the proper number of guides and by the correct use of a follower block behind the guides and folders. **Follower blocks** (or *compressors*) may be moved back and forth in a drawer to allow for contraction or expansion of its contents (See Figure 4-6). A follower block that is too loose will allow the drawer contents to sag; one that is too tight will make it very difficult to get a folder in or out of the drawer. In an over-compressed drawer, as in an overcrowded drawer, locating and removing a single sheet of paper is almost impossible. Instead of follower blocks, some file drawers have slim steel upright dividers placed permanently throughout the file drawer to keep the contents vertical.

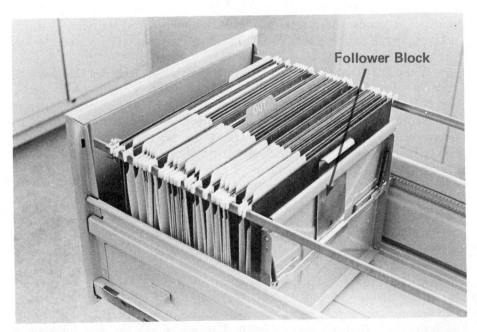

FIGURE 4-6 — Follower Block

OUT Indicators

OUT indicators are control devices that show the location of records at all times. When a borrowed record is returned to storage, the OUT indicator is removed, to be reused, thrown away, or saved and later used to check the activity at the files or to determine which records are active or inactive. The more commonly used indicators are OUT guides, OUT folders, and OUT sheets.

OUT Guide.   An **OUT guide** is used to replace any record that has been removed from storage. When the borrowed record is returned, the filer can thus quickly find the exact place from which the record was taken. An OUT guide is made of heavy card stock—similar to cardboard—with the word OUT printed on its tab in a large size and in a distinctive color. In Figure 4-1 an OUT guide is located between the Adams and Amalfi and the Ah Wing Wah Cafe individual folders. Instead of an OUT guide, however, one of the two indicators explained next may be used.

OUT Folder.   An **OUT folder** is used to replace a complete folder that has been removed from storage. The OUT folder remains in the file as a temporary storage place for records that will be transferred to the permanent folder when it is returned to storage.

OUT Sheet.   An **OUT sheet** is a form that is inserted in place of a record or records removed from a folder. An OUT sheet is often the same size and color as an OUT guide, but its thickness is that of a sheet of paper. An OUT sheet, too, remains in the file until the borrowed material is returned to storage.

OUT guides and sheets have spaces on them for writing the name of the person borrowing the record, the date it was borrowed, a brief statement of the contents of the record, and the date it should be returned to storage. An OUT folder has a pocket or slot into which a card is placed bearing the same information concerning who took the folder, the date it was taken, its contents, and the date the folder should be returned to storage.

Most efficient alphabetic storage systems follow the arrangement you have just studied: primary and special guides followed by individual and special folders, with a general folder as the last item in a section. Occasionally you will find a general folder as the first item within an alphabetic section.

ILLUSTRATIVE ALPHABETIC RECORDS STORAGE SYSTEMS

Many manufacturers have produced trade-named alphabetic systems with special characteristics intended to speed records storage and retrieval and to provide a double check against misfiling. These systems use color extensively, as you will see in the four specialized alphabetic systems that are shown and described on the following pages. Other trade-named alphabetic systems are available; the ones shown here are thus representative but not inclusive.

The use of color has two meanings: (1) **color coding**, where different colors are used to divide the alphabetic sections in the system; and (2) **color accenting**, where different colors are used for the different supplies in the system—one color for guides, various colors for folders, one color for OUT indicators. Both color coding and color accenting are found in the systems illustrated here.

To obtain maximum understanding of each system, study the text material carefully and refer to the illustrations frequently. Give special attention to the sequence of items in the illustrations.

Jeter Top Coder Color-Coded System

The Jeter Top Coder Color-Coded System (Jeter Systems Corp., Akron, OH, Color Illustration A) shows drawer storage with folder labels color coded according to the first and second letters of the key unit. The color coding is applied by adhesive labels toward the right of the folder top, with the extreme right position reserved for OUT folders. White labels on the middle of the folders contain full names, typed and arranged alphabetically.

Other color codes to the left of the folder top can signify a variety of additional information, such as (1) types of allergies or whether the individual is on Medicare or Medicaid (if the folders are those of a doctor's office) and (2) the date of last reference to the folder, for retirement of inactive records. Other information you might wish to indicate could be color coded at the left positions on the folder top.

The alphabet is divided into 13 colors with two different label patterns. Letters A through M have solid color labels; letters N through Z have a solid line that separates the label into two parts. The following colors and patterns are used.

Solid Label Letters	Label Color	Two-Part Label Letters
A	Red	N
B	Brown	O
C	White	P
D	Gray	Q
E	Orange	R
F	Beige	S
G	Yellow	T
H	Dark Blue	U
I	Light Blue	V
J	Light Green	W
K	Black	X
L	Dark Green	Y
M	Magenta	Z

The insert on Color Illustration A shows alphabetic, numeric, date, and solid-color block labels; alphabetic, numeric, and OUT folders for open-shelf storage are also shown. Note the position of the OUT tab on the open-shelf guides. Two guide books come with this system for use by the filer to assure that the color coding is done correctly.

Alpha-Z® System

The Alpha-Z System (The Smead Manufacturing Company, Hastings, MN, Color Illustration B) shows part of a lateral drawer with side-labeled folders. Divisions of the alphabet are very visible on extended label holders attached to the tops of heavy black guides (See A and B in Color Illustration B). Folders have end tabs with score marks for three labels. Labels in 13 color combinations are available with white letters on solid color backgrounds for the letters A through M and white letters on a color background with a white stripe through it for letters N through Z.

The first of the three labels bears a color block, the typed name, and the letter of the alphabet for the key unit in the name. The second label is color coded to the second letter of the key unit of the name being stored. The color sequence is: A-red, B-dark blue, C-dark green, D-light blue, E-purple, F-orange, G-gray, H-dark brown, I-pink, J-yellow, K-light brown, L-lavender, and M-light green. The sequence is repeated for letters N through Z. The third label, if used, color codes the third letter of the key unit. All labels are easily read from either side of the folder.

Inset A shows the 26 alphabetic characters on self-adhesive labels. Each label may be used for either of two alphabetic characters by stripping away the letter not needed.

Inset B shows the color-coded labels used for the second letter of the key unit. They are self-adhesive and available in the same 13 colors as are the name labels.

Folders can be added very easily as they are needed. Because labels for the second letter of the key unit are covered with a protective laminate, smudging and smearing are avoided. This protection gives greater strength to the part of the folder that receives the greatest wear because that is where the filer would grasp the folder for insertion or removal.

Colorscan

The Colorscan system (Kardex Systems, Inc., Marietta, OH, Color Illustration C) uses color folders in 10 hues and is, therefore, a color accented system. To store or retrieve any folder in the system, use the first letter of the key unit to find its location. (See the alphabetic guides that protrude from the folders in Color Illustration C.) The guides separating the alphabetic divisions are not color.

Then use the first letter of the second unit to find the color of the folder, as follows:

AB - Red	KL - Brown
C - Yellow	MNO - Blue
DEF - Pink	PQR - Orange
GHI - Green	ST - Violet
J - White	U-Z - Tan

All ten colors are used behind every alphabetic guide. For example, the Gary Lewis folder is stored behind the L guide, and the folder color would be green for Gary. Folders within each alphabetic section are stored in random sequence—active folders remain in the front because of frequency of use, and less active folders are in the rear. (See arrangement of folders in the A section of Color Illustration C.) If a folder has only one unit (Tiffany's, for example), the first letter determines both position and color—T and violet.

In Color Illustration C, lower left, side or lateral storage is shown. At the top right of Color Illustration C, an open-shelf arrangement is shown. The preprinted vertical alphabetic boxes on the edge of the folders are used when storage is on open shelves. Blacking out the letter of the alphabet by which the key unit begins creates a black horizontal line throughout a section of the alphabet when folders are stored side by side. (See in Color Illustration C that all As are blacked out.) Misfiling is then very evident, as a black block will be out of place.

Accu-Find

The Accu-Find system (Shaw-Walker, Muskegon, MI, Color Illustration D) is a color-accented and color-coded shelf filing system. The color folders are in sequence through the alphabet with 13 colors. The 13 colors are repeated on labels with color bands; the letters A through L have solid color bands; the letters Mc through Z have solid color bands with black crossbars on them. (See the lower right corner of Color Illustration D.)

Each folder bears a printed letter, being the first letter of the key unit. A pressure sensitive, two-inch label is color banded and bears a typed name. The color band is coded to the second letter of the key unit. One-inch pressure-sensitive labels may be used for additional coding (usually the first letter of the second unit). In Color Illustration D at the top left, the F folder is green; the yellow-banded label indicates that the second letter of the key unit is E (See Ferguson on the label); the one-inch blue-banded J label indicates that the second unit begins with the letter J (See John on the label). Misfiles are easily seen when colors do not match. (See Color Illustration D for the misfile in the B section, where the gray folder does not match the other folders in the red B section.)

ADVANTAGES AND DISADVANTAGES OF ALPHABETIC RECORDS STORAGE

The advantages of alphabetic records storage are as follows:

1. You can refer directly to an alphabetic arrangement to find a name. This is called **direct reference**—you look directly for a specific name.
2. The dictionary (A to Z) order of arrangement is simple to understand.
3. Storage is easy if standard procedures are followed.
4. Misfiles are easily checked by examining alphabetic sequence.
5. Costs of operation may be lower than for other methods because of the direct reference feature.
6. Only one sorting is required—by alphabet.

The disadvantages of alphabetic records storage are:

1. Misfiling is prevalent when there are no established rules for alphabetic storage and filers follow their own preferences.
2. Similar names may cause confusion, especially when spellings are not precise.
3. Transposition of some letters of the alphabet is easy, causing filing sequence to be out of order.
4. Selecting the wrong name for storage can result in lost records.
5. Names on folders are instantly seen by anyone who happens to glance at an open storage container. Consequently, confidential or classified records are not secure.
6. Labeling of folders can be a laborious task if names and full addresses are placed on labels.

SELECTION AND DESIGN OF ALPHABETIC RECORDS STORAGE SYSTEMS

At the time a new office is opened, a decision must be made on the kind of storage system to be selected or designed. For already established offices, the system in use may prove to be ineffective because it no longer serves the needs of those who request records. If the records are to be requested by names of individuals, businesses, and organizations with few subjects, then an alphabetic system is best for that office.

When the alphabetic method of storage is selected, utmost care should be exercised in its selection or design because, once installed, it is likely to be used for a long time. In order to select an alphabetic system, or to redesign one, the records manager should know:

1. The total volume of records to be stored.
2. The number of records in each alphabetic section and which letters of the alphabet have a large number of records in them.
3. The expected activity in the files—an estimate of how many times records may be requested.
4. The length of time records are to be kept.
5. The efficiency of the filing personnel.
6. The training time available for personnel.

In some cases, the person in charge of the records may seek the help of a records management consultant or a representative of a filing system manufacturer. These people study the needs of the office, consult with the person in charge of the records, and make recommendations.

It is important that the person in charge of the records keep the needs of the office in mind rather than being swayed by the beauty of a system, the expert sales techniques of a representative, or the apparent low cost of one system as compared to another. The ultimate test of any successful storage system (alphabetic or any other) is whether or not records that have been stored within the system can be quickly found when needed.

Regardless of the arrangement chosen, records can become lost if those who handle the records do not consistently follow the same procedures. Rules for alphabetic storage can be carelessly handed from person to person by word of mouth instead of in writing. At times of sickness, during vacation periods, or when employees leave the firm, chaos may result because no one knows what rules and procedures have been followed. The necessity to develop and use standardized procedures and written rules, available to all and followed by all, is obvious.

PROCEDURES FOR STORING RECORDS ALPHABETICALLY

The actual storing operation is an exacting responsibility. It must be done with concentration and the knowledge that a mistake may be costly. No matter whether records storage is centralized, decentralized, or centrally controlled, the filing procedures remain the same: Records must be (1) inspected, (2) indexed, (3) coded, (4) cross-referenced if necessary, (5) sorted, and (6) stored. Therefore, the filer must enjoy detailed work, be dexterous, have a good memory, be willing to follow set procedures, be interested in developing new and better procedures, and realize the importance of correctly storing all records so that they may be found immediately when needed. Each of the procedures will be discussed, in turn.

Inspecting

Checking a record for its "readiness to be filed" is known as **inspecting.** A business record must not be stored until its contents have been noted by someone with authority. And storing must not take place before whatever needs to be done with the record has been done. Anyone who stores records should be absolutely certain that the actions required by the contents of the records have been taken or noted on a reminder calendar so that the records will be brought to the attention of the proper person at a future date. Storing records before their contents have been noted and before appropriate action has been taken can sometimes cause embarrassment to a business and might even result in financial loss or loss of goodwill. After a record has been put into storage, it is often left there for some time. If the contents of the record require urgent action which is not taken before the record is stored, a great deal of time and money could be lost as a result.

It may be assumed that the copy of an outgoing letter or other communication is ready to be stored when it is received by the filer for storage. But in most offices every original (or incoming) record to be stored must bear a **release mark** showing that the record is ready for storage (See "RK" on Figure 4-7). This mark, usually put on the record by the person who has typed the reply or otherwise handled the matter, may be in the form of initials, a code or check mark, a punched symbol, a stamped notation, a lightly drawn pencil line through the contents, or some other agreed-upon mark. A missing mark is a signal to the filer that an inquiry as to why it is missing must be made. Someone may have forgotten to place the release mark on the record, or the record may have gotten into the filing basket by mistake. A time stamp (See JUN 22 19— 2:30 PM in Figure 4-7) is not a release mark. The person who opens mail often stamps the correspondence with a time stamp showing the date and time received, for reference purposes only.

A cardinal rule that all filers must observe, therefore, is:

> Be sure that the record to be stored has been released for storage.

Indexing

Before any record is stored in a container, it is read or scanned to determine the **filing segment** (or name) by which it is to be stored. The mental process required to determine the filing segment is called indexing or classifying. In alphabetic storage, indexing means determining the name that is to be used.

The indexing step is more difficult when correspondence is being stored than it is when cards are being put in alphabetic order. On a card, the name is instantly recognizable; on correspondence, the name may appear in various places on the page. Because accurate indexing is necessary for quick retrieval, the indexing step is extremely important. *Careful, accurate indexing is perhaps the most exacting step in the storage procedure.* In an alphabetic arrangement, the selection of the right name by which to store (the filing segment) means that the record will be found quickly when it is needed. If the wrong name is selected, much time will be wasted trying to locate the record when it is eventually requested.

In order to select the filing segment, the following rules are to be kept in mind:

1. The name most likely to be used in calling for the record, usually the most important name, is the one to be used for storage.
2. On original correspondence, the most likely name for storage purposes is usually in the letterhead.
3. If a letterhead has no relationship with the contents of the letter, the location of the writer, or the business connection of the writer, the letterhead name is disregarded for filing purposes. An example is a letter written on hotel stationery by a person who is out of town on a business trip.
4. Original correspondence on plain paper (paper without a letterhead) is most likely to be called for by the name in the signature line, which will be the one used for storage, therefore.
5. When both the company name and the name of the writer seem to be of equal importance, the company name is used.
6. On the file copy of an outgoing letter, the most important name is usually the one contained in the inside address.
7. When both the company name and the name of an individual are contained in the inside address of the file copy of an outgoing letter, the company name is used for filing unless the letter is personal or unless a name in the body is the correct name to index.
8. On the copy of a personal letter, the name of the writer may be the most important and should be used for storage.
9. If a special subject is used in an alphabetic arrangement (such as Applications), the subject is given precedence over both company and individual names appearing in the correspondence. Often, the subject name is written on the correspondence at the top right.
10. If a subject or a name given in the body of the letter is the most important, it should be used for storage purposes.
11. In case of real doubt as to the most important name, clarification should be requested from the supervisor or the department from which

the record came. If a records manual is in use in the office, it should be consulted.

12. Sometimes two names seem equally important. One name is selected as the name by which the record is to be stored and the other name is cross-referenced (explained later in this chapter) at the time the record is coded.

Coding

Coding is the actual marking of the record to indicate its placement in storage. Coding is a physical act, as contrasted to indexing, which is a mental determination. In order to code properly, a set of rules for alphabetic storage must be faithfully followed. (These rules are presented in Chapters 5 and 6.) When a record has been released for storage, the filing segment may already have been coded. If this has been done, the filer's job is that of skimming the contents of the record to confirm that the coding has been done correctly.

Often the filer is responsible for coding the record. In coding, the filing segment may be marked in any one of several ways. Figure 4-7 shows a straight underline and numbering method of coding. In some offices a colored pencil is used for coding to make the code stand out; in other offices, coding is done with a pencil, to keep distracting marks at a minimum.

Coding saves time when refiling is necessary. If an uncoded record is removed from storage and brought back at a later date to be refiled, it then must be indexed and coded. If the coding has been done originally, time is not required to reread the record. Coding that is done too quickly may result in choosing the wrong name or incorrectly coding the right one, resulting in storing the record in the wrong place.

Cross-Referencing

While indexing a record, the filer may determine that the record could be requested by a name other than the one selected for coding. Since that record may be requested by the *other* name or names that were not coded, it is desirable to prepare an aid called a **cross-reference.** The record is stored under the name the filer assumes to be the most important. The other names are then cross-referenced as explained below and in Chapters 5 and 6 more fully.

Assume that the letter shown in Figure 4-7 comes to the filer for storage. The record is indexed and coded for *Weekly Investments Magazine* by underlining the key unit and numbering the other units. The letter is then coded for cross-referencing since it may be called for by *Hyde Consulting Services*. A wavy line is drawn under *Hyde Consulting Services*; an X is written in the margin; and the units are numbered for the cross-referenced name. The cross-reference coding marks are different from those used for the regular coding of a record. Figure 4-8 shows the cross-reference made for the letter shown in Figure 4-7.

A separate cross-reference sheet, as shown in Figure 4-8, may be prepared for the alternative name, or an extra copy of the original record may be coded for cross-reference purposes. The cross-reference sheet shown in Figure 4-8 is a type that may be purchased in quantity and filled in with the required information as needed. Note that the name at the top of the cross-reference sheet is coded for storage in exactly the same way as is any record—the key unit is underlined with a straight line and the succeeding units are numbered.

At times a **permanent cross-reference** takes the place of an individual folder. The permanent cross-reference is a guide with a tab in the same position as the tabs on the individual folders. The caption on the tab of the permanent cross-reference consists of the name by which the cross-reference is actually filed, the word "SEE," and the name by which the correspondence may be found. In Figure 4-1, a permanent cross-reference guide for Babcock Crafts SEE Warren Industries appears in proper alphabetic sequence on the right side of the file drawer.

A permanent cross-reference may be used, for instance, when a company changes its name. The company's folder is removed from the file, the name is changed on the folder, and the folder is refiled under the new name. A permanent cross-reference guide is prepared under the original name and is placed in the position of the original folder in the file. For example, assume that Maynard and Phelps changes its name to Bayshore Products, Inc. The Maynard and Phelps folder is removed from the file, the name on the folder is changed to Bayshore Products Inc and the folder is filed under the new name. A permanent cross-reference guide is made and filed in the M section of the file:

Cross-referencing must be done with discretion. Each cross-reference requires valuable time, creates at least one additional sheet

CROSS-REFERENCE

FIRM NAME or SUBJECT *Hyde Consulting Services*   FILE NO.

DATE	REMARKS	*Survey conducted for*
		Weekly Investments Magazine

SEE *Weekly Investments Magazine*   FILE NO.
Chicago, Illinois
1106 Michigan Blvd

DATE *6/22/--*   SIGNED *L. L. Crandell*

FILE CROSS-REFERENCE UNDER NAME or SUBJECT LISTED AT TOP OF THIS SHEET, AND IN PROPER DATE ORDER THE PAPERS REFERRED TO SHOULD BE FILED UNDER NAME OR SUBJECT LISTED UNDER 'SEE'.

FORM NO. O99CR

FIGURE 4-8 — Cross-Reference for Letter Shown in Figure 4-7

weekly
investments²
magazine³   1106 Michigan Boulevard Chicago, IL 60610-2109

June 20, 19--

JUNE 22, 19-- 2:30 PM

Mr. Robert Peppard
11961 Terminal Tower
Public Square
Cleveland, OH 44102-1190

Dear Mr. Peppard

In order to improve our magazine and serve our subscribers to an even greater extent, we have hired the
Hyde Consulting Services firm to conduct a survey of
the investment objectives of the subscribers to our
magazine.

In the near future Hyde Consulting Services will send
to each of our subscribers a questionnaire that will
provide spaces for the listing of total yearly income,
approximate yearly expenses, amount available for savings
and investment, financial objectives, and other perti-
nent information. The questionnaire need not be signed.
Therefore you can give accurate information without
sacrificing the confidential nature of the survey. Hyde
Consulting Services will analyze the data received from
all those who return the questionnaire and will then
make recommendations for types of special articles and
departments that will be of greatest interest and benefit
to our readers.

We ask that you fill out the questionnaire completely
as well as accurately and return it to the Hyde firm
shortly after you receive it.

We shall greatly appreciate your cooperation in this
matter.

Sincerely yours

David Simpson

David Simpson, Editor

li

FIGURE 4-7 — Letter Properly Released and Coded

that must be stored, and therefore requires additional space in the equipment. Cross-referencing is explained in detail in Chapters 5 and 6.

Sorting

Sorting is the act of arranging records in a predetermined sequence, such as alphabetic or numeric, according to the storage method used. In most instances, a sorting step precedes the actual storing. It is very important that sorting be done as soon as possible after coding and cross-referencing, especially if storage must be delayed. Sometimes coding and **rough sorting** are done in sequence. After each record has been coded, it is immediately put into a pile of like pieces—all of the A, B, Cs are together, all of the D, E, Fs are together, and so on. Coordination of inspection, indexing, coding, and sorting means handling each record only once. Records can be found with less delay if they have been roughly sorted instead of being put in a stack on a desk or in a "to-be-filed" basket.

A delay in sorting until all records have been coded means handling each record twice, consumes more time and energy, and results in greater record-handling costs. If sorting is delayed until all coding is finished, the records may then be grouped into another rough-sort arrangement: all the As together in no special order; all the Bs together at random; all the Cs together in mixed order; and so forth. This sorting may be done on top of the desk, with the records placed in separate piles. The sorting will be easier if a desk-top sorter that has holders or pockets for various sections of the alphabet is used (Refer again to page 65 in Chapter 3).

After the records have been roughly sorted according to the alphabetic sections, they are removed section by section, alphabetized properly within each section, and replaced in order in the sorter for temporary storage. This step is often called **fine sorting.** The records in all sections have thus been alphabetized and are now ready to be stored. The records are removed in sequence from all divisions of the sorter and taken to the storage containers.

Using these rough and fine sorting procedures saves time. Wasted motion will be minimized because all records are in strict alphabetic order. The greater the number of records to be stored, the more precise or fine the sorting should be so as to make the work easier, quicker, and less tiring.

Storing

Storing is the actual placement of records in containers, a physical task of great importance in an office. A misfiled record is often a lost record; and a lost record means loss of time, money, and peace of mind while searching for the record.

The time at which records are actually put into the storage containers depends on the work load during the day. In some offices, storing is the job performed first in the morning; in others, all storing is done in the early afternoon; in others, storing is the last task performed each day. In still other offices, storing is done whenever records are ready and when there is a lull in other work. In a centralized filing department, there is no lull; storage takes place all day every day—storing, retrieving, and re-storing.

Prior to the actual storage of records, the filer must remember to:

1. Remove paper clips and pins from records to be stored.
2. Staple records together (if they belong together) in the upper *right* corner so that other records kept in the folder will not be inserted between them by mistake.
3. Mend torn records.
4. Unfold folded records to conserve storage space unless the folded records fit the container better than when unfolded.

Then, when at the storage equipment, the filer should:

1. Glance quickly at the label on the container to locate the place to begin storage.
2. After locating the place, scan the guides until the proper alphabetic section is reached.
3. Pull the guides forward with one hand, while the other hand searches quickly for the correct folder.
4. Check to see if an individual or a special folder for the filing segment has been prepared. If there is none, locate the general folder.
5. Slightly raise the folder into which the record is to be placed. Avoid pulling the folder up by its tab, however, as continual pulling will separate the tab from its folder. If the folder is raised, the record will be inserted *into* the folder and not in front of or behind it.
6. Glance quickly at the label and the top record in the folder to verify further the fact that the piece to be stored is correctly placed, since all records will bear the same coded name.
7. Place each record in the folder with its top to the left (Figure 4-9). When the folder is removed from storage and placed on a desk to be used, the folder is opened like a book with the tab edge to the right; all the records in it are then in proper reading position.
8. Jog the folder to straighten the records if they are uneven.

FIGURE 4-9 — Proper Insertion of Papers into File Folder

9. Never open more than one drawer in a cabinet at the same time; a cabinet can fall forward when it becomes overbalanced because two or three loaded drawers are open.

Special points to be remembered include:

1. The most recently dated record in an individual folder is always placed at the front and therefore is on top when the folder is opened. The record bearing the oldest date is the one at the back of the folder.
2. Records that are removed from a folder and later refiled must be placed in their correct chronologic sequence, not on top of the contents of the folder.
3. Records within a general folder are arranged first alphabetically by correspondents' names and then by date within each correspondent's records. The most recently dated record is therefore on top of each group.

Efficient alphabetic records storage is the result of (1) good planning to choose the right equipment, supplies, and system; (2) proper training of personnel who recognize the value of the release mark, know and consistently apply the rules for alphabetic indexing, code papers carefully, prepare cross-references skillfully, invariably sort papers before storing, and carefully store records in their proper containers; and (3) constant concerned supervision by records managers or others responsible for the storage and retrieval functions.

IMPORTANT TERMS AND CONCEPTS

as-written order
closed (double) notation
color accenting
color coding
cross-reference
direct reference
filing segment
fine sorting
follower blocks
indexing order
inspecting
multiple-closed notation
open (single) notation
OUT folders

OUT guides
OUT sheets
period folders
permanent cross-reference
primary guides
release mark
rough sorting
score marks
sorting
special folders
special (auxiliary) guides
storing
straight order

REVIEW AND DISCUSSION

1. What kinds of alphabetic arrangements have you encountered in your daily life? Can you think of examples not given in the text? (Obj. 1)

2. Comment on the advisability of using a bright red drawer label, a deep brown folder label, a buff-colored folder label with a vivid green band across its top. (Obj. 2)

3. A label on a file cabinet drawer bears the following information:

   Sa - Sm

   (Se - Sl)

   What does the label mean? What is this type of caption called? (Obj. 2)

4. What is the difference between a primary guide and a special guide? (Obj. 3)

5. How can guides be a source of trouble in storage containers? (Obj. 3)

6. What is the difference between an individual folder and a general folder? How are they similar? (Obj. 3)

7. What is a score mark on a folder? What is its use? (Obj. 3)

8. When are new folders necessary in a storage container? (Obj. 3)

9. Of what value would a set of guide and folder tabs preprinted by a manufacturer be? When would blank ones be of greater use? (Obj. 3)

10. Why are OUT indicators important? How are they used? (Obj. 3)

11. What are the advantages and disadvantages of the alphabetic storage method? (Obj. 4)

12. Why should one carefully inspect and study an alphabetic record-storage system before purchasing it? (Obj. 5)

13. What are the six steps (in order) necessary for storing a record properly? Which one is the most important? Why? (Obj. 6)

14. What are the kinds of release marks you might find on records that are ready to be stored? (Obj. 6)

15. What is a filing segment? (Obj. 6)

16. What is the difference between indexing and coding? (Obj. 6)

17. Why should cross-referencing be done with discretion? (Obj. 6)

18. What is the distinction between rough and fine sorting? (Obj. 6)

DECISION-MAKING OPPORTUNITIES (DMO)

DMO 4-1: Coding Choice

On the copy of an outgoing letter, both the company name and the name of the individual receiving the letter appear in the inside address:

> Dr. Jayne DeSales Bertram, President
> Microform Equipment Sales & Services, Inc.
> Conway Towers #47
> Dallas, TX 75202-1847

Which name is coded for storage? Why? (Obj. 6)

DMO 4-2: Deciding on Supplies

If stored correspondence requires 100 standard file drawers to contain it and there is a great amount of daily reference to the folders, why would an 80-division set of alphabetic guides be inadequate? How many guides would you estimate would be required and how did you arrive at that decision? (Obj. 3)

DMO 4-3: Analyzing an Alphabetic System

Here is an illustration of part of an alphabetically arranged drawer that you find your first day on the job. Do you believe efficient storage is enhanced or hindered by this system? Why? Do you have any suggestions to improve this arrangement? What are they and why do you make the suggestions? (Objs. 3, 5)

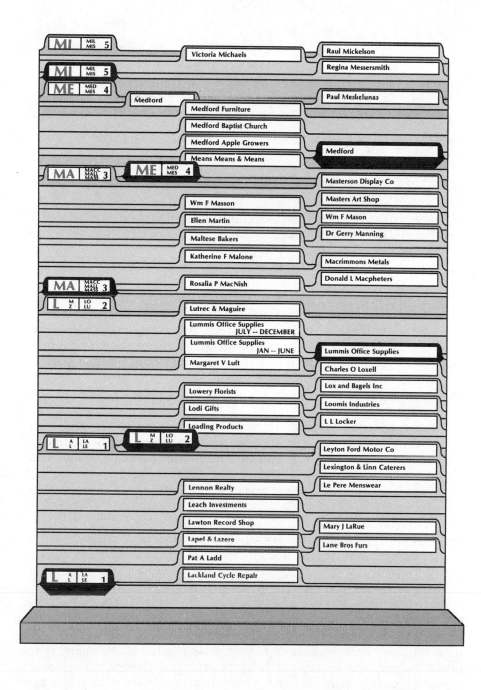

ALPHABETIC RULES FOR INDEXING PERSONAL AND BUSINESS NAMES

After you have completed this chapter, you will be able to:

1. Explain the necessity for indexing rules for names to be stored alphabetically and the importance of following these rules consistently.
2. Index, code, and arrange in alphabetic order personal and business names.
3. Index, code, and arrange in alphabetic order personal and business names containing hyphens, punctuation, prefixes, or particles.
4. Index, code, and arrange in alphabetic order personal and business names containing abbreviations, nicknames, and shortened names.
5. Index, code, and arrange in alphabetic order personal and business names containing titles.
6. Index, code, and arrange in alphabetic order identical names of persons and businesses.
7. Index, code, and arrange in alphabetic order business names containing prepositions, conjunctions, articles, symbols, and numbers.
8. Index, code, and arrange in alphabetic order business names composed of single letters.
9. Prepare cards for alphabetic arrangement and arrange them correctly in a card file.
10. Understand and explain cross-referencing.
11. Explain SEE ALSO cross-references and how they are used.
12. Describe coding procedures for original and cross-reference cards.

In Chapter 4, mention was made that an extremely important procedure for successful alphabetic storage is that of carefully following a set of rules. No one universal set of rules for alphabetic arrangement is followed by everyone because of office preferences. However, the Association of Records Managers and Administrators, Inc. (ARMA) has published *Guidelines to Alphabetic Filing*, containing rules for storing records alphabetically. The rules in this chapter and in Chapter 6 are written to agree with the ARMA Simplified Filing Standard Rules and Specific Filing Guidelines and are explained in detail.

Variations do exist in the procedures for storing records alphabetically. Therefore, the procedures that are to be used in any one office must be determined, written down, and followed with no deviation. Without written rules for storing records alphabetically, procedures will vary with time, changes in personnel, and spoken explanations. Unless those who maintain the records are consistent in their procedures for storage, they will be unable to locate records when they are needed. And the real test of an efficient storage system is being able to *find* records once they have been stored.

If you thoroughly understand the rules in this textbook, you will be able to adjust to any exceptions encountered in the specific office where you may work. Records managers who adopt these rules for their offices will find them understandable, logical, workable, and comprehensive enough to provide answers to the majority of storage questions that arise. In this chapter, you will learn the rules for alphabetic arrangement and how to cross-reference. Cross-referencing is used so that records can be retrieved quickly, even if they are requested by a filing segment other than the originally coded one.

The rules for alphabetic storage are presented here with illustrative examples and problems to help you understand the application of the rules. These rules for alphabetic arrangement are understood best if studied in three groups: (1) persons' names, (2) business names (sometimes referred to as "company names" or "firm names"), and (3) other names. In this chapter you will study the rules for personal and business names; in Chapter 6, rules for other names will be presented. Study carefully the illustrative examples accompanying each rule in these chapters because the examples clarify the rules.

The correct way to study is first to read the rule carefully, making sure you understand the meaning of the words used to state the rule. Then look at the examples. Note that the complete name as written or printed is given at the left. Then the name is separated into indexing units at the right according to the rule you are studying. Be sure you understand why the name has been separated as it has.

In determining alphabetic order, compare the units in the filing segments for differences. If the key units are alike, move to the second units, the third units, and succeeding units until a difference occurs. It is at that point of difference that alphabetic order is determined. Marks that appear over or under some letters in foreign names are disregarded (such as Señora, Marçal, René, Valhallavägen). In this text, you will find an underline in each example except the first one; this underline indicates the letter of the unit that determines alphabetic order. Examples are numbered for ease in referring to them. Be sure you understand each rule before going to the next.

RULES FOR NAMES OF PERSONS

Eight rules explain the way in which the names of persons are arranged in alphabetic order:

1   Order of Units

A. A person's name is indexed in *transposed* order: the last name (surname) is the key unit; the given name or initial is the second unit (2); and the middle name or initial is the third unit (3).

B. Unusual names are indexed in the same manner. If it is not possible to determine the surname of an unusual name, consider the last name as written to be the surname. Cross-reference the unusual name, using the first name written as the key unit (See page 124).

Indexing Order of Units

Name	Key Unit	2	3
1. M. Pal Laker	Laker	M	Pal
2. Mary P. Laker	Laker	Mary	P
3. Mary Paula Laker	Laker	Mary	Paula
4. Bills Lillard	Lillard	Bills	
5. Sayed Loussiran	Loussiran	Sayed	

2   Hyphens and Punctuation

The hyphen and any other punctuation (commas, periods, and apostrophes) within a person's name are disregarded. Hyphenated names are considered as one indexing unit.

Indexing Order of Units

Name	Key Unit	2	3
1. Karin D'Angelo	DAngelo	Karin	
2. Marie-Thérése Dann-Young	DannYoung	MarieTherese	
3. David Dartt-Haven	DarttHaven	David	
4. J. Mark Dellarobia	Dellarobia	J	Mark
5. William Van Dello-Fair	DelloFair	William	Van
6. Lee-Ann O'Brien	OBrien	LeeAnn	

3   Prefixes or Particles

A prefix or particle in a person's name is part of the name following it, regardless of spacing or capitalization. Examples of particles or prefixes are a la, D', Da, De, Del, De la, Della, Den, Des, Di, Dos, Du, El, Fitz, Il, L', La, Las, Le, Les, Lo, Los, Lu, M', Mac, Mc, Me, O', Per, Saint, San, Santa, Santo, St., Ste., Te, Ten, Ter, Van, Van de, vander, Ver, Von, Von Der.

Indexing Order of Units

Name	Key Unit	2	3
1. Delores D'Amico	DAmico	Delores	
2. DeLorry d'Amico	dAmico	DeLorry	
3. Maurice de la Croix	delaCroix	Maurice	
4. Samuel El Soudani	ElSoudani	Samuel	
5. Donald Il Agan	IlAgan	Donald	
6. Esperanza Ilagan	Ilagan	Esperanza	
7. John L. SantaCruz	SantaCruz	John	L
8. L. Nancy St. Clair	StClair	L	Nancy
9. Kurt K. Von der Haar	VonderHaar	Kurt	K
10. Emma von Korff	vonKorff	Emma	

4   Abbreviations, Nicknames, and Shortened Names

Abbreviated given names (Edw., Jas., Jos., Thos.) are considered as written; nicknames and the brief form of a given name (Don, Liz, Pat) are also considered as written.

Indexing Order of Units

Name	Key Unit	2	3
1. Sam R. Sandburg	Sandburg	Sam	R
2. Sam'l P. Sandburg	Sandburg	Saml	P
3. Nick Sanders	Sanders	Nick	
4. Wm. Nicholas Sanders	Sanders	Wm	Nicholas
5. Bett St. Clair	StClair	Bett	
6. Betty St. Clair	StClair	Betty	
7. Liz L. Swanson	Swanson	Liz	L
8. Liza Beth Swanson	Swanson	Liza	Beth
9. Pat Swanson	Swanson	Pat	
10. Ptk. Swanson	Swanson	Ptk	

5   Seniority Designations

A seniority designation (Jr., Sr., II, III, and the like) is considered the last unit in abbreviated form. Numeric designations (II, III, IV, etc.) are filed in numeric sequence before alphabetic designations (Jr., Sr.). Arabic designations are filed in numeric sequence before Roman designations (2, 3; II, III).

Indexing Order of Units

Name	Key Unit	2	3	4
1. C. M. Wright	Wright	C	M	
2. C. M. Wright, 2d	Wright	C	M	2d
3. C. M. Wright, II	Wright	C	M	II
4. C. M. Wright, IV	Wright	C	M	IV
5. C. M. Wright, Junior	Wright	C	M	Jr
6. C. M. Wright, Sr.	Wright	C	M	Sr

6   Titles and Degrees

A. Titles with Complete Names. A title (military, religious, personal, educational, professional, etc.) is considered as the last indexing unit whenever it appears.
B. Royal and Religious Titles without Complete Names. When a name contains a royal or religious title followed by a surname only or by a given and sometimes a middle name only, the name is indexed as written.
C. Degrees. Professional degrees (DD, DVM, EdD, MD, PhD, and the like) are considered the last unit and arranged alphabetically as written.
D. Professional Certifications. Earned certificates of accomplishment in some professions (CLU, CPA, CPS, CRM) are considered the last unit.

Indexing Order of Units

Name	Key Unit	2	3	4
1. Brother Francis	Brother	Francis		
2. Joan B. Flanagan, CLU	Flanagan	Joan	B	CLU
3. Senator Joan B. Flanagan	Flanagan	Joan	B	Senator
4. Dr. John Flanagan	Flanagan	John	Dr	
5. Lady Margaret Ann	Lady	Margaret	Ann	
6. Michael P. Maguire, EdD	Maguire	Michael	P	EdD
7. Rev. Michael P. Maguire	Maguire	Michael	P	Rev
8. Señora Rosa Masón	Mason	Rosa	Senora	
9. Sister Rosa Kathleen	Sister	Rosa	Kathleen	
10. Rosa Kathleen Sister, CRM	Sister	Rosa	Kathleen	CRM

7   Names of Married Women

A married woman's name is indexed as she writes it and according to Rule 1. Many married women are using their maiden names hyphenated to their married names. Such a hyphenated name is indexed according to Rule 3. If an alternate form of a married woman's name is known, a cross-reference is made (See page 125).

	Indexing Order of Units			
Name	**Key Unit**	**2**	**3**	**4**
1. Jean Parker King (Mrs. Roy G. King)	King	Jean	Parker	
2. Mrs. Jeanette R. King	King	Jeanette	R	Mrs
3. Ms. Jeanette R. King	King	Jeanette	R	Ms
4. Mrs. Joan King-Holt	KingHolt	Joan	Mrs	

5. Ms. Justine Kinghorn
   (Mrs. Arthur L. Dye)
   (also signs Justine Kinghorn Dye)
	Kinghorn	Justine	Ms	

8   Identical Names of Persons

If all units, including titles, in the names of two or more persons are identical, order is determined by addresses. Cities are considered first, followed by states or provinces, street names, and then house numbers or building numbers, in that order.

A. When the first units of street names are written as figures, the names are considered in ascending numeric order and placed together before alphabetic street names.
B. Street names with compass directions are considered as written. Numbers after compass directions are considered before alphabetic names (East 3d, East Pinehurst, SE Third, Southeast Third, etc.).
C. House numbers are arranged in ascending numeric order if street names are identical.
D. Building numbers are arranged in ascending numeric order and placed together before spelled-out building names.
E. If a street address and a building name are included in an address, disregard the building name.
F. State or province names are considered by their two-letter abbreviated form and are arranged alphabetically by the two letters.
G. ZIP Codes are not considered in indexing.

Indexing Order of Units

Name	Key Unit	2	3	4	5	6	7	8
1. Dan King Canton, OH	King	Dan	Canton	OH				
2. Dan King Columbus, GA	King	Dan	Columbus	GA				
3. Dan King Columbus, IN	King	Dan	Columbus	IN				
4. Leslie Knight 1214 34th St. Provo, UT	Knight	Leslie	Provo	UT	34	St	1214	
5. Leslie Knight 2572 34th St. Provo, UT	Knight	Leslie	Provo	UT	34	St	_2572_	
6. Leslie Knight 1214 May St. Provo, UT	Knight	Leslie	Provo	UT	_May_	St	1214	
7. Leslie Knight Trent Bldg. Provo, UT	Knight	Leslie	Provo	UT	_Trent_	Bldg		
8. Leslie Knight 1100 W. May St. Provo, UT	Knight	Leslie	Provo	UT	_W_	May	St	1100
9. Leslie Knight 2717 W. May St. Provo, UT	Knight	Leslie	Provo	UT	W	May	St	_2717_
10. Leslie Knight 2946 W. May St. Worley Apts. Provo, UT	Knight	Leslie	Provo	UT	W	May	St	_2946_

CHECKING KNOWLEDGE OF THE RULES

1. As your instructor directs, indicate the key, second, and third units in each of the following persons' names:

a. Miss Louisa Marçal
b. Juan Image
c. Miss Jane W. O'Briant
d. Clyde St. John Clavel, Jr.
e. Thos. Hubert LeBar, CRM
f. Rev. Marie Pat Ambler
g. Ms. Mildred McCubbins-Rhodes
h. Bishop Madeiros
i. F. Roosevelt George III
j. Sister Mary Francesca
k. N. Ruth Hamilton
l. Jo-Nell Hanson, CPS
m. Dr. Maurine Heeger
n. S. Joseph DeBrum

o. Ms. Jeannette Nadeau
p. Colonel H. A. Cresta
q. M. Belle C. Haithcock
   (Mrs. Herbert Haithcock)

r. Mark Brown-Campbell, DVM
s. Sui Sang Tong
t. Mr. D. Garcia

2. Are the two names in each of the following pairs in correct alphabetic order? Explain.

a. Roberta L. Newstadter
   Robert L. Newstadtler
b. Darlene A. Newman
   Darlene B. Neuman
c. Tita Tan, MD
   T. Tan Tang
d. Butch Sangrinette
   Anthony Sangrinetti
e. Victor San Miguel
   Victoria San
f. Jake Sasser, Jr.
   1748 Oakmont Ave.
   Troy, NY
   Jake Sasser, Sr.
   2917 Oakdale Ave.
   Troy, NY

g. Miss Connie P. Nelson
   Ms. Chas. P. Nelson
h. Edward O'Connell
   Edwin O. Connell
i. Wallace Dunham, PhD
   Ms. Wallace C. Dunham
j. Miss Jane Jones
   Wheaton, IL
   Miss Jane Jones
   Wausau, WI
k. Miss Joanne Ursprung
   Joe Urroz
l. Valerie A. David
   David A. Valentine

3. The three names in each of the following groups of names are in correct alphabetic order. A fourth name is given in parentheses below each group. Indicate where this name should be placed so as to be in correct alphabetic order with the other three. Explain your choice.

Example: 1. D. Louis Cooper
            2. Louisa H. Cooper
            3. Louisa Henry Cooper
            (4. Louis Cooper)

Answer: Between 1 and 2, because the key units are alike and order is determined by the second units: Louis precedes Louisa.

a. 1. Brother Marshall
    2. Scott L. Marshall
    3. Sharon Marshall-Medlin
    (4. Anne B. Marshall)

b. 1. James Simmons, CPA
    2. James Simmons, Jr.
    3. Professor James Simmons
    (4. James Simmons III)

c. 1. Bill Sister
    2. Willard Orville Sister
    3. Antoinette Sisters
    (4. Sister Silvia)

d. 1. B. L. Lorcal
    2. Miss Bea Lord
    3. Lord Beaverbrook
    (4. Lana B. Beaven)

e. 1. Isabel Gregg-Sanchez
    2. J. Gregg Sanchez
    3. Jose Sanchez
    (4. Annette Sanches)

f. 1. Dr. Sally MacFarlane
    2. Judge Janet Mahoney
    3. Patrick McFarland
    (4. Ms. Sarah McFarlan)

RULES FOR BUSINESS NAMES

Eight rules explain the way in which the names of businesses are arranged in alphabetic order:

9   Order of Units

A. Each word in a business name is a separate indexing unit.
B. Units in a business name are considered as written, including a person's name within a business name (See Example 1 below).
C. Each word in compound business and place names with spaces between the parts of the name is considered a separate unit.
D. Each separate word in a foreign business name is considered to be a separate unit, as written.

Indexing Order of Units

Name	Key Unit	2	3	4
1. Betty Gruber Plumbing Company	Betty	Gruber	Plumbing	Company
2. Forest View Apartments	Forest	View	Apartments	
3. Graham, Payne, Silva, Attorneys	Graham	Payne	Silva	Attorneys
4. Grantland Gift Shoppe	Grantland	Gift	Shoppe	
5. Lake Side Variety	Lake	Side	Variety	
6. Lakeside Animal Shelter	Lakeside	Animal	Shelter	
7. Mid America Bakery	Mid	America	Bakery	
8. Pan American Airlines	Pan	American	Airlines	
9. South Western Insurance	South	Western	Insurance	
10. Trois Rivières Marine Supplies	Trois	Rivieres	Marine	Supplies

10   Prepositions, Conjunctions, Articles, and Symbols

A. All complete English words, including prepositions, conjunctions, and articles, are separate indexing units.

B. If "The" is the first word in a business name, it is the *last* indexing unit (See Example 3 below).

C. Symbols, such as the ampersand (&), ¢, $, #, %, are indexed as if spelled in full—and, Cent, Dollar, Number, Percent.

Indexing Order of Units

Name	Key Unit	2	3	4	5	6
1. A Special Place	A	Special	Place			
2. $ and ¢ Store	Dollar	and	Cent	Store		
3. The Downbeat Record Shop	Downbeat	Record	Shop	The		
4. Fruit of the Loom Company	Fruit	of	the	Loom	Company	
5. In Harmony Dance Studio	In	Harmony	Dance	Studio		
6. New York Fifty % Off Showroom	New	York	Fifty	Percent	Off	Showroom
7. Night & Day Deliveries	Night	and	Day	Deliveries		
8. Side by Side Spa	Side	by	Side	Spa		
9. Ted & Mary Boutique	Ted	and	Mary	Boutique		
10. Travel with Tanya	Travel	with	Tanya			

11   Hyphens and Punctuation

All punctuation and hyphens are disregarded in indexing business names. Hyphenated names are considered as one indexing unit.

Indexing Order of Units

Name	Key Unit	2	3	4
1. A-Jay-Zee Company	AJayZee	Company		
2. Anti-Freeze Distributors	AntiFreeze	Distributors		
3. Beef-N-Ale Cafe	BeefNAle	Cafe		
4. Brill/Best Drug Store	BrillBest	Drug	Store	
5. Farmers' Co-Op Warehouse	Farmers	CoOp	Warehouse	
6. Franklins' Self-Serve Store	Franklins	SelfServe	Store	
7. Franklin's Trans-Canada Truck Lines	Franklins	TransCanada	Truck	Lines

(continued)

Indexing Order of Units

Name	Key Unit	2	3	4
8. Home Pub'ns	Home	Pubns		
9. South-East Suppliers	SouthEast	Suppliers		
10. Tri-City U Drive	TriCity	U	Drive	

12   Single Letters and Abbreviations

A. Single letters in business names are indexed as written. If there are spaces between each single letter, each letter is a separate indexing unit. Periods and hyphens are disregarded and not considered as spaces when names with single letters are being indexed.

B. Acronyms (words formed by taking the first, or the first few, letters of several words) are indexed as one unit.

C. Abbreviations in business names are indexed as one unit, regardless of punctuation or spacing.

D. Radio and TV station call letters are indexed as one word.

Indexing Order of Units

Name	Key Unit	2	3	4	5
1. B & B Gifts, Ltd.	B	and	B	Gifts	Ltd
2. Bailey Bros. Co.	Bailey	Bros	Co		
3. BMOC (Burlington Mfrs. Outlet Center)	BMOC				
4. Carolina AAA Motor Club	Carolina	AAA	Motor	Club	
5. D U K E U-Drive	D	U	K	E	UDrive
6. D.U.K.E. Showcase, Inc.	DUKE	Showcase	Inc		
7. Dwight A. L. Sanders, Inc.	Dwight	A	L	Sanders	Inc
8. Gen'l Mtge. Assn.	Genl	Mtge	Assn		
9. Radio Station WDNC	Radio	Station	WDNC		
10. WUNC-TV	WUNCTV				

13   Titles in Business Names

Titles in business names are indexed as written.

Indexing Order of Units

Name	Key Unit	2	3	4	5
1. The Captain Kidd Toy Store	Captain	Kidd	Toy	Store	The
2. Doctor Benshoof's Pet Store	Doctor	Benshoofs	Pet	Store	
3. Father Flanagan's Boys' Home	Father	Flanagans	Boys	Home	
4. General Robert E. Lee Museum	General	Robert	E	Lee	Museum
5. Madame Marie's Salon	Madame	Maries	Salon		
6. Mlle. Paulette's Graphic Analysis	Mlle	Paulettes	Graphic	Analysis	
7. Mr. TV Repair Shop	Mr	TV	Repair	Shop	
8. Prince George Hotel	Prince	George	Hotel		
9. Professor John Flynn's Bookstore	Professor	John	Flynns	Bookstore	
10. Señorita Rosa's Mexican Foods	Senorita	Rosas	Mexican	Foods	

14   Prefixes or Particles

A prefix or particle in a business name is part of the word following it regardless of spelling, capitalization, or spacing. Examples of prefixes and particles are given in Rule 3, page 111.

Indexing Order of Units

Name	Key Unit	2	3	4
1. Donna St. Pierre Real Estate	Donna	StPierre	Real	Estate
2. La Belle Grande Maison	LaBelle	Grande	Maison	
3. L'Espérance Retirement Center	LEsperance	Retirement	Center	
4. Notre Dame du Lac Resort	Notre	Dame	duLac	Resort
5. San Diego Sailing Club	SanDiego	Sailing	Club	
6. Santa Barbara Antiques	SantaBarbara	Antiques		
7. St. Clair Bicycle Repair	StClair	Bicycle	Repair	
8. Ste. Agathe Society, Inc.	SteAgathe	Society	Inc	

15   Numbers in Business Names

A. Numbers spelled out in business names are indexed as written and arranged in alphabetic order (See Example 10).

B. Numbers written as figures in business names are considered as one unit (See Example 6).

C. Names in which a number written as figures is the first word are arranged in ascending order before all alphabetic names (See Examples 1 through 7).

D. Arabic numbers are filed before Roman numerals (2, 3; II, III) (See Examples 6 and 7).

E. Names with inclusive numbers (23-37 Worth Road Apartments) are arranged by the lowest number only (See Example 4).

F. If numbers comprise a unit of a name other than the key unit (Palma's 420 Boutique or Palma's & Paul's 300 Club), and all units preceding the numbers are identical, the numbered units precede units composed of letters (See Examples 8 and 9, 11 and 12).

G. If numbers contain st, d, or th endings, ignore the endings and consider only the digits (See Example 2).

Indexing Order of Units

Name	Key Unit	2	3	4	5
1. 2 Grand Painters	2	Grand	Painters		
2. 3d Floor Bistro	3	Floor	Bistro		
3. 4 Mile House	4	Mile	House		
4. 4-40 Mission Hill Bldg.	4	Mission	Hill	Bldg	
5. 10¢ Novelty Nook	10	Cent	Novelty	Nook	
6. 2900 Parkway Apts.	2900	Parkway	Apts		
7. II by IV Gallery	II	by	IV	Gallery	
8. Bell's 490 Main Shoes	Bells	490	Main	Shoes	
9. Bells and Bangles Jewelry Store	Bells	and	Bangles	Jewelry	Store
10. Fifty Park Avenue Condo	Fifty	Park	Avenue	Condo	
11. #10 Office Supply Depot	Number	10	Office	Supply	Depot
12. Number One Card Shop	Number	One	Card	Shop	

16   Identical Names of Businesses

When names of businesses are identical, order is determined by the addresses. Cities are considered first, followed by states or provinces, street names, and then house numbers or building numbers, in that order. Follow Rule 8 pertaining to identical personal names, page 113, when alphabetizing identical business names.

Indexing Order of Units

Name	Key Unit	2	3	4	5	6	7	8
1. Quasar Co. Wellesley, MA	Quasar	Co	Wellesley	MA				
2. Quasar Co. Wellesley, ON Canada	Quasar	Co	Wellesley	ON				
3. Quick Copy 7200 28th Ave Dallas, TX	Quick	Copy	Dallas	TX	28	Ave		
4. Quick Copy 107 138th Blvd. Dallas, TX	Quick	Copy	Dallas	TX	138	Blvd		
5. Quick Copy 7272 Gaston Ave. Dallas, TX	Quick	Copy	Dallas	TX	Gaston	Ave		
6. Quick Copy 1134 Green Ave. Dallas, TX	Quick	Copy	Dallas	TX	Green	Ave	1134	
7. Quick Copy 5030 Green Ave. Dallas, TX	Quick	Copy	Dallas	TX	Green	Ave	5030	
8. Quick Copy Hyatt Regency Hotel Dallas, TX	Quick	Copy	Dallas	TX	Hyatt			
9. Quick Copy 206 W. Green Ave. Dallas, TX	Quick	Copy	Dallas	TX	W	Green	Ave	206
10. Quick Copy Wright Bldg. 20700 W. Green Ave. Dallas, TX	Quick	Copy	Dallas	TX	W	Green	Ave	20700

CHECKING KNOWLEDGE OF THE RULES

1. As your instructor directs, indicate the key, second, and succeeding units in each of the following names:

a. Triple City Record Bar

b. UCB S.A. Pharmaceuticals

c. Frances B. Perkins Bookstore

d. The Last Chance Store

e. Sterling-on-the-Hudson Roller Rink

f. B Sharp Music House

g. J. W. Brannon, Inc.

h. Ship 'n Shore Travel Agency

i. % Off Discount House

j. Used USAF & USMC Uniforms, Inc.

k. Station WOW Coffee Shop

l. Doctor Ellen's Pet Shop

2. Are the following names in alphabetic order? If so, indicate by writing "OK." If not, write "No." Then determine the correct alphabetic order and show it by rearranging the numbers.

Example: 1. St. Joseph's Florists
          2. Second Time Around
          3. Señora Marguerita's Hair Styles

          Answer: No, 2-3-1

a. 1. New York Furriers
   2. Newark News Stand
   3. Newport Donut Shop

f. 1. Los Angeles Candle Co.
   2. Las Vegas Novelties, Inc.
   3. Lasvegan & Nettle, Ltd.

b. 1. Miss Minnie's Tot Tenders
   2. Miss & Mr. Clothing
   3. Ms. Smith's Dress Designs

g. 1. Self-Serve Grocery
   2. The Self-Service Barn
   3. Tammy Self Dance Studio

c. 1. A to Z Advertising Co.
   2. AAA Used Cars
   3. A. Wilson Enterprises

h. 1. Balihai Hardware Store
   2. Bali Hai Village Deli
   3. Bali H. Vestry Wear

d. 1. Goode, Will & Fowler
   2. Goodwill Card Shop
   3. Good Will Industries

i. 1. San Diego Sailboats, Inc.
   2. San Diego 300 Club
   3. 300 San Diegans, Inc.

e. 1. 50 Townehouse Apts.
   2. Fifty Trenton Towers
   3. Fifty-five Hammond Place

j. 1. Ann Park's Jewelry Store
   2. The Parks Market
   3. Anna Parker's Bakery

3. Are the two names in each of the following groups correctly arranged in alphabetic order? Indicate by writing "Yes" or "No," and explain your answer.

a. Norton-Simon Co.
   Norton-Simon, Inc.

g. Northwestern Airlines
   North Western Appliances

b. Charles Norberg Pharmacy
   Norberg-Carlson Co.

h. Fair Trade Meat Market
   Fait Accompli Guest House

c. In and Out Diner
   IFC Repair Shop

i. 962 North Side Apts.
   #9 Nachos Mfg. Co.

d. Madam Nguyen Dressmaking
   Erma Nguyen

j. Orton, James & Varga
   2265 Smith Avenue
   Chicago, IL 60605-6655
   Orton, James & Varga
   1600 Michigan Blvd.
   Chicago, IL 60603-6658

e. Six-City Opticians
   6th Sense Camera Shop

f. North Bellevue Gift Shop
   North Bellavue Auto Parts

ALPHABETIC CARD FILING

In many offices, card files of the names and addresses of persons and businesses are kept in alphabetic arrangement. These cards are prepared according to the style selected by the files supervisor or records manager so that the cards can be handled with maximum efficiency and ease.

Preparation of Cards

Data that are typed on each file card must follow the same pattern in order to ensure consistency and ease in referring to the names. As you read the following explanation, refer frequently to Figure 5-1, which shows one style that is commonly used.

1. Type the name of the person or business in indexing order beginning on the third space from the left edge of the card and on the third line from the top edge. The key unit is always the first word typed, (See A in Figure 5-1) followed by the second and succeeding units. A person's title should be typed if it is known (See B in Figure 5-1). A variation in typing style is to type the names with slashes between each unit, such as Robertson/Susan/A or Tillman/Air/Conditioning/and/Heating/Company.
2. Retype the name and address a triple space below the name that is typed at the top of the card in the order it would be typed on an envelope, but with upper and lower case letters and with punctuation (Note C in Figure 5-1).
3. If the name on the file card is to be used with a numeric system, type the code number in the upper right corner of the card (See D in Figure 5-1).

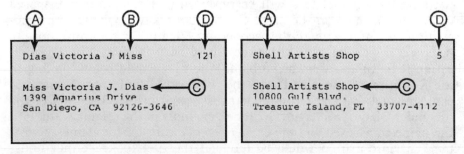

FIGURE 5-1 — Typed File Cards

Cross-Referencing

Some records of persons and businesses may be called for by a name that is in a different sequence from the way in which it was stored. This is particularly true if the key unit is difficult to determine. When a record is likely to be requested by any of several names, it is desirable to prepare a cross-reference. A cross-reference card shows a name in a form other than that used on the original card, and it indicates the location of the original card. The filer can then find requested records regardless of the name used in the request for those records. A cross-reference card may be identical with all other cards in size and color, or it may be distinctively different in color so that it will stand out clearly from the other cards.

Two types of persons' names should be cross-referenced:

1. Unusual and foreign names.
2. Married women's names.

Types of business names for which cross-references are usually prepared are:

1. Acronyms and abbreviations.
2. Names of companies doing business under more than one name.
3. Business names composed of two or more surnames.
4. Names of companies that are affiliates or branches of other companies.
5. Company names that have been changed.

An explanation of the procedure to be followed in cross-referencing each of these kinds of names follows.

Unusual and Foreign Names of Persons.   A cross-reference is made for an unusual or foreign name in the exact form in which the name is written. The original card will be typed with the name in transposed order. For example, in the name Dr. Kuniko Okawa, Okawa is considered the key unit, Kuniko the second unit (2), and Dr. the third unit (3). If, however, someone called for the record of Dr. Okawa Kuniko, indicating that Kuniko was the surname, the filer would begin looking in the K section of the file. There, the filer would find a cross-reference card showing that the record is actually stored in the O section of the file under Okawa. See Figure 5-2 for an example of the original card with the name transposed and the cross-reference card for the name as written. The information would be found if the filer looked either under Kuniko or under Okawa as the key unit.

```
Okawa Kuniko Dr


Dr. Kuniko Okawa
Fidelity Plaza
112 North Port
Spokane, WA  99201-1244
```

```
Kuniko Okawa Dr

SEE

Okawa Kuniko Dr
```

FIGURE 5-2 — Original and Cross-Reference Cards for Unusual or Foreign Person's Name

Married Women's Names. A married woman's name can be written in many ways, but it is indexed according to Rule 7. Cross-reference cards are prepared for any known alternate forms of the name. The illustration in Figure 5-3 shows the original card for Mrs. Justine King-Tyler. Below that card are two cards: (1) a cross-reference card showing her husband's name, Mrs. Arthur L. Tyler, which she sometimes uses, and (2) a cross-reference card for another alternate name she sometimes uses: Ms. Justine King. Each cross-reference card gives the filer the correct name by which Mrs. King-Tyler's name was indexed originally.

```
KingTyler Justine Mrs


Mrs. Justine King-Tyler
2015 Aspen Circle
Norman, OK  73069-2031
```

```
Tyler Arthur L Mrs

SEE

KingTyler Justine Mrs
```

```
King Justine Ms

SEE

KingTyler Justine Mrs
```

FIGURE 5-3 — Original and Cross-Reference Cards for Name of Married Woman

Acronyms. Many businesses and associations are commonly referred to by acronyms or abbreviations of their names rather than by their full names. Cross-references are to be prepared for all names of this type. Two examples of such cross-reference cards are given in Figure 5-4.

To be certain of the correct words making up an acronym or abbreviation, use a source such as the telephone directory, the dictionary, or a secretarial reference book. Do not guess!

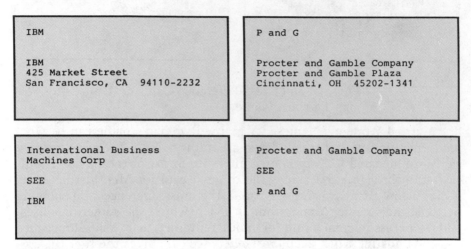

```
IBM                              P and G


IBM                              Procter and Gamble Company
425 Market Street                Procter and Gamble Plaza
San Francisco, CA  94110-2232    Cincinnati, OH  45202-1341



International Business           Procter and Gamble Company
Machines Corp
                                 SEE
SEE
                                 P and G
IBM
```

FIGURE 5-4 — Original and Cross-Reference Cards for Abbreviations

Names of Companies Doing Business under More than One Name. If a company is organized under one name but conducts business under another name, records should be kept under the name by which it does business. A cross-reference is prepared for the correct organization name in case records are requested by that name at some future time. For example, if the Gamble Manufacturing Company does business under the name of Gamco, Inc., its records would be stored under Gamco, Inc. In a card file, the cards would be those appearing in Figure 5-5.

```
Gamco Inc                        Gamble Manufacturing Company

                                 SEE
Gamco, Inc.
1351 West Losey                  Gamco Inc
Galesburg, IL  61401-2337
```

FIGURE 5-5 — Original and Cross-Reference Cards for Name of Company Doing Business under Another Name

A company with a long name may, for the sake of convenience, be commonly known by an abbreviated form of the name. In such a case, the cards would be prepared according to Figure 5-6.

```
Shortys


Shorty's
Box 1032
Iowa City, IA   52240-3233
```

```
Shortbridge Bros and Bergenfeld

SEE

Shortys
```

FIGURE 5-6 — Original and Cross-Reference Cards for Name of Company Doing Business under Shortened Name

Business Names Composed of Two or More Surnames. When a business name is composed of two or more surnames or names that appear to be surnames, records pertaining to that business are stored according to the name as written. A cross-reference is prepared for each last name except the first one so that if a request is sent to the filer with the names in incorrect order, the filer will more quickly find the material. For example, in a card file, the original card for Kennon, O'Sullivan, and Levin is indexed under Kennon. Cross-reference cards are prepared for the other two surnames (See Figure 5-7).

The important point to remember is to use each of the surnames once as the key unit in a cross-reference. All possible combinations of the names are not cross-referenced, to avoid overcrowding the file.

```
Kennon OSullivan and Levin


Kennon, O'Sullivan, and Levin
400 Wachovia Bank Building
Durham, NC   27702-1355
```

```
OSullivan Levin and Kennon

SEE

Kennon OSullivan and Levin
```

```
Levin Kennon and OSullivan

SEE

Kennon OSullivan and Levin
```

FIGURE 5-7 — Original and Cross-Reference Cards for Business Name Composed of Two or More Surnames

Names of Companies that are Affiliates or Branches of Other Companies.   When one company is affiliated with or is a branch of another company, the name appearing on the letterhead of the branch or affiliate is the one indexed on the original card. A cross-reference is made under the name of the parent company. Figure 5-8 shows the original and cross-reference cards prepared for the Sav-Well Grocery Store in Tucson, Arizona, whose parent company is National Grocers, Inc.

As names of other branches or affiliates of the National Grocers, Inc., are added to the file, their names will be added to the cross-reference card beneath Sav-Well Grocery Store.

```
SavWell Grocery Store


Sav-Well Grocery Store
1800 Broadway
Tucson, AZ  85701-2321
```

```
National Grocers Inc

SEE

SavWell Grocery Store Tucson AZ
```

FIGURE 5-8 — Original and Cross-Reference Cards for Names of Companies that are Affiliates or Branches of Other Companies

Company Names that Have Been Changed.   At times a company may change its name. The records must then also be changed to indicate the name change and to ensure that the new name will be used for storage purposes. The records already in storage are usually refiled under the new name, and the former name is put in the records as a cross-reference. Figure 5-9 shows the original card for Helen Henning Hat Company. At the time its name was changed to Chapeau Designers, the original card was changed to reflect the new name. That card now be-

```
Helen Henning Hat Company


Helen Henning Hat Company
1st Bank Bldg., Suite 200
Denver, CO  80202-1345

SEE

Chapeau Designers
```

```
Chapeau Designers


Chapeau Designers
1st Bank Bldg., Suite 200
Denver, CO  80202-1345
```

FIGURE 5-9 — Original and Cross-Reference Cards for Company Name Change

comes a cross-reference card and a new original card is made for Chapeau Designers.

If, however, moving the Helen Henning Hat Company records to the new position (Chapeau Designers) would be a tremendous job because of an accumulation of years of records, a new type of cross-reference might be needed. This cross-reference is called a SEE ALSO cross-reference, described in the next section.

SEE ALSO Cross-References.   The SEE ALSO cross-reference is used to refer the filer to additional information related to the name for which he or she is looking. For instance, in the example of the Helen Henning Hat Company, the filer might prefer to leave all the old records stored under Helen Henning Hat Company. Then, in the Chapeau Designers file, the filer would insert a SEE ALSO cross-reference (as the first item in the file folder) reading:

```
Chapeau Designers

SEE ALSO

Helen Henning Hat Company for
records previous to (date of
name change)
```

Anyone who looked for Chapeau Designers, then, would be referred also to Helen Henning Hat Company for more information.

Another use of the SEE ALSO cross-reference is as follows: Many grocery stores are affiliated with the Independent Grocers Association (IGA) chain. The name and address of each grocery store would be typed on a separate original card, and that card would be filed alphabetically. The SEE ALSO cross-reference card, bearing the name of the Independent Grocers Association, would read as follows:

```
Independent Grocers Association

SEE ALSO

Owl Grocery Priest River Idaho
Pantry Pride Cayuga Indiana
Quick Stop Lawrence Kansas
Sprint Grocery Des Plaines Illinois

(and all other groceries affiliated with IGA)
```

Anyone finding the Independent Grocers Association card would then immediately know all of the names of the stores affiliated with the Independent Grocers Association.

Another form of the SEE ALSO cross-reference is found in large files that have a number of similar names. Difficulty may arise in locating last names that are pronounced the same but spelled differently. A SEE ALSO reference may be prepared for insertion at the beginning of each spelling of the name to direct the filer to other suggested spellings. The following are examples of five cards that would be prepared:

Beal—SEE ALSO Beale, Beall, Biehl, Bielle
Beale—SEE ALSO Beal, Beall, Biehl, Bielle
Beall—SEE ALSO Beal, Beale, Biehl, Bielle
Biehl—SEE ALSO Beal, Beale, Beall, Bielle
Bielle—SEE ALSO Beal, Beale, Beall, Biehl

Still another SEE ALSO cross-reference found useful in card files reflects a change in the spelling of a name when it has been translated from a foreign spelling to an English spelling. For example:

```
Mueller

SEE ALSO

Miller
Moller
Muller
```

After all original and cross-reference cards have been prepared, they are filed alphabetically. Coding may or may not be done on the cards themselves, but the mental process of indexing always takes place in determining alphabetic order.

Coding Procedures

If the names on cards are coded, the name on the first line of the card is always used to determine placement in the file. This applies to original cards and to cross-reference cards, including SEE ALSO cards. The key unit is underlined, and the remaining units are numbered 2, 3, etc.

REVIEW AND DISCUSSION

1. If a person knows the alphabet, why is a set of rules necessary for indexing and coding records to be filed alphabetically. (Obj. 1)

2. How are names of married women coded for alphabetic filing? (Obj. 2)

3. How are hyphens and punctuation handled in persons' names and in business names when coding for alphabetic filing? (Obj. 2)

4. Explain an acceptable form for typing names on cards to be arranged alphabetically in a card file. (Obj. 9)

5. What is the purpose of a cross-reference? Why can too many cross-references be undesirable? When is a cross-reference prepared? How are cross-references coded? (Obj. 10)

6. Give at least two examples of names that should be cross-referenced. (Obj. 10)

7. What are SEE ALSO cross-references? When are they used? (Obj. 11)

DECISION-MAKING OPPORTUNITIES (DMO)

DMO 5-1: Arranging Cards in Alphabetic Order

A. On 5" by 3" cards or on slips of paper of that size, type or print in indexing order the names given below. Also type the number of the name in the top right corner of the card.
B. Prepare cross-reference cards where necessary, according to the suggestions given in this chapter.
C. Code each card for alphabetic filing.
D. Arrange all cards, including cross-references, in alphabetic order.
E. In a vertical column on a separate sheet of paper, list the numbers typed or printed on the cards that you have now arranged in alphabetic order.
F. Save the cards for possible later use. (Obj. 2-12)

1. Charles C. Norris, Jr., 622 Idaho Blvd., Boise, ID 83701-7610

2. Norrish-Halaby Corp., Columbia at Main, Saint Paul, MN 55107-4238

3. N-and-Out Diner, 2295 Adams Lane, St. Louis, MO 63111-4981

4. MacNeill & North, Florists, 4160 Light Drive, Las Vegas, NV 89102-7946

5. Father Norman, 10 Sea Breeze Blvd., Juneau, AK 99801-8999

6. Madame Norris Creations, Lua Lua Bldg., Honolulu, HI 96803-8601

7. 962 North Side Apt., 962 North Blvd., Helena, MT 59601-3629

8. Norman, Jones & Norris, 2265 Smith Avenue, Chicago, IL 60605-6655

9. Charles Norrish Pharmacy, 169 Second Avenue, Terre Haute, IN 47801-4588

10. North Miami Gift Shop, 22 Ocean Way, North Miami, FL 33121-2918

11. Mrs. Charles (Rita) Norris, 1606 Cherry Grove, Eugene, OR 97401-9470

12. NFC Repair Shop, 62 Chaney Avenue, Norwood, CA 91340-9622

13. Chas. Norman-Jones, 365 Cottage Lane, Denver, CO 80210-7821

14. No-Waste Meat Market, 33 Elm Avenue, Houston, TX 77006-7777

15. Edith M. Nakai, d/b/a/ Edie's Enterprises, Inc., 641 Waiakamilo Road, Honolulu, HI 96816-8603

16. North West Auto Parts Co., 3d and Plum, Portland, ME 04102-1138

17. Charles C. Norris, Sr., 290 Tenth Avenue, Boise, ID 83701-7610

18. Non-Skid Carpet Mfrs., Albany, NY 12202-1216

19. Mrs. Charles C. Norris Riding Farm, 22 Joyce Blvd., Canton, OH 44702-4321

20. Northside #3 Variety Store, 222 Long Street, Evanston, IL 60201-6520

21. Norman, Jones & Norris, 1600 Michigan Blvd., Chicago, IL 60603-6653

22. Marsha Norris Insurance Co., 2101 Magnolia, Sioux City, IA 51106-4334

23. #7 Nachos, 3605 Espejo NE, Albuquerque, NM 87111-2016

24. N M N, Inc., Box 1166, Wake Forest, NC 27587-1693

25. Northwest Airlines, Inc., 435 Market St., Seattle, WA 98102-1331

APPLYING THE RULES

Job 1, Card Filing—Persons' Names; Job 2, Card Filing—Business Names

All supplies necessary for completing Jobs 1 and 2 and all other jobs in *Records Management Projects*, 4th ed., are contained in the practice set.

6 ALPHABETIC RULES FOR INDEXING OTHER NAMES

Objectives

After you have completed this chapter, you will be able to:

1. Index, code, and arrange in alphabetic order the names of schools.
2. Index, code, and arrange in alphabetic order the names of religious institutions.
3. Index, code, and arrange in alphabetic order the names of organizations and associations.
4. Index, code, and arrange in alphabetic order the names of financial institutions.
5. Index, code, and arrange in alphabetic order the names of guardians, trustees, receivers, and agents and understand their importance.
6. Index, code, and arrange in alphabetic order the names of newspapers, periodicals, and other publications.
7. Index, code, and arrange in alphabetic order United States government and foreign government names.
8. Select subject categories judiciously to be used within an alphabetic arrangement.
9. Cross-reference foreign language names of businesses and governments, and names of guardians, trustees, receivers, and agents.
10. Select the correct name to code for alphabetic arrangement when there are several names on a business record.

Chapter 5 contains the rules for alphabetically arranging names of persons and of businesses. Many names, however, do not fit into either the "persons" category or the "business names" category. This chapter, therefore, gives the information necessary to arrange alphabetically names that may be referred to as "other names." The seven rules explained in this chapter require the same careful study that you gave to the rules in the previous chapter. Note especially the examples, as they will help you to understand the rules. All of the rules about hyphens, punctuation, single letters, particles, etc., apply to these names in the same way that they were used for personal and business names.

RULES FOR OTHER NAMES

17   School Names

A. **Elementary and Secondary Schools.**   Elementary and secondary school names are indexed in the order written. "The" used as the first word in these names is considered the last unit. In the case of identically named schools, city names are used to determine alphabetic order as explained in Rule 16. State or province names are considered only if the city names are identical.

Indexing Order of Units

Name	Key Unit	2	3	4	5
1. Alamo Elementary School Alamo, CA	Alamo	Elementary	School		
2. Alamo High School Alamo, GA	Alamo	High	School		
3. Carter High School Easton, KS	Carter	High	School	Easton	KS
4. Carter High School Easton, MD	Carter	High	School	Easton	MD
5. The Des Moines Middle School Des Moines, IA	DesMoines	Middle	School	The	
6. E. K. Powe High School Carrboro, NC	E	K	Powe	High	School
7. John Adams School Rutland, VT	John	Adams	School	Rutland	
8. John Adams School Tucson, AZ	John	Adams	School	Tucson	

B. **Colleges, Universities, and Special Schools.**   The name of a college, university, or special school is indexed in the order written. In the case of identically named schools, city and state or province names are used in that order to determine alphabetic arrangement.

Indexing Order of Units

Name	Key Unit	2	3	4	5
1. Bethune Kindergarten	Bethune	Kindergarten			
2. Bethune-Cookman College	BethuneCookman	College			
3. College of the Pacific	College	of	the	Pacific	
4. Iowa State University	Iowa	State	University		

Indexing Order of Units

Name	Key Unit	2	3	4	5
5. Janet Allen Design School	Janet	Allen	Design	School	
6. The Montessori Schools	Montessori	Schools	The		
7. Port Huron Community College	Port	Huron	Community	College	
8. School of Mines Portland, ME	School	of	Mines	Portland	ME
9. School of Mines Portland, OR	School	of	Mines	Portland	OR
10. South Eastern Baptist University	South	Eastern	Baptist	University	
11. St. Thomas Seminary	StThomas	Seminary			
12. University of Missouri	University	of	Missouri		

18   Religious Institutions

The names of cathedrals, churches, synagogues, temples, and the like, are indexed as written. In the case of identical names, city and state or province names are used to determine the alphabetic order.

Indexing Order of Units

Name	Key Unit	2	3	4	5	6
1. Baha'i Center	Bahai	Center				
2. Calvary Cross Church Galesburg, IL	Calvary	Cross	Church	Galesburg		
3. Calvary Cross Church Modesto, CA	Calvary	Cross	Church	Modesto		
4. Cathedral of St. Paul	Cathedral	of	StPaul			
5. Church of God	Church	of	God			
6. Congregation Ner Tamid	Congregation	Ner	Tamid			
7. Disciples of Christ	Disciples	of	Christ			
8. First Church of Science	First	Church	of	Science		
9. Idaho Falls Community Church	Idaho	Falls	Community	Church		
10. Our Lady of Mercy of Troy	Our	Lady	of	Mercy	of	Troy
11. Ste. Brigid's Church	SteBrigids	Church				
12. Taft Street Baptist Church	Taft	Street	Baptist	Church		
13. Temple Shalom Israel	Temple	Shalom	Israel			
14. Yoseikan Zen Buddhist Center	Yoseikan	Zen	Buddhist	Center		

19   Organizations and Associations

The names of clubs, fraternal orders, health organizations, lodges, societies, unions, and similar groups are indexed as written. When the names of organizations are identical, city and state or province names are considered in that order.

Indexing Order of Units

Name	Key Unit	2	3	4
1. American Federation of Musicians	American	Federation	of	Musicians
2. Audubon Society of Alaska	Audubon	Society	of	Alaska
3. Better Business Bureau Provo, UT	Better	Business	Bureau	Provo
4. Better Business Bureau St. Paul, MN	Better	Business	Bureau	StPaul
5. Delta Pi Epsilon	Delta	Pi	Epsilon	
6. Fraternal Order of Eagles	Fraternal	Order	of	Eagles
7. International Brotherhood of Teamsters	International	Brotherhood	of	Teamsters
8. Jewish Family Service	Jewish	Family	Service	
9. Mary's Help Hospital	Marys	Help	Hospital	
10. Matt Mann Rehabilitation Center	Matt	Mann	Rehabilitation	Center
11. Medical Arts Clinic	Medical	Arts	Clinic	
12. Ohio State Employees Credit Union	Ohio	State	Employees	Credit
13. Rotary Club	Rotary	Club		
14. University of Iowa Alumni Association	University	of	Iowa	Alumni

20   Financial Institutions

The names of banks, trust companies, savings and loan associations, and other financial institutions are indexed as written. When the names are identical, city and state or province names are considered. Branch names are considered after the institution, city, and state or province names.

Indexing Order of Units

Name	Key Unit	2	3	4	5	6
1. Bank of Hawaii Kaiko'o Branch Hilo, HI	Bank	of	Hawaii	Hilo	HI	Kaikoo
2. Bank of Hawaii Kalakaua Branch Honolulu, HI	Bank	of	Hawaii	Honolulu	HI	Kalakaua
3. Bank of Hawaii Pali Branch Honolulu, HI	Bank	of	Hawaii	Honolulu	HI	Pali
4. Boston Savings & Loan Assn. Boston, MA	Boston	Savings	and	Loan	Assn	
5. First National Bank Muncie, IN	First	National	Bank	Muncie		
6. First National Bank Omaha, NE	First	National	Bank	Omaha		
7. First Savings Bank Calgary, AB (Alberta)	First	Savings	Bank			
8. Guaranty Trust Co. Bozeman, MT	Guaranty	Trust	Co			
9. North Carolina National Bank Chapel Hill, NC	North	Carolina	National	Bank		

21   Guardians, Trustees, Receivers, and Agents

Guardians, trustees, receivers, or agents act for another person or organization and their names are not indexed. Such guardians, receivers, trustees, and agents may be persons, financial institutions, or companies. *Records are filed by the name of the person or organization for whom the guardian, trustee, receiver, or agent is acting.* For instance, if the Pacific Security National Bank is the trustee for Angela Dixon, a minor, the original records are filed by the name of Angela Dixon. Later in this chapter you will see how a cross-reference is made, using the name of the guardian, trustee, receiver, or agent.

Indexing Order of Units

Name	Key Unit	2	3
1. Pacific Security National Bank, Trustee for Angela Dixon	Dixon	Angela	
2. Forrest W. Work, Guardian for William E. Nadeau	Nadeau	William	E
3. Brockman & Clattenburg, Agents for Rytex Trucking	Rytex	Trucking	
4. Colfax Webb, Receivers for Samuelson Instrument Co.	Samuelson	Instrument	Co

22   Newspapers, Periodicals, and Other Publications

The names of newspapers, magazines, pamphlets, and other periodicals and publications are indexed as written. If names are identical, city names are used to determine order, followed by the state or province name if necessary.

Indexing Order of Units

Name	Key Unit	2	3	4	5
1. ARMA Records Management Quarterly	ARMA	Records	Management	Quarterly	
2. Business Education Forum	Business	Education	Forum		
3. The Daily Record Baltimore, MD	Daily	Record	The	Baltimore	
4. The Daily Record Dunn, NC	Daily	Record	The	Dunn	
5. How to Grow Azaleas	How	to	Grow	Azaleas	
6. PC	PC				
7. P.S. for Private Secretaries	PS	for	Private	Secretaries	
8. Ruff Times News Letter	Ruff	Times	News	Letter	
9. Sylvia Porter's Personal Finance Magazine	Sylvia	Porters	Personal	Finance	Magazine
10. Travel-Holiday	TravelHoliday				
11. U. S. News & World Report	U	S	News	and	World
12. Words	Words				

23   Government Names

Of primary importance in the alphabetic arrangement of government records is a method that will effectively separate the many types of American names at the various government levels. These include local, regional, state, and national, as well as names of foreign governments. Because of the similarity of names at all levels of government, careful attention to detail is very important.

If many records accumulate that pertain to one branch of the government, a special storage section may be set aside for these records. The names of agencies, departments, bureaus, and offices are then stored alphabetically within the special section. An authentic list of United States Government agencies and offices can be secured from the U. S. Superintendent of Documents in Washington, D.C. *The U.S. Government Manual* and the *Congressional Directory*, published annually, contain such lists also.

If government records are stored with other correspondence, the following rules apply:

A. **Federal Names.**   The first three units for any federal government name are *United States Government*. These words should be written on any record to which they apply if they do not already appear. The fourth and succeeding units are the distinctive name of the office, bureau, department, etc., as it appears on the letterhead. The words *Department of, Office of, Bureau of, Division of,* and the like, are transposed and used as units only *if needed* to distinguish between otherwise identical names.

Indexing Order of Units

Name	4*	5	6	7
1. Department of Agriculture Agricultural Marketing Service	Agricultural	Marketing	Service	
2. Department of Justice Drug Enforcement Administration	Drug	Enforcement	Administration	

---

*Remember that the key unit and the next two are always *United States Government*.

Indexing Order of Units

Name	4	5	6	7
3. Department of Labor U. S. Employment Service**	Employment	Service		
4. Department of Justice Federal Bureau of Investigation	Federal	Bureau	of	Investigation
5. Department of the Army Fort Cronkite	Fort	Cronkite		
6. General Services Administration	General	Services	Administration	
7. Department of the Treasury Internal Revenue Service	Internal	Revenue	Service	
8. Department of Labor Bureau of Labor Statistics	Labor	Statistics	Bureau	of
9. Department of the Interior Bureau of Mines	Mines	Bureau	of	
10. Department of Commerce National Weather Service	National	Weather	Service	
11. U. S. Postal Service**	Postal	Service		
12. Department of Health and Human Services Social Security Administration	Social	Security	Administration	

B. **State, Province, Commonwealth, and Territory Names.** The key unit is the name of the state, province, commonwealth, or territory. It must be written on any record on which it does not already appear. (To be technically correct, Kentucky, Massachusetts, Pennsylvania, and Virginia are Commonwealths; however, we will follow common usage and consider them as states.) The next unit is the word *State, Province, Commonwealth,* or *Territory,* to distinguish between this governmental level and the next lower one (city, county, township, and the like). The succeeding units are the principal words in the name of the bureau, department, board, or office. The words

---

**If *U. S.* appears again in the name, disregard it. Do not index it twice since it has already been used as the first three indexing units.

Department of, Bureau of, and the like, are not indexed unless needed to distinguish between identical names. If they are needed, they are transposed.

Indexing Order of Units

Name	Key Unit	2	3	4	5
1. Colorado State Board of Education	Colorado	State	Education	Board	of
2. Territory of Guam Board of Health	Guam	Territory	of	Health	Board
3. Maine Highway Patrol	Maine	State	Highway	Patrol	
4. New York State Athletic Commission	New	York	State	Athletic	Commission
5. North Carolina Committee for the Aged	North	Carolina	State	Aged	Committee
6. Oklahoma Department of Revenue	Oklahoma	State	Revenue	Department	of
7. Texas Dept. of Energy Conservation	Texas	State	Energy	Conservation	Dept

C. **County, Borough, Parish, City, Town, Township, and Village Names.** The key unit is the name of the county, borough, parish, city, town, township, or village. It must be written on any record on which it does not already appear. The next unit is the word *County, City, Town, Township,* or *Village.* The words *Parish* and *Borough* customarily follow the parish or borough name and are indexed in order as written. (Alaska is our only state with boroughs; Louisiana is our only state with parishes.) The succeeding units are the principal words in the name of the department, bureau, board, or office. Such words as *Department of, Bureau of,* and the like, are transposed and used only *if needed* to distinguish between otherwise identical names.

If all the names are identical, state names are considered as units immediately after county, borough, parish, city, town, township, and village names.

Indexing Order of Units

Name	Key Unit	2	3	4	5
1. Waste Department Ada, OK	Ada	City	Waste	Department	
2. Welfare Department Adams County, CO	Adams	County	CO	Welfare	Department
3. Welfare Department Adams County, IL	Adams	County	IL	Welfare	Department

Indexing Order of Units

Name	Key Unit	2	3	4	5
4. Police Department Albany, NY	Albany	City	NY	Police	Department
5. Police Department Albany, OH	Albany	City	OH	Police	Department
6. Albany County Court House Albany, NY	Albany	County	Court	House	
7. Kenai Peninsula Borough Protective Association Kenai, AK	Kenai	Peninsula	Borough	Protective	Association
8. Ecology Commission of the Parish of Orleans New Orleans, LA	Orleans	Parish	Ecology	Commission	

D. **Foreign Government Names.** The distinctive English name of the foreign country is the key unit. This is followed by the name of the office, bureau, or department, in the same manner as are government names in the United States. If foreign-language names are to be stored with English names, the foreign-language names should be translated into English and indexed accordingly. An excellent source for understanding systems of government and their divisions is *World Encyclopedia of Political Systems and Parties*, George E. Delury, Editor (1983), available in most libraries.

The names of foreign countries may be on the original records in English or in the native spelling. To ensure uniformity, the filer should keep a complete list of countries with their foreign spellings and the English translations used in the office. A good reference source for determining translations is the *Statesman's Year-Book*, available in the library. Records from foreign countries should be marked with the English spelling before storage. A cross-reference may be made to the foreign language spelling (See page 146).

Indexing Order of Units

Name	Key Unit	2	3	4	5	6
1. Republic Österreich	Austria	Republic	of			
Bundesrat	Austria	Federal	Council			
Oberster Gerichtshof	Austria	Supreme	Court	of	Justice	

Name	Key Unit	Indexing Order of Units				
		2	3	4	5	6
2. República Federativa do Brasil	Brazil	Federal	Republic	of		
Banco Central da República do Brasil	Brazil	Central	Bank	of	the	Republic
3. Kongeriget Danmark	Denmark	Kingdom	of			
Folketing	Denmark	Parliament	.			
Højesteret	Denmark	Supreme	Court			
4. République Française	France	Republic	of			
Conseil Supérieur de la Défense Nationale	France	High	Council	of	National	Defense
Tribunaux de Police	France	Police	Courts			
5. Elliniki Dimokratia	Greece	Democracy	of			
Trapeza Tis Ellados	Greece	Bank	of	Greece		
Elliniki Radiophonia Teleorasis	Greece	Greece	National	Radio	and	TV
6. Bharat	India					
Rajya Sabha	India	Council	of	States		
7. Estados Unidos Mexicanos	Mexico	United	States	of		
Ferrocarriles Nacionales de México	Mexico	Mexican	National	Railways		
Tribunal Supremo de Justicia	Mexico	Supreme	Court			
8. Kroninkrijk der Nederlanden	Netherlands	Kingdom	of	the		
Staten-Generaal	Netherlands	Parliament				
Raad van State	Netherlands	State	Council			
9. Schweiz -- Suisse -- Svizzera	Switzerland					
Bundesrat	Switzerland	Federal	Council			
Nationalrat	Switzerland	National	Council			

SUBJECTS WITHIN ALPHABETIC ARRANGEMENT

Within an alphabetic arrangement, records may sometimes be stored and retrieved more conveniently by a subject title than by a specific name. Beware, however, of using so many subjects that the arrangement becomes primarily a subject arrangement with alphabetic names as subdivisions! A few typical examples of acceptable subjects to use within an otherwise alphabetic name arrangement are:

A. Applications—the job for which applications are being made is more important than are the names of the applicants.
B. Bids or projects—similar records are kept together regardless of the names of the writers, as all records pertain to the same bid or the same project.
C. Special promotions or celebrations—all records relating to the event are grouped together by subject instead of being spread throughout storage under the names of the writers or those of the companies.
D. Branch office memos and duplicated information sent to many different offices—material of this nature is kept together to keep storage containers from becoming filled with duplicate records in many different places.

The procedure for the subject storage method is explained in detail in Chapter 8. Its application in this chapter consists of writing the subject title on the record if it does not already appear there. The main subject is the key unit. Subdivisions of the main subject are considered as successive units. The name of the correspondent is considered last. For example, on all records pertaining to applications, the word *Applications* is written as the key unit. The specific job applied for is a subdivision of that main subject and is the next unit (Accountant in the first example). Further subdivisions may be necessary (See Factory Clerk/Typist in the third example and Office Clerk/Typist in the fourth example). The applicant's name is coded last.

Indexing Order of Units

Key Unit	2	3	4	5
1. Applications	Accountant	McCance	Zenna	
2. Applications	Administrative	Assistant	Wingler	Carmen
3. Applications	ClerkTypist	Factory	Rebozo	Morton
4. Applications	ClerkTypist	Office	Hill	Jack
5. Applications	Data	Processing	Nguyen	Van
6. Applications	Maintenance	Factory	Stein	Carolyn
7. Applications	Maintenance	Headquarters	Apple	Faye
8. Applications	Word	Processing	Deal	Evelyn

CROSS-REFERENCING OF OTHER NAMES

Many of the records that are indexed according to the rules studied in this chapter may be called for by a name other than the one used for storage. When you know that this may be the case, cross-referencing at the time of storage will be a great help in finding requested records. Names in this chapter for which cross-references are very often made include:

A. Names of guardians, trustees, receivers, and agents.
B. Foreign language names of businesses and governments.

Guardian, Trustee, Receiver, and Agent Names

A cross-reference is made in the name of the guardian, receiver, trustee, or agent in order to refer the filer to the name of the individual or organization for whom the agent is acting. Cross-references for the four examples given on page 139 can be seen in Figure 6-1.

```
Pacific Security National          Work Forrest W Guardian
Bank Trustee
                                   SEE
SEE
                                   Nadeau William E
Dixon Angela
```

```
Brockman and Clattenburg          Colfax Webb Receivers
Agents
                                  SEE
SEE
                                  Samuelson Instrument Co
Rytex Trucking
```

FIGURE 6-1 — Cross-Reference Cards for Guardian, Trustee, Receiver, and Agent Names

Foreign Language Names of Businesses and Governments

The spelling of the name of a foreign business or a foreign government and its agencies is often the original spelling in the foreign language that is then usually translated into English for coding. The translation should be written on the document to be stored. When requests for records come in the native language, the filer will find that a cross-reference bearing the original spelling is an aid in finding the records.

Special care should be taken to type correct spellings and markings since these may differ greatly from the English form. Figures 6-2 and 6-3 illustrate cross-references that would be very helpful:

```
Little Mermaid The


Copenhagen Denmark
```

```
Den Lille Havfrue

SEE

Little Mermaid The
```

FIGURE 6-2 — Original and Cross-Reference Cards for a Foreign Language Business Name

```
Sverige

SEE

Sweden
```

```
Lyovel dio Island

SEE

Iceland
```

FIGURE 6-3 — Cross-Reference Cards for Foreign Language Names of Governments

Although the preceding discussion about cross-references was illustrated by reference to a card file, the procedures are exactly the same when working with any other kind of records. The original record is stored in one place according to the alphabetic rules being used. A cross-reference is made, if necessary, for any of the reasons just discussed. The cross-reference will, in all probability, be on a label affixed to the tab of a guide or on a sheet of paper inserted into a folder. The guide or the sheet may be of a distinctive color so that it is easy to find.

CHECKING KNOWLEDGE OF THE RULES

1. As your instructor directs, indicate the key unit in each of the following names:
   a. Eastern Kentucky University
   b. Independent Order of Foresters
   c. First National Bank

    d. Plumbers Local 59 Credit Union
    e. Garden Club of Toledo
    f. Raleigh/Durham Writers' Club
    g. Cleveland Chamber of Commerce
    h. Theta Alpha Delta
    i. All Saints Episcopal Church
    j. Cathedral of Divine Grace
    k. Yukon Credit Bureau
    l. 3d Street Gospel Mission
    m. St. Christopher Church
    n. Nat'l Assn. of Broadcasters
    o. Olin T. Binkley Memorial Church
    p. Central Bank & Trust Co.
    q. Toledo Savings & Loan Assn.
    r. John Carroll School of the Arts
    s. Franklin D. Roosevelt High School
    t. West Bend Elementary School
    u. Temple Beth Israel
    v. Texas Assn. of Hotel Employees
    w. Beth-El Baptist Church
    x. "Tiny Tots" Kinder School

2. As your instructor directs, indicate the succeeding units after the key unit in each of the names in the list in #1.

3. Is the alphabetic order of the names in each of the following pairs correct or wrong? Explain your answer.

    a. Catholic University of America, Washington, DC
       Catholic University of Puerto Rico, Ponce, Puerto Rico
    b. Katherine Grant Business College, Las Vegas, NV
       Kathryn Grant Business College, Las Cruces, NM
    c. *The Los Angeles Times*
       Los Angeles Theatrical Association
    d. Austin Guaranty Trust Co., Guardian for Vernon Austin
       Austin University, Austin, MN
    e. *Apartment Life*
       Apartment Living
    f. School of Performing Arts
       School of Performing Artists

g. Senior High School, Hazard, KY
   Senior High School, Hazen, AR
h. Jamestown College
   Jamestown Historical Society
i. Saint Mary's Hospital
   St. Mary's Academy
j. Contemporary Dramatic School, Dallas, TX
   Contemporary Drama School, Fort Worth, TX
k. College of the Desert, Palm Desert, CA
   College of the Dessert, New York, NY
l. Hart Institute of Electronics, Fargo, ND
   Electronics Institute of Fargo, Fargo, ND
m. *New York Daily News*
   New York Day Center Reporter
n. Ellen Cushing Junior College
   Ellen-Dale Corners Junior College
o. Hudson School of Commerce, Troy, NY
   Hudson/Belk Fashion Academy, Troy, NY

4. Each of the following sets of three names is arranged in correct alphabetic order. Study the arrangement and then indicate where the 4th name should be placed so as to be in correct alphabetic order with the other three.

Example: 1. Cathedral of the Divine   Answer: Between 2 and 3.
           2. First Presbyterian Church
           3. Temple Judea

           4. St. Paul's Methodist Church

a. 1. *Long Island Press*
   2. *The Los Altos Tribune*
   3. *The Lottery Digest*

   4. *The Los Angeles Times*

c. 1. Caycroft Elementary School
   2. Christ Church Episcopal
   3. *Consumers Digest*

   4. Charles Christman Middle
      School

b. 1. *Bon Appétit*

   2. *Good Housekeeping*
   3. *Potter's Weekly*

   4. *Savvy*

d. 1. Loyola University Alumni
      Assn.
   2. Lyons Elementary School
   3. Lyons Vocational School

   4. Lyonne School for the Deaf

e. 1. San Diego Trust Co., Trustee for Miss Tina A. Potter
   2. San Jose State University
   3. Santa Clara Hospice
   4. Salt Lake City Animal Hospital

f. 1. *The Record*, Cadiz, KY
   2. *The Record*, Louisville, KY
   3. *The Record*, New Castle, VA
   4. *The Record*, Jal, NM

5. Print or type the correct order of the indexing units for the following names. If you think cross-references are necessary, prepare them. Use 5" by 3" cards or slips of paper cut to that size on which to type or print.

a. Internal Revenue Service
Department of the Treasury
Covington, KY

b. State Highway Patrol
Tulsa, OK

c. Board of Health
Newark County
Newark, NJ

d. City Purchasing Department
Pittsburgh, PA

e. Veterans Employment Service
U. S. Department of Labor
Knoxville, TN

f. Public Library
Johnson County
Iowa City, IA

g. Federal Bureau of
Investigation
Department of Justice
Washington, DC

h. Consumer Protection Board
New York, NY
(a state agency)

i. Bureau of International
Commerce
U. S. Department of
Commerce
Washington, DC

j. State Department of Industrial
Relations
Houston, TX

k. U. S. Army Recruiting Service
Department of the Army
Detroit, MI

l. Office of the Director
Bureau of the Mint
Department of the Treasury
Washington, DC

m. Banque Centrale d'Algérie
(Central Bank of Algeria)
Algiers

n. Ferrocarriles de Costa Rica
(Costa Rican National
Railways)

o. Board of Elections
Hamilton County
Cincinnati, OH

p. Department of Public Works
County of San Francisco
San Francisco, CA

6. After you have checked your work and corrected any errors, arrange the names in #5 in correct alphabetic order (including cross-references).

REVIEW AND DISCUSSION

1. School names are often identical in different cities. If you had several of these identically named schools to arrange in alphabetic order, what would determine the alphabetic arrangement? (Obj. 1)

2. How would you code the name, "The Good Shepherd Convent"? Why? (Obj. 2)

3. Arrange the following names in alphabetic order and explain their arrangement. List the numbers of the items in correct alphabetic order. (Obj. 3)

   a. Kiwanis Club, Sioux City, IA
   b. Kiwanis Club, Sac City, IA
   c. Triangle Kiwanis Club, Raleigh, NC
   d. Kiwanis Club, Springfield, MA
   e. Kiwanis Club, Springfield, IL
   f. Kiwanis Club, Spring Valley, CA

4. Arrange the following three names in alphabetic order and explain your reasons. (Obj. 4)

   a. First Savings Bank, Midland, ON (Ontario, Canada)
   b. First Savings Bank, Regency Plaza Branch, Midland, MI
   c. First Savings Bank, Eastowne Branch, Midland, MI

5. Assume that your company does business with the First National Bank which serves as the Trustee for Arthur G. Hunter. Under what name would the records be stored? Why? (Objs. 5, 9)

6. Many newspapers have the same name but are published in different cities. How would you arrange alphabetically correspondence from:

   a. *Daily News*, Anchorage, AK
   b. *Daily News*, Wellington, KS
   c. *Daily News*, Van Nuys, CA
   d. *Daily News*, Bowling Green, KY
   e. *Daily News*, Effingham, IL (Obj. 6)

7. Explain how you would prepare to store alphabetically correspondence from each of the following governmental agencies in Norway. "Norge" is the native spelling. Indicate the alphabetic order of the items. (Obj. 7)

Foreign Name	English Translation
a. Storting	a. Parliament
b. Statsråd	b. Council of State
c. Høyesterett	c. Supreme Court of Justice

If you did not know the English translation for each of the three names, what source might you use to help you?

8. In the alphabetic arrangement of U. S. government names, separation of the names according to their proper levels of government is of prime importance. What are the various levels of government for which you may have records to store? (Obj. 7)

9. In arranging federal government correspondence alphabetically, what are always the first three key units to be coded? (Obj. 7)

10. Why are subject categories ever found in an alphabetically arranged name file? Give at least two examples of subjects that might be found. (Obj. 8)

11. The Finnish spelling for Finland is Suomen Tasavalta. If you had correspondence from a government agency in Finland, in the native language, and you had forgotten what Suomen Tasavalta stood for, what might you have in storage to aid you? (Obj. 9)

DECISION-MAKING OPPORTUNITIES (DMO)

DMO 6-1: Arranging Cards in Alphabetic-Order

A. On 5″ by 3″ cards or on slips of paper of that size, type or print the names given below in filing order. Also type the number of the name on the top right corner of the card.

B. Prepare cross-reference cards where necessary according to the suggestions given in this chapter.

C. Code each card for alphabetic filing.

D. Arrange all cards, including cross-references, in alphabetic order.

E. In a vertical column on a separate sheet of paper, list the numbers on the cards that you have now arranged in alphabetic order.

F. After you have checked your work and corrected any errors, merge these cards with the cards you prepared for DMO 5-1 in Chapter 5, page 131. (You have already checked these latter cards and corrected any errors.)

G. In a vertical column on a separate sheet of paper, list the numbers of all the cards that you have arranged in alphabetic order (cross-references included). (Objs. 1, 7, and 9)

26. First Christian Church
27. Lihue Community College (Lihue is a city in Hawaii.)
28. International Brotherhood of Electrical Workers
29. Chicago Guaranty Trust Co.
30. James Carter Middle School
31. Fischer High School
32. Constance Murray Dance School
33. National College of Osteopathy
34. North Eastern Iowa Technical College
35. Judea Temple
36. Jokelson Holistic Medicine Institute
37. Svoboda Lodge #3
38. Margaret Nystrom, Guardian for Lottie McCauley
39. *New Office Topics*
40. Fisher Cosmetology School
41. *Durham Morning Herald*
42. U. S. Postal Service, Duke Station
43. U. S. Environmental Protection Agency
44. Kansas City Human Relations Commission
45. Chicago Parks and Recreation Department
46. Durham County Department of Social Services
47. Banque Nationale pour le Commerce et l'Industrie
        (translation: National Bank of Commerce and Industry)
48. *Svenska Bokförlagets* (translation: *Swedish for Tourists*)
49. Lihue Police Department
50. National Association of TV Artists

APPLYING THE RULES

Job 3, Card Filing—Other Names; Job 4, Card Filing—Review; Job 5, Correspondence Storage—Persons' Names

7 MANUAL RECORDS RETRIEVAL AND TRANSFER

Objectives

After you have completed this chapter, you will be able to:

1. Explain the meaning of retrieval and how it has changed over the years.
2. Identify ways in which requests are made for stored records.
3. State the interdependence between storage and retrieval.
4. Name the three procedures necessary to control stored records.
5. Describe the forms used for requisitioning a stored record and explain their use.
6. Explain charge-out and its importance to records control.
7. Describe the forms used in charging out records.
8. Explain follow-up procedures, the reasons why they are necessary, and the forms used for follow-up.
9. Describe a tickler file and how and why it is used.
10. Explain how to find misfiled or lost records.
11. List reasons for transferring stored records.
12. Describe two methods of records transfer.
13. Identify the procedures used in the transfer of active records to semi-active and to inactive records storage.

As you will recall from previous chapters, two steps in the record cycle are retrieval and transfer of stored records. These two steps, as they relate to the manual retrieval of paper records or to information from them, are discussed in this chapter.

Stored records may (1) be requested for use again, (2) be left for some predetermined period in temporary storage, (3) be transferred to permanent storage, or (4) be disposed of. Careful management of stored records requires that agreed-upon procedures be followed for each of these situations.

All retrieval consists of comparing requested information with stored information. Whether the retrieval is done manually, mechanically, or automatically, the process of comparison takes place. And when the information being searched for matches the information found, retrieval is accomplished.

RECORDS RETRIEVAL

With the development of more sophisticated records systems, records terminology takes on newer, more significant meanings. Initially, to "retrieve" information meant only to find it. Now, however, *information retrieval* is the term commonly used to mean both the *storage method* and the *reference system* to the stored records. For example, a common storage and retrieval problem is that of finding a name and telephone number in a telephone directory. The storage method is an alphabetic listing of names on the pages of a book; the reference system is a table search (scanning of tabulated telephone lists) according to name. Similarly, nonfiction library books are stored on shelves in numbered sequence; the shelves are searched by reference number to retrieve a desired book.

Retrieval of a record or of information from it can be done in two ways: (1) manually—a person goes to the storage container and takes by hand the record wanted or notes the information requested from it; or (2) mechanically—a person uses some mechanical means to locate a record. The physical record may not need to be removed from storage; but the inquirer is informed as to where it can be found or the information requested is shown to the inquirer in some way, perhaps on a screen.

Requests for stored records may come in many ways: orally (from the next desk, over the telephone or intercom, or by messenger); or in writing (by memo, by letter, or on a special form). The request may be delivered in person or sent by some mechanical means such as a pneumatic tube or conveyor system. The gist of a request, for example, might be, "Please get me the recent letter from Sears & Scanlon that has the lumber quotation in it." Or, "Let me have the tape that has Bill's annual meeting speech on it." Or, perhaps, "Get me the current price of XXX and let me have the microfilm it's on." All of these records have previously been stored manually according to some agreed-upon method of storage. The letter, tape, or film must be found quickly in storage and given to the requester. Every minute of delay in finding the record is costly—in executive waiting time and in clerical searching time—to say nothing of possible loss of business as an ultimate result.

If filer and requester use the same filing segments for storing and for requesting a record, the system works well. If, however, records relating to Jane Nystrom-Sandburg were stored under Nystrom but requested under Sandburg, retrieval would be extremely difficult because the searcher would look in the S section of storage instead of in the N section.

Manual Retrieval and Restorage Cycle

The same set of general steps to retrieve are used for handling all types of records. Only the specific operating procedures will differ. The steps making up the retrieval and restorage cycle are shown in Figure 7-1. The crucial step, the point at which a problem is most likely to arise, is in Step 1 with the words used to request a record. Ideally, the one who stores the record should be the one who searches for and removes it from storage when it is requested. In practice, however, the record may be stored by one person and retrieved by someone else when that record or information from it is requested.

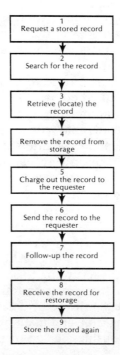

FIGURE 7-1 — Steps in Manual Retrieval and Restorage

Effective records control includes following standard procedures for requesting records, charging them out, and seeing that they are returned. In records management terminology, the procedure is referred to as *Requisition, Charge-Out, and Follow-Up.*

Effective records control enables the records manager or searcher to retrieve requested records on the first try and to answer correctly these five questions:

1. *What* records are out of storage?
2. *Who* took the records?
3. *When* were the records taken?
4. *How long* will the records be out of storage?
5. *Where* will the records be refiled when they are brought back to storage?

Control is achieved and the questions can be answered if standard procedures have been established and are followed. Each of these procedures will be discussed.

Requisition Procedures

Preparation of a request is the first step in the retrieval sequence. A **requisition** is a written request for a record or information from a record. Even if the borrower orally requests the information or record, that request is put in writing and referred to as a requisition. The form may be (1) prepared by the requester or (2) made out by the filer from information given orally or in writing by the requester. Two of these forms are discussed below.

Simple Requisition Form. One of the most frequently used requisition forms is a 5″ by 3″ or 6″ by 4″ card or slip of paper printed with blanks to be filled in. Figure 7-2 shows an example of such a requisition

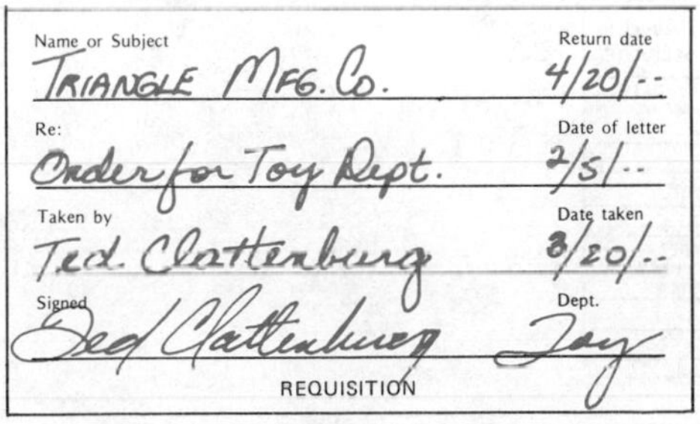
Name or Subject: TRIANGLE MFG. Co. Return date: 4/20/..
Re: Order for Toy Dept. Date of letter: 2/5/..
Taken by: Ted. Clattenburg Date taken: 3/20/..
Signed: Ted Clattenburg Dept.: Toy
REQUISITION

FIGURE 7-2 — Requisition Card

form. By studying it, you can see that on March 20 Ted Clattenburg of the Toy Dept. asked for the February 5 letter concerning an order from Triangle Manufacturing Company. (The return date, one month later, is a control that is explained on page 161.)

The requisition form may be prepared in duplicate. The original copy usually stays in the storage container as part of an OUT indicator, and the second copy is held as a reminder (discussed later).

On-Call (Wanted) Cards.   A record that has already been borrowed will occasionally be requested from storage. When this occurs, the filer must immediately notify the requester that the record has been loaned. If the request is urgent, the filer notifies the original borrower that some-one else wants the record and asks that it be returned to storage. The notification may be made orally or in writing on an **on-call card** or a wanted card (See Figure 7-3). The card is similar to an OUT card.

Two copies of an on-call card are usually made; one going to the original borrower, and the other being attached to the original OUT in-dicator in storage. As soon as the borrowed record is returned to storage, it is charged out to the second borrower by the usual method of charge-out or by noting on the on-call card the date on which the record was delivered to the second borrower. (See the "Delivered" column at the right of the card in Figure 7-3.)

Although the practice of keeping on-call or wanted cards in a sepa-rate reminder file is followed in some offices, it is much better to put the on-call or wanted cards at the place where the requested record is customarily stored. When the record is returned to storage by the origi-nal borrower, the filer immediately sees that the record is wanted by someone else. If the request has been placed in a reminder file, it might be several days before reference to the reminder file reveals that the rec-ord is wanted by a second person.

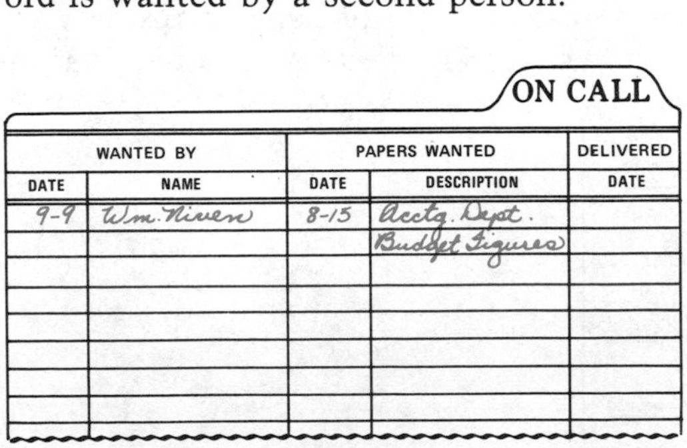

ON CALL				
WANTED BY		PAPERS WANTED		DELIVERED
DATE	NAME	DATE	DESCRIPTION	DATE
9-9	Wm. Niven	8-15	Acctg. Dept. Budget figures	

FIGURE 7-3 — On-Call Card or Wanted Card

Requests for Confidential Records.   All stored records are considered valuable or they would not be stored. Some, however, are so valuable as to be marked *Confidential, Classified, Secret, Vital, Personal,* etc. The filer must be sure not to release these records from storage without proper authority. In some offices, a written request bearing the signature of a designated officer of the company is required for the release of such records.

Some records are so valuable or confidential that they are not to be taken from storage under any circumstances. They must be inspected at the storage container. This inspection is not accompanied by any requisition form other than the required signature of someone in authority before the inspection is allowed.

Charge-Out Procedures

The term **charge-out** means exactly what it says: A record is "charged out" to the borrower, who is held responsible for returning it to storage. A management-oriented person will develop a procedure for keeping track of the records that are taken from storage. This procedure should be followed in every instance, regardless of who removes material from storage. Less than one minute is needed to note the name of the person who borrowed a record, while hours can be spent searching for a lost or misplaced record. Borrowers, too, are much more conscientious about returning records to storage when they know that records have been charged out in their name. The charge-out procedure consists of (1) using OUT indicators to show that records have been removed from storage, (2) sometimes using carrier folders to transport borrowed records, and (3) disposing of OUT indicators when the borrowed records have been returned to storage.

Use of OUT Indicators.   When requested records are found, they are removed from storage and an OUT form is inserted in place of the records just removed. The four types of OUT indicators in general use were explained in Chapter 4—OUT guides, folders, cards, and sheets.

Use of Carrier Folders.   To preserve the life of a folder, the original folder may be left in storage but its entire contents transferred to a temporary, brightly colored **carrier folder**. That name is given to this folder because it carries the requested records to the person who asked for the original folder. An OUT form is placed in the original folder in storage with information indicating the whereabouts of the folder contents and the number of items that were borrowed. Lending the contents of an entire folder raises the possibility that some of the records will be missing when the folder is returned. Unless the records are fastened together securely, some may be lost. Occasionally each record that is borrowed is numbered in pencil on the back of the record and a note is made on the OUT indicator of the total number of records loaned.

The color of the carrier folder serves as a reminder to the borrower that the records must be returned to storage. Often the carrier folder has "Return to Files" printed prominently on its front cover as a further reminder to the borrower.

A major advantage of using a carrier folder is that the original folder is not subjected to wear and tear, as it would be if it were removed from the storage container. When the carrier folder is returned to storage, its contents are transferred to the original folder. If they have been numbered, the pages are checked to make sure that all have been returned. The OUT form is removed, and the carrier folder is ready to be used again.

Disposition of OUT Indicators.   When borrowed records are returned to storage, all OUT forms inserted while the records were gone must be immediately removed. If the charge-out information has been written on the OUT form itself, this information is crossed out and the form is stored for reuse. In some offices, OUT forms are kept for tallying purposes, to see how many records are being requested, to determine the work load of employees, and to see which records are being used frequently and which are not. Totals are often kept by day, week, month, or year. Requisition cards that are removed from holders may be destroyed, and the holders are then stored for reuse. If any duplicates of OUT slips or OUT cards have been made (for reminder purposes, for instance), they should be located and immediately destroyed also.

Follow-Up Procedures

Whoever is responsible for retrieving records from storage and charging them out is also responsible for checking on their return within a reasonable length of time. This checking is known as **follow-up**. The length of time records may be borrowed from storage depends on the type of business, the number of requests that come in for the records, the use made of copying machines, and the value of the records. Experience has shown that the longer records remain out of the files, the more difficult their return becomes. Many businesses stipulate a week to ten days, with two weeks being the absolute maximum time records may be borrowed. Other businesses allow less time because records can be so easily and quickly copied that the original may be returned to storage within a few hours. Doing a follow-up may mean calling a borrower as a reminder that records must be returned to storage, or a follow-up may take the form of a written request that borrowed records be returned.

Following Up Confidential Records.   The rule concerning confidential records is usually that the records (if they may be borrowed at all) must be returned to storage each night. A special memory device should be used by the filer as a reminder to see that these records are returned. Notation of their location is made in the same way as that used for any other borrowed record—by using a requisition and an OUT indicator. An *additional* reminder must be made to make sure that the filer will not forget to secure the return of the record before leaving for the day. This reminder may be a simple card note prominently displayed on the desk, a copy of the requisition impaled on a spindle reserved for urgent matters that require attention before the day's end, or a special flag or signal in plain view on the desk as a memory jogger. Whatever the device used, it should be unusual because it must never fail to remind the records manager or the filer that some confidential records are out of storage and must be recovered.

Tickler Files.   Many requisitions are made in duplicate so that the second copy can be used for follow-up purposes. The follow-up or reminder method most frequently used is the **tickler file**. Other names sometimes used to describe such a file are *bring-up file, suspense file,* and *pending file.* The basic arrangement of a tickler file is always the same: chronologic. This arrangement usually takes the form of a series of 12 guides in a **card tickler file** (Figure 7-4), or folders in a **folder tickler file** (Figure 7-5), with the names of the months of the year printed on their tabs. One set of guides or folders with tabs printed with 1 through 31 for the days of the month are also used. Guides or folders for the years following the present one may also be used.

Card Tickler File.   Card-size requisition forms or index cards are filed in card tickler files. In an office where duplicate copies of requisitions are made for all records requested from storage, the second copy of the requisition becomes the card placed in the tickler file. The date by which it is filed is the date on which the records are to be returned

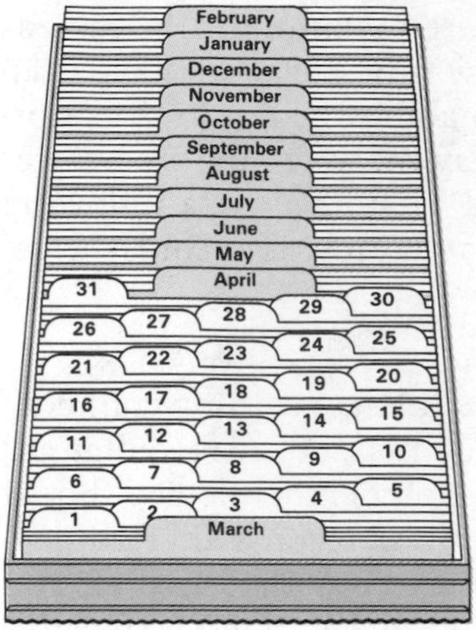

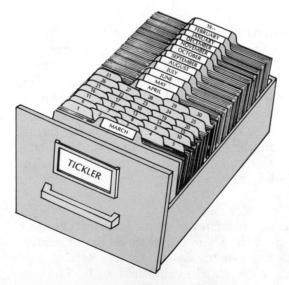

FIGURE 7-4 — Card Tickler File

to storage. The card shown in Figure 7-2 is filed behind the April guide because the record is to be returned on April 20.

If an oral request or a request written on a form other than a requisition slip or card is received and a record is to be removed from storage, the filer completes a requisition card or types a separate index card containing complete information. An example of a separate index card made for a letter loaned on March 6, to be returned on March 20,

FIGURE 7-5 — Folder Tickler File

is shown in Figure 7-6. The card would be placed behind the "20" guide since March is the current month in the illustration. If the letter were to be returned on April 6, the card would have April 6, 19--, on its top line and it would be filed behind the April guide in the card tickler file.

Many executives use a card tickler system to remind them of events that happen yearly, such as birthdays and anniversaries; membership expiration dates and dues payments; insurance premium payments; weekly, monthly, or annual meetings; subscription expiration dates; and the dates on which certificates of deposit or bonds are due.

Folder Tickler File. Figure 7-5 illustrates a folder tickler file. If a folder tickler file is used, duplicates of OUT sheets and cards are filed in the folder tickler file according to the dates on which the OUT slips need attention. Using a duplicate requisition system eliminates the need for writing information twice, eliminates errors, and saves time.

Another satisfactory way to use a folder tickler file is to make an extra copy of any record that will be needed at a future date. The extra copy is placed in the tickler folder bearing the date on which the original record will be needed. If the record reveals an action to be taken on a date within the current month, the copy of it would go into the correct *date* folder. If the date falls in a succeeding month, the copy of the record would go into the folder bearing the name of that month. The filer makes this extra copy since original records belong in storage.

The tickler file must be the first item checked each day. Information on the notes found in the tickler file reminds the filer to get records from storage and bring them to the attention of a specific person. If the tickler file notation shows that certain borrowed records are due to be returned that day, they are requested from the borrowers.

If a borrower wants to keep records beyond the due date, that date may be extended if no other request for the records has been received. The date on the tickler file reminder is then changed to the new due date, and the card or sheet is returned to the tickler file and put behind the new due-date guide.

```
March 20, 19--

9/3/-- letter from Amy Lee, 2819 East Third
Street, Springfield, IL  61108-2813, should be
returned today.  Taken by C. H. Coppedge,
(Sales Dept.) on 3/6/--.
```

FIGURE 7-6 — Typed Requisition Card

On the last day of each month, the person in charge of the tickler file checks through the date cards or folders so as to be certain that nothing has been inadvertently overlooked during the month. Then that person removes all the cards or papers from behind the next month's guide and redistributes them behind the daily guides (numbered 1 through 31). At the end of November, for instance, the spaces behind all the daily guides would be checked, the November guide would be moved to the back of the file, and the December guide would be put in the front. All reminders that were filed behind December would then be redistributed behind the daily guides according to the dates on the reminders.

No matter which type of tickler file is used, it is a means of controlling records. When records are returned to storage, any tickler notation (the card, requisition, or sheet) relating to the records is destroyed. Any extra copies are disposed of. This destruction must be done carefully, as it is possible to destroy the wrong card, requisition, or copy if attention to detail is lacking.

If the file is small, no tickler system may be necessary for the follow-up of borrowed records since the filer can open the drawers daily and quickly scan the folders for OUT indicators. Each OUT indicator can be checked individually to see if the records should be returned that day. If so, a request for them can be made immediately. The use of a tickler file to remind the filer of some future action, however, is important. And the use of OUT indicators is also important, no matter how small the file.

Misfiled and Lost Records

Even with care, some records are misfiled and become lost. And if storage is done haphazardly or with no concern for the importance of following consistent procedures, lost records are even more numerous. Lack of attention to spelling, careless insertion of records into the storage equipment, distractions such as unnecessary conversation or paying more attention to office festivities than to coding of records—these reasons and others cause records to be misfiled and, therefore, "lost."

Experienced filers use the following techniques in trying to find missing records:

1. Look in the folders immediately in front of and behind the correct folder.
2. Look between the folders.

3. Look under all the folders, where the record may have slipped to the bottom of the drawer or shelf.
4. Look completely through the correct folder because alphabetic or other order of sequence may have been neglected due to carelessness or hurry.
5. Look in the general folder in addition to searching in the individual folder.
6. Check the transposition of names (Hayes Benjamin instead of Benjamin Hayes).
7. Look for the second, third, or succeeding units of a filing segment rather than for the key unit.
8. Check for misfiling because of misreading of letters—e for i, n for m, t for l, k for h, C for G, etc.
9. Check alternate spellings (Jon, Jahn).
10. Look under other vowels (for a name beginning with Ha, look also under He, Hi, Ho, and Hu).
11. Look for a double letter instead of a single one (or the reverse).
12. Look for anglicized forms of a name (Miller, Moller, or Muller for Mueller).
13. Check for transposition of numbers (35 instead of 53).
14. Look in the year preceding or following the one in question.
15. Look in a related subject if the subject method is used.
16. Be aware that the records may be en route to storage.
17. Look in the sorter.
18. Ask the person in whose desk or briefcase the record may be to search for it!

If every search fails to produce the missing record, some records managers try to reconstruct the record from memory, typing up as much as is known. This information is placed in a folder labeled "LOST," in addition to the name of the original folder. This new folder is stored in its correct place as a constant reminder to the filer to be on the alert for the missing record.

The loss of records may sometimes be prevented by permanently binding them at their top edges or in book form. Binding in this manner assures neatness and precludes the borrowing of individual records. Bound volumes can be placed on shelving, which releases drawer space and utilizes space that might not otherwise be used. But binding creates bulk; the transporting of bound volumes is difficult; loss of individual sheets from bound volumes is almost impossible to detect; bound volumes are often stored in hard-to-reach places; and many unnecessary records must be loaned along with the one that is requested. The binding of correspondence, therefore, is not recommended.

RECORDS TRANSFER

Once a record is stored somewhere, it does not stay there forever—think of the thousands of storage containers (cabinets, shelves, and other equipment) that would be required in offices if that were the case! At some point in the life of a record, it is moved. As you will recall from Chapter 2, this movement may be according to the retention schedule that the well-managed records program is following. Sometimes the record may be destroyed, or it may be transferred and retained. If it is transferred, the main basis for making such a decision may often be the activity (frequency of use) of the record. Other reasons also have a great bearing on when and why transfer takes place. Some of these reasons are:

1. No more records storage space is available.
2. Costs of more storage equipment and extra office space are rising and less costly areas of nearby storage or offsite storage become attractive alternatives.
3. Stored records are no longer being requested and, therefore, are ready for transfer.
4. Work loads have lightened and there is time for records transfer activity.
5. Case or project records have reached a closing or ending time (the shopping mall has been built and sold or the divorce case is settled and closed).
6. Established company policy requires every department to transfer records at a stated time.

Once transfer is decided upon, the records manager who is concerned about records control must find answers to four important questions:

1. WHAT records are to be moved?
2. HOW are the records to be prepared for transfer?
3. WHEN are the records to be transferred?
4. WHERE are the records to go?

The answers to WHAT, HOW, and WHEN will depend on the transfer method selected. The answer to WHERE will depend not only on the method selected but also on the availability of in-house or offsite records storage areas. (A brief discussion of this point is contained in Chapter 2.) After answering those questions, the records manager then follows transfer procedures as explained in this chapter to move the selected records.

Transfer Methods

Two of the most common methods of transferring records are the perpetual transfer method and the periodic transfer method. Each will be explained with procedures for ensuring efficient transfer.

Perpetual Transfer Method. Under the **perpetual transfer method**, records are continuously transferred from active storage to semiactive or inactive storage areas, whenever the records are no longer needed for reference. Examples of records that can be transferred by the perpetual method include legal cases that are settled; research projects when results are finalized; medical records of cases no longer needing attention; prison and law-enforcement case records; and construction or architectural jobs that are finished. Each of these examples is a well-defined unit; when the records are no longer needed for active reference, they are transferred.

The perpetual transfer method is not recommended for business correspondence or records that are continually referred to and that must be quickly available. The perpetual transfer method is, therefore, not practical for most offices.

Periodic Transfer Method. The **periodic transfer method** keeps together records of a certain time period, usually one year. At the end of the period, all records for that year are removed from active storage and placed in inactive storage. New folders are made for records that are then allowed to accumulate in active storage until the next transfer period. If transfer takes place once or twice a year, it is called the **one-period transfer method**. At the end of *one period of time*, records are transferred. The chief advantage of this method is its ease of operation. The chief disadvantage is that some frequently called-for records will be in inactive storage, and time will be lost in making frequent trips to the inactive storage area. At times, records of some correspondents will need to be retrieved from both active and inactive storage if the requested records cover several time periods.

If transfer is from active records storage to semiactive records storage to inactive records storage, the term **two-period transfer method** is used. Two folders, one for active and one for semiactive records, are maintained in the office. Figure 7-7 shows an arrangement of four-drawer file cabinets in which active records are kept either in the top two drawers or in the middle two drawers. Semiactive records are housed in either the lower drawers or the top and bottom drawers—the drawers that are most difficult to reach.

A-E ACTIVE	L-R ACTIVE
F-K ACTIVE	S-Z ACTIVE
A-E SEMIACTIVE	L-R SEMIACTIVE
F-K SEMIACTIVE	S-Z SEMIACTIVE

A-E SEMIACTIVE	I-O SEMIACTIVE
A-B ACTIVE	M-N ACTIVE
C-F ACTIVE	O-S ACTIVE
G-L ACTIVE	T-Z ACTIVE
F-H SEMIACTIVE	R-Z SEMIACTIVE

FIGURE 7-7 — Active and Semiactive Storage Arrangements in Four-Drawer File Cabinets

If the records are kept in five-drawer file cabinets, the active records are often stored according to the drawer arrangements shown in Figure 7-8. In Figure 7-8A, the arrangement of active and semiactive records allows easy access to current records and less convenient space is reserved for the semiactive records. In Figure 7-8B, the active and semiactive records are side by side for ease in locating like records from two time periods. If records are stored on shelves, the middle three shelves would house the active records, and the semiactive records would be stored on the upper and lower shelves (the harder places to reach).

Transfer under the two-period method is usually done once a year with the semiactive records being sent to inactive storage. Active records are transferred to the semiactive containers, and new folders are made to contain active records.

The advantage of the two-period method is that it is very suitable for small offices where storage space may be limited. The two-period method keeps the records of two time periods accessible even though they are separated. The disadvantage is that expensive equipment and

A-B ACTIVE	A-B SEMIACTIVE	K-L ACTIVE	K-L SEMIACTIVE
C ACTIVE	C SEMIACTIVE	M-N ACTIVE	M-N SEMIACTIVE
D-E ACTIVE	D-E SEMIACTIVE	O-R ACTIVE	O-R SEMIACTIVE
F-G ACTIVE	F-G SEMIACTIVE	S ACTIVE	S SEMIACTIVE
H-J ACTIVE	H-J SEMIACTIVE	T-Z ACTIVE	T-Z SEMIACTIVE

A-B SEMIACTIVE	D-E SEMIACTIVE	K-L SEMIACTIVE	O-R SEMIACTIVE
A-B ACTIVE	F-G ACTIVE	K-L ACTIVE	S ACTIVE
C ACTIVE	H-J ACTIVE	M-N ACTIVE	T-Z ACTIVE
D-E ACTIVE	F-G SEMIACTIVE	O-R ACTIVE	S SEMIACTIVE
C SEMIACTIVE	H-J SEMIACTIVE	M-N SEMIACTIVE	T-Z SEMIACTIVE

A.   B.

FIGURE 7-8 — Two Arrangements of Active and Semiactive Storage in Five-Drawer File Cabinets

space are needed for the semiactive records that, in reality, may be mostly inactive. The semiactive records are simply records of another time period, retained in the office until the next periodic transfer takes place.

Transfer Procedures

Once the transfer method has been determined, transfer procedures are communicated to every department. The records manager must see that adequate storage equipment is available and at the correct place to receive transferred records before the actual transfer begins. If records are to be moved to a distant storage area, as is usually the case with inactive records, transfer equipment and supplies are needed, as discussed below.

Transfer from Active to Semiactive Storage.   If records are moved from one file cabinet drawer to another close by, or from one place on the storage shelves to another nearby, the required physical activity involves taking care not to drop the folders, being sure that the order of the records is kept, and checking to be sure that no records remain in active storage. All guides are left in the active storage containers; only the folders are moved. New folders are prepared, in advance of transfer time or as needed, to receive records in active storage.

An alternate method of transferring from active to semiactive storage takes more time but keeps actively consulted records together. On the transfer date, folders having records bearing recent dates are kept in active storage. All other folders are transferred to semiactive storage. "Recent" must mean a specified date—and each folder, therefore, must be opened and checked before determining whether it should be moved or should stay in active storage. This method necessitates looking through the general folders carefully and removing only those correspondents' records that have dates prior to the "recent" date decided upon. This will mean preparing a new general folder to be stored in semiactive records, since the original general folder will remain in active storage. Because guides are left in active storage, the general folder is often used as the first item in its section in semiactive storage and becomes the substitute for a guide.

Transfer from Active or Semiactive to Inactive Storage.   Preparing records for transfer involves completing the necessary forms and boxing or packaging the records for inactive storage. The forms used will vary;

Figure 7-9 shows a records transfer form used by a large pharmaceutical company. Typed or clearly written on the form, to be attached to the storage box, is information about its contents, such as a description, the time span covered, the department name, and retention data.

At the time records are transferred, the transferring department completes four copies of the records transfer form. One copy is retained by the transferring department while the box is in transit to storage. The original and two copies accompany the box to inactive storage where the box is logged in and its location on the storage shelves is noted on all copies. One copy of the form is returned to the sending department and retained there for reference when a record from that box is required. The copy that was first retained in the department is now destroyed.

The fourth copy of the transfer form is kept in the storage center office. The storage center will have its own system of keeping track of the boxes—by department, by number, by project, and the like. Some inactive storage centers use computers for locating records and for keeping track of disposal times. Information from the records transfer form is either keyed into or read into the automated equipment (further discussed in Chapter 14). When records are borrowed from inactive storage, the same controls are needed as are used in active storage—requisition, charge-out, and follow-up.

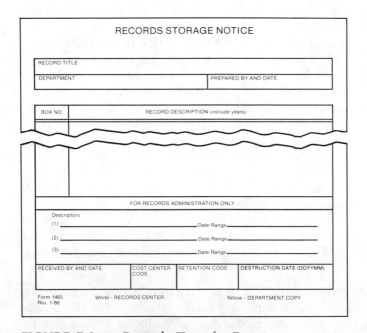

FIGURE 7-9 — Records Transfer Form

FIGURE 7-10 — Inactive Storage Containers
Fellowes Manufacturing Co.

If the storage center does not provide boxes of uniform size in which to store records to be transferred, the records manager must see that all departments use the same size box, to facilitate stacking and to use space most economically. Transfer cases are made of heavy fiberboard with sliding drawers. Transfer boxes, also of heavy fiberboard, have lift-up or lift-off tops or lift-out sides and are more difficult to retrieve records from than are transfer cases. Figure 7-10 shows two types of transfer boxes. (See Figure 2-6, page 47, for an illustration of boxes stored in an inactive records storage center.)

IMPORTANT TERMS AND CONCEPTS

card tickler file	one-period transfer method
carrier folder	periodic transfer method
charge-out	perpetual transfer method
folder tickler file	requisition
follow-up	tickler file
on-call (wanted) card	two-period transfer method

REVIEW AND DISCUSSION

1. How has the meaning of the phrase "to retrieve records from storage" changed over the years? (Obj. 1)

2. Name at least five ways that requests for stored records may come to the filer. (Obj. 2)

3. How are storage and retrieval related? (Obj. 3)

4. What procedures should the records manager establish to maintain control over stored records? (Obj. 4)

5. Why is it difficult to explain "requisition" without talking about "charge-out" also? (Objs. 5, 6)

6. Three dates are usually written on a requisition form. What are they? Why are all three necessary? (Obj. 5)

7. Explain why an on-call or wanted card is used. (Obj. 5)

8. How are OUT indicators used in the charge-out procedure? How are they disposed of? (Obj. 7)

9. What is a carrier folder and how is it used? (Obj. 7)

10. What is the reason for follow-up procedures? (Obj. 8)

11. What is a tickler file and how is it used? (Objs. 8, 9)

12. What does searching for a lost record involve? What should be done if the record cannot be found? (Obj. 10)

13. Why is it necessary to transfer records? (Obj. 11)

14. What are four important questions to be answered before records transfer takes place? (Obj. 11)

15. Explain the two most common methods of records transfer. (Obj. 12)

16. How can active and semiactive records be kept separate and yet be housed in the same five-drawer file cabinets or the same six-shelf files? (Obj. 12)

17. How does transfer of records to inactive storage differ from transfer to semiactive storage? (Obj. 13)

18. How is a records transfer form used? (Obj. 13)

DECISION-MAKING OPPORTUNITIES (DMO)

DMO 7-1: Solving Retrieval Problems

You are one of two administrative assistants in the office of a small Certified Public Accountant firm where there are 2 CPAs, 1 junior accountant, and 2 administrative assistants—you and Nick. Since you do not have a records manager, you and Nick are responsible for keeping the records stored so that they can be found quickly. All of the 5 people in the office have access to the files—removing and refiling records as needed. You and Nick do the refiling about 50 percent of the time.

The business is growing and so is the volume of records to be stored. You are using conventional five-drawer file cabinets which seem to be adequate for the number of records you anticipate will be stored for several years to come. Because the office is small, no controls are presently being used; there is no way to tell who has a client's records except to ask. There is no separation of active from inactive client records. Misfiling occurs frequently because someone is in a hurry when records are refiled, and you and Nick spend unproductive time searching for records you *know* should be in storage but that are not there.

What kind of records control procedures would you recommend? Do you believe additional supplies or equipment are needed to provide adequate control of the records? If not, explain why. If so, what would you recommend? Be specific in your answers. (Objs. 6, 7, 8)

DMO 7-2: Finding a Lost or Misplaced Record

A handwritten requisition comes to you. It is difficult to read, but you believe it is a request for a letter from Stubbs, Prentis, and Cole, dated the 17th of last month. You spend several minutes searching in your alphabetically arranged storage for a folder labeled *Stubbs Prentis and Cole* but cannot locate it in its correct alphabetic position. What would you do to find this letter? (Obj. 10)

DMO 7-3: Recommending Records Transfer Methods

What method of records transfer would you recommend for each of the following records situations? Explain your decision. (Objs. 12, 13)

A. Doctors' clinic office: Medical cases of deceased patients.
B. Law office: Client folders with 10 years' accumulation in the folders.
C. Department store: Correspondence and billing records of customers, kept for five years in active storage.
D. Shopping center developer: All folders related to a shopping center that has just been completed, all space rented, and the Grand Opening held last Saturday. Folders are those of contractors, lessees, insurance carriers, and governmental agencies containing permits.

APPLYING THE RULES

Job 6, Correspondence Storage—Business Names; Job 7, Correspondence Storage—Other Names and Tickler File Usage; Job 8, Requisition and Charge-Out Procedures; Job 9, Transfer Procedures.

3 – Adaptations of Alphabetic Storage and Retrieval

8 – Subject Records Storage
9 – Numeric Records Storage
10 – Geographic Records Storage

Part 3 continues the study of storage methods with three methods of records storage based on the alphabetic method. The equipment and procedures for storage and retrieval of records using subject, numeric, and geographic methods are discussed. The advantages and disadvantages of each storage method are presented.

8 SUBJECT RECORDS STORAGE

Objectives

After you have completed this chapter, you will be able to:

1. Store and retrieve records by the subject method.
2. State the differences and similarities exhibited by the alphabetic and subject records storage methods.
3. Explain the straight dictionary arrangement of subjects.
4. Explain the encyclopedic arrangement of subjects.
5. Explain the importance of a written list of subjects as used in the subject storage method.
6. Describe a master index used with the subject method.
7. Describe a relative index used with the subject method and tell how it differs from a master index.
8. Explain the relationship between cross-referencing and the relative index in the subject method.
9. State advantages and disadvantages of the subject method of records storage.

In Part 2 of this text you studied in considerable depth the alphabetic method of records storage. You will recall that within the alphabetic records storage method, several subjects might be found, such as applications, projects, branch office memos, etc. Storing records solely by subject matter or by topic instead of by the name of an individual, business, or organization is known as the **subject records storage method.**

OVERVIEW OF SUBJECT RECORDS STORAGE METHOD

As you study this chapter, you will see the parallelism between the subject and alphabetic methods and the necessity to again use the rules for alphabetic indexing presented in Chapters 5 and 6, as you store records according to subjects.

The subject storage method is used somewhere in almost every office. Some of the types of businesses and their uses of this method are:

1. Department stores that keep all records together relating to advertising, appliances, customers, home furnishings, housewares, menswear, special promotions, store maintenance, window displays, etc.
2. School offices where records are stored according to accidents, accreditation, athletics, budget, cafeteria, curriculum, graduation, library, personnel/certificated, student records, etc.
3. Engineering departments of firms manufacturing specialized equipment where records are arranged according to each type of equipment.
4. Research departments where records are stored by project titles.
5. Airplane manufacturers where records may be stored according to the types of planes being manufactured.
6. Construction companies whose records are stored by the types of construction: apartment houses, bridges, condominiums, individual homes, multifamily homes, office buildings, roads, etc.
7. Purchasing agents who keep records according to the names of the items being bought or being considered for purchase, rather than according to the names of the vendors.
8. Production managers whose records are stored by subjects such as equipment, grievances, labor contracts, safety, etc.

Subject storage is a very costly and difficult method of storage. The labor costs are high since every record must be carefully read to determine the one or more subjects to which its contents refer. In an alphabetic system, the filing segment that is selected is a name and the name *Wood* is not confused with the name *Rivera*. With the subject method, however, two persons can easily think of one topic by similar or synonymous terms, such as *Doctors* for *Physicians*; *Rugs* for *Floor Coverings*; and *Athletic Field* for *Stadium*. Because of the similarity of terms and since some records refer to more than one subject, much cross-referencing is necessary, as will be explained later in this chapter.

The selection of a word or phrase to be used as a subject (the filing segment) is of prime importance. The persons responsible for choosing subjects must be thoroughly familiar with the material to be stored, which implies a deep knowledge of every phase of the operations and activities of their business. The subject must be short and clearly descriptive of the material it represents. Once a subject has been chosen, it must be used by everyone in the organization; and all future subjects should be chosen so that they will not duplicate or overlap any subject previously assigned.

If filers use headings or subjects assigned at random by members of different departments, soon the same type of material may be stored under two or more synonymous terms. Such storage of related records at two or more places will not only separate records that should be stored together but will also make retrieval of all related records exceedingly difficult. Good subject selection means (1) agreement by everyone on the subjects to be used, (2) flexibility to allow for growth within the subjects chosen and for expansion to include new material, and (3) simplicity so that the users of the records can understand the system.

With the rapid acceptance and use of word processing and the storage of word information in computers and on magnetic media, the importance of proper selection of subjects is further increased. To find information that has been stored on the media, the searcher must know what subject or filing segment has been used to store that information before he or she can key into the equipment the words needed to retrieve the information quickly. Further discussion of mechanical and automated storage and retrieval will be found in Chapter 14.

A records manager can seldom find a ready-made list of subjects easily adaptable to the company's needs since each company's subjects are specialized. However, some equipment and supplies manufacturers have prepared prepackaged subject listings for some professional and industrial fields. These packaged systems contain main subjects and subdivisions that typically will be useful to school administrators, human resource managers, hospital administrators, and other executives. Such prepackaged sets may well be excellent starting points for determining subject classifications, but the records manager must study carefully the needs of the office in order to be in a position to adapt such a system.

Printed subject lists that a records manager might use as guides for setting up the subject listings for the office can also be secured from some professional associations and organizations. Library sources that might provide helpful listings include *Business Periodicals Index, Public Affairs Information Services Bulletin, Engineering Index, Applied Science and Technology Index, Readers' Guide to Periodical Literature, Index Medicus* (medical subject headings, a National Library of Medicine publication), and *Social Sciences and Humanities Index.* The H. W. Wilson Company (950 University Avenue, Bronx, NY 10452) publishes a free catalog each September that contains a number of subject lists: applied science and technology, art, biology and agriculture, education, general science, humanities, law, library literature, American paintings, plays, short stories, and social sciences.

Even the most thoughtful selection of subjects is worthless unless the subjects are arranged so that the storage of records can be done easily and their retrieval can be quick. Suggestions for the arrangement of records stored by subject follow.

ARRANGEMENT OF RECORDS STORED BY SUBJECT

The standard arrangements for subject storage are (1) the straight dictionary arrangement and (2) the encyclopedic arrangement, both of which are explained in the following paragraphs. Other arrangements using numbers are explained in Chapter 9.

Straight Dictionary Arrangement

In the **straight dictionary arrangement**, the subject folders are arranged behind A to Z guides in their correct alphabetic order according to the subject title. Subjects that are exceptionally active may be made conspicuous by the use of auxiliary guides (See OWNERS in Figure 8-1). Color coding is often used to distinguish one subject from another. The illustration in Figure 8-1 shows a drawer of file folders arranged in straight dictionary order, used by the secretary of a condominium owners association. A-to-Z guides occupy first position. OUT indicator tabs are in second position. Auxiliary guides are in third position. Subject folders are in combined fourth and fifth positions in straight-line arrangement. Expansion within this type of arrangement is simple as each new subject can be added in its correct alphabetic position.

Encyclopedic Arrangement

The encyclopedic arrangement differs from the straight dictionary arrangement in that in the **encyclopedic arrangement** the subjects are subdivided so that several folders contain small portions of the records pertaining to one main subject. The labels on these folders show them to be subdivisions of the main subject. Figure 8-2 shows part of an encyclopedic arrangement used by an advertising agency. The main subjects are arranged in alphabetic order in first position. Subject labels have been typed and inserted into the metal holders of the fourth-cut guide tabs. The typed subdivision labels are affixed to guides in second position and bear the main subject title and the subdivision subject. Individual folders have typed labels affixed to tabs in combined third and

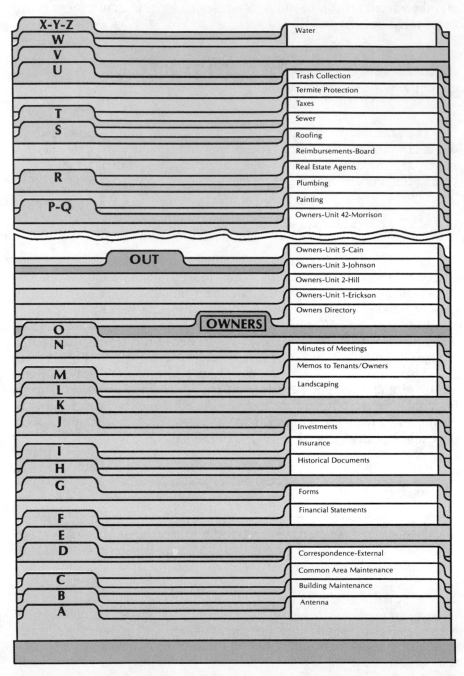

FIGURE 8-1 — Straight Dictionary Arrangement of Subjects

fourth positions. These tab captions include the main subject, the sub-division subject, and the words that indicate the subject contents of the folders.

Refiling is easy when the main subject heading and its subdivision are typed on the folder labels. The storage section into which the folder should be returned is easily found because that subject is typed on the label. Very often, each subject will have a color band that is repeated on all guides and folders of that subject. Or all captions of one subject will be one color, the color changing when the subject title changes. Or each subject will have guides and folders of one color only; another color will be used for guides and folders of the next subject.

Note that the OUT indicator has a third-cut, third-position tab in Figure 8-2. The OUT indicator is a distinctive color and is placed in the drawer to show the removal of a folder behind *Exhibits Associations Regional*.

The equipment needed for subject storage is the same as that used for alphabetic storage. There is one difference in supplies, as will be explained in the following section.

SUPPLIES FOR SUBJECT RECORDS STORAGE

The supplies used for subject arrangement are guides, folders, OUT indicators, and indexes. Each item will be briefly explained in the following paragraphs.

Guides

The guides used in subject records storage are determined by the kind of subject arrangement used. If the subject headings are long, wide tabs will be needed to accommodate the words needed for the subjects chosen. Primary guides contain the main subject headings; secondary guides contain the main subject headings and their subdivisions.

Folders

The folders used in subject arrangement have captions that include the main subject and any subdivision thereof. Individual folders following each subject guide often have double-width tabs because a great deal of information may have to be typed on the label.

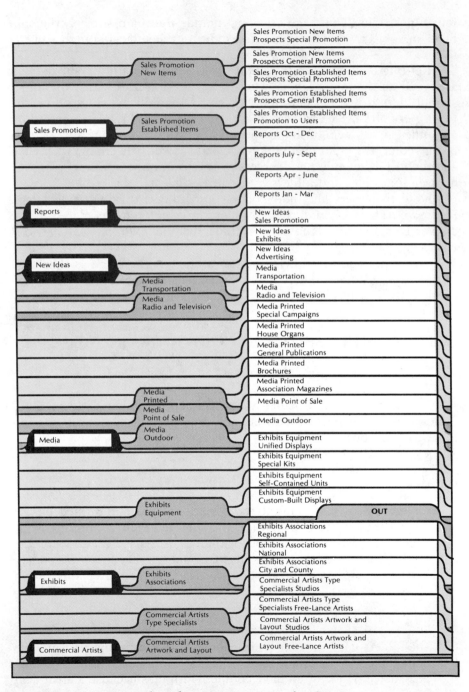

FIGURE 8-2 — Encyclopedic Arrangement of Subjects

The use of general folders should be avoided. A general or miscellaneous category usually indicates an incomplete selection of subject headings or divisions. If there seems to be no place to store a record except under the heading of *General*, careful study should be given to the subjects in use.

Main subjects may be typed in all capital letters to distinguish them from subdivisions. Uniformity of typing is important for ease of recognition. The size of the label used is determined by the size of the tab to which it is to be affixed. If color is used, the typist must be careful to select the correct color for the subject title to be typed.

OUT Indicators

OUT indicators are used in the subject storage method just as they are used in the alphabetic storage method. The order of the information on the OUT indicator will show the subject first because the method of storage is the subject method. As in all storage methods, these OUT indicators are control devices that show the location of records at all times.

Indexes

The subject storage method cannot function efficiently without indexes. The use of indexes is the one difference between the supplies used for alphabetic storage and those used for subject storage. Two types of indexes are extremely valuable to the filer—the master index and the relative index. In addition, a special subject index and a name index can be helpful. Each is explained below.

Master Index.   A **master index** is a typed alphabetic listing of all subjects (filing segments) used for storage. It is updated as new subjects are added and old ones eliminated or modified. When new subjects are to be added, the index will provide guidance to those in charge of subject selection so as to avoid duplication. The index may be typed on sheets of paper, on cards, or on some kind of visible file—usually a strip file, described in Chapter 11. A subject list on sheets of paper or on visible strips is easier to see at a glance than are subjects typed on individual cards. If a word processor or computer is available, adding and deleting subjects can be done quickly and easily as is shown in Chapter 14. Subject information on visible strips is arranged alphabetically. As subjects change, the strips can be easily slipped in and out. The important point is that the list must be kept up-to-date at all times.

If a card file is used, each card bears a subject name and the cards are filed alphabetically by subject. The use of cards has two advantages over listings on sheets of paper: (1) As new subjects are added, new cards are made and are inserted in the existing card file in alphabetic order. On sheets of paper, new subjects are added in ink wherever space will allow and an arrow is drawn to their correct alphabetic order. When the list becomes difficult to decipher, retyping will be necessary. (2) Color can be used advantageously. Cards of one color might identify main subjects; another color might identify subdivisions. Another way to use color is similar to color coding on file folders: All cards pertaining to one subject (the main subject and its subdivisions) are of one color; when the subject changes, the card color changes. Usually, the sequence of color is kept the same throughout the file. For example—pink, buff, green, white, yellow, blue; and then it begins again with pink, buff, green, etc., through the entire range of subjects.

Relative Index.   A more complex subject arrangement requires a **relative index** in which all main headings and subdivision headings and all likely variations of subjects are listed. The word *relative* is used because the subjects are *related* to each other in the manner in which they are used or requested. An excellent example of a relative index is found in many telephone directories preceding or following the Yellow Pages. This index contains all the subjects listed in the Yellow Pages as well as additional related subjects.

The relative index may be a typed list or a card file, the card file being preferred because of constant addition of subjects to it. A relative index is a cross-reference device since it contains all the subjects by which a record might be requested. Whenever someone requests a record by a subject that is not the one selected for use, the filer checks the relative index to see if that requested subject has been included with the correct subject beside it. If not, the filer adds the requested subject to the index listing as soon as the requested record has been located.

Figure 8-3 shows a section of the card file containing the relative index that accompanies part of the subject file shown in Figure 8-2. The list of entries on the cards in the card file given here is only a partial list. Study it while referring to Figure 8-2 to see the related subjects by which records might be requested.

The relative index contains SEE ALSO cross-references (See top left card in Figure 8-3) in addition to the usual SEE cross-references. A SEE ALSO card is very helpful in bringing together related materials and in

Advertising
SEE New Ideas
SEE ALSO Media Printed

Agency Fees
SEE Commercial Artists Art-work and Layout Studios
Commercial Artists Type Specialists Studios

Artwork
SEE Commercial Artists Artwork and Layout

Association Magazines
SEE Media Printed Association Magazines

Brand Names
SEE Media Printed Brochures
Media Printed House Organs

Brochures
SEE Media Printed Brochures

Campaigns
SEE Media Printed Special Campaigns

Car Cards
SEE Media Transportation

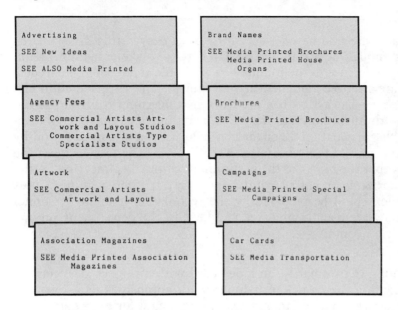

FIGURE 8-3 — Part of Relative Index for Figure 8-2

explaining the nature of a subject. A SEE ALSO card for Commercial Artists is shown in Figure 8-4.

Special Subject Index. A **special subject index** can save valuable time when someone needs to find information contained in corporate minutes, annual proceedings of trade associations, and regular meeting minutes of organizations. Finding what action has been taken on any topic (such as Convention Arrangements, Jewelry, Pensions, Sales Meetings, or the Branch Office in Kansas City) over the past 25 or more years is a time-consuming process if all minutes for those years must be carefully read.

Commercial Artists

SEE ALSO

Agency Fees
Artwork
Fees
Free-Lance Artists
Layout
Studios
Type Specialists

FIGURE 8-4 — A SEE ALSO Cross-Reference Card Showing Related Subjects

To make the finding of a certain subject easy, cards are prepared containing enough detail, including dates, to give skeletal information and the page reference to the minute books, should more detail be needed. The cards are arranged alphabetically by subject. The sample card in Figure 8-5 shows what action has been taken concerning *Convention Arrangements* through the years. The first entry indicates that the arrangements for the first national convention held in Miami can be found by referring to page 7 of the minutes of April 7, 1976. The last entry on the card shows that the report of the preliminary committee meeting for the 1986 convention is on page 14 of the February 11, 1985, minutes. Cards for this index could be prepared by the records department personnel although they are usually prepared and kept in the department serving the convention committee.

Name Index.   Customarily, an index used with a subject arrangement does not contain the names of individuals or companies. However, for many businesses, a **name index** may contain a card for each correspondent. The name and address of each correspondent and the subject under which the records are stored are included on the card. The cards are arranged alphabetically by name. Because records may sometimes be requested by the name of an individual or a company, cards containing this information can save the filer hours of time that would otherwise be spent searching through the records stored by subject.

```
Convention Arrangements

First National convention--Miami     4- 7-76 p.  7
Report of convention committee      10- 1-76 p. 19
Exhibitors' plans for 1972           2- 6-78 p. 11
Cancellation of L.A. convention      4- 4-78 p.  6
Resumption of national conven-
   tion--Minneapolis                 4- 8-80 p. 15
Report of convention committee       8- 6-80 p. 16
Joined with Rotary Club--Chicago     4- 4-82 p.  4
Exhibit plan--1982                   2-10-82 p.  6
Report of convention committee--
   Reno convention                   4- 8-82 p. 12
Exhibitors' plans for 1984           2- 9-84 p. 14
Report of convention--Vancouver      4-10-84 p.  3
Prelim committee meeting --
   1986 convention                   2-11-85 p. 14
```

FIGURE 8-5 — Special Subject Index Card

	S/P	
	R	D

QUANTITY	STOCK NUMBER	=	LOCATION	R	D
001	1	K69		C5023	EXAM	X
002	1	T38		C6716	EXAM	X
003	1	T38M		C6717	FREE	F
004	1	K69A		C6834	FREE	F

26   130

* **SHIPPED FROM:**

1 - CINCINNATI, OHIO
2 -
3 - WEST CHICAGO, ILLINOIS

4 - LIVERMORE, CALIF.
5 - CARROLLTON, TEXAS
6 - TUCKER, GEORGIA
7 - BACK ORDERED

8 - NOT YET AVAILABLE, WILL SHIP LATER
9 - OUT OF STOCK AND OUT OF PRINT.

STORING AND RETRIEVING PROCEDURES FOR THE SUBJECT METHOD

All the steps studied in Chapter 4 for storing and retrieving records are as important in the subject method as they are in any other storage method. A brief description of each step follows, together with an explanation of its importance to the subject method.

Inspecting

In any storage system, the inspection of every record is necessary to see that it has been released for storage. No record should be stored until someone with authority has indicated that it is ready for storage.

Indexing

Indexing, or classifying, consumes more time with the subject method than with any other storage method. The filer must examine the contents of each record carefully in order to determine the filing segment under which it is to be stored. If the record relates to one subject only, indexing is comparatively simple; the correct subject is chosen from the subject list. If someone else has previously indicated the subject under which the record is to be stored, the filer must recheck the accuracy of the subject selection.

If the record contains information about more than one subject, indexing will consist of the determination of the most important subject by which the record is to be stored. Then place a check mark beside the other subjects that must be cross-referenced.

Coding

Coding of the main subject heading and of any subdivisions of it consists of underlining or otherwise marking the selected words (filing segment) if they appear on the record. If the subject is not mentioned, it must be legibly written at the top of the record, sometimes with a colored pencil. Some filers prefer to write the filing segment on the material to be stored instead of underlining or circling the information. When more than one subject is indicated, only the most important one is coded;

all other subjects are marked in some distinctive manner (with a wavy line, checked, x-ed, etc.) for cross-referencing.

The filer should not rely on memory to determine the subject under which a record should be stored. The subject list should always be consulted to make sure that the correct filing segment is selected and coded.

Cross-Referencing

Many cross-references may be made for one record. If the record to be stored refers to several important subjects, sometimes copies (typed, photocopied, or otherwise reproduced) are made of the record, and those copies are stored under the different subject headings involved to eliminate the need for cross-references for that record. To avoid clogging the storage containers with many copies, cross-references may be made for the card file only.

In Figure 8-6, the illustration on the left shows a card of a distinctive color to show the filer the correct filing segments under which to look for information about automobiles. A cross-reference of this type is a SEE reference used for synonymous or similar terms. The SEE ALSO reference shown on the middle card in Figure 8-6 is a reference to two places where helpful material connected with claims may be found.

The illustration on the right in Figure 8-6 shows a card made for a correspondent whose name is often used in calling for records. Since the records relate to the Plaza Shopping Center, they have been stored under that filing segment. The cross-reference card will be stored in the card file containing correspondents' names, not in the subject card file.

Instead of placing a cross-reference in the card file, a permanent cross-reference guide may be placed in the regular storage container. Figure 8-7 shows the tab of a permanent cross-reference guide with a label directing the filer to the correct place in storage where records on Automobiles may be found. No record, therefore, would ever be stored under the heading *Automobiles*.

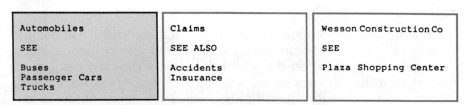

FIGURE 8-6 — Three Cross-References for a Relative Index

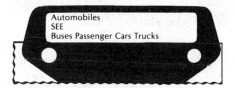

FIGURE 8-7 — Tab of Permanent Cross-Reference Guide

Sorting

The sorting of records to be stored alphabetically by subject is usually done in an A-to-Z sorter. Records are sorted by main subjects; any resorting by subdivisions is done at the time the records are inserted into the file folders. If the volume of records to be stored is great and many subdivisions are used, the sorter might be subdivided to save the filer's time.

Storing

Careful placement of records into folders is always important. A quick look at the folder tab to see that the subject on it agrees with the filing segment coded on the record will help to avoid misfiling. A slight raising of the folder by one hand before the record is inserted by the other hand will also avoid mistakes.

Records in a single subject folder are placed in alphabetic order according to the names of the correspondents. Each correspondent's records are then arranged by date with the most recent date in front.

Retrieving

Retrieval procedures for the subject storage method are the same as those used in any other method of storage. Knowing who has taken the records, the contents of those records, what date the records were borrowed, and when the records are supposed to be returned to storage is important in maintaining control over all records. Follow-up is necessary to assure that the records are returned, to extend the charge-out time, or to call to the attention of someone any matters needing consideration in the future.

ADVANTAGES AND DISADVANTAGES OF THE SUBJECT STORAGE METHOD

The advantages and disadvantages of subject storage are numerous and they depend somewhat on the type of subject storage used. As in all storage methods, carelessness, inattention to detail, improper reading of the contents of the records, and undue haste will cause mistakes that will mean hours of wasted time if retrieval cannot be done quickly.

Advantages of the Subject Storage Method

Subject storage saves time since all written records on a specific topic, a situation, a project, or a problem requiring managerial decision are grouped rather than being separated into folders by the names of the correspondents.

Subject lists can be expanded easily by adding subdivisions to main subjects. For example, if Transportation were a main heading and Airplanes, Automobiles, Buses, and Trains were subheadings, Space Shuttles could easily be added.

Since, in a subject system, all related material has been brought together at a common point of reference, statistical relationships stand out and statistical data become available. This important characteristic is not present in the other storage systems that have been discussed.

When you have finished studying Chapter 9, the Numeric Storage Method, you will find additional advantages that result when numbers and subjects are combined. All the advantages inherent in numeric storage are also found in the combination of numbers and subjects.

Disadvantages of the Subject Storage Method

The disadvantages of the subject method are many. Unless extreme caution is taken, subject lists and subdivisions grow until there are too many overlapping subjects chosen. The selection of subject classifications is difficult in that subject titles must be concise, clearly defined, and uniformly stated. The development and installation of subject storage usually requires the assistance of experienced records analysts.

Unless the chosen subjects are used consistently, new personnel will find retrieval extremely difficult because the original filer deviated from the subject list. An inadequate subject index often prevents or seriously delays records retrieval. Furthermore, a subject classification is not effective when the titles used are not clear; a folder bearing the title *Office Memos* or *General* contains, in reality, unsorted records.

As was mentioned previously, but which bears repeating here, the subject method of storage is the most expensive method to maintain because it requires very experienced filers. Preparation of materials for subject storage always takes longer than for any other method of storage, since the content of every record must be thoroughly and carefully read; skimming will not suffice. When a subject folder contains records that are often called for by the name of the writer, and no cross-reference card has been prepared, a delay in retrieval results. Again, the use of folders for officers' names leads to difficulty when the name of an officer is unknown or forgotten or when personnel changes have been made. Too often records are stored in folders made for the name of the officer (Lotus Wong) who is in charge of the department, instead of for the name of the department (Accounting Department). Personnel may change in organizations, but the name of the department or position usually remains. If cards are not prepared for the alternate subjects by which records may be requested, retrieval is delayed. An up-to-date relative index is very necessary in addition to the master list of subjects.

Records that are stored by subject in order that statistical information may be easily compiled or that mailing lists can be quickly prepared require an extensive cross-referencing system that is impractical. It would be costly, for instance, to store customers' correspondence and orders under the headings of *Accounts—Out-of-Town* and *Accounts—City* just to find sales statistics for each sales representative's territory or for each state or each city.

Most of the disadvantages mentioned here are based on inappropriate uses of the subject method. If reference to records is to be made by the name of an individual, by a firm name, or by location, subject storage is not the recommended method. However, after careful study of the needs of a company, a records manager may rightly decide that a subject arrangement is the best method by which to store a portion of the company's records.

IMPORTANT TERMS AND CONCEPTS

encyclopedic arrangement	special subject index
master index	straight dictionary arrangement
name index	subject records storage method
relative index	

REVIEW AND DISCUSSION

1. State the differences between and the similarities of the alphabetic and subject storage methods. (Obj. 2)

2. Why is the subject storage method said to be more costly than the alphabetic storage method? (Obj. 2)

3. What is the difference between the straight dictionary arrangement and the encyclopedic arrangement of subjects? (Objs. 3, 4)

4. Why must every subject arrangement be accompanied by a written list of subjects used? (Obj. 5)

5. What indexes are necessary for use with the subject storage method? Explain their use. (Objs. 6, 7)

6. What is the relationship between cross-referencing and the relative index? (Obj. 8)

7. List at least three advantages of the subject storage method. (Obj. 9)

8. List at least three disadvantages of the subject storage method. (Obj. 9)

DECISION-MAKING OPPORTUNITIES (DMO)

DMO 8-1: Selecting Subjects

Refer to Figure 8-1. You will recall that it shows a file drawer of subject folders used by the secretary of a condominium owners association. The secretary is contemplating the addition to the drawer of folders as labeled below. What do you think of the secretary's selection of new subjects? Why? (Objs. 5, 6)

A. *Current*—in which will be placed matters needing attention at the next Board meeting.

B. *Budd Piper Roofing Co.*—in which will be placed all paid bills and correspondence related to building repairs for which this company is responsible. After each heavy rainstorm, the services of Budd Piper are necessary to caulk windows and fix leaky roofs of unit owners' condos.

C. *Applications—Condo Management*—in which will be placed correspondence to and from persons desiring to manage the condo complex.

D. *H & E Development Co.*—in which will be placed correspondence and memos between the association and its developers, the H & E Development Co.
E. *Dues Ledger Sheets*—in which will be placed all noncurrent ledger sheets for all owners. The sheets show the monthly record of payments made by the owners over the years.

DMO 8-2: Storing Records by the Subject Method

You are in charge of storing all the records of three departments. You have set up a master index of subjects and a relative index of variations of the subjects. Records come to you:

A. with the filing segment coded that agrees with the subjects that are on your master index,
B. not coded at all,
C. coded with subjects that do not appear on your master or relative indexes. (Obj. 1)

What would be your procedure for storing each of the records in those three categories? For instance, in A you would:

1. Read the records to see if the coded filing segment agrees with the content of the records. If not,
2. either check . . .
3. if so, ...

APPLYING THE RULES

Job 10, Correspondence Storage—Subject Method.

9 NUMERIC RECORDS STORAGE

Objectives

After you have completed this chapter, you will be able to:

1. Identify and explain some of the number codes used in our everyday lives.
2. Explain the difference between consecutive and nonconsecutive numbering storage methods.
3. Identify and explain the use of the supplies needed for storing records according to consecutive numbers.
4. Describe in detail the coding procedure for the consecutive numbering method.
5. Explain the steps necessary to convert from an alphabetic arrangement of records to a consecutively numbered arrangement.
6. State the advantages and disadvantages of consecutive numeric records storage.
7. Explain the way in which records are stored by terminal digit and middle digit storage methods.
8. Explain the way in which records are stored by skip numbering.
9. Describe combinations of numeric and subject storage methods.
10. Suggest the most appropriate numeric storage method to be used in a specific business situation.

In previous chapters, alphabetic and subject methods of records storage were discussed. In this chapter, a third method by which records can be stored is explained—**the numeric storage method**. As its name suggests, the numeric method of records storage is storage by *number* instead of by name or by topic. Records are assigned numbers and then stored in a sequence to be explained later in this chapter. Two major reasons for using a numeric storage method are the infinite set of numbers available (relative to the limitation of 26 alphabetic characters) and the ease with which people recognize and use numbers. Machines, too, are capable of great speed in the use of numbers; and the increase in the use of machines is abundantly apparent in our lives.

Numbers as a means of classifying data are common in our everyday routines. For example, numbers identify our:

bank checks and accounts	charge accounts
social security records	school courses
driver's licenses	legal cases
ZIP Codes	permits of many kinds (boating,
insurance policies	hunting, fishing)
hospitalization/health plans	post office boxes
residential addresses	safe-deposit boxes
telephones	student records

Products in grocery stores are coded with a Universal Product Code for use by computers. Mail-order houses sometimes store their merchandise in numbered areas, rows, and bins and retrieve the items by mechanical robots or arms called "pickers." As businesses become more reliant on computers, and as the number of personal computers in homes increases, the use of numbers to classify data further stresses the need for knowledge about the numeric method of storage.

The numeric method of records storage is particularly useful to:

1. Insurance companies that store records by policy and claim numbers.
2. Social welfare agencies that maintain records by case numbers.
3. Firms in the building trades that use contract or job numbers and stock or parts numbers, store records accordingly.
4. Architects who assign contract numbers to their clients' projects to ensure clear-cut identification of all pieces of correspondence and other records pertaining to contracts and projects.
5. State automobile license departments and social security offices where records are arranged by number because of their large-scale operations.
6. Real estate agencies that list properties according to a code number that is keyed to a price category. (Such a code might be 00–19 for listings under $20,000; 20–29 for listings $20,000 to 29,999; ... 100–149 for listings $100,000 to $149,999; etc.)
7. Physicians, dentists, and veterinarians who assign numbers to patient history records and to X-ray records.
8. Companies whose personnel records are stored by either employee number or social security number.
9. Savings and loan associations and banks whose mortgage and loan departments store records by the number assigned to the mortgage or loan.

10. Law firms that assign a case number to each client. Such a number could be subdivided as different actions on a client's behalf are undertaken. For instance, the number for James L. Howie, a client, might be 2070. This number would be assigned when Howie first sought legal advice on the purchase of a home. If Howie initiated divorce proceedings, 2070.2 might be the number used (.2 always indicating divorce work). At Howie's death, estate matters would be handled under the number 2070.9 (.9 being the number assigned for all estate and probate matters of clients).

Hundreds—perhaps thousands—of numeric identification codes are used in businesses throughout the country. Two of these codes are mentioned here to show the possibilities for different numbering systems.

One of the most commonly used numeric identification methods is a code assigned to parts, equipment, or prices. These codes are known only to the persons in an organization who are responsible for their creation and who use the codes. Each has a natural memory jogger built in. Here are examples of these codes:

A catalog number for a piece of office equipment might be assigned the number CF 4770–5315, meaning:

> card file (signified by CF)
> 47" high (the first two numbers)
> 70" wide (the next two numbers)
> containing 5" by 3" cards (the next two numbers)
> in 15 drawers or tiers (the last two numbers)

The number CF 3860–5312 in this same system would then mean a card file 38" high, 60" wide, containing 5" by 3" cards in 12 drawers or tiers.

Another use of a numeric code is to identify the wholesale price of an item on its retail price tag. An organization selects a 10-letter word as the code, with each letter being different. For instance, CHARLESTON may be selected. Each letter is assigned a number in sequence from 1 to 0: C (1), H (2), A (3), R (4), L (5), E (6), S (7), T (8), 0 (9), N (0). The code on a price tag of a package of batteries might be AL, meaning that the wholesale price was 35 cents (while the selling price on the tag might read 89 cents). Some companies use a phrase or several words for the code, always 10 letters and none repeated. MARBLE TOPS is an example.

This chapter contains a detailed description of the basic features of numeric arrangements and the procedures for storing records numerically. Also included in this chapter is information about the use of color, illustrative trade-named systems, conversion from an alphabetic arrangement to a numeric arrangement, using numbers to store by sound (phonetically) instead of by spelling, terminal and middle digit storage, and the advantages and disadvantages of the various numeric arrangements. Consecutive and nonconsecutive numbering methods are discussed, and combined subject and numeric storage methods are explained in the following pages.

CONSECUTIVE NUMBERING METHOD

The easiest-to-understand method of numeric storage uses numbers arranged in sequence. This method is called the **consecutive numbering method**, also sometimes referred to as serial or sequential numbering. The numbers begin with 1 and progress upward; or they may begin with 100, 1000, or some other number and progress upward. For example, office forms such as invoices, sales tickets, and purchase orders are frequently numbered in consecutive order. Even though these forms may be filled in at various locations within a business, the forms are ultimately stored together in consecutive numeric sequence.

Correspondence may also be stored numerically by consecutive numbers. The supplies needed and procedures to be followed to store correspondence so that it may be found easily will be explained and illustrated. The numeric method is an **indirect storage method**—more steps are needed in the numeric method than are necessary with the alphabetic method to store a record in its proper container.

Basic Features of the Consecutive Numbering Method

The consecutive numbering method requires the following supplies:

1. Numbered guides and folders
2. Alphabetic guides and folders
3. An alphabetic card file
4. An accession book

Numbered Guides and Folders.   Two arrangements of the contents of a consecutively numbered file drawer are shown in Figure 9-1. A series of primary guides, numbered 100, 110, and 640, 650 in Figure 9-1, divide the drawer into easy-to-find numeric segments. The guides may be purchased with numbers printed on their tabs; numbered labels may be inserted into blank slots on the tabs; self-adhesive numbers may be attached to blank tabs; or numbers may be stamped on tabs with a numbering machine or typed on. Handwriting or printing should be avoided because of its lack of uniformity.

Numbered guides may be arranged in a straight line, as are the primary guides in Figure 9-1, or guides may be staggered across the drawer. Usually, one guide is provided for every ten folders.

In the two illustrations in Figure 9-1, consecutively numbered folders 100 through 109 and 640 through 650 are placed behind the guides that begin the correspondingly numbered sections. Folders at the right in Figure 9-1 also show the names of the correspondents since secrecy is not a factor, and office policy requires names in addition to numbers. The names are stored in random order, not alphabetically, as names are assigned numbers; and the *numbers* are in consecutive order. Since the sequence of numbered folders will never vary (1, 2, 3, etc.; or 100, 101, 102, etc.), the folder tabs may be placed in one position or staggered. In Figure 9-1, the illustration on the left shows a staggered arrangement; the illustration on the right, a straight-line arrangement.

Alphabetic Guides and Folders.   An alphabetic general section found in many numeric arrangements holds records of correspondents whose

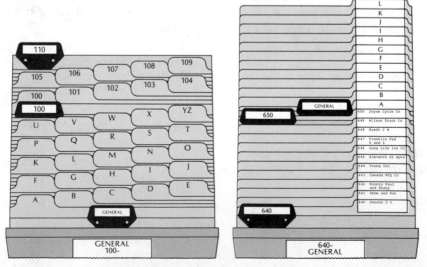

FIGURE 9-1 — Two Arrangements of a Consecutively Numbered File Drawer

volume is very small. In most offices, an individually numbered folder is not used until at least five pieces of correspondence that relate to one correspondent have accumulated. Until those five pieces accumulate, correspondence is stored by customer or client name in the general section in the same manner as names are stored by the alphabetic method.

The entire general section of guides and folders may be placed at the beginning of the numeric sequence (as shown on the left in Figure 9-1) or at the end of it (as shown on the right in Figure 9-1). Because expansion occurs at the end of a consecutively numbered arrangement, placement of the general section at the beginning is recommended.

The general section contains a primary guide labeled GENERAL. This guide may be followed by other guides to indicate the alphabetic divisions. In Figure 9-1, the GENERAL guide is in center position. Behind the GENERAL guide are the alphabetically captioned folders that hold records of correspondents who have not yet been assigned numbers.

Alphabetic Card File.   A numeric arrangement cannot function without an **alphabetic card file** of the names of the correspondents (and of any subjects, such as Applications or Shipments or Warranties) for whom records may be stored. The cards, arranged alphabetically, show the numbers that have been assigned to the filing segments. According to office policy, cards may or may not be made for correspondents whose records are stored in the GENERAL section. If cards are made for those correspondents, the cards bear the letter G to show that the correspondence with those individuals or companies is in the general section of storage. Figure 9-2 shows a portion of a card file with cards arranged alphabetically, not numerically.

Since each correspondent is assigned a different number and thousands of correspondents' records may be in storage, remembering the numbers for all of those names is impossible. Therefore, the card file serves as the "memory," for each card shows either the complete name and address of one correspondent and its assigned number or the name of one subject and its assigned number. Mistakes made in the card file are very serious because the card file is the first place to which the filer goes to locate any requested name or subject. Great care must be taken to keep the card file up-to-date and accurate.

Accession Book.   The **accession book** is sometimes called an *accession record*, an *acquisition book*, or a *number book*. It is a book containing numbered blank lines on which is written information showing (1) those numbers already assigned to correspondents and subjects and

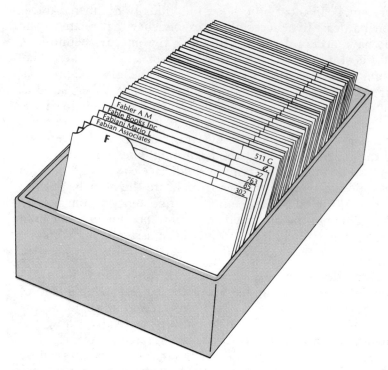

FIGURE 9-2 — Card File for Use with Consecutive Numbering Method

(2) the next number available for assignment (See Figure 9-3). The proper use of an accession book prevents a filer from assigning the same number twice.

If a numbered folder is lost or misplaced, reference to the accession book would provide the name that had been assigned that number; and the full information can then be obtained from the card file to help in locating the folder. Only complete names, not addresses, need be written in the accession book since the card file shows all the information about each correspondent. The accession book is never used to locate numbers previously assigned to correspondents since that information is instantly available in the card file.

An accession book in bound form with prenumbered lines is usually purchased at an office supplies store. Unnumbered, lined pages may be used if extreme care is exercised to number the lines in sequence. Figure 9-3 shows two pages of an accession book. This figure indicates that 1298 was the last number used and that 1299 is the next number to be assigned.

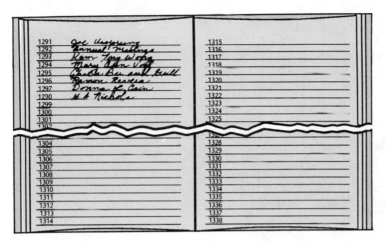

FIGURE 9-3 — Accession Book

Illustrative Consecutive Numbering Systems

Most ready-made systems for numeric storage use color as well as numbers to indicate sequence. These systems may use color folders as well as color labels for different numbers. The numbers are always consecutive so that color-blind persons need not depend on color to locate or replace folders. In the illustrative systems that follow, mentally visualizing the colors will be a distinct aid in understanding the figures and explanations.

Color Sentry® (Safeguard Business Systems, Inc., 400–T Maryland Drive, Ft. Washington, PA 19034). This system (Figure 9-4) is designed for open-shelf storage with end tab folders.

The label colors used are: 01 to 09—brown; 10 to 19—red; 20 to 29—blue; 30 to 39—pink; 40 to 49—green; 50 to 59—yellow; 60 to 69—olive; 70 to 79—tan; 80 to 89—purple; 90 to 99—orange. Every digit in a number except the last two has its own color label. The last two digits of any number bear the same color label. This creates a larger uniform color band at the bottom of each group of 10 file folders. In each 100 folders, therefore, there will be 10 groups of 10 having identical color bands at the bottom label position of the file folder. The color-coded label that is second from the bottom will change every 100 folders; the third, every 1,000 folders; and the fourth, every 100,000 folders.

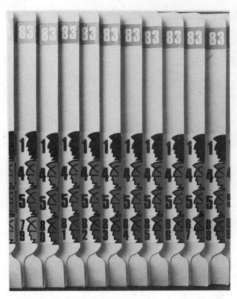

FIGURE 9-4 — Safeguard Color Coded Numeric System
Safeguard Business Systems, Inc.

CompuColor® (TAB Products Co., 1400–T Page Mill Road, Palo Alto, CA 94304). The color bars corresponding to the 10 digits, 0 through 9, are printed on labels that are applied to the edge of the file folders according to this sequence: 1 = red; 2 = light orange; 3 = dark orange; 4 = emerald; 5 = dark green; 6 = blue; 7 = purple; 8 = lilac; 9 = brown; 0 = pink. In Figure 9-5, the numbers on each folder have a different color bar. The colors at the bottom of each folder tab change from folder to folder as the sequence of numbers changes. The colors on the bars that are second from the bottom will change with every 10 folders. If a folder is misfiled, the color blocks will not match, automatically indicating to the filer that the folder is out of sequence.

Storage and Retrieval Procedures for the Consecutive Numbering Method

The steps for storage (inspecting, indexing, coding, cross-referencing, sorting, and storing) and retrieval (requisitioning, charging out, and following up) are as important in the numeric method as they are in all

FIGURE 9-5 — CompuColor's Sequential Numeric Shelf Filing System
Tab Products Company

other storage methods. The procedures to be followed in storing and retrieving records numerically are discussed below.

Inspecting and Indexing.   Records are first inspected for release marks. Then records are mentally indexed to determine the name or subject by which each record is to be stored.

Coding.   Coding for numeric storage requires two steps: (1) coding the name or subject (the filing segment) to which the record refers (as is done in all storage methods) and (2) assigning a number to the record.

If the alphabetic coding of the name or subject has been previously done, the filer checks the coding for accuracy. If the coding has not been done, the filer marks the record according to the practice of the office. If cross-references should be prepared, the coding should include a notation to that effect (usually an X written on the record).

When many records are to be stored, a rough preliminary alphabetic sorting at this time will speed the storing process later because reference to the alphabetic card file is the next step. Consulting the card file will show whether or not a card has already been prepared for that correspondent or subject and, if so, whether a number or the letter G (indicating records in the general section of storage) has been assigned. In some offices, a number is automatically assigned to every correspondent when the first record arrives, or an officer of the company may indicate that a new correspondent is of such importance that a number is to be assigned immediately even though only one piece of correspondence has been received.

Correspondents or Subjects with Numbers Already Assigned. Since the card file will contain a card for the correspondent, the record is coded with the number found in the upper right corner of the card (See Figure 9-2). The number is written at the top right on the record to be stored, and the coded record is then placed in a numeric sorter for later storage in its properly numbered folder. The letter on the left in Figure 9-6 is coded by name for the alphabetic card file and also coded "419" because the card file showed that 419 had previously been assigned to the name of that organization.

Correspondents or Subjects with the Letter *G* Already Assigned. If the card file shows a G, the previous correspondence for that person, organization, or subject has been stored in the general alphabetic section of numeric storage. The record now to be stored is therefore coded with G in the upper right corner. The record is then placed in an alphabetic sorter for later storage in the general section of numeric storage. The letter at the right in Figure 9-6 shows the G coding.

New Correspondents or Subjects to be Assigned Numbers. If a correspondent is to be immediately assigned a numbered folder, the filer should take the following steps:

1. Consult the accession book and on the first unused numbered line write the correspondent's name or the subject.
2. Write the assigned number on the record in the upper right corner.
3. Type a file card for the correspondent or subject. For all correspondents, include complete information (See Figure 9-7). For subjects, type the subject and the assigned number.
4. If any cross-referencing needs to be done, prepare cross-reference cards to be placed in the card file only.

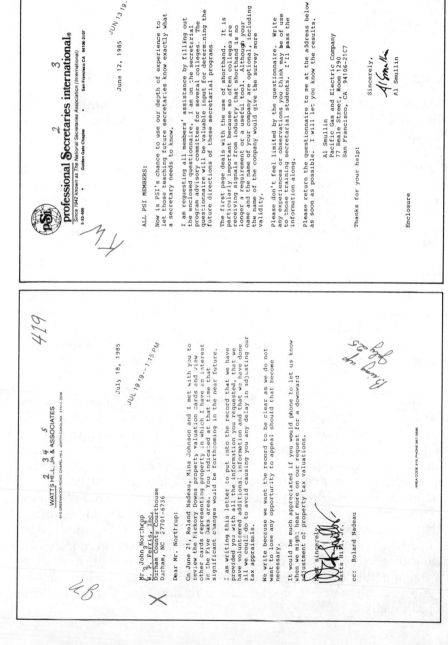

FIGURE 9-6 — Coding of Correspondence for Numeric Method

```
┌─────────────────────────────────────────┐
│  Grayson Carolyn R              133       │
│                                           │
│  Carolyn R. Grayson                       │
│  167 Wellington Street West               │
│  Toronto, Ontario                         │
│  CANADA M2H 9P4                           │
│                                           │
│                                           │
└─────────────────────────────────────────┘
```

FIGURE 9-7 — Card for the Consecutive Numbering Method

5. Prepare a new folder, placing on its tab the assigned number (and, if the procedure in the office requires it, the correspondent's name or the subject).
6. Place the record with top to left in the folder.
7. Place the folder in the sorter to be stored later in numeric order. Or, the folder may be laid aside in a separate pile to be taken to storage at the time the storing of other records is done.

   New Correspondents or Subjects to be Assigned the Letter G.   If the filer does not find a card for the correspondent or subject in the card file and the correspondent or subject does not warrant a numbered folder immediately, a card is prepared for the name of that correspondent or the subject. G is typed in the upper right corner. Any necessary cross-reference cards are made also, and the letter G is placed on each of those cards. The record is marked G in the upper right corner and placed temporarily in the alphabetic sorter until it is stored. The newly typed cards are then inserted in their correct alphabetic sequence in the card file.

Cross-Referencing.   Cross-referencing of names and subjects follows the same rules and procedures as were explained in Chapter 4. No cross-references are stored in numeric file folders—all cross-references are on cards placed in the alphabetic card file. In order to emphasize the fact that a card is a cross-reference, the filer should use a card of distinctive color. The cross-reference card should bear the number assigned to the original card, followed by X to indicate clearly that the card serves as a cross-reference. Figure 9-8 shows an original card on the left with the number 690 assigned to the correspondent, Flavelle & McGinnis. The accompanying card on the right in Figure 9-8 bears the number 690X, showing that it is a cross-reference card. The typing format, capitalization, and punctuation should be consistent on all cards; the style shown here is an excellent one to use because it is simple and, therefore, can be typed rapidly.

```
┌─────────────────────────────────────┐  ┌─────────────────────────────────────┐
│  Flavelle and McGinnis        690    │  │  McGinnis and Flavelle       690X   │
│                                      │  │                                      │
│  Flavelle & McGinnis                 │  │  SEE                                 │
│  841 Bishop Street                   │  │                                      │
│  Honolulu, HI   96802-8411           │  │  Flavelle and McGinnis               │
│                                      │  │                                      │
└─────────────────────────────────────┘  └─────────────────────────────────────┘
```

FIGURE 9-8 — Original and CR Cards Used in Numeric Method

Sorting. If rough sorting has been done as the records were prepared for storage, the sorter and its contents may be moved to the storage area for ease of use. If sorting has not been done, a quick rough sorting before storage will save time. Stacking the records randomly in groups by hundreds is one helpful sorting method that eliminates moving back and forth from drawer to drawer or shelf to shelf. The filer would store all 100s, move to the 300s, and finally move to the 600s, eliminating much retracing of steps.

Storing. All records coded with numbers are stored in the correspondingly numbered folders, with the latest date on top. All records coded with G are stored in the general alphabetic folders, first alphabetically according to the units in the filing segments and then by date within each name group, with the most recent date on top.

Office policy governs the point at which accumulated records in the general folder require the assignment of a permanent number. When that accumulation has occurred, the filer should remove the records from the general folder and take the following steps:

1. Consult the accession book to ascertain the next number to be used and write the name of the correspondent or the subject in the accession book beside that number.
2. Locate the file card that has already been typed with the subject or the correspondent's name and address, showing the code letter G.
3. Change the G to the assigned number by crossing out the G and writing the assigned number above it or beside it (See Figure 9-9).
4. If cross-reference cards have been prepared, locate the cards, cross out the G on them and write the assigned number followed by an X in the upper right corner (See Figure 9-9).
5. Insert cards in their proper alphabetic sequence in the card file.
6. Recode all records with the newly assigned number, crossing out G and writing the number beside it.

```
Flagg Zenser Marina          204¢


Flagg Zenser Marina
33 The Moorings
Clarksville, VA  23927-3472
```

FIGURE 9-9 — Original Card Marked to Show Change from General to Numbered Folder

7. Prepare a new folder with the assigned number on its tab (and, possibly, the correspondent's name or the subject).
8. Place all records into the new folder, with the most recently dated record on top.
9. Place the numbered folder in its correct numeric sequence in storage.

Retrieving.   Whenever records are removed from numeric storage, requisitions, charge-out cards or slips, and OUT indicators must be used in the same way as they are used for alphabetic or subject records storage. Many records are stored by number in computers and information is retrieved electronically from the computer file, either by being shown on a screen or by being printed on paper. A discussion of this aspect of numeric records storage is included in Chapter 14.

Follow-up procedures to locate borrowed records include the use of a tickler file or other reminder system. These procedures are identical to those used in the alphabetic method, as described in Chapter 4.

Conversion from Alphabetic Arrangement to Consecutively Numbered Arrangement

An organization may decide that numeric arrangement would provide for quicker records storage and retrieval than would an existing alphabetic arrangement. Or, an organization may decide to change from alphabetic storage to consecutively numbered storage for security reasons. A number on a storage container or file folder does not convey information to inquisitive persons; a name on a folder is instantly recognizable to anyone who sees it. Whatever the reason for a conversion, the procedure is not difficult; it is only time consuming.

In the conversion process, folders that are presently arranged alphabetically are relabeled with numbers assigned consecutively. As numbers are assigned, a card is prepared for each subject or for each correspondent's name (the filing segment). The alphabetic card file and the sequence of numbered folders will parallel each other since folders are usually removed from their containers in A to Z order. As new folders are added to numeric storage, however, this parallel sequence will stop. The card file will *always* be in alphabetic order, but new folders will be added at the end of the numbered sequence as they are assigned the next numbers in order.

Steps to be followed in converting from an alphabetic arrangement to a consecutively numbered arrangement are as follows:

1. Numbered guides are prepared for every 10 folders in storage according to the sequence of numbers decided upon, such as 1–10–20; 100–110–120; 1000–1010–1020; etc.
2. Each individual folder is removed from storage and is assigned a number from the accession book. Notation of the filing segment (the name of each correspondent or of any subject) is made in the accession book beside the assigned number.
3. A new label with only a number on it is made and affixed to the folder—or the newly assigned number is added to the old label. *Caution: General folders must not be removed from alphabetic storage, as will be explained later.*
4. A card is typed for each filing segment, and all necessary cross-reference cards are typed immediately. The assigned number is typed on each card for reference purposes; the number and X are then typed on cross-reference cards.
5. Cross-reference sheets and SEE ALSO sheets are removed from the individual folders since the cross-reference cards now take the place of those sheets.
6. If any permanent cross-reference guides are within the group of folders being converted to the numeric method, the guides are removed and cross-reference cards are made bearing the same information as was on the guides.
7. All cards, including cross-reference cards, are placed in the card file alphabetically by name or subject.
8. Each record in every folder is coded with its newly assigned number in the upper right corner of the record.
9. The numbered folders are returned to storage in their correct numeric sequence.

10. After all individual folders have been removed from alphabetic storage, converted to numbered folders, and refiled numerically, the folders remaining in alphabetic storage will be the general A to Z folders. These become the general section of the numeric storage arrangement. All records in each general folder are coded with the letter G.
11. A card is typed for the name of each correspondent, or the subject, in every general folder. The cards are placed in the card file in alphabetic order.

Advantages and Disadvantages of the Consecutive Numbering Method

Every storage method has advantages and disadvantages. Consecutive numbering is no exception.

Advantages. The major advantage is speedy storage and retrieval because the majority of people know the sequence of numbers better than they know the sequence of the letters of the alphabet. Other advantages of the consecutive numbering method are:

1. Refiling of coded records is rapid because of the reasoning given above.
2. Expansion is easy and unlimited. New numbers may be assigned without disturbing the arrangement of the existing folders.
3. Transfer of inactive records is easy, especially in the offices where case numbers or contract numbers are used. The oldest cases or contracts have the lowest numbers and are together in storage rather than being scattered throughout the storage equipment, as would be the situation if cases were stored by name. This transfer then provides space for active records, eliminating the need to buy more equipment.
4. All cross-references appear in the card file and do not congest the file folders, drawers, or shelves.
5. A file drawer filled with guides and folders with tabs containing *only* numbers is secure from curious eyes or intentional seekers of information. This need for secrecy may be important for patents, research projects, formulas, or clients' names.
6. Orders, invoices, ledger accounts, and correspondence of one customer all bear the same number, keeping like records together. Fewer errors may occur in matching invoice and payment, for example.
7. A complete list of correspondents' names and addresses is instantly available from the alphabetic card file.
8. Time and effort in labeling are saved because numbers can be affixed much more quickly than can correspondents' names or subjects. Folders may be numbered in advance of their use.

9. Misfiled folders may be easily detected because numbers out of place are usually easier to locate than are misfiled records arranged alphabetically.

Disadvantages. Disadvantages, too, are found in the consecutive numbering method. They are:

1. Transposition of numbers, inaccuracy in copying, and the omission of a digit are frequent errors that may not be easily detected. Carelessness results in misfiling—carelessness by the person who wrote the original number as well as carelessness by the filer who stored the record.

2. Numeric storage is an indirect method. Reference to an alphabetic file is necessary to ascertain whether or not a number has been previously assigned to the case, contract, or correspondent whose records are being stored. Whenever more steps are required to store records, more mistakes can be made.

3. More guides are necessary for the numeric method than for other methods; the cost of numeric storage is therefore somewhat higher.

4. Since it is necessary to consult an alphabetic file in order to store records by the numeric method, congestion around the card file can arise if there is frequent reference to its contents by more than one person.

5. Two storage methods are involved—alphabetic and numeric. All of the disadvantages inherent in the alphabetic method are therefore found in the numeric method in addition to the disadvantages of the numeric method.

6. Since it is necessary to check each record against an alphabetic card file, sorting alphabetically must usually be done first. Then resorting is done numerically prior to storage. This double sorting requires extra time.

7. If the card file and the accession book are not very carefully kept, one correspondent's records might be assigned more than one number and be stored in more than one folder. Or a number could be assigned twice, resulting in a mixture of records within one folder.

8. If the card file is not checked, some of the records of one correspondent could be placed in a general folder and some of the records in a numbered folder.

9. As the numbers used become larger, remembering them becomes harder and misfiling can easily result if memory fails.

10. In the consecutively numbered method, folders are added in consecutive order at the end of storage. Usually the folders with the highest numbers are the ones referred to most often, and reference

to them by several people simultaneously is physically difficult because the filers get in each other's way.

The consecutively numbered method is used infrequently for ordinary correspondence storage because the alphabetic method is less costly to operate. However, in offices such as those mentioned on page 195 of this chapter, numeric storage can fill a definite need.

NONCONSECUTIVE NUMBERING STORAGE METHODS

The term **nonconsecutive numbering** means a system of numbers that either has no logical sequence or that may have logical sequence but the numbers follow one another with blocks of numbers omitted. Very useful storage methods and systems that use numbers in random order are the subject of this section. These methods include terminal and middle digit storage, skip numbering, and phonetic (sound) storage.

Terminal Digit Storage

Terminal digit storage was developed to avoid the disadvantage of working with large numbers. This method also overcomes the disadvantage of congestion at the storage area. The terminal digit storage method is used most effectively with thousands of folders whose numbers have reached at least five digits. The words *terminal digit* refer to the end digits of a number, and you will see how they are referred to *first* as you study this method.

Description. In **terminal digit storage,** numbers are assigned to records in the same manner as was explained previously under consecutive numbering, using an accession book and creating an alphabetic card file. After the numbers are affixed to folders, they are sorted by being read in groups from *right to left* instead of from left to right. The digits in the number are usually separated into groups of twos or threes. For example, the number 293746 could be divided 293 746 or 29 37 46 (sometimes written with hyphens: 29–37–46). The numbers would be *read* as 46 37 29 (beginning with the terminal or end numbers). Because of this backward reading, the terminal digit method seems difficult. Very careful study and some rereading of the explanation may be necessary before you understand it.

The groups of digits will be identified in this text as terminal, secondary, and tertiary numbers reading from right to left.[1]

29   37   46

(tertiary)   (secondary)   (terminal)

The terminal digits usually indicate a drawer or shelf number. If the volume of records stored is great, more than one drawer or shelf may be needed to hold all records with numbers ending in the same terminal digits. (As you read this explanation, refer often to Figure 9-10; the meaning of *terminal digit* will soon become clear.) Figure 9-10 shows the arrangement of folders or numbered cards in a portion of drawer 46. All records within that drawer bear numbers ending in 46.

The guide numbers in the drawer are determined by the numbers of the *secondary* digits, beginning with 00 and ending with 99 in each terminal-numbered section of storage. If space had permitted, the entire

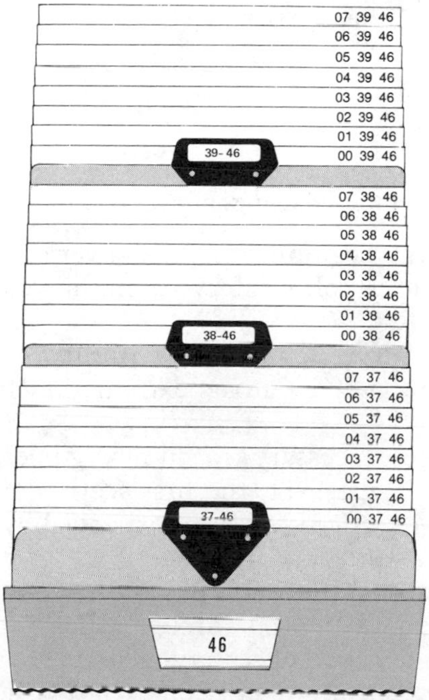

FIGURE 9-10 — Terminal Digit Arrangement

---

[1]The Color Sentry system mentioned on page 201 refers to these numbers as terminal, section, and file. Other systems have labeled them primary, secondary, and final or terminal, middle, and tertiary.

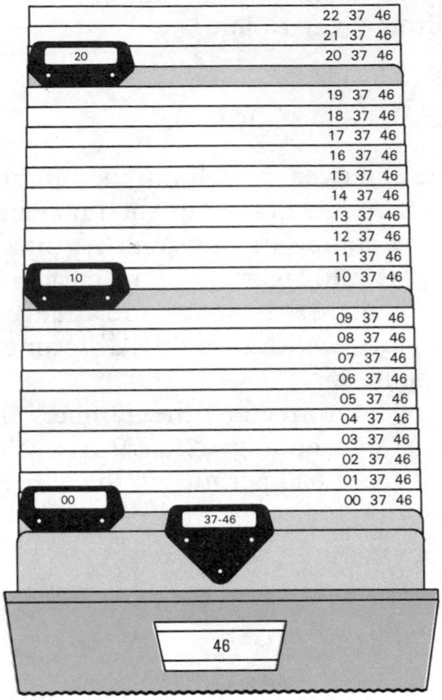

FIGURE 9-11 — Expansion of Terminal Digit Arrangement

46 section would show guide 00–46 at the beginning of the drawer and guide 99–46 at the end of the drawer, each followed by its numbered folders.

The order of arrangement behind a certain guide is determined by the *tertiary* digits. Remember, these are the digits at the extreme LEFT of the number.

As new folders are stored, it becomes necessary to add new guides to separate each group of 10 folders. In Figure 9-11, the first section of the file shown in Figure 9-10 (the 37–46 section) has been expanded by the addition of folders bearing numbers 10–37–46 through 19–37–46. The terminal number is 46; the secondary number is 37; the tertiary numbers now have increased from the previous 00 through 07 to 00 through 19. Therefore, guides 00, 10, and 20 are necessary as dividers.

If the next folder added to storage were numbered 08–37–47, the folder would not be placed in this drawer but would be placed in the 47 drawer. Thus, as numbered folders are added to storage, the new folders will be distributed among different drawers according to the last two digits of the new numbers. (In a consecutively numbered drawer all new folders would go at the end, as numbers increase consecutively.)

Assume that folders having the following numbers are ready to be stored:

a.	67 38 24	c.	00 52 93
b.	67 38 25	d.	42 52 93

To store each of the folders correctly requires the following procedure:

a. Locating the terminal number 24 drawer or shelf; locating the secondary number 38–24 guide; locating the 60 guide and placing the 67 in its proper numbered sequence behind 66.
b. Locating the terminal number 25 drawer or shelf; locating the secondary number 38–25 guide; locating the 60 guide; and placing the 67 in its proper numbered sequence behind 66.
c. Locating the terminal number 93 drawer or shelf; locating the secondary number 52–93 guide; locating the 00 guide; and 00 will be the first folder behind that guide as there is no number smaller than 00!
d. Locating the terminal number 93 drawer or shelf; locating the secondary number 52–93 guide; locating the number 40 guide within the 52–93 section; and placing the 42 in its proper numbered sequence behind 41.

Although the terminal digit storage method is designed to be used in a situation where there are many file folders, it can be used in smaller offices by arranging the secondary and tertiary numbers in combined numeric sequence. For example, 12345, 12445, and 12545 would all be stored in the 45 section, with 123, 124, and 125 stored in sequence.

Illustrative System. Ten-Color Terminal Digit Filing System (Kardex Systems, Inc., Marietta, OH 45750). The Kardex system is designed for shelf storage and is color accented, using colored folders in addition to numbers. The folder color is based on the fourth digit from the right. If the number were 12 37 86, for example, the 3 would determine the color of the folder. Color equivalents to numbers are: 0—white, 1—red, 2—yellow, 3—pink, 4—green, 5—brown, 6—blue, 7—orange, 8—purple, 9—tan.

Two series of boxes numbered 0 through 9 are printed on the right edge of the back flap of each folder (See Figure 9-12). The last two digits (the terminal digits) are blacked out in these boxes. In the example 12 37 86, 8 would be blacked out in the top series and 6 would be blacked out in the bottom series. Therefore, if the folder is stored correctly, the

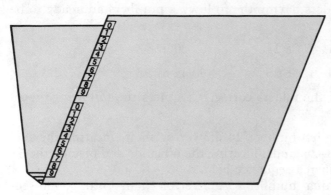

FIGURE 9-12 — Folder for Use with Ten-Color Terminal Digit System

black boxes will be in line with the black boxes on the other folders in the 86 section (See Figure 9-13). Similarly, since the secondary numbers are assigned different colored folders, if the secondary number 43 in a green folder were stored in the 34 section, the green folder would immediately be seen as misfiled because it would be in a pink section. Color eliminates the need for secondary guides in this system.

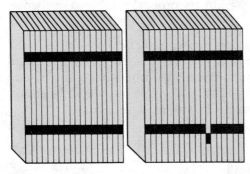

FIGURE 9-13 — Folders Filed Correctly and One Folder Misfiled in Ten-Color Terminal Digit System

Advantages and Disadvantages of Terminal Digit Storage. Because of the difference in the way numbers are read, some people are inclined to think that the terminal digit method has few advantages. A thorough study of the method, however, will show the following advantages:

1. Fewer errors in number transposition are likely to occur with this method than with consecutive numbering because the numbers on

the folders are divided into groups of two or three digits, and the filer is concerned with only two or three numbers at one time.

2. Misreading of numbers is less likely to occur with shorter groups of numbers than with one long number.
3. Several persons can be storing or retrieving consecutively numbered folders at the same time with no congestion or waiting for someone to move in the storage area because filers will be working at different places.
4. Folders are distributed throughout the drawers or shelves as new ones are added because the terminal numbers determine storage placement. Additions to storage occur at various places in the storage area.
5. The use of color coding on folders reduces misfiling and in some systems eliminates the need for additional guides to separate every ten folders, as the change in color effectively separates every ten numbers. Eliminating guides cuts costs.
6. If a color system is used, the color association simplifies training of filers because they quickly learn the color associated with the secondary number.
7. Sorting by secondary number is eliminated when this sorting is accomplished on the basis of color.
8. In especially large storage installations, a filer is assigned to a specific section of the equipment and fixed responsibility for records storage and retrieval can be effectively placed.

Disadvantages of the terminal digit storage method are:

1. People are fearful of the method because it appears complex.
2. Training of filers may take longer with this method than with any other method. Part of this difficulty is caused by the habit of reading numbers from left to right. It takes time to change to reading groups of numbers from right to left.
3. As is true with any filing method, inattention and carelessness will result in misfiled folders; a misfiled numbered folder (unless it is color coded in some way) is extremely hard to find because of number similarity.
4. When a large block of consecutively numbered folders is requested, the filer must go to each of many locations in storage to retrieve the folders. This retrieval takes much more time than would be required to retrieve a block of consecutively numbered folders from a consecutively numbered arrangement. Since such a request does not occur often, the disadvantage is not great.

Middle Digit Storage

Description. In **middle digit storage**, a modification of the terminal digit method, the middle numbers are considered first. Numbers are usually written with spaces or hyphens between the groups to aid the filer, with 764303 being written as 76 43 03. The number 43 (the middle group) is considered first; 76 is considered second, and 03 is the last number to be considered. In Figure 9-14 all records with the middle digits 43 are stored in one section. The sequence within the 43 drawer is determined first by the digits on the left and then by the digits on the right. Guide numbers are determined by the left digits.

In the middle digit method, a block of 100 (00 through 99) sequentially numbered records is kept together. Middle digit arrangement is often used in large insurance companies where it is desirable to keep together blocks of policies issued by one agent. Each agent is assigned a number, which becomes the secondary number. In Figure 9-14, three agents' numbers are shown: 76, 77, and 78. Figure 9-14 shows that agent 76 has on file four policies (4300, 4301, 4302, and 4303) and that there is space in that section for storing 96 additional policies. The largest number that could be affixed to a folder for agent 76 would be 76 43 99, making 100 folders possible—00 to 99.

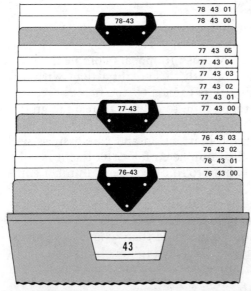

FIGURE 9-14 — Middle Digit Arrangement

Reference again to Figure 9-14 shows that agent 77 has six policies on file (4300 through 4305). Agent 78 has two policies on file.

The middle digit method is most effective with numbers not exceeding six digits. If more than six digits are used, the numbers are separated so that the left grouping has three digits instead of two: 246 81 39.

Advantages and Disadvantages of Middle Digit Storage.

Two advantages are claimed for middle digit storage, and one major disadvantage is evident. The advantages are:

1. Conversion is easier from a consecutively numbered filing arrangement to a middle digit filing arrangement than it is from a consecutively numbered arrangement to a terminal digit arrangement. This is true because blocks of 100 consecutively numbered folders can be moved at one time to the middle digit arrangement. For instance, if folders were numbered from 764300 through 764399, they would be moved as a block to middle digit storage in the 43 section.
2. If color is used, misfiling is reduced in the same manner as is true in the terminal digit storage method.

The disadvantage of the middle digit storage method is again related to the complexity of the method—people fear it. A period of retraining of filers is necessary since the reading of numbers begins with the *middle* digits. Then reading moves to the left and then to the right, contrary to normal reading habits.

Skip Numbering Storage

Description. A third nonconsecutive numbering method is known as **skip numbering**. When the number of records that will ultimately be stored will increase somewhat slowly and an alphabetic sequence is desired in storage as well as in the card file, the numbers that are assigned to names or subjects may be spaced quite far apart from each other—numbers are skipped.

Folders are often assigned numbers with spaces or skips of 100 between them. The assumption is made that no more than 100 new numbered folders will be added in these spaces. As new numbered folders need to be stored between the original folders, the new ones are assigned numbers between those originally numbered, again leaving intervals between numbers. In this manner, an alphabetic arrangement is still maintained.

In Figure 9-15, on the left, a record sequence was started (100, 144, 168, and so on). Note the spaces for additional folders that are shown in the figure. As new folders are added, they will be assigned numbers 101 through 143, 145 through 167, and so on.

As the number of records to be stored increases, it may become necessary to add a folder between the one assigned the number 100 and the one assigned the number 101. In this event, the alternatives are (1) to accept less than strict alphabetic sequence by assigning a number out of order; (2) to renumber all folders, allowing perhaps 200 unassigned numbers between folders this time; or (3) to add a zero to the end of the number of each already numbered folder so that nine new numbers are provided between folders. By adding a zero to the numbers of all previously numbered folders, they become 1000, 1010, 1020, 1030, 1040, 1050, 1060, and so on. The drawer on the right in Figure 9-15 shows the capacity gained in the drawer by adding a zero to the end of the numbers already on the folders.

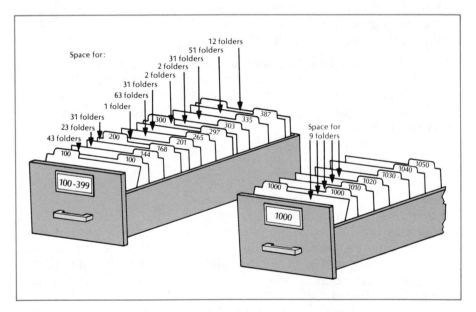

FIGURE 9-15 — Skip Numbering Storage

Block Codes.   **Block codes** are a second form of skip numbering often used to classify data by categories. For example, each department of a business may be assigned a block of numbers to use on its forms as the forms are designed. If the accounting department, for instance, were assigned the numbers 100 to 149 for its exclusive use, the first form designed would be numbered 100, the second form would be 101, the next form would be 102, etc. The purchasing department might be assigned the numbers 150 to 199; sales, 200 to 249; human resources, 250 to 299; and so on.

Group Coding.   A third form of skip numbering is known as **group coding**. Round numbers (100, 200, 300, 400, etc.) are assigned to specific groups, such as main subjects. Subdivisions of these subjects are then assigned numbers within the main numbers (110, 120, 130, 140, 150, etc., within the 100 group; 210, 220, 230, etc., within the 200 group; and so on). One application of group coding is an **alphanumeric storage method**, used with subject storage. Subjects are assigned numbers that indicate main divisions and subdivisions, but the subjects are arranged alphabetically. The method, therefore, is alphabetic and numeric, thus alphanumeric. In Figure 9-16 the main subject guides are in alphabetic order in first position in the drawer; and behind each main subject, the folders for the subdivisions are also arranged alphabetically. Skips or gaps in the assigned numbers allow for later expansion.

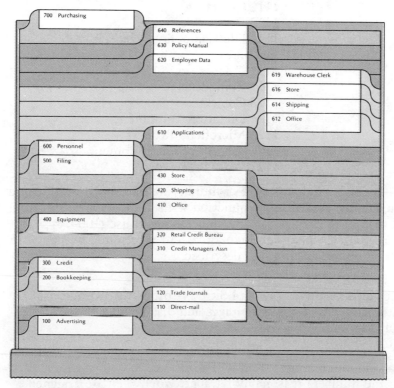

FIGURE 9-16 — Skip Numbering Arrangement of Subject Storage

The captions on the guide and folder tabs may show both the subjects and the numbers assigned to them, or they may show only the numbers. If the captions consist of numbers only, a supplementary card file must be set up to arrange the subjects alphabetically. The records manager decides which practice to follow, depending on the requirements of the office.

Another example of group coding can be found in an equipment inventory system. For example, code numbers might be assigned in this way: 1000 would mean Equipment. All pieces of equipment would then be coded with a number beginning with 1000. The major types of equipment would be designated 1100, 1200, 1300, and so on. Within each of these blocks, numbers would be assigned for subdivisions. Here is a typical example of such group coding:

```
1000 Equipment
    1100 Office Equipment
        1110 Furniture
            1111 Bookcases
            1112 Chairs
            1113 Desks
            1114 File Cabinets
        1120 Machines
            1121 Calculators
            1122 Computers
            1123 Copiers
            1124 Dictation Equipment
            1125 Microfiche Readers
            1126 Transcription Equipment
            1127 Word Processors
```

Several variations of this type of numbering have been tried, using letters or a decimal system in conjunction with numbers. The resulting numbered categories become quite cumbersome to use (100–A–2b, for instance, or 1000.112). Errors are likely to occur more quickly than with the simpler four-digit system just described.

Advantages and Disadvantages of Skip Numbering Storage.   Every numeric storage method has advantages and disadvantages. Specific advantages of skip numbering are:

1. If great increase in the number of records to be stored is not anticipated, a skip numbering system will work well, provided care is used to keep the numbers reasonably far apart when they are assigned.

2. Renumbering by adding a zero at the end of existing numbers is a relatively easy way to secure additional numbers for use.
3. If group codes are assigned, the addition of new groups and subgroups is easily effected by either expanding the number or adding decimals or letters to the basic numbers.

Disadvantages of skip numbering include:

1. Renumbering takes time that would not have to be spent if either consecutive numbering or terminal or middle digit arrangement had been used.
2. Adding new groups and subgroups by expanding the number or adding decimals or letters to the basic numbers can result in lengthy numbers that may be difficult to decipher. If extreme care and attention to detail are not practiced, the wrong combinations can easily be assigned and misfiling will result.
3. Carelessness or inattention while reading or assigning numbers may result in transposing digits or in copying numbers incorrectly.

Phonetic Storage

Description.   An unusual adaptation of the numeric method is **phonetic storage**, one that combines sound and spelling into a numeric code. In the alphabetic method, described in Chapter 4, names are stored as they are spelled. Since so many surnames can be spelled in more than one way (Reid, Reed, Reede), the potential for errors in storage is great, especially when a request comes to find a record for which the exact spelling of the name is not known.

The request may come by telephone from someone who knows only the pronunciation, not the spelling of the name. It may come in a poorly written note or in typed form with misspellings. For example, the surname Johnson can be spelled Jonson, Jahnson, Johnsson, Jonsson, Johnsen, Jahnsen, among others, but all are pronounced the same. In a large file based on the alphabetic method, records for these correspondents might be far apart, and the time consumed in locating the names would be extremely great unless the filer knew the correct spelling.

Large storage areas containing many folders for common surnames (such as Anderson, Brown, Johnson, and Smith) have an extreme congestion of similar names with the resulting problem of correct storage. For any storage operation in which a large number of names and spellings offers almost endless possibilities for error, a method employing *sound* may be more efficient.

Computer programs are now available that search for names by sound. "The Telephone Assistant," for example, is a computer program (BASIC) that uses the Soundex system. **Soundex** helps telephone operators, airline reservationists, detectives, and researchers locate names when the exact spelling is not known.

Illustrative System. Soundex (Kardex Systems, Inc., Marietta, OH 45750).

The Soundex system has been in existence for many years but is not used extensively because of the skill required to code and the necessity for a huge number of names to store to make its use worthwhile. The Soundex system groups together names that are spelled or pronounced in a similar manner but that would be widely separated if they were arranged in alphabetic order. This method of storage is especially useful where there are many similar surnames; for example, in hospitals, credit bureaus, insurance companies, banks, public utilities, and government offices.

In the Soundex system, the key unit of the filing segment (the surname of an individual or the first coded unit of a company name) is given a code consisting of one letter and three digits. The letter in the code is the first letter of the key unit (such as *S* in *Scotia Ski Lodge* or *N* in *Pamela Nichols*). The three digits are numbers that are assigned to, and therefore represent, certain *consonants* in the surname or key unit. Once the key unit in a name is coded by the Soundex method, the filing order can be roughly determined by that alphanumeric code. However, many names will have identical code numbers. The order is then determined by looking at the second unit in the name. If the second units are identical, the order is determined by going to the third and succeeding units, exactly as is done in determining the order in any alphabetic method. As the coding procedure is quite complicated, and extensive training is required to use it, a detailed explanation of the Soundex system will not be presented in this text.

Advantages and Disadvantages of the Phonetic Method.

Some of the advantages claimed for the Soundex system are:

1. Every name has a positive, unchanging number.
2. Approximately 98 percent of all family names are automatically grouped regardless of spelling.
3. Only 7 numbers are used instead of the 26 letters of the alphabet.
4. Numeric sorting, storing, and retrieving—the speediest of all methods—is used.
5. File folders used in other types of storage can be easily converted into folders suitable for a Soundex system by adding the code number.

6. Cross-references are not used in a Soundex system and do not, therefore, add bulk to the contents of storage containers.

   Disadvantages of the Soundex system are:

1. The training of filers to code properly is a time-consuming job.
2. Because of the complexities of rules, mistakes in coding can and do occur because of carelessness or haste.
3. Retrieval of records can be slowed or halted if codes are not correctly assigned.
4. Regional pronunciations differ and many people cannot pronounce words phonetically, never having been trained to read in that way. If consonants are omitted or inserted incorrectly in the pronunciation, wrong codes will result.
5. Since cross-references are not used, searching for names incorrectly or incompletely given can be an extremely time-consuming task.
6. If an unusual name is encountered, it is possible to assign two codes to it unknowingly. For instance, Tjoslien might be pronounced Josleen and, therefore, coded with a J. If the next reference to it is by Fosleen, the filer will look in the F section of storage and not find the name and assign another number to it. The filer must be especially alert to recognize unusual spellings, pronunciations, and variations.
7. Because of the grouping of like names together and the necessity of using second and succeeding units to determine alphabetic order, the system can be confusing to the inexperienced filer.

COMBINATIONS OF NUMERIC AND SUBJECT STORAGE METHODS

Group coding of subjects was discussed as one form of the skip numbering method. Other combinations of numeric and subject storage methods used in offices or in libraries are the simple numeric, the duplex numeric, and decimal arrangements.

Simple Numeric-Subject Arrangement

In **simple numeric-subject arrangement**, each subject, as it is selected, is assigned a number from the accession book. Then, instead of storing by alphabet, the subject folders are stored in numeric sequence. An alphabetic index of subjects with a relative index, usually a card file, is maintained and should be consulted each time a record is stored or requested from storage. The assigned number must appear on every file card and on every record in storage.

Duplex Numeric Arrangement

The **duplex numeric arrangement** of subject storage is similar to simple numeric arrangement. Duplex means that in addition to a number, there is a printed subject, rarely arranged in alphabetic order. Main subject headings are numbered in the order in which they are added to storage. An accession book and an alphabetic card file are used as in simple numeric arrangement. For example, if the first subject placed in storage is Equipment, the folder number will be 1. The card in the file will be as follows:

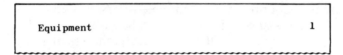

The guide in storage, in addition to being numbered, will also bear the subject title (which is different from the simple numeric arrangement). The guide caption will be as follows:

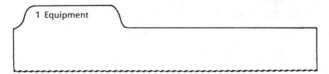

Another difference between the duplex numeric method and the simple numeric method is that each main subject is subdivided. The subdivision receives the number assigned to the main heading and also a number that indicates its place in the classification. For example, subdivisions of the 1 Equipment section will have folders with labels as follows:

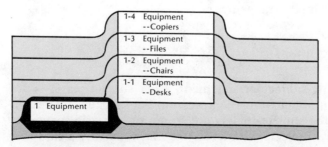

When a subdivision folder becomes overcrowded, it may be further subdivided by adding a letter to the numbers assigned to the main heading and first subdivision. For example, the *1–1 Equipment—Desks* folder may become so full that the contents bulge over the top of the folder. Records will be removed from it and separated into three folders to show the three types of desks referred to. The labels on the three new folders will read:

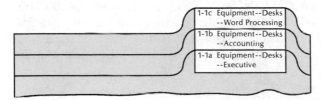

A card for each subject and each subdivision must be made for the card file, with the number assigned to each. The card file arrangement will be alphabetically by major subject and numerically by subdivision. Reference to the card file will show the last number that has been assigned within any subject. For instance, in Figure 9-17, the E (for Equipment) section of the card file shows the following arrangement:

1-4	Equipment	-	Copiers	
1-3	Equipment	-	File Cabinets	
1-2	Equipment	-	Chairs	
1-1c	Equipment	-	Desks	- Word Processing
1-1b	Equipment	-	Desks	- Accounting
1-1a	Equipment	-	Desks	- Executive
1-1	Equipment	-	Desks	
1	Equipment			

FIGURE 9-17 — Duplex Numeric Card File

By referring to the card file, the filer knows the next subdivision of Equipment must be assigned the number 1–5. And the next subdivision of Equipment—Desks must be assigned the number 1–1d. If more than 26 subdivisions are anticipated, letters are not feasible because the alphabet has only 26 letters. An additional number would have to be used, separated from the other numbers by a colon, a dash, a period, or some other distinguishing symbol. Such notations as 1–3c4 or 1–2–3a or 1:4/7–6 are confusing and increase the possibility of storage error.

Masterformat—a master list of section titles and numbers for the construction industry—was jointly published by the Construction Specifications Institute and Construction Specifications Canada. The listing is a sample of the duplex numeric and skip-numbering methods. There are 17 numbered and labeled major divisions with their names and numbers appearing on guide tabs: 0 = Bidding and Contract Requirements, 1 = General Requirements, 2 = Sitework, 3 = Concrete, 4 = Masonry, 5 = Metals, and so on. Subdivisions of each main division are skip numbered to correspond to their main subject numbers and allow for expansion. For instance, 4 Masonry has the following subdivisions: 04050 Masonry Procedures, 04100 Mortar, 04150 Masonry Accessories, 04200 Unit Masonry, 04400 Stone, 04500 Masonry Restoration and Cleaning, 04550 Refractories, and 04600 Corrosion Resistant Masonry. Each of these subdivision titles will appear on folder tabs, placed to follow their main division guides.

Decimal Arrangement

The **decimal arrangement** was first used in 1873 by Dr. Melvil Dewey for classifying library materials. In 1876, Dewey published "A Classification and Subject Index for Cataloguing and Arranging the Books and Pamphlets of the Library." Many public and private libraries in the United States and in other countries use Dewey's method because every subject upon which anything has been written is included. The system has ten general classes or main divisions:

000 Generalities
100 Philosophy and related disciplines
200 Religion
300 The social sciences
400 Language
500 Pure sciences
600 Technology (Applied sciences)
700 The arts
800 Literature (Belles-lettres[2])
900 General geography and history and their auxiliaries

Each of these major groups is divided into ten parts, which in turn can be divided into ten additional groups, and so on indefinitely. For example, group *300 The Social Sciences* (where most books about business are stored) is subdivided as follows:

---

[2]Belles-lettres is a French expression meaning beautiful writing.

300 The Social Sciences
      310 Statistics
      320 Political science (politics and government)
      330 Economics
      340 Law
      350 Public administration Executive branch of government
           Military art and science
      360 Social problems and services, association
      370 Education
      380 Commerce, communications, transportation
      390 Customs, etiquette, folklore

The *370 Education* group has these subdivisions:

370 Education
      371 Generalities of education
      372 Elementary education
      373 Secondary education
      374 Adult education
      375 Curriculums
      376 Education of women
      377 Schools and religion
      378 Higher education
      379 Education and the state[3]

Although books on business subjects are stored on the library shelves in the 300 and 650 numbers, the Dewey Decimal System is not adaptable to general office usage. The system is used only when classifying library material. (The Library of Congress Classification System is an alphabetic system of subject storage that is growing in popularity and may take the place of the Dewey Decimal System.)

Many government offices and private companies have devised systems based on the decimal classification principle because their records will fit into ten or fewer main headings. The success of any decimal system depends primarily on the original classifications selected. If the main divisions prove to be too specific or limiting, if they overlap or fail to cover the entire subject, the system will not work. Mere knowledge of the subject matter is not sufficient; ability is needed to analyze and classify clearly and accurately. A records manager or perhaps a trained filer should be able to set up and operate a decimal system efficiently.

---

[3]*Dewey Decimal Classification and Relative Index*, devised by Melvil Dewey, 19th ed., 1979; Forest Press, Inc., of Lake Placid Club Education Foundation (publishers), Lake Placid Club, New York, 12946.

IMPORTANT TERMS AND CONCEPTS

accession book
alphabetic card file
alphanumeric storage method
block codes
consecutive numbering method
decimal arrangement
duplex numeric arrangement
group coding
indirect storage method

middle digit storage
nonconsecutive numbering
numeric storage method
phonetic storage
simple numeric-subject arrangement
skip numbering
Soundex
terminal digit storage

REVIEW AND DISCUSSION

1. Give examples of various numbers that may be used to identify you. (Obj. 1)

2. What is another name for a consecutive numbering method? (Objs. 1, 2)

3. What is the difference between the consecutive numbering method and a nonconsecutive numbering method of storing records? (Obj. 2)

4. Is the numeric method a direct or an indirect storage method? What is the difference between the two? (Obj. 3)

5. What four supply items are needed for an efficient consecutive numbering method? (Obj. 3)

6. Why is it recommended that a general alphabetic section of folders be placed at the beginning (not the end) of a consecutively numbered storage arrangement? (Obj. 3)

7. Of what value is an alphabetic card file in the numeric storage method? (Obj. 3)

8. Why is an accession book necessary in numeric storage? (Obj. 3)

9. Describe several uses of color in numeric storage. (Obj. 3)

10. How does the coding step for storing records by numbers differ from the coding step for storing records alphabetically? (Obj. 4)

11. Why will some cards in the alphabetic card file bear a code of G; some will have a crossed-out G and a number (G̶178); and other cards will have only a number (93)? (Obj. 4)

12. How do you cross-reference in the consecutive numbering method? Are cross-references numbered? Why or why not? (Obj. 4)

13. In converting from an alphabetic arrangement to a consecutively numbered arrangement, you will not assign numbers to the general folders in alphabetic storage. Where will these folders be located in the numeric storage arrangement? Will records in these folders be coded with a number? Why or why not? (Obj. 5)

14. Why are misplaced folders bearing numbers on their tabs easier to locate than are misplaced folders that have complete names typed on their tabs? (Obj. 6)

15. What is the major advantage of the consecutive numbering method? Why? Mention at least five more advantages and disadvantages of the consecutive numbering method and discuss them briefly. (Obj. 6)

16. Assume you are talking with someone who does not know about the nonconsecutive numbering storage methods. Clearly explain three nonconsecutive numbering storage methods, including advantages and disadvantages. (Objs. 7, 8)

17. How does the addition of folders in terminal digit or middle digit storage differ from the addition of folders in a consecutively numbered storage container? (Obj. 7)

18. Why is skip numbering used? (Obj. 8)

19. What is the difference between simple numeric-subject arrangement and duplex numeric arrangement of subjects? (Obj. 9)

20. What is the most commonly known decimal subject system in use today? Is it suitable for storing business records? Why or why not? (Obj. 9)

DECISION-MAKING OPPORTUNITIES (DMO)

DMO 9-1: Improving the Present Storage Method

You are presently working in a large insurance company at a job requiring you to refer to clients' records many times each day. Records are stored by insurance policy numbers in consecutive order in an open-shelf arrangement. The records of the last 10 years are included in the active storage area.

The records are in excellent condition and are relatively easy to find because all of the employees are very careful about refiling the numbers correctly. Sometimes, however, a record you need will not be in storage, and you have no idea where to look for it. The company charge-out policy (which is closely adhered to) is that any record removed from storage in the morning must be returned to storage that afternoon; any record removed in the afternoon must be returned the next morning. This policy often means you have to wait half a day or overnight to find the record you need.

The folders are in good shape, with typed labels bearing both policy number and client's name. Each January 1, the color of the folders and labels is changed. Last year they were yellow; this year they are pink; next year they will be buff, in keeping with the sequence of five repeated colors: pink, buff, blue, white, yellow. The labels look like this:

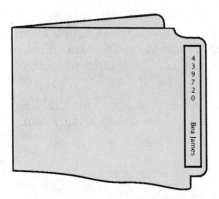

A master card file containing about 400,000 cards is arranged alphabetically by the names of clients. The card file occupies many drawers, similar to what you see in a library. Congestion at the card file is becoming a problem, and many times several people need to work at the same place in the storage area.

Your supervisor customarily holds a staff meeting each Monday morning. On the agenda for the next meeting is the question of records storage. Your supervisor has asked every employee who uses clients' records to come to the meeting with suggestions of any kind about what to do to make the records more readily accessible. You have been reminded that the company policy is to keep at least 10 years of records together in one area, so transfer at this time is not possible. Also, the company is not yet ready to computerize any of the records. Improvement in storage method seems to be the only solution.

What suggestions do you have? Be specific. Your supervisor will welcome *every* suggestion. Offering unusual solutions to a problem often brings out ideas that would not otherwise be advanced, and your supervisor can adapt or change ideas that at first do not seem workable. List your suggestions so that you can not only give them orally but also have them ready to hand to your supervisor at Monday's meeting. (Helps: a better numbering method? color usage expanded? label change?)

DMO 9-2: Recommending a Numeric Method of Storage

A new archery club is being organized in your school (under the auspices of the student government) to which every interested student may belong upon payment of minimal dues. The dues structure is such that there are several different payment categories. (Your instructor will indicate which categories you are to use. They might be any of the following or any other: freshmen, sophomores, juniors, seniors; first-term, second-term, third-term students; full-time, part-time, special, continuing education students.)

You are on a committee to recommend a numeric method for keeping account of the dues collections and for keeping all other records of the club. The method should be easy to understand, simple to maintain, and capable of unlimited expansion as the membership changes and increases. The financial records will be kept on computer but you will undoubtedly have limited correspondence with students concerning their dues payments. The club may also have limited correspondence with organizations outside the school concerning special programs, social events, celebrations, and the like. Rules, regulations, some memos, and various communications from within the school and your periodic financial statements will also need to be stored.

The equipment available to the club consists of one five-drawer file cabinet and a box into which approximately one thousand 5" by 3" cards will fit. About $50 is available to you for whatever supplies you may need.

You are asked to bring to the next committee meeting your description of the method of records storage to be used by the club. Your discussion may include a list of questions that your committee needs to have answered before submitting their recommendation to the student government body. Be prepared to present your points in writing as well as orally.

DMO 9-3: Adding Records to a Skip Numbering Arrangement

In your small office, conversion from the alphabetic method to the skip numbering method has just taken place. Your drawer storage contains folders labeled with numbers only, arranged consecutively in skip numbering arrangement. The customers' names are on cards in the card file. The B, C, and D sections of that card file are shown below with the assigned numbers opposite the names.

DRC Forms Inc – 350
Drambo Cypter Dr – 299X
D B G Theatre – 301
Cyranos Shoes – 300
Cypter Drambo Dr – 299
Cylo and Butterfield – 298
Cycle Shop The – 295
Cut and Curl Shop – 290
Custer Insurance Co – 275
Crane George L – 250
Cooper Carole E – 200
Butterfield and Cylo – 298X
Branson Word Processing Corp – 150
Barnes Engineering Company – 125
(Front of File)

What numbers would you assign to the following names to maintain strict alphabetic order in storage? Explain your decision.

1. Dougherty Computer Store
2. Coronet Hotel
3. Barons Floor Coverings
4. Cutter Bakatsias and Sons
5. Cyclops Record Bar
6. Charlotte P Cyne Hospital
7. Crew Sports Shop
8. Cyne Auto Repair

APPLYING THE RULES

Job 11, Correspondence Storage—Consecutive Numbering Method;
Job 12, Correspondence Storage—Terminal Digit Method

10 GEOGRAPHIC RECORDS STORAGE

Objectives

After you have completed this chapter, you will be able to:

1. List the differences and similarities between the geographic and alphabetic methods of records storage.
2. Describe the kinds of businesses that might use the geographic method of storage.
3. Explain the difference between the location name guide plan and the lettered guide plan of geographic arrangements.
4. Describe the sequence of guides and folders in the most commonly used geographic arrangement—by states and by cities within states.
5. Explain the use of an alphabetically arranged card file in the geographic method of storage.
6. Describe the difference in labels or captions as they appear on guides and folders used for the geographic method as opposed to those used on guides and folders for the alphabetic method.
7. List the types of cross-references used in the geographic storage method.
8. List advantages and disadvantages of the geographic storage method.
9. Give examples of the combination of the geographic method with other storage methods.

The last of the alphabetic methods to be discussed in this text is the **geographic storage method**. This is a method of storing and retrieving records by *place* or *location* as the first filing segment and then by individual or business name. Because you may encounter it where you work or you may find the method needed in your office situation, the geographic method is discussed here. Although limited in usage because there is no widespread need to store information by geographic area, its principles and procedures are necessary for your study if you are to have a complete understanding of the four primary methods of records storage. As you study this chapter, you will see again the necessity for using the rules for alphabetic indexing that were presented in Chapters 5 and 6. You will also see the parallelism between the alphabetic and geographic methods.

Businesses that may store records by the geographic method include:

1. Multinational companies—those businesses with overseas branches and customers outside the boundaries of the United States, whose records are arranged first by country.
2. Businesses that have many branches (possibly sales branches) at different geographic locations within the country and often a great deal of intracompany correspondence.
3. Businesses that are licensed to operate in some states but not in others (such as insurance companies, franchised operations, investment firms) and their records are kept according to the states in which business is conducted.
4. Mail-order houses and publishers whose business is conducted through the United States mail and who refer to their customers' records first by geographic location.
5. Companies that direct their advertising promotions to specific geographic areas, such as to the West Coast states.
6. Utility companies (electricity, gas, telephone, water) whose customers are listed by street name and address first.
7. Real estate firms that list their properties by areas; sometimes the area may be quite unusual, such as islands, or castles and estates in foreign countries; sometimes the areas are divisions of countries or cities; and sometimes in a metropolitan area, the listings may be grouped by subdivision names or by street boundaries within the city itself.
8. Government agencies whose records might be stored according to geographic areas, such as state, county, township, etc., depending upon the scope of the governmental function.

Several geographic record arrangements will be illustrated and explained. The supplies needed for geographic arrangement and the procedures for storing and retrieving records geographically will be discussed. The advantages and disadvantages of the geographic method will also be listed.

ARRANGEMENT OF RECORDS STORED BY THE GEOGRAPHIC METHOD

The geographic arrangement that is used in an office will depend upon:

1. The type of business being operated
2. The way that records are referred to (by state, by geographic region, by country, etc.)
3. The geographic areas to which the records are related.

Generally, a geographic arrangement is organized according to one of two plans: (1) the location name guide plan or (2) the lettered guide plan. You will find the location name guide plan used more often than is the lettered guide plan. Each of these plans is explained in detail in the following paragraphs. As you study them, refer often to the illustrations to help your understanding.

Location Name Guide Plan

A geographic storage arrangement based on the **location name guide plan** has location names (such as names of countries, provinces, states, counties, or cities) as the filing segments that comprise the main divisions. Probably the most frequently found location name guide plan arrangement is that based on state names as the first filing segment.

States.   The main divisions in storage are the names of the states. The subdivisions necessary within each state depend on the number of records to be stored behind each state name. For instance, a national pharmaceutical company uses one guide for each state. Behind each state guide are 12 numbered folders corresponding to the 12 months of the year (1 = January, 2 = February, etc.). The color of the folder for each month is different, the same color sequence being used behind each state. In these folders are stored returned goods authorizations and claims and adjustments in random order because the number of records is small.

A national fast food chain, which constructs its buildings according to a master plan throughout the United States, stores its architect's drawings geographically in large flat drawers labeled for each state. City names also appear on the labels in alphabetic order. Within the drawers the drawings are arranged first by city name and within cities, by street address.

Figure 10-1 shows part of a drawer based on the location name guide plan by states. Illinois is shown here; Indiana will follow it and Idaho will have preceded it. As you study the arrangement, refer frequently to the figure. The circled numbers on it correspond to the following numbered paragraphs.

1. The first item in the drawer is the primary guide for the state name, *Illinois*. Since this arrangement uses the state names as the largest geographic divisions, the guide tab with the state name on it is double width and centered to give the guide prominence. A different color may be used for each of these guides as a further aid in storing and retrieving records. All folder and guide tabs following the color state guide would then bear the same color as does the state guide.

2. The second item in the drawer is a city guide for *Alton*, the first location name guide after the state guide. Since this city guide usually stays in the drawer in its correct position, it does not need the name of the state on it.

3. The third item is a general city folder for *Alton*. In this folder are stored the records from all correspondents located in Alton for whom only a few records have accumulated. When their number increases to a predetermined figure (usually five), the records are removed and an individual folder is prepared. Since the *Alton* folder may be removed from storage, it bears the name of the state to which it belongs (using the two-letter state abbreviation as approved by the Postal Service) in addition to the city name. There are undoubtedly other Altons in the United States, and failure to put the state name on the tab will require the filer to look inside to see to what state the folder belongs when it is to be refiled. This folder is the last folder in the city section.

4. The fourth item is a city guide for *Aurora*.

5. The fifth item is an individual folder for the *Kelly Manufacturing Company* in Aurora. The first piece of correspondence from Kelly Manufacturing Company was placed in the *IL—Aurora* general city folder (No. 6 in Figure 10-1). When records of the company increased to a sufficient number of pieces (perhaps five), it was necessary to make an individual folder and place it between the *Aurora* guide and the *Aurora* general city folder. Note that the caption on the individual folder bears state and city as the first filing segment. Then the name of the correspondent and the address are given.

6. The sixth item is the general city folder for *Aurora*, in which are stored the records from all correspondents located in Aurora for whom only a few records have accumulated. This step is identical to No. 3 above.

7. The last item in the A section of this drawer is a general state folder with the caption *IL—A*. In this folder are stored records from Illinois correspondents located in cities beginning with the letter A for which there is not yet a city folder (because five records relating to any one city have not yet accumulated).

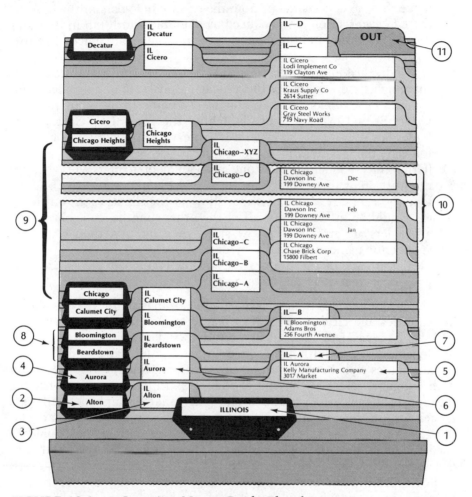

FIGURE 10-1 — Location Name Guide Plan for a State

8. The next six items in the drawer are those that relate to B city names. Study them carefully so that you understand the placement of each one.

9. Since Chicago is the location of so many correspondents, one general city folder is not large enough to contain the records. Therefore, the names of those correspondents whose records will have to be stored in a *Chicago* general folder are grouped alphabetically. The groups are separated into lettered folders. (See IL Chicago—A, IL Chicago—B, IL Chicago—C, IL Chicago—O, and IL Chicago—XYZ, the intervening letters having been omitted to conserve space.) To

make these folders stand out from the other city folders in the drawer, the *Chicago* section is introduced by a double-width tab in first and second positions, and the *Chicago* general folders are placed in third position.

Individual folders for correspondents located in Chicago are placed in alphabetic order among the Chicago alphabetic folders according to the first letter of the key unit of the name filing segment. (See Chase Brick Corp. Its folder is behind the general IL Chicago—B folder but in front of the general IL Chicago—C folder.) The general folder is the last item in its section.

10. If the correspondence with one individual or firm is very heavy, monthly individual folders are provided (See Dawson, Inc.). Only January, February, and December show in the illustration; but folders would be in storage for all of the other months, too. Note that all folders are arranged first by state, then by city, then by correspondent's name, and finally by date.

11. Near the back of the file drawer, an OUT guide is placed in fifth position, where it is easy to see.

If a business needs to have a geographic arrangement of states showing counties and cities, the location name guide plan shown in Figure 10-2 can be used. Here, fifth-cut first-position guides show the state names in alphabetic order. Fifth-cut second-position guides and folders show county names alphabetically arranged (Anderson, Knox, Marion, Shelby) with a general folder at the end of the items in each county. Fifth-cut third-position guides and folders show city names alphabetically arranged within their counties. The corresponding general folders are the last items within their sections. Fourth and fifth combined positions are used for individual folders in order to provide room for typing all the necessary information on the tab. Note that the state, county, and city names appear on the first line of the captions; correspondents' names appear next in indexing order, followed by their addresses. OUT indicators in fifth position are easy to see.

Because of the great number of different guide and folder tabs necessary, the appearance of the storage drawer tends to be cluttered. Care must be taken to see that new guide and folder tabs, when provided with labels, occupy the same position and are of the same cut as the ones in use.

Districts within States. If the nature of the business requires a breakdown of the states into regions or districts, the storage arrangement can reflect this aspect by means of the captions on the general guides and folders. Figure 10-3 shows how the geographic method is used to

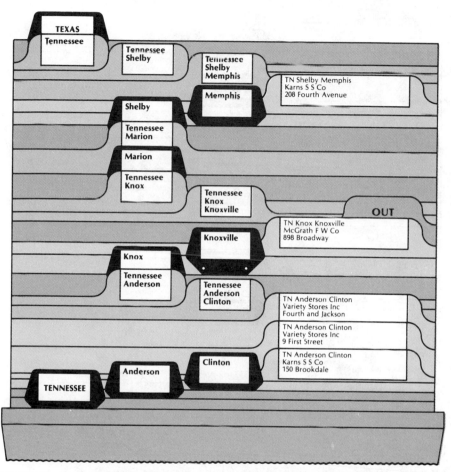

FIGURE 10-2 — Location Name Guide Plan Showing Both Counties
and Cities

divide the state of California into northern and southern regions. The
cities within each region are listed (in alphabetic order) on fifth-cut tabs
in third position with their general folders having tabs of the same size
and in the same position—the last item within their sections. Individual
folders have tabs in fourth and fifth combined positions. The sequence
of information on the tabs is state, region, city, and correspondent's name
and address. Again, OUT indicators are in the fifth position, easy to see.
A map of California must be readily available, showing the boundary
between southern and northern California, so that all filers will store
records in the correct region.

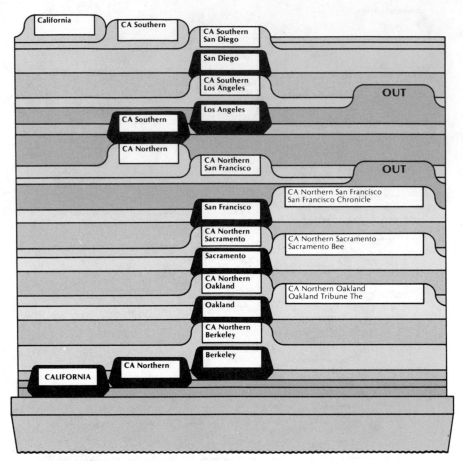

FIGURE 10-3 — Location Name Guide Plan for State Regions

Local Areas. Some businesses (utility companies, for example) that have customers in a restricted area, such as a city or a county, store records by the street locations of their customers. Such an arrangement may indicate names of suburbs and must show names of streets and names of customers with their house or building numbers (See Figure 10-4). In this arrangement there are no general folders; each folder is an individual one for one specific location. Guides in first position bear the names of suburbs; second-position guides have the street names on them; individual folders are on the right. No city name is necessary since this business serves only one city.

Many times the required information is too long to fit on the individual folder tabs as easily as that shown in Figure 10-4. If names are

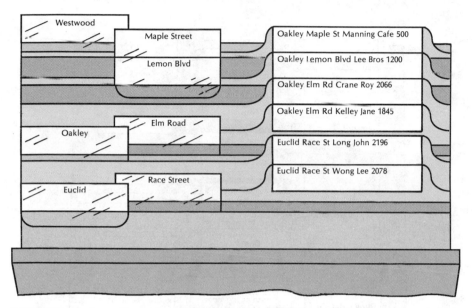

FIGURE 10-4 — Location Name Guide Plan for Local Use

long, two lines must be used but the sequence of information is the same: suburb name, street name, customer name in indexing order, and house or building number last. The house or building number takes precedence over the name of the customer in the storage arrangement. This arrangement is needed because reference to the records is made by the *location* of the customer first; the customer's name is the least important.

Foreign Countries.   The location name guide plan can be readily adapted to the needs of organizations that do business in or with foreign countries. For example, if a business has correspondence with several individuals and firms throughout the world, it might have a storage arrangement similar to that shown in Figure 10-5. The word FOREIGN appears on the drawer label, but the label might have read: Foreign A—M. The arrangement is alphabetic by country and alphabetic by city within each country. Individual folders are arranged alphabetically by correspondents' names if there are two or more folders within the same country or city (See Montreal in Figure 10-5). The arrangement in Figure 10-5 is as follows (paragraph numbers correspond to circled numbers):

1. The first item in the drawer is the permanent guide for the country name, *Canada* (third cut, second position). Since the arrangement uses

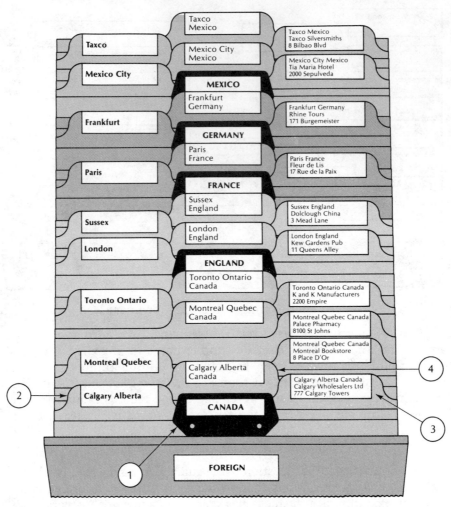

FIGURE 10-5 — Location Name Guide Plan for Foreign Countries

    the country names as the largest geographic divisions, the tab of each country's guide is heavy and centered, to give it prominence. If color is used, a different color is assigned to each country as a further aid to storing and retrieving. All folder and guide tabs for a country would then be of one color.

2. The second item in the drawer is the city guide for *Calgary Alberta* (third cut, first position). The name of the province is also given since all Canadian location names include city and province in their addresses. Since this guide is never removed from the drawer in regular

storage activity, the name of the country does not need to be written on it.

3. The third item in the drawer is an individual folder for *Calgary Wholesalers Ltd* (third cut, third position).
4. The fourth item in the drawer is the general folder for *Calgary Alberta* (third cut, second position). In it are stored records for all correspondents whose address is in Calgary until their volume increases to a predetermined number (usually five pieces) at which time the records are removed and an individual folder is prepared.

If many Canadian records are to be stored, the arrangement might be slightly different. Guides and folders might be arranged alphabetically first by province and then by city (instead of by city first, as shown in Figure 10-5).

As you glance through the drawer, you will see nine city guides in first position. Behind each city guide are the individual folders related to that city. Behind the individual folders, in second position, are the general folders labeled the same as each of the city guides. You will recall that for each guide, there must be a correspondingly labeled general folder. The general folders bear the name of the city and country for ease in returning the folders to storage once they have been removed.

The arrangement of guides and folder tabs is a matter of personal preference. Straight-line arrangement (as is shown in Figure 10-5) is preferred because additions may be made to the drawer contents without disturbing the orderly arrangement of either guides or folders.

Each foreign country has its own unique geographic divisions. The use of a world gazeteer or a world almanac would be very helpful to the filer.

Special Folder Arrangements.   All of the arrangements of folders explained thus far have been in alphabetic order. However, a geographic arrangement may be of more value if the alphabet is disregarded. For instance, sections may be set up for storage according to areas outlined on a map. Records might be arranged in an order as follows: Canada, Northern U.S., Eastern U.S., Southern U.S., Midwestern U.S., Mountain States U.S., Western U.S., Alaska-Hawaii U.S., Mexico. Or the guides and folders might be arranged alphabetically by those regions: Alaska-Hawaii U.S., Canada, Eastern U.S., Mexico, Midwestern U.S., Mountain States U.S., Northern U.S., Southern U.S., and Western U.S. Another special arrangement may be by distance zones from a central point, such as those used in the post office to figure parcel post rates. Any such nonalphabetic arrangement, however, requires the use of a plainly marked map to show the area boundaries. If a map is not used, misfiling results because people guess at the location of a correspondent instead of checking it.

Lettered Guide Plan

The lettered guide plan can be used in any geographic arrangement. However, the plan is not used frequently because of the cluttered appearance within the storage container. If the volume of records stored geographically is very large, alphabetic guides will cut storage and retrieval time by guiding the eye quickly to the correct alphabetic section of storage. As its name implies, the **lettered guide plan** uses guides printed with alphabetic letters—sometimes with letters and numbers—in addition to guides with location names printed on them.

Figure 10-6 shows part of a drawer of Michigan records stored by the lettered guide plan. Refer to the figure often as you study the arrangement, where circled numbers are explained by similarly numbered paragraphs below.

1. The first item in the drawer is the guide for the name of the state, *Michigan*; states are the largest geographic division in this storage plan. The guide tab is double width and centered to give it prominence.
2. The primary guides are sixth-cut *alphabetic* guides that divide the state into alphabetic sections. The guides are staggered in first, second, and third positions (A–1, B–2, C–3, D–4). Each guide indicates the section of the alphabet within which are stored records with city names in that section. The guide tabs are numbered consecutively so that they will be kept in correct order.
3. Each primary guide is accompanied by a corresponding general alphabetic folder, which is placed at the end of that alphabetic section. The folder has the same caption as that of the primary guide, and it is placed in the same position as the primary guide. Each general alphabetic folder contains records from correspondents located in cities with names beginning with the letter of the alphabet on the folder. For instance, the general A 1 folder would contain correspondence from organizations and people in Addison, Adrian, Albion, Allegan, Anchorville, Athens, Auburn Heights, and Avoca, but not from Ann Arbor since that city has its own general folders.
4. In fourth position appear several types of guides and folders: (a) special city guides to indicate cities for which there is a considerable

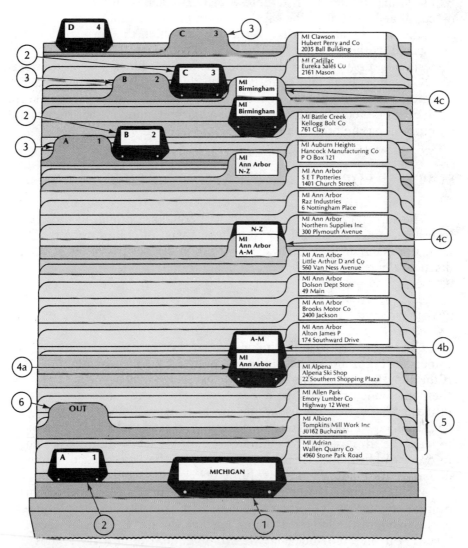

FIGURE 10-6 — Lettered Guide Plan

volume of records (MI Ann Arbor); (b) special alphabetic guides that provide a breakdown of correspondents' names in the cities identified by the special city guides (A–M and N–Z); and (c) special general city folders to accompany the special city guides (MI Ann Arbor A–M; MI Ann Arbor N–Z; and MI Birmingham).

5. Individual folders with double-width tabs appear in fifth and sixth combined positions. The caption for an individual folder contains the name of the state and that of the city in which the correspondent is located as the first line on the label. The second line bears the correspondent's name; the third line, the street address or box number.
6. OUT guides have tabs slightly to the right of first position, to avoid interference with primary guides and so that OUT may be easily seen. Such guides customarily are also of a distinct color so that they stand out among the other items in the drawer.

SUPPLIES FOR THE GEOGRAPHIC METHOD

The supplies used in the geographic method are similar to those used in other storage methods. The supplies consist of guides, folders, OUT indicators, and an alphabetic card file. Each of these supplies is briefly discussed here.

Guides

Guides printed with the names of states or provinces, counties, and important cities are available for purchase from a few manufacturers of filing supplies. If such sets of preprinted guides fit the needs of the office, then their purchase may be a timesaver. However, since the needs of offices are so varied, the usual practice is either (1) to have the filer prepare labels for folder tabs and for insertion in guide tabs as needed or (2) to have the filing supplies manufacturer print a set of guides and folders to order. Additions are made in the office as they are needed, and subdivisions are made when the volume of records stored requires them.

Whatever the arrangement decided on, the primary guides ordinarily bear the names of the largest divisions. An exception is the placement of the name of the largest division, such as the name of a country or of a state, on the container label. If this is done, the primary guides can bear the names of the next largest divisions, such as states or provinces. Secondary guides are used to subdivide the divisions indicated by the primary guides.

If the guides are secured to the equipment by rods or clips and cannot be taken out of their containers by mistake, their captions need not contain the name of the largest division as well as that of the next largest division. If, however, the guides can be taken out of the drawer or off the shelf or changed in position by mistake, the guide captions need to include the name of the largest division as well as the name of the next largest division.

Folders

For every primary guide there is usually a similarly labeled general folder containing records pertaining to the geographic location indicated on the folder tab until individual folders are warranted.

Folder labels may be typed in several ways, but all folder labels should be consistent in style. The first typed line shows the *location* of the correspondent; the second line of information contains the *name* of the correspondent.

In every instance, both the name of the largest division and the name of the subdivision thereof must appear on the tabs of folders so as to insure their proper replacement in storage. Because of the duplication of city names in several states, confusion would result if state names were omitted from the folder labels. The same principle holds true for general folders. If such folders were labeled only with letters of the alphabet or with city names only, for instance, it would not be possible to determine in which geographic location they belonged without opening them to inspect the contents.

OUT Indicators

OUT guides, slips, and folders are inserted into a geographic arrangement in the same manner as they are in all other records storage arrangements. Information on the OUT indicators is arranged so that the location information is given first, followed by the correspondent's name and address.

Alphabetic Card File

An alphabetic card file is very important to a geographic storage arrangement. Correspondence may be requested by the *name* of the person or organization rather than by the address. A file consisting of cards on which are typed the names of the correspondents in alphabetic indexing order, followed by their complete addresses, gives all the necessary information when the filer must locate records without knowing the location. The usual typing format used on the cards is that shown in Figure 10-7.

```
Seligman Rose S Dr


135 Font Boulevard
San Francisco, CA  94132-4108
```

FIGURE 10-7 — Card for Alphabetic Card File

STORAGE AND RETRIEVAL PROCEDURES FOR THE GEOGRAPHIC METHOD

The same basic steps to store records in alphabetic, subject, and numeric methods (inspecting, indexing, coding, cross-referencing, sorting, storing) are also followed in the geographic method. Small differences will be explained in the following paragraphs. Retrieval procedures (requisitioning, charging out, and following up) are also basically the same.

Inspecting and Indexing

Inspecting and indexing take place at the time a record is ready to be stored. Checking to see that the record has been released for storage (inspecting) and scanning it for content to determine its proper place in storage (indexing) are always necessary. In Figure 10-8 the handwritten letters RC indicate that the letter is released for storage.

Coding

Coding in the geographic method requires marking the correspondent's *location* (address) first. Coding can be done by circling the filing segment (See Figure 10-8, Muncie, IN). The order in which the words are to be considered for alphabetizing is sometimes indicated by numbers written above or below the units. The name of the correspondent

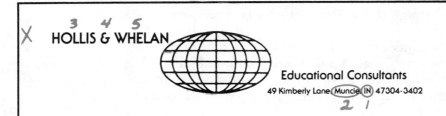

X   3   4   5
HOLLIS & WHELAN

Educational Consultants
49 Kimberly Lane, (Muncie,) (IN) 47304-3402
2 1

RC   May 4, 19--

MAY 5 19-- 9:31 AM

Dr. Ester L. Dawes
School of Business
Yorkshire University
Terre Haute, IN 47805-5410

Dear Dr. Dawes

Your request for 50 brochures explaining in detail the
programmed learning materials we have available for use in
summer workshop programs has been referred to our Pittsburgh
office.

Interest in this exciting and novel material has been
extremely high, and we have been pleased that professors
are finding it so worthwhile. Because of the extraordinary
number of requests we have had for this brochure, it is
temporarily out of stock. We expect a supply within the
next two weeks, however, and will send your 50 copies as
soon as we receive them.

Thank you for letting us provide you with helpful materials
for your workshop.

Sincerely

H. A. Hollis

H. A. Hollis
Educational Consultant

dw

2 1
Branch Office: 2964 Broadway, (Pittsburgh) (PA) 15216-7523   X

FIGURE 10-8 — Letter Coded for Geographic Method

is then coded in the usual manner (by underlining, checking, starring, etc.). Figure 10-8 shows a letter properly coded for the geographic storage method.

At this time, too, the card file is consulted to see if a card has previously been made for this correspondent. If not, one is typed (See Figure 10-9) and placed in the H section of the card file. Note that both addresses of the correspondent are typed on the original card.

```
┌─────────────────────────────┐   ┌─────────────────────────────┐
│ Hollis and Whelan           │   │ Whelan and Hollis           │
│                             │   │                             │
│                             │   │ SEE                         │
│ 149 Kimberly Lane           │   │                             │
│ Muncie, IN  47304-3402      │   │ Hollis and Whelan           │
│                             │   │                             │
│ and                         │   │                             │
│                             │   │                             │
│ 2964 Broadway               │   │                             │
│ Pittsburgh, PA  15216-7523  │   │                             │
└─────────────────────────────┘   └─────────────────────────────┘
```

FIGURE 10-9 — Original and Cross-Reference Cards for Alphabetic Card File Used with Geographic Method

Cross-Referencing

Cross-referencing is as necessary in the geographic storage method as it is in the alphabetic storage method. In Chapter 4, page 99, a list is given of the names for which cross-references are customarily prepared. In addition, cross-references should be prepared for names of companies that have more than one address and for companies located at one address and doing business under other names at other locations.

In the geographic method, cross-references are inserted into: (1) the alphabetic card file and (2) the storage containers. In the alphabetic card file, it is necessary to have a card for every name by which a correspondent may be known or by which records may be requested. For the letter shown in Figure 10-8, a cross-reference is indicated because the name is composed of two surnames. Therefore, the cross-reference card (See Figure 10-9, right) is prepared and inserted in the W section of the alphabetic card file. This cross-reference card is both a *name* and a *location* cross-reference.

In the storage containers, three kinds of cross-references may be used: (1) cross-reference sheets that are stored in folders to refer the filer to specific records, (2) cross-reference guides that are placed in storage as permanent cross-references, and (3) SEE ALSO cross-reference notations on sheets or on folder tabs. Each of these cross-references is explained below.

A *cross-reference sheet* is used to call attention to a specific record stored in a folder other than the one in which the filer is searching. The cross-reference sheet in Figure 10-10 refers to the letter shown in Figure 10-8. The letter itself would be stored in the I section of the geographic storage (for Indiana), but the cross-reference sheet would be stored in the P section (for Pennsylvania). Some filers prefer to make a copy of the record that needs the cross-reference and place the copy in the alternate folder. When this procedure is followed, the filer need not go to another part of the storage area to find the record, since a copy is at the place being searched.

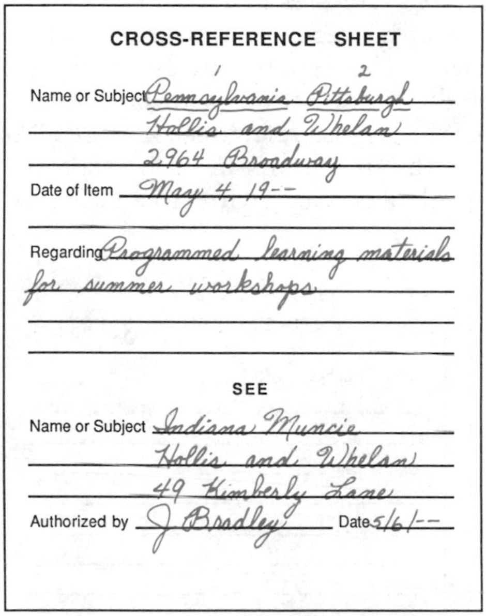

CROSS-REFERENCE SHEET

Name or Subject _Pennsylvania Pittsburgh_
Hollis and Whelan
2.964 Broadway

Date of Item _May 4, 19--_

Regarding _Programmed learning materials_
for summer workshops.

SEE

Name or Subject _Indiana Muncie_
Hollis and Whelan
49 Kimberly Lane

Authorized by _J. Bradley_   Date _5/6/--_

FIGURE 10-10 — Cross-Reference Sheet for Geographic Method

A *cross-reference guide* (See Figure 10-11) may be placed in storage to indicate to the filer that all records pertaining to a company that has several branches, for instance, are stored under the home office address. If the home office of Mortenson, Incorporated, is in San Francisco, and if a branch office is in Monterey, CA, all the correspondence may be stored under the home office location. A cross-reference guide would be placed in storage at the proper place for Monterey, CA—the guide shown in Figure 10-11. This cross-reference indicates that all records are stored

CA Monterey
Mortenson Incorporated
SEE   CA San Francisco
        Mortenson Incorporated

FIGURE 10-11 — Cross-Reference Guide for Geographic Method

under the San Francisco address even though the record bears a Monterey address. The words *San Francisco* must be written on each record when it is coded. The cross-reference guide is stored according to the location on the top line of its caption, in alphabetic sequence with other geographically labeled guides and folders.

SEE ALSO cross-references are used to direct the filer to sources of related information. If a company has two addresses and records are stored under both addresses, two SEE ALSO cross-references would be used (for instance, Wills Supply Company, Inc., in Chicago, IL, and also in Peoria, IL). The references would indicate that information is to be found in both places in storage. If these SEE ALSO cross-references are sheets of paper, they would always be kept as the first items in their respective folders so that they would not be overlooked (See Figure 10-12). Instead

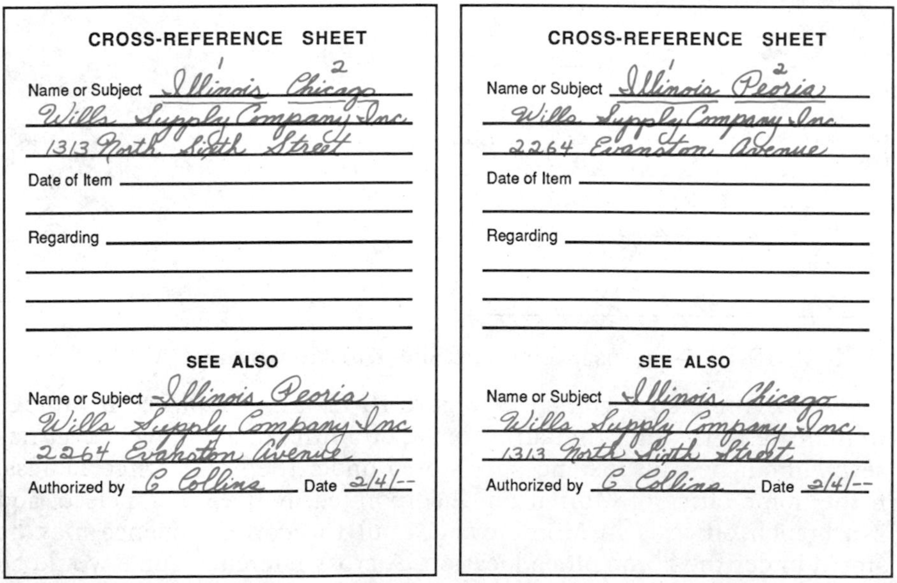

CROSS-REFERENCE SHEET	CROSS-REFERENCE SHEET
Name or Subject *Illinois Chicago* *Wills Supply Company Inc.* *1313 North Sixth Street*	Name or Subject *Illinois Peoria* *Wills Supply Company Inc.* *2264 Evanston Avenue*
Date of Item _____	Date of Item _____
Regarding _____	Regarding _____
SEE ALSO	**SEE ALSO**
Name or Subject *Illinois Peoria* *Wills Supply Company Inc.* *2264 Evanston Avenue*	Name or Subject *Illinois Chicago* *Wills Supply Company Inc.* *1313 North Sixth Street*
Authorized by *C Collins* Date *2/4/--*	Authorized by *C Collins* Date *2/4/--*

FIGURE 10-12 — Cross-Reference Sheets for SEE ALSO References

of being written on separate cross-reference sheets, this SEE ALSO information may be typed on the tabs of the two folders for the Wills Supply Company, Inc. (See Figure 10-13).

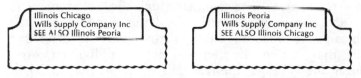

FIGURE 10-13 — SEE ALSO Reference on Folder Tabs

Sorting

Records are sorted by location, the distinctive feature of the geographic method. Records are sorted first by the largest geographic unit (perhaps a state), next by the first subdivision (such as a city), and last by the names of the correspondents, in alphabetic arrangement. The use of a rough sorter would be very helpful.

Storing

Because of the complexity of a geographic arrangement—individual correspondents' folders, special city folders, alphabetic subdivisions of cities with their corresponding general folders, general folders for alphabetic groupings of cities, and general state or regional folders—the filer must be extremely careful when storing. It is easy to place a record in the wrong folder!

Location Name Guide Arrangement.   Assuming the arrangement is by state and city, the filer first finds the state, then looks for the correct city name. If a city guide is found, the filer then searches for an individual correspondent's folder. And if one is found, the record is stored according to date.

If there is no individual folder, the record is stored in the correct general city folder according to the geographic location of the correspondent and then by name, in alphabetic order with the other records within the folder. If more than one record is stored for a correspondent, the records are arranged chronologically with the most recent date on top.

If there is no general city folder, the record is placed in the general state folder, first according to the alphabetic order of the city name and then by correspondent's name and street address (if necessary), according to the rules for alphabetic indexing.

Lettered Guide Arrangement. Again, assuming the arrangement is by state and city, the filer finds the state. The lettered guides are then used to locate the alphabetic state section within which the city name falls. After finding that section, the filer looks for an individual correspondent's folder. If one is found, the record is stored in that folder in chronologic order.

If there is no individual folder, the filer must look for a general city folder. If it is found, the record is stored according to the correspondent's name in the same manner as in an alphabetic arrangement. If there is no general city folder, the record is stored in the general alphabetic folder within which the city name falls. Again, arrangement is by city name according to the rules for alphabetic indexing.

Within a city, the names of correspondents are arranged alphabetically; and the records of one correspondent are grouped together with the most recent date on top. If there are identically named correspondents in one city, the rules for identical names are followed (See Chapter 5 for review).

When enough correspondence has accumulated to warrant making a separate folder for a certain city, a certain geographic section, or an individual correspondent, the filer removes the records from the general folder and prepares a new folder with the geographic location on its tab as the first item of information. The filer then prepares a similarly labeled guide, if one is needed, for the folder. The folder and guide are then placed in their correct positions in storage.

While the practice varies on the requirements for preparing a separate folder for a specific geographic location, a good rule of thumb is: *When five or more records accumulate that pertain to one specific geographic location (such as a state, a city, or a region), a separate folder should be made for that location.*

Retrieving

Retrieval of a record from the geographic arrangement involves these four steps: (1) asking for (requisitioning) the record, (2) searching in the storage containers to find it, (3) charging it out by some means, and (4) following up to see that the record is returned to storage within a specified time.

Requisitioning.   When a record is requested from a geographic arrangement, it may be asked for by location or by correspondent's name. If the request is made by location, finding the record should be simple. If the request is made by name, however, reference to the alphabetic card file is necessary in order to locate the address by which the record was originally stored (unless the filer's memory is superb and can supply this information without reference to the card file!).

Charging Out Records.   Once the record is located, the process of charging it out from a geographic arrangement is the same as that for charging out records from any other method of storage. An OUT indicator is inserted where a folder or record is removed.

Follow-Up Procedures.   The follow-up procedures used with the geographic method, to secure the return of borrowed records, are the same as those used with any other storage method. A tickler file or other reminder system is used to make sure that records are returned to storage at designated times and to remind the filer of records that need to be brought to someone's attention in the future.

ADVANTAGES AND DISADVANTAGES OF THE GEOGRAPHIC METHOD

As is true of any storage method, the geographic method has advantages and disadvantages. Human problems (carelessness, inattention to detail, and inexperience) may be added to the specific disadvantages discussed in the following paragraphs.

Advantages of the Geographic Method

Speedy reference to specific geographic areas to retrieve information of a geographic nature is the main advantage of geographic storage. All the advantages of alphabetic storage are inherent in this method also since this is basically an alphabetic arrangement. Many geographic systems use color as a safeguard to give the filer a check against misfiling.

The number of records generated in various geographic areas can be compared by looking at the space required by the stored records within those areas. An analysis of those records can be used in sales work to note areas with the most complaints; to note aggressive selling effort or the lack thereof; to note areas that need special attention; or to show where territories need to be combined, separated, or subdivided. If territories are changed, geographic guides and folders may be readily rearranged. Each location is a unit or a group, and the shifting of groups is relatively easy because it simply means moving an entire group from one place to another.

Disadvantages of the Geographic Method

One disadvantage of the geographic method may be the complexity of the guides and folders. Because the nature of the geographic method calls for many subdivisions, a geographic arrangement requires more time to set up than does an alphabetic arrangement. Getting records into and out of storage is time consuming because reference must be made first to an area (such as a state), then to a certain point within that area (such as a city), and finally to a correspondent's address and name.

Keeping a card file of correspondents' names arranged alphabetically is a time-consuming job. If the location of a correspondent is not remembered and no alphabetic card file is kept, much time is lost by the filer in trying to remember the address or in locating the correspondence by chance. Even with the use of a card file of alphabetized names, delay occurs because two operations are necessary in order to store material—a quick check of the card file to be sure the correspondent's name is stored correctly in it, plus the actual storage of the record in its correct geographic section. Two operations may also be necessary in order to find records—a check of the card file, if only the individual correspondent's name is given, to find the address to which reference must be made, and then the actual searching in storage for the records of the correspondent.

Misfiling can result because of the similarity of state names (Ohio and Iowa, North Carolina and South Carolina, North Dakota and South Dakota, Vermont and Virginia). If two-letter abbreviations are used, carelessness may confuse CO and CA, NV and NE, SD and SC. The frequency of identical city names within various states can also lead to misfiling. (Springfield is found in at least 18 states!)

COMBINATIONS OF THE GEOGRAPHIC METHOD AND OTHER STORAGE METHODS

Geographic arrangements are often found in an otherwise alphabetic arrangement. For instance, correspondence with ABC Company may accumulate to such volume that one folder becomes overcrowded. Inspection of the contents reveals that the correspondence concerns ABC Company in two or three different states or cities. By separating the correspondence into folders arranged geographically by state or by city, the overcrowding will be eliminated. Such an arrangement is found in Figure 10-14. The I–L–M Products folders are arranged geographically (in alphabetic order by location) by state names. A distinctively colored guide precedes this arrangement to help the filer locate that section of storage easily.

Another geographic arrangement within an alphabetic arrangement might be helpful if correspondence were received from and sent to several officers of one organization that has, for instance, a vice-president

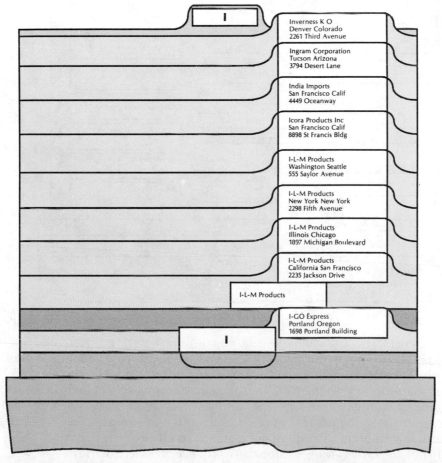

Inverness K O
Denver Colorado
2261 Third Avenue

Ingram Corporation
Tucson Arizona
3794 Desert Lane

India Imports
San Francisco Calif
4449 Oceanway

Icora Products Inc
San Francisco Calif
8898 St Francis Bldg

I-L-M Products
Washington Seattle
555 Saylor Avenue

I-L-M Products
New York New York
2298 Fifth Avenue

I-L-M Products
Illinois Chicago
1897 Michigan Boulevard

I-L-M Products
California San Francisco
2235 Jackson Drive

I-L-M Products

I-GO Express
Portland Oregon
1698 Portland Building

FIGURE 10-14 — Combination of Geographic and Alphabetic Methods

in each of several different districts. Because their terms of office are for only one year, the names of the vice-presidents are not important. The districts in which vice-presidents are located are the important filing segments. Figure 10-15 shows the five district folders of the National Office Workers, in which correspondence with the five vice-presidents is stored. The five folders are alphabetically arranged with other N folders and are also arranged alphabetically by their location names (Great Lakes, Northeast, etc.).

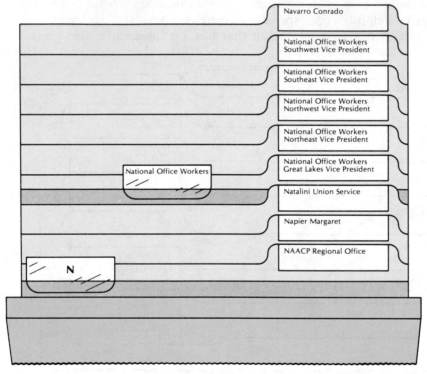

FIGURE 10-15 — Combination of Geographic and Alphabetic Methods

Geographic arrangements can be combined with numeric designations, also. One of the country's largest filing supplies manufacturers with branches in hundreds of cities combines geographic storage with the numeric arrangement. Correspondence from each branch office is stored in numbered folders, the numbers having been assigned by the home office to the names of the cities in which the branches are located. Since remembering the numbers assigned to all the cities is impossible, a list of the cities arranged alphabetically is necessary, with the assigned number appearing beside each city name. If there are identically named cities, they are arranged alphabetically by state. For instance, note the order of the following four names:

> Greenwich – 41
> Greenville SC – 93
> Greenville NC – 107
> Greensboro – 67
> (Front of file)

Unless city names are identical, state names are not used in the alphabetic listing. Within these cities, another subdivision occurs if there is more than one salesperson in the office. For instance, the number of Research Triangle Park (a city) is 235 and there are three salespeople in that office. The folders for that location would bear the following identification:

> 235 Tan Tita
> 235 Diaz A
> 235 Adams Bill
> (Front of file)

This is a numbered geographic arrangement, with alphabetic order according to salespersons' names.

The combinations of alphabetic, subject, numeric, and geographic arrangements are many. Yet the basic rules for alphabetic indexing determine placement in each of the storage methods or combinations.

IMPORTANT TERMS AND CONCEPTS

geographic storage method
lettered guide plan
location name guide plan

REVIEW AND DISCUSSION

1. How does the geographic storage method differ from the alphabetic storage method? How does it resemble the alphabetic method? (Obj. 1)

2. What types of businesses might use the geographic storage method rather than the alphabetic name storage method? (Obj. 2)

3. How does the location name guide plan differ from the lettered guide plan? (Obj. 3)

4. What is the sequence of guides and folders in a geographic arrangement where the names of states are the major divisions, with subdivisions by city and by location within the city? Use a state of your choosing to explain your answer. (Obj. 4)

5. Why is an alphabetic card file a necessity in geographic storage? (Obj. 5)

6. How do the labels on individual folders used in geographic storage differ from the labels used in alphabetic storage done by customer name? (Obj. 6)

7. What types of cross-references are used in the geographic method? Where are they stored? (Obj. 7)

8. What are the advantages and disadvantages of the geographic storage method? (Obj. 8)

9. Give two examples of the combination of the geographic method with either the numeric or the alphabetic methods. (Obj. 9)

DECISION-MAKING OPPORTUNITIES (DMO)

DMO 10-1: Selecting the Most Efficient Geographic Arrangement

Refer to Figures 10-1 through 10-6 as you complete this DMO. For each of the situations listed below, recommend a geographic arrangement and explain your choice. Be prepared to sketch a rough picture of the arrangement you recommend.

1. A large oil company has its home office in Texas. It stores correspondence and records to and from stations, refineries, suppliers, and branch offices in cities in all 50 states and in foreign countries, as well.

2. The French tire manufacturer Michelin has its U.S. headquarters in New York City. Its sales department records in NYC include distributors in many parts of the United States and Canada.

3. A professional organization has its headquarters in Boulder, CO. Its organizational structure is such that each one of its many chapters belongs to one of five geographic areas in the United States. It also has Canadian chapters and Mexican chapters as well as affiliate chapters in other foreign countries. Correspondence and other records are

stored by chapter. Because much of the organization's business is done by computer, each chapter has been assigned a number.

DMO 10-2: Checking Geographic Arrangement of Folders

The geographic storage method being used at Steve Herrara Corp. is one of state name as the first filing segment, followed by city name, then individual or organization name, and then street designation. In each of the following pairs, the folders are arranged in the order you see (reading from front to back). Are they correctly arranged? Explain your answer.

Example x.

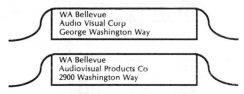

Answer: x. Wrong. *Audio* should precede *Audiovisual.*

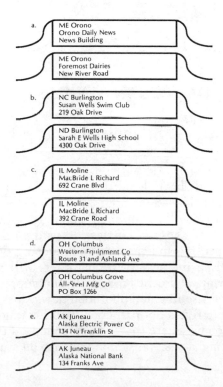

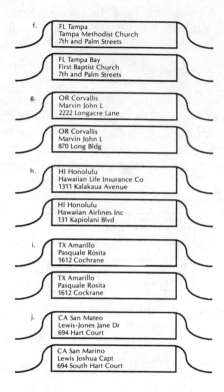

COMPREHENSIVE CASE 2

Planning, Organizing, and Implementing a Records Program for a Small Business Operation

You and two friends have decided to start a small service business. You will work during nonschool hours and on weekends, as you can, doing all sorts of jobs. You'll repair small appliances; help with moving; clean out basements, garages, and attics; do yard work; do small paint jobs and minor carpentry; and provide bookkeeping or accounting services to other small businesses. Your customers will provide all painting, cleaning, repairing, and other materials and supplies needed.

You plan to advertise in a neighborhood newspaper, *The Village Advocate*, and distribute flyers door to door. You have no office but work out of one of your rooms where there is a telephone, a typewriter, a two-drawer file cabinet, and a desk (at which you also do studying). You have no letterhead stationery or business cards but your business will be known as A–1 HELP!

Each of you has a special task, to get your business under way. One of you is taking care of setting up the books or financial records you must have. One of you is preparing the flyers and contacting the newspaper. *You* have volunteered to set up the nonfinancial office records.

Your task is to plan the type of paper records that you will be generating and will need to keep for reference and for keeping track of jobs (future, in progress, and completed). Then you must organize your thinking by doing the following:

1. List the supplies you believe to be absolutely necessary, in addition to the two-drawer file cabinet you already have. Keep your list short, as the three of you have very little money to spend.
2. Determine what method(s) of storage (filing) you believe your business should use—alphabetic, subject, numeric, or geographic. Write the reasons for your choice(s) and also why the other method(s) may not be as suitable as is/are your choice(s).
3. List the guide captions you believe will be necessary. Assume that the following customers noted on your calendar have already given you jobs:

   (1) Diaz Nissan Motors, 100 West Main—Basement cleaning
   (2) Dameron Tax Service, 151 Front Street—Painting
   (3) Ms. Dorine George, 3918 Stone Park Blvd.—Toaster repair
   (4) Navarro Asphalt Co., 118 East Main—Bookkeeping
   (5) Donald R. Ambler & Brothers, 412 West Main—Bookkeeping
   (6) Mrs. Denise Neuman, 3900 Stone Park Blvd.—Carpentry
   (7) Newman & Dorris, Attorneys, 235 Front Street—Painting
   (8) Dock and Doris De Angelo, 4200 Erwin Road—Moving help
   (9) Deborah DeAngelo-Newman, 4318 Erwin Road—Sweeper repair
   (10) D & D Office Supply, 357 Front Street—Bookkeeping
   (11) Dorton Arena Copy Center, 6900 Stone Park Blvd.—Cleaning
   (12) David L. Camp, 1400 Warren Avenue—Carpentry
   (13) C. A. M. Parts Co., 533 East Main—Painting
   (14) CAMP Costumes, Ltd., 600 Front Street—Bookkeeping
   (15) Don R. Ambler, 4208 Erwin Road—Yard work
   (16) Mrs. Daisy Newman, 1543 Warren Avenue—Yard work
   (17) Noriko Nozaki, 4301 Erwin Road—Moving help
   (18) D. J. Newmann, Chickory Downs #3—Cleaning
   (19) Mary Chan, 3906 Stone Park Blvd.—Yard work
   (20) Dr. Roger Rodriguez, 4200 Stone Park Blvd.—Yard work

4. List the order of your guides (and folders) as they will appear in your storage drawer.
5. Record the arrangement you have made for transferring inactive records—or will you have any in the near future?
6. As a conclusion to this case, list the evaluation steps you will take after you have been in business for a few months, to see if your records needs are being met.

APPLYING THE RULES

Job 13, Correspondence Storage—Geographic Method

4 – Special Records Storage and Retrieval

11 – Card Records Systems
12 – Special Records
13 – Microrecords
14 – Mechanized and Automated
      Records Systems

Part 4 centers on special records and the equipment and procedures required for storing and retrieving special records. Discussion in the first half of the Part focuses on manual records systems while the second half of the Part introduces you to two of the most important concepts in modern records management— microrecords and mechanized and automated systems for managing records.

11 CARD RECORDS SYSTEMS

After you have completed this chapter, you will be able to:

1. Compare card records with correspondence and other records, such as business forms.
2. Identify the main classifications of card records.
3. Discuss the advantages and disadvantages of card records systems.
4. Explain how vertical card systems differ from visible card systems.
5. List the typical types of equipment and supplies used in vertical card systems.
6. List the typical types of equipment and supplies used in visible card systems.

In this chapter, two types of card records are discussed: (1) vertical card records and (2) visible card records. The equipment and supplies needed to operate each card records system are also described briefly.

THE NATURE OF CARD RECORDS SYSTEMS

In every department of an organization, much frequently used information is stored on cards. A **card record** is a small piece of card stock, used for storing information, that provides the durability to withstand large-volume use. Such a card record is usually stored in special filing equipment rather than in the folders used in storing correspondence.

Types of Card Records

Card records are classified in three ways: (1) by their physical makeup or construction, (2) by use, and (3) by the filing method used.

Classification by Physical Construction.   As a rule, card records are standardized in size by the paper manufacturers. The most common sizes of cards are 5" × 3", 6" × 4", 8" × 5", and 9" × 6", with the horizontal measurement of the card listed first. Each of these sizes has been standardized so that the card fits the commonly used storage equipment to be discussed later.

Cards may be blank or have horizontal and/or vertical rulings, such as accounting journals, sales department quotation forms, medical patient histories, and the like. Cards may also be of single thickness, folded, or hinged to provide additional sides for recording information, as shown in Figure 11-1. Other cards are designed as special records and discussed in Chapter 12.

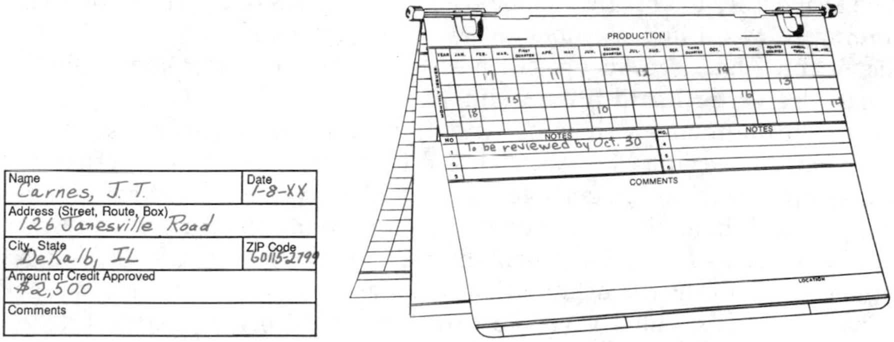

FIGURE 11-1 — Two Types of Card Records

Classification by Use. Card records that contain information used *for reference only* are called **index records**. Index records are found in most offices and contain the following kinds of information:

1. Names and addresses of customers, clients, or patients
2. Employee or membership lists
3. Names and addresses of suppliers or vendors
4. Locations of assets within the organization
5. Prospective customer lists
6. Most frequently used telephone numbers
7. Subscription or donor lists

An alphabetic card file of names and addresses of customers would be consulted, for example, in order to answer such questions as: "What is the telephone number of the Baker Insurance Company?" "What is the customer number of the Kendall Tool and Die Company?" and "What is the address of Savage, Leff, and Favor law firm?"

A second type of record classified by use is the posted record. A **posted record**, sometimes called a **secondary record**, contains information which is continually updated; that is, added to, deleted, or changed in some other way to reflect the current status. New information is posted on the card record either by hand or by machine. Examples of posted records are:

Credit and collection cards	Medical and dental record cards
Department ledger cards	Payroll cards
Hospital records	Stock control cards
Inventory cards	

Classification by Filing Method. Card records are maintained according to two filing methods. Many card records are filed *vertically*; that is, on edge or in an upright position. A collection of such records is called a **vertical card file**, or simply a *vertical file*. This is the most popular filing method—it is commonly used in filing papers as well—and is discussed in a later section of this chapter. A second method of filing cards is to store such records *horizontally* in an overlapping arrangement. When the cards overlap, one margin of the card—usually the bottom margin—is visible when the tray in which the card is held is pulled out from the file cabinet. For this reason, a collection of this type of card record is called a **visible card file**, or simply, a *visible file*. A horizontally filed card record need not be removed from the file to be used.

The information on the visible margin of the card summarizes the detailed information entered on the other areas of the card. In a lumberyard inventory file, for example, the visible margin of the card may show "2 × 4 Grade A pine," while the remaining areas of the card show a history of the receipts and withdrawals of such lumber from inventory over a period of time. Figure 11-2 shows a vertical card file and a visible card file with one record tray pulled out for retrieving information from or posting information to the record card.

In addition to cards, many visible record systems use one-line strips of card stock. The information on the strips may identify a customer name, address, or telephone number or some other readily used item from a list.

Advantages and Disadvantages of Card Records

To understand the advantages and disadvantages of card records, remember the basic difference between card records and records kept in other forms. When information is stored on cards rather than as lists of

FIGURE 11-2 — Vertical and Visible Card Files
DEMCO, INC.   *The Shaw-Walker Co.*

information on sheets of paper in a book or in a loose-leaf notebook, one main item or unit of information is stored on each card. For this reason, a card has often been called a **unit record**, a term widely used to describe the punched cards used earlier in data processing systems.

Cards as unit records offer many advantages to the records manager. These advantages include the saving of space because of their size and the easy visibility of the record; one employee can work with a great deal of information without changing position. Also, cards are handled more easily than are papers because of the more uniform size of cards; and the thickness of cards, compared with that of paper, makes handling easier.

Card records offer several other advantages over records that are maintained on sheets of paper as lists of information that are subject to frequent change. With only one key information item, such as a customer name or the name of a cataloged library book, on each card, information is easy to locate. If a change occurs in the address of a customer, or if a new book is added or an old book removed from the library stacks, the new information can be quickly inserted and the obsolete information deleted, crossed out, or the card physically removed from the file.

Because only one main item of information appears on each card, the information on such cards can be easily rearranged in any sequence desired. For example, assume that a sales department's information needs require that customer name cards be arranged alphabetically by customer name. At another time, the cards are rearranged by customer name according to the numeric codes assigned to products purchased. In a third instance, the cards are rearranged geographically by the sales territories in which each customer is located. Cards can also be divided into groups or stacks, which permits several records clerks to use the entire file at once.

Card record systems also have disadvantages. For example, cards that are removed from the file can easily get out of sequence, especially when a stack is dropped. Small-size cards are easily lost, misfiled, or misplaced when removed from the file. Under certain conditions, it may be difficult to add, delete, or change information on a card without removing the card from the file; and in manual systems, it is sometimes difficult to type information on the top or bottom margins of the card. When information is recorded on cards from another document, errors can easily occur if the person posting the information is careless or inattentive to detail. Time is also required to transfer information from one record to another.

EQUIPMENT AND SUPPLIES FOR CARD RECORD SYSTEMS

The equipment and supplies required for card record systems depend solely on the type of filing method—vertical or visible—used. The equipment and supplies used in both types of card record systems are discussed in this section.

Vertical Card Systems

Remember that vertical card systems store records "on end," as compared with the type of storage used in visible systems. To operate an effective vertical card system, manufacturers provide special equipment and supplies, the most important of which are explained here.

Equipment.   Cards may be filed vertically in two types of housing or filing equipment: (1) manual equipment that includes drawers, boxes, trays, and rotating wheel equipment; and (2) motorized or power-driven equipment.

Drawer Cabinets.   Perhaps the most widely used housing for vertical card records is the **drawer cabinet**, which has drawers similar to but smaller than correspondence file cabinet drawers. Filed records rest on their longest edge in these files; thus, the 8″ edge of an 8″ × 5″ card rests on the bottom of the drawer. In cases where card records are used in conjunction with other types of records, such as correspondence, a file cabinet is selected that provides drawers for vertical card record storage and other drawers that accommodate business forms or correspondence. Such cabinets may be purchased in many heights, ranging from two to six or more drawers (See Figure 11-3).

FIGURE 11-3 — Drawer Cabinet for Vertical Card Storage
DEMCO, INC.

Boxes.   Boxes of heavy cardboard are sometimes used to store card records, which are most often found in 5″ × 3″, 6″ × 4″, and 8″ × 5″ card sizes. Box files are commonly used for home and small-office record storage (See Figure 11-4).

Trays.   Card records may be stored on trays, either individually as shown in Figure 11-5, or as a set of multiple trays placed side by side. Such an arrangement makes the trays portable. Individual trays may be removed from the multiple group of trays for use on the desktop or for storage in a desk drawer, or for distribution of trays to various departments in the firm. A mechanized version of tray storage is discussed in

FIGURE 11-4 — A Two-Drawer Cabinet and a Box File
Gaylord Brothers, Inc.

a later section of this chapter. By mixing card and tray sizes, a variety
of card records may be stored in a mechanized unit.

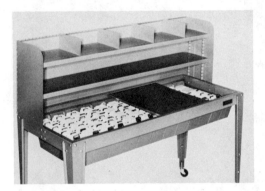

FIGURE 11-5 — Tray Unit for Storing Card Records
E-Z-Way Systems

Rotary Wheel Equipment.   Two types of rotary wheel equipment
are used for storing card records: (1) wheel files and (2) rotary file cabinets. **Wheel files** provide an arrangement in which the card records are
attached directly to the equipment frame that is operated manually or
driven by motors. Such equipment provides storage for card records and
guides that are snapped into place over a center rod, and the records are
kept within bounds by the outer rims of the wheel. Wheel files may
contain one or more rows of card records side by side. Figure 11-6 shows
one row of records in a small, compact desktop unit. The entire file is
rotated by hand to the position of the desired record. Wheel files are
frequently used for storing inventory records, price lists, name and address lists, and so on.

FIGURE 11-6 — Single-Row Wheel File
Rolodex Corporation

Larger versions of rotary wheel equipment, called **rotary file cabinets**, are also available. These cabinets rotate horizontally around a hub, as shown in Figure 11-7, an arrangement that permits several persons to access the file at the same time. Records kept in such files require less floor space than would be needed to house the same number of records in drawer cabinets. Such files, placed between workstations, eliminate

FIGURE 11-7 — Rotary Files
Delco Associates, Inc.

walking, since the cards can be rotated to the persons who use them. Fewer misfilings occur because fatigue, discomfort, and poor visibility (often found when using drawer cabinets) are reduced. Also, records need not be duplicated since one set of records can serve several departments; and sliding covers with locks are available on some models for making the records more secure.

Motorized Card Record Equipment. **Motorized** or **power-driven card record equipment** provides shallow trays on movable shelves for the storage of records. Such shelves are powered by an electric motor and mounted on a frame inside the cabinet using a revolving motion similar to the operation of a Ferris wheel. Any shelf can be brought to the front of the machine by pressing one or more of a series of buttons mounted on a control panel. Figure 11-8 illustrates such a motorized unit with trays of cards appearing in a horizontal side-by-side arrangement. The trays can, if desired, be removed from the shelves; or the operator may consult the card records without removing any of the trays from the unit.

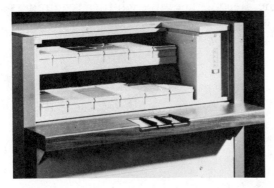

FIGURE 11-8 — A Motorized Card Record Storage Unit
Kardex Systems, Inc.

Supplies.   In the typical correspondence system, records are stored in folders that act as separators between the many records stored. In vertical card files, since no folders are required, cards are filed upright and separated by guides into the desired sections. Guides and signals are the main supplies used in vertical card systems.

Guides.   Guides used in vertical card files are much the same as those used in correspondence files, varying only in size. Therefore, in order to separate cards into sections, guides are available for cards filed in drawer cabinets, boxes, trays, rotary wheel equipment, and motorized records storage equipment. Guides also help the filer to file the cards in an orderly fashion and, when needed, to locate quickly the section of the file in which the requested record is stored. In vertical card record systems, the guide tab is visible, protruding above the height of the card.

The most important consideration in selecting guides is durability, which in turn depends on the type and weight of the guide material. Guides are made from various materials. However, bristol board or pressboard is usually used for guides in vertical card record files. The thickness of the stock used for guides is referred to in terms of *points*, a point being 1/1000 of an inch. The greater the number of points, the thicker and more durable the paper. Common thicknesses of paper stated in terms of points are shown as follows:

> 11 points = heavyweight paper
> 14 points = extra heavyweight paper
> 17 points = bristol board
> 25 points = pressboard
> 35 points = fiberboard

Vinyl guides in opaque colors are also available for vertical record files. Vinyl guides are washable and will not warp, crack, or become dog-eared from extensive use—problems that may develop if paper-based guides, such as bristol board or pressboard products, are used.

Signals.   Two types of **signals** are used in vertical card record systems to convey to the filer special information about the cards. Special add-on or clip-on markers of movable transparent or opaque materials are frequently attached to the top of selected cards. In other cases, a distinctive color is placed on the signal, on the tab, or on the cards themselves, and different colors may be used to show different types of information on the marked cards. For example, the names of customers in a certain geographic area may be indicated by green cards. Signals draw immediate attention to the cards bearing the identifying markers and thus speed up the location of such special card records. Signals are shown in Figures 11-2 left, 11-9, and 11-13.

Visible Record Systems

The kinds of equipment and supplies used for visible records depend on the following factors: (1) the requirements of the organization as reflected by the number of cards or strips to be filed; (2) the importance of their location to their use; (3) whether the files must be portable, that is, able to be carried from one location to another for use; (4) the frequency of use; and (5) whether the visible records are to be used for reference or for posting purposes.

Equipment.   The main types of visible card equipment are (1) card visible equipment, and (2) reference visible equipment. Each type of equipment is discussed in this section.

Card Visible Equipment.   A number of different forms of **card visible equipment**, often called **posting visible equipment**, are available. The most frequently used visible equipment is the cabinet with shallow drawers or trays, each one labeled to show the contents. Each drawer contains a number of overlapping cards held horizontally by hangers or hinges or in slots called **pocket holders**. Figure 11-2, page 269, shows such equipment with drawers that can be pulled out and down but that remain attached to the cabinet by a hinge. Card holders are attached to the trays by wires that snap in and out of the drawer. Cards are held in by slots in the holders, and both sides of the card may be used.

By raising the set of cards preceding the card that requires posting, the filer can quickly post the desired information on the card. Note the insert in Figure 11-9 that shows an example of the contents of the visible margin on such a card. In this case, the name identifies a customer in the credit department of a manufacturing company.

Cards are inserted into the holders so that one or two lines of each card are visible. Pocket holders are slotted to accommodate cards of various sizes. Some holders have transparent edge protectors, while some have the complete pocket made of transparent material. This see-through covering protects the edge or the entire card from wear, tear, moisture, and dirt.

When portability of cards is a factor and the volume of cards to be filed is small, or when many employees need to post simultaneously, **hinged pocket books** may be used instead of other methods of storage. These card books may have fastenings at the top of the cards for ease in posting, or the cards may be snapped in and out at any point. Looseleaf books with removable panels of cards provide portability and contain much data in a small space. Labeling of the contents of the book is done on the back binding.

Racks and cabinets are used to house card books. On the racks, books stand in an upright, closed position with the aid of bookends. Cabinets have compartments, and the books are stored in an upright position. The cabinet may revolve so that several persons can refer to the information.

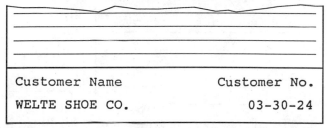

Customer Name	Customer No.
WELTE SHOE CO.	03-30-24

FIGURE 11-9 — Common Type of Visible Record Cabinet and Illustration of Contents of Visible Margin on the Card

Acme Visible Records

Reference Visible Equipment. If only one line or a few lines of information are needed for reference purposes, using an entire card on which to record a small amount of information is unnecessary and wasteful. In such cases, **reference visible equipment** in which information is placed on narrow strips of card stock that are inserted into holders attached to panels, trays, or frames is used. Figure 11-10 shows one-line strips of information on panels attached to a revolving center post. The insert in the figure illustrates a common use of such one-line strips—a name and address list of members of a farmers' cooperative society. This is **single tier rotary equipment**, but double and triple tiers are also available.

Square rotary units that provide four reference sides at once may be purchased. With round rotaries, when one frame is in use, all other frames

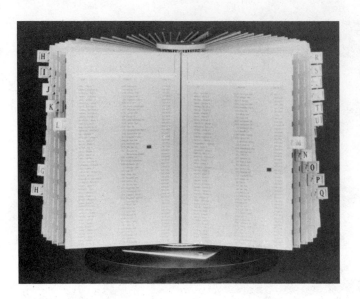

Kane, Jay	121 W. Main St.	761-2963
Keller, May	206 E. Olive	842-8880
Kitler, J. H.	R.R. 8	531-3061
King Farms	R.R. 1	290-7349
Kuster, P. T.	R.R. 5	651-2003

FIGURE 11-10 — Single Tier Rotary Visible Equipment with Illustration of Contents of One-Line Strips

Acme Visible Records

are automatically compressed. See Figure 11-11 for a desktop stand for visible reference files with one reference side.

Room for expansion is provided at the top of each panel; and as names are added, the strips may be shifted upward since each strip is simply snapped into place. Removal of a strip allows the strips above it to shift downward.

Panels of these visible strips may be arranged in book form, in the form of flip-up indexes, or on stationary panels. Strips ordinarily are purchased in sheet form with perforations between them. They may be typed on, separated, and flexed into place (See Figure 11-12), or they may be inserted into transparent tubes that are then snapped into position in the trays.

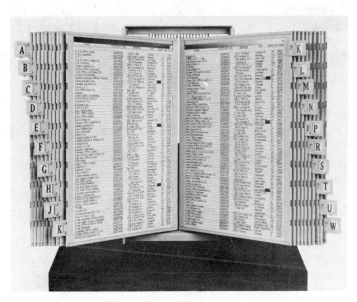

FIGURE 11-11 — Desk Stand Visible Strip File
Acme Visible Records

FIGURE 11-12 — Placing a Strip in a Visible File
Acme Visible Records

Other types of cabinets have more than one panel of horizontally held cards within the same drawer, to increase the capacity of the equipment. The capacity varies with the size of the equipment and the size and thickness of the cards used.

The features of well-constructed visible record equipment include:

1. Glare-free finishes
2. Trays on nylon or ball-bearing rollers for quick, effortless gliding
3. Easy hand grips on the front of the trays
4. Large label holders on the trays for easy visibility and quick reference
5. Low side edges on the trays for reduced interference in posting activities
6. An almost flat lay-back angle of posting-record equipment (See Figure 11-13)
7. 1/4-inch to 1/2-inch visible margin exposure on cards
8. Protection on the bases of desktop equipment to prevent marring and slipping (thick corrugated rubber pads or small rubber "bumpers" or knobs attached to the equipment).

Supplies.   Visible records housed in horizontal trays do not need guides. When the trays are pushed into their cabinets, labels on the front of the trays indicate the range of the tray contents. Thus the only guides used for visible records are those found on strip file panels in vertical equipment such as that shown in Figure 11-11. Guide tabs at the sides of the panels are the primary dividers that indicate the range of the names on each panel. Upright visible frames used for constant reference should have several places for label holders along their edges so that the information may be speedily read from both sides.

Visible card systems also use signals or markers that call attention to some specific condition or content of the card. Signals that may be used with visible equipment include colored card stock, special printed edges that may be cut in various ways, and removable metal or plastic tabs of various colors and shapes (See Figure 11-13). Paper strips along the edge of the card may be tinted in many different colors. Other methods of signaling include perforations in the card edge to allow different colors to show through from color tabs inserted behind the holes. Card corners may be clipped to indicate special information. Some cards are made so that their tabs can be progressively cut (half cut when the name is a prospect, for instance, and one-fifth cut when the prospect becomes a customer).

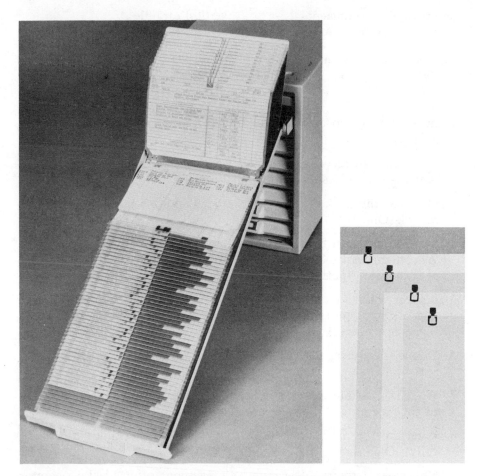

FIGURE 11-13 — Signals Used in Visible Card Systems
Acme Visible Records

IMPORTANT TERMS AND CONCEPTS

card record
card visible equipment
drawer cabinet
hinged pocket books
index records

motorized/power-driven card record
   equipment
pocket holders
posted record/secondary record
posting visible equipment

reference visible equipment   vertical card file
rotary file cabinets   visible card file
signals   unit record
single tier rotary equipment   wheel file

REVIEW AND DISCUSSION

1. In what ways do card records differ from correspondence records? (Obj. 1)

2. How are card records classified? Give an example of a card record that fits each classification. (Obj. 2)

3. Describe the nature and purpose of an index record and a posted record. (Obj. 2)

4. Explain the term *unit record* as it is used in card record systems. What significance does this term have for the use of cards as holders of stored information? (Obj. 3)

5. List the main advantages and disadvantages of card record systems. Discuss which of the two—advantages or disadvantages—outweighs the other. (Obj. 3)

6. Define the concept of vertical filing as it is used in card record systems. (Obj. 4)

7. What is a visible card system? When could such a system be used to good advantage? (Obj. 4)

8. What are the main types of equipment used for filing cards vertically? (Obj. 5)

9. How does a rotary file cabinet arrangement offer special operator efficiency that is not offered by other types of vertical card equipment? (Obj. 5)

10. Explain the operation of motorized or power-driven card record equipment. What type of information is needed in order to justify buying and using this type of equipment? (Obj. 5)

11. Why are guides and signals used in a vertical card system? (Obj. 5)

12. What types of equipment are commonly used in visible card systems? (Obj. 6)

13. Identify the main types of supplies used in card record systems. What skills are needed for working efficiently with visible card equipment and supplies? (Obj. 6)

DECISION-MAKING OPPORTUNITIES (DMO)

DMO 11-1: Analyzing the Use of Card Record Systems

To get a broader understanding of the use of card record systems in either manual or automated systems or both, go to your school or community library. Observe carefully the following aspects of such systems: (1) the types of information on each of the catalog cards that record each book stored in the library; (2) the kinds of guides and signals provided in each card drawer and the purposes of each; (3) the use of visible files and why they are used instead of vertical card records; (4) to what extent mechanized or power-driven record systems are used; and (5) any problems that you are able to detect in the use of these card record systems.

Take detailed notes on your observations to be used for class discussion or for other forms of class assignments as outlined by your instructor.

DMO 11-2: Selecting Filing Equipment and Supplies for a New Business

Two former graduates of your school, Rita Montez and Tami Osaki, have recently visited your instructor on campus. During their visit, these women asked the instructor for help in selecting filing equipment and supplies for a new business (to be called Info-Shopping Services) they are starting in the basement of Osaki's home. The main service to be offered by this new firm is that of providing rapid answers to persons and business organizations in the surrounding community of 200,000 regarding the names and addresses of organizations and their products—information that is not readily available from the Yellow Pages of the telephone directory or from the Chamber of Commerce. Retail, wholesale, and manufacturing information will be provided as well as an over-the-phone shopping service. Handicapped persons and senior citizens who cannot leave their homes will be able to call in orders for food, clothing, and other staple merchandise items for delivery to their homes by high school youths. Local businesses will finance this new firm.

Your instructor feels that this request offers an excellent learning challenge to your class. Thus, class members individually are asked to complete such a decision-making assignment in two closely related parts:

1. To develop a set of questions that your class as problem solvers would need to ask Montez and Osaki before you could make specific suggestions to them about what filing equipment and supplies are needed.

The guidelines for selecting equipment and supplies discussed in various chapters of this textbook would be useful for completing this first phase of your assignment. Other records management, office management, and systems references can be found in your college and community libraries as aids in securing additional information.

2. To make some practical assumptions about the types of information that persons using the services would request. Put yourself "in their shoes." For example, assume that most requests would be made over the telephone. Assume, too, that many of the callers would be calling before going to work in the morning or after returning home from work in the late afternoon or early evening. Thus, certain forms would be needed and appropriate files for filing such forms. Other assumptions about typical *calls* and typical *callers* must be made.

Be prepared to discuss orally the answers to your assignment (take some appropriate notes to class), in written form as specified, or in both oral and written form. Your instructor will provide detailed instructions and deadlines.

12 SPECIAL RECORDS

Objectives

After you have completed this chapter, you will be able to:

1. Define special records.
2. Identify the methods of storing common accounting records.
3. Compare the methods of storing drawings and other large special records with the methods used to store legal documents.
4. Cite several examples of magnetic records and indicate how these records are stored.
5. Discuss the usage of photographic records and the types of equipment used for storing and retrieving such records.
6. Explain how published materials, such as books and catalogs, are stored and why each is stored in that way.
7. Compare the procedures for storing and retrieving special records with the procedures for storing and retrieving common records.

The two most common types of records discussed earlier in this book are correspondence and business forms. As a rule, these records appear in paper form, frequently in 8 1/2" x 11" size for letters and many business forms, or as heavier card stock as discussed in Chapter 11.

Special records are files of unconventional size, shape, or weight commonly used in business and professional offices. Such records often cause difficulty for the filer who does not have an effective method of storing these items so that they can be found quickly. Therefore, efficient methods of storing each of the many types of special records are needed and are discussed in the first section of this chapter. The second section reviews briefly storage and retrieval procedures as they are applied to special records.

METHODS OF STORING SPECIAL RECORDS

Many of the special records discussed in this section have been created because of the advances made by technology in the office. Thus, microfilm technology has created its own types of special records, and automated offices produce large volumes of computer output that require special types of files. These records and their storage systems are discussed in Chapters 13 and 14, respectively.

In traditional offices, special records continue to be produced and used in large numbers. These records are special because they differ in size, shape, and construction from the regular office records and are stored in specialized equipment. The nature of the information, especially the manner by which the information is retrieved, dictates how these records are stored.

Accounting Records

Noncomputerized offices continue to use large numbers of records that are prepared by hand or by relatively simple machines, such as typewriters and accounting machines. Of special importance are those records, such as cash receipts journals and ledgers, that store administrative information about the accounting system—a system that is vital to the survival of the organization. Two of the most common accounting records—checks and vouchers—are discussed in this section.

Checks.   Although automated operations in banks and other financial institutions are changing the check-handling procedures, the typical method of handling canceled checks still requires many manual operations. As a rule, canceled checks are returned by a bank to its customers along with a list of all deposits and withdrawals.

Business firms usually store returned checks in small drawers housed in vertical record storage equipment. Usually checks are stored according to the number on the check, which is typically chronologic in nature. Lightweight portable boxes can be used for storing a small volume of checks. Figure 12-1 shows typical equipment for storing checks.

Vouchers.   **Vouchers** are documents used in business to confirm that a business transaction has occurred. Vouchers are usually larger than checks but smaller than correspondence and are stored alphabetically or numerically in special equipment in keeping with the size of the vouchers. For example, vouchers 8" x 5" in size would be stored in drawers of a corresponding size near the workstation.

FIGURE 12-1 — Equipment for Storing Checks
Kardex Systems, Inc.

Drawings

Large organizations with highly specialized departments require a wide variety of nonstandard records. For example, art and advertising departments store posters, art prints, tracings, and other types of graphic art. Also, engineering departments commonly use blueprints, charts, maps, and other types of drawings some of which are very large and bulky. Maps and engineering drawings are often rolled and stored in pigeonholes for convenience. However, this practice is not recommended because rolled records are difficult to use after they have been rolled for any length of time.

For storing large flat items, two methods are recommended: (1) placing the records in flat shallow drawers in cabinets made for this purpose, and (2) hanging the items vertically using hooks or clamps. Figure 12-2 shows a type of flat-file cabinet commonly used for storing bulky records. The labels on the drawers show the range of the contents, arranged either by alphabet or number.

Legal Documents

Many of the records maintained in the offices of attorneys are different in size from those found in nonlegal offices. In fact, 8 1/2" x 14"

FIGURE 12-2 — A Flat-File Cabinet for Storing Large Records

paper continues to be called "legal size" and is widely used for legal records, such as abstracts, affidavits, certificates of incorporation, contracts, insurance policies, leases, and mortgages. Frequently legal-size records are stored in document boxes on open shelves. Numbers are assigned to the boxes, and an alphabetic card file and accession book are required as discussed in Chapter 9. These boxes are labeled appropriately to show their contents.

Magnetic Records

In addition to the special records stored on paper, many offices store information on magnetic records. Perhaps the most commonly used magnetic records are the cassettes and other media used for storing dictation. A growing number of records stored on tape, disks, and diskettes are used in data processing and word processing systems. Chapter 14 treats these automated systems records in detail.

Cassettes.   **Magnetic tape cassettes** are small containers in which magnetic tape is stored for the convenience of the dictator and transcriber to facilitate immediate playback and dictation. Also, cassettes protect magnetic records against dirt and destruction. Several equipment options for storing cassettes may be used:

1. Albums or binders with molded plastic page forms that can hold six or eight cassettes on each side of a page are available (See Figure 12-3A). Cassette albums and binders are stored on shelves.
2. A hanging panel may be used that fits into conventional desk drawers. Each panel holds six or eight cassettes.
3. Carousels (rotary storage devices) may be chosen. Carousels are often placed on desk tops for easy reference (See Fig. 12-3B).
4. Small shelves into which cassettes will slide are also popular. Cassettes are housed in their own plastic holders.
5. Desk or table drawers or cabinets are also used for cassette storage. Drawers having dividers are available to separate cassettes (See Figure 12-3C).

Each of the pieces of equipment discussed in this section must have labels affixed to an outer surface to show the contents of the cassettes being stored. Labeling may be by subject, name of the person dictating, name of the person transcribing, date of the dictation, or the cassette number. Cassettes are usually labeled on their flat, broad surfaces; however, the edges of the plastic containers holding cassettes may be correspondingly labeled so that each cassette can be quickly retrieved and later returned to its proper place in the file.

Other Dictating Machine Records.   In addition to cassettes, plastic belts and disks are used to record and store dictation. After these magnetic records have been transcribed by the word processing operator or typist, they are usually retained for a specified period of time. Temporary storage is usually provided in boxes, drawers, or folders and arranged chronologically by date of dictation or by record number. Sometimes, too, these "used" records are arranged alphabetically by the names of the dictators.

Photographic Records

Cameras are used to photograph many types of records, some of which are highly specialized in nature. However, only the most common photographic records are discussed here.

A. Album
Dennison National

B. Carousel
Luxor Corporation

C. Drawer
Luxor Corporation

FIGURE 12-3 — Equipment for Storing Cassettes

Films and Filmstrips. Motion-picture films are commonly placed in canisters that are stored vertically in open wire racks. These photographic records may be stored alphabetically by subject or film title or numerically by film number. Thus, when a numeric storage system is used, an alphabetic card file is required for reference to titles or subjects; and an accession book is necessary for assigning numbers. The equipment used for storing motion-picture films is similar to that used for storing computer magnetic tapes shown in Figure 14-7, page 339.

Filmstrips are ordinarily kept in cabinets with shallow drawers to hold the small metal containers, as shown in Figure 12-4. The drawers may have compartments formed by adjustable or fixed dividers. The top of the small container is labeled for identification of the contents in much the same way as the large motion-picture film canisters are labeled. Like films, filmstrips are stored using subject, alphabetic title, or filmstrip number; and each drawer is labeled to show the range of its contents.

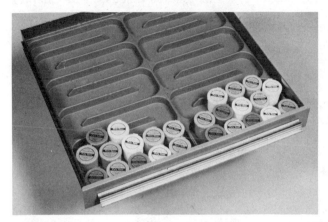

FIGURE 12-4 — Filmstrip Storage
Luxor Corporation

Slides.   Slides are usually stored in boxes with compartments, or in ring binders. Oblong or rotary slide trays that fit into a projector may store in sequence all slides relating to one subject, with the tray being labeled to indicate the subject. Numbered slots in drawers in which slides may be stored correspond to numbers written on the slides. In addition, a master list of numbers with slide identification is kept either on cards or on separate sheets of paper. A microcomputer, if available, may be used to maintain an inventory of these records.

Published Materials

Large organizations maintain extensive libraries related to the special interests and needs of their personnel. Small offices, too, store many types of published materials. The most common methods of storing published materials, such as books, catalogs, periodicals, and pamphlets, are discussed briefly in this section.

Books. To save office space and still provide convenient access, books should be stored in bookcases or on other types of shelves. Books may be arranged alphabetically by book titles or by the names of their authors, or numerically by the decimal method. As a rule, books are labeled on the back binding or spine. Frequently used reference books, such as dictionaries and secretarial office manuals, are kept at the workstations where the reference books are used. Charge-out procedures, similar to the procedures used for other types of records discussed in Chapter 7, should be developed to ensure proper control over these important and expensive records.

Catalogs. Catalogs are highly useful references and need to be carefully stored in the office. Office equipment catalogs, educational program catalogs, and catalogs representing a growing number of mail-order firms are examples of the types of printed publications that require storage in the office.

Catalogs are best housed on shelves or in bookcases. The following procedures have proved effective for storing catalogs:

1. Place the catalogs in alphabetic order by the names of the firms issuing the catalogs. Also, prepare a separate subject card file listing the names of all firms issuing catalogs on each specific subject.
2. Assign numbers to the catalogs according to the order of their receipt and store them numerically. An accession book to use when assigning numbers and a card file are necessary. Such a file contains (a) cards showing the names of the firms in alphabetic order, with their assigned numbers, and (b) subject cards listing by number all catalogs on a given subject.

Frequently the publishers of catalogs send supplements to their catalogs rather than publish an entirely new catalog, thereby saving considerable publishing and mailing expense. Since these supplements often contain but a few pages and therefore are quite flimsy, file folders are used for storage to provide the needed rigidity. When this practice is used, the folders are labeled according to the storage system used (alphabetic, numeric, etc.) and stored adjacent to the respective catalogs.

Periodicals. Periodicals, or magazines, comprise a growing problem for office managers and records managers. Current issues of magazines are usually kept in stacks and arranged in chronologic order by date of publication, with the most recent issue on top. The order of the stacks on the shelves is usually alphabetic by magazine name. Sturdy fiberboard or metal boxes with open backs may also be used to house current issues to keep them from becoming worn and dusty. Some publishers sell boxes with the names of their magazines already printed on them, in which case only date information need be added to the label on the back of the box. These boxes are stored chronologically by date of publication.

Pamphlets.   Pamphlets cannot be stored satisfactorily side by side on shelves or in drawers. Therefore, storing pamphlets in folders according to subjects is recommended. Pamphlet folders are stored in alphabetic order by subject.

PROCEDURES FOR STORING AND RETRIEVING SPECIAL RECORDS

Steps required to store and retrieve special records are the same steps needed to store and retrieve other manually processed records. However, special records have certain unusual features that more traditional records do not possess. These special features affect the procedures for storage and retrieval. In this section, an abbreviated discussion of storage and retrieval procedures is presented.

Inspecting Special Records

The step of inspecting special records requires much more time than does the inspection of regular paper records. This is the case because many special records are used with mechanized equipment that will not function properly with damaged records. Inspection of special records means checking to see if the record is in good condition or damaged as well as determining if it is complete in all respects. Also, such a record should be inspected to be sure that it is clean, properly encased (if a protective cover is required), and that the record bears a cross-reference to its source if it is a partial copy or excerpt of an original.

Indexing Special Records

The indexing step requires carrying out the same procedures that are used to index and classify regular paper records. The filer analyzes the contents of the record to determine under what category the record should be classified and stored.

Coding Special Records

In the efficient records system for regular as well as special records, coding is always done. Because of the wide variety of special records, coding procedures will vary also. For example, coding could involve gluing a number on a canister holding film, labeling by subject envelopes containing photographs, or affixing labels to the backs of books. The purpose of coding, however, is always the same—to make the task of storing records easy as well as to facilitate the task of replacing in storage a record that has been charged out and returned.

Cross-Referencing Special Records

In some instances, special records do not require cross-references, for such records are so unique that there may be only one place for them to be stored. If, however, a record is requested by an alternate name, by a subject, or by number, a cross-reference should be prepared and inserted in the alphabetic card file or the subject listing in the usual manner. Chapter 4 contains detailed information on cross-referencing procedures.

Sorting Special Records

If a number of special records of the same type must be stored, a separate sorting procedure will save time when the filer takes the records to the equipment to be stored. For instance, if fifteen numbered filmstrip boxes need to be stored, arranging such boxes in sequential order in a carrying tray would save time at the storage cabinet.

Storing Special Records

Special records should be stored as soon as possible after they are approved for storage. Because they are unusual and often bulky, special records may be unsightly and give a cluttered, inefficient appearance to the office if they are allowed to accumulate over long periods of time. Care must be taken to turn all special records of the same type in the same direction (covers of books facing forward and spines of magazines readable from the same direction, and so on). And because of the varying sizes of special records, as discussed earlier, large records frequently must be stored alongside small records. Thus, the filer needs to be alert to see that the smaller records do not get crushed among the larger ones.

Retrieving Special Records

The efficient retrieval of special records will follow these steps:

1. Whenever a special record is removed from storage to be used by someone other than the filer, a requisition form should be presented.
2. After the record is found and removed from storage, an OUT or IN USE indicator is inserted in place of the borrowed item.

With this information on hand, the office manager or records manager knows where every record has gone, when it was taken from storage, and when it is due to be returned.

IMPORTANT TERMS AND CONCEPTS

magnetic tape cassettes
special records
vouchers

REVIEW AND DISCUSSION

1. What are special records? How do they differ from correspondence and business forms? (Obj. 1)

2. Describe how bank checks are filed. According to your present knowledge, to what extent are the banks in your community using manual bank-check storage or automated systems of storage? Explain. (Obj. 2)

3. What is a voucher? How are vouchers filed? (Obj. 2)

4. Besides checks and vouchers, what other special accounting records may be stored in the office? How is each stored? (Obj. 2)

5. What are some of the large, bulky records that are frequently stored in organizations? In what departments are such records typically stored and used? (Obj. 3)

6. How do legal documents, as discussed in this chapter, differ in size, purpose, and storage equipment required from the large, bulky records mentioned in Question 5? (Obj. 3)

7. What types of magnetic records are used for dictation purposes? (Obj. 4)

8. List several storage options for cassette records. (Obj. 4)

9. Identify three types of records that are produced by photography. How is each type of record stored? What procedures would you follow to retrieve each of these records from storage? (Obj. 5)

10. How are books and other published materials stored in the office? Why should office personnel be concerned about these records since each is usually associated with a library? (Obj. 6)

11. What particular problems are associated with the storage of magazines and pamphlets that do not arise in the storage of books? (Obj. 6)

12. In what ways are special records coded? How does the coding process for special records differ from the way common records are coded? (Obj. 7)

DECISION-MAKING OPPORTUNITIES (DMO)

DMO 12-1: Storing and Retrieving Personal Checks

Assume that you have an active personal checking account—that is, one against which you write from 35 to 50 checks each month. Because you frequently refer to your canceled checks once they are stored, it seems important to install an efficient system for storing and retrieving such valuable records.

Based on this information, make sound decisions for answering these questions:

1. What types of systems information (volume of checks written, how they are retrieved, and so on) do you need to complete this assignment?

2. What storage equipment and supplies are needed to maintain such a file?

3. How long should such records be retained?

Report your answers as directed by the instructor. (Objs. 2 and 7)

DMO 12-2: Planning Special Records for a New Department Office

In answering this DMO, you are asked to make some management decisions about equipping the special files for a new academic (teaching) department responsible for business communication courses. Assume that this department's office area must provide space for a department chairperson and a secretary. For this assignment you need to know what courses are taught and what types of instructional materials (films, transparencies, etc.) are used as well as the special administrative records that may be used.

Assume that the department chairperson and the six instructors use many audiovisual materials, most of which are stored in the department office since they are owned by the department. For teaching dictation skills, magnetic records are used; and the overhead projector and film projectors are used on a daily basis.

In order to simulate the kinds of decisions made by a department chairperson, you will need to provide answers to the following questions:

1. What kinds of special records would probably be stored in this department office?
2. What types of equipment and supplies would be needed for storing such records?
3. What information should be considered in order to estimate the costs of such equipment and supplies?

Answer these questions in a short memo report to your instructor. (Objs. 4, 5, and 6)

13   MICRORECORDS

After you have completed this chapter, you will be able to:

1. Define the following terms: micrographics, microrecords, and microforms.
2. Identify the four requirements for ensuring microfilm quality.
3. List the most common microforms and their uses.
4. Explain the steps required to produce computer output microfilm (COM) and computer input microfilm (CIM).
5. Outline the general steps involved in filming, processing, and duplicating a microrecord.
6. List ways of protecting microrecords from the hazards found in storage and usage environments.
7. Describe the types of procedures and equipment used in storing and retrieving microrecords.
8. State the differences between basic and advanced computer-assisted retrieval (CAR).
9. Outline important management considerations regarding when to use microrecords, how to determine the legality of microrecords, and how to evaluate microrecord systems.
10. Describe microrecord applications in large and small firms.

Paper records discussed in earlier chapters continue to grow at an increasing rate, causing major problems for the records manager, even in the computer age. To save space and increase efficiency, many companies are microfilming their records, an important process that is discussed in nontechnical terms in this chapter.

The microfilm process creates miniature or micro (very small) images of records called **microrecords.** The full range of services for creating, storing, retrieving, using, and protecting microrecords is known as **micrographics.** These microrecords, in turn, may be packaged in a variety of convenient and easily usable forms—**microforms**—of which the most common varieties are *roll film, microfiche, microfilm jackets,* and *aperture cards*. Because a single unit or file of records may be contained on one microfiche, on a jacket, or on an aperture card, these microrecords are called **unitized microforms**. Each of these microforms is discussed later in this chapter.

MICROFILMING

The microfilming concept is simple. It involves the use of an appropriate type of camera to photograph records and reduce them in size for storage. To be used, the microrecord must be enlarged to the original record size and projected on a viewing screen. Special procedures and equipment for using a microrecord are required, as will be discussed later in this chapter. In addition, special types of film must be used and a high level of microrecord quality must be maintained if the microrecord system is to fulfill its purposes.

Sizes of Film

Microfilm comes in various widths measured in millimeters (mm) of which the three most common are 16mm, 35mm, and 105mm. The narrowest film (16mm) is most frequently used for filming small documents, such as checks and standard- and legal-size records. When larger records, such as newspapers, maps, and engineering drawings, are filmed, 35mm microfilm is used; 105mm microfilm is commonly used in the preparation of microfiche.

Microfilm is also available in various lengths and thicknesses. The length of microfilm varies from 100 feet to over 200 feet. The thickness may vary from .06mm to .175mm. Consequently, the thinner the film, the greater the number of feet of film that can be stored on a standard reel.

Microfilm Quality

Microrecords must be carefully prepared, filmed, processed, and protected during storage and retrieval in order to represent a true facsimile of the original record. Four factors relating to the filming process are (1) resolution, (2) density, (3) reduction ratio, and (4) magnification ratio.

Resolution.   **Resolution** is a special microfilm term that refers to the sharpness of lines or fine detail on a microimage. To ensure good resolution, a high quality of film and a camera with a good lens are required. Resolution is an important factor, for there must be good, clear images on the microrecord so that when it is enlarged, clarity of detail is not lost.

Density.   **Density** is a numeric measure of the contrast between the dark and light areas of the film as determined by a device called a **densitometer**. A high-quality microrecord has a wide variation in the dark and light areas of the film. The higher the contrast, the easier it is to read the images on the microrecord.

Reduction Ratio.   The term **reduction ratio** refers to the size of the microimage as compared to the original document. A ratio stated as 24 to 1 (usually shortened to 24X) means that the image on the film is 1/24th the size of the original record. Reduction ratios range from 5X to more than 2400X, although the most common reduction is 24X. The higher the reduction ratio, the smaller the images, and the greater the number of images that can be photographed on one square inch of film. For example, 8,100 regular-size bank checks can be photographed on 100 feet of microfilm at 24X reduction and 16,600 such checks at 50X. An interesting example of the reduction ratio is shown in Figure 13-1 in which all 773,746 words in the Bible are reduced to this incredibly small space. This microrecord can be read with appropriate reading equipment.

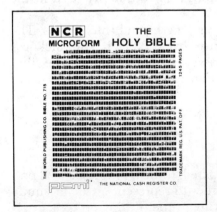

FIGURE 13-1 — The Bible in Microform
NCR Corporation

Magnification Ratio.   In order to be read by the user, a microrecord must be enlarged or magnified. The **magnification ratio** describes the relationship between the size of the microrecord and the enlarged record on a microfilm reader screen. For example, a one-inch square microrecord that is magnified ten times (a magnification ratio of 10X) appears in its enlarged form as ten square inches.

MICROFORMS

Early usage of microrecords was on rolls of film. As time passed, manufacturers developed a wide variety of other forms on which filmed records are made, stored, and used.

Each microform shown in Figure 13-2 has a wide range of applications to meet special needs of an office. Microfilm, microfiche, jackets, and aperture cards are discussed in detail in this chapter, as these microforms are the most commonly used.

Roll Film

The most inexpensive microform is **microfilm,** a roll of film containing a series of pictures or images much like a movie film. Roll film is normally used for information that needs to be stored in sequence, such as employee records. A 100-foot roll can hold up to 4,000 images. These images may be either positive (black characters on a clear background) or negative (white characters on a black background).

Typically roll film is used to photograph records that are not used frequently or records that do not require changes. Large volumes of information can be stored on film in very little space at low cost. If changes in records do not occur often, such changes can be made by cutting out the old information and splicing in the new film. However, such changes in the film are expensive and may weaken the film as well as make it inadmissible as legal evidence in a court of law.

Reels of 16mm microfilm are used primarily for storing rolls of microrecords containing alphabetic and numeric data, such as correspondence, checks, and invoices. The wider 35mm reels of film are used for storing microrecords of larger documents, such as maps, X rays, engineering drawings, and newspapers. This type of packaging provides **file integrity**—the assurance that none of the documents filmed in sequence is lost or misfiled.

Microfilm **cartridges,** as shown in Figure 13-2, serve as convenient packages for rolls of microfilm and permit automatic threading of the film into the viewer. Cartridges are plastic film cases that protect the film from fingerprints and other possible sources of damage. **Microfilm cassettes** provide even greater convenience for the handling of continuous rolls of microfilm. Each cassette contains two film reels—the feed and the take-up—which eliminate the need for rewinding a cassette when it is removed from a reader.

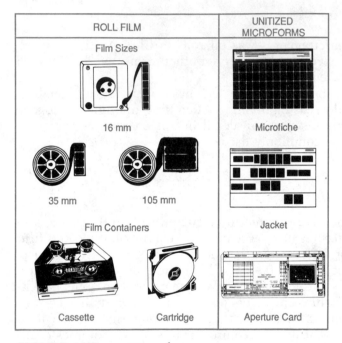

ROLL FILM	UNITIZED MICROFORMS
Film Sizes	
16 mm	Microfiche
35 mm 105 mm	Jacket
Film Containers	
Cassette Cartridge	Aperture Card

FIGURE 13-2 — Microforms

Microfiche

Microfiche, usually shortened to *fiche* and pronounced "feesh," is the French word for *index card*. Fiche is a sheet of film containing a series of microrecords arranged in rows and columns on a card. Although fiche is available in a variety of sizes, the 6″ × 4″ fiche is most commonly used and has been designated by the microfilm industry as the standard-size sheet. The maximum number of images that can be contained on a fiche depends on the amount of reduction. Most fiche are filmed at ratios ranging from 18X to 24X. At a 24X reduction, 98 original documents can be stored on one microfiche, arranged in a grid of seven rows and fourteen columns. Most commonly, 16mm film is used in the preparation of standard microfiche. Recent product developments enable microfiche to be updated so as to provide a current record for use in the office. **Updatable microfiche** permits changes to be made in the records stored on microfiche.

In Figure 13-3, notice the arrangement of pages (labeled "Pa") in each section (labeled "Sec") in an employee handbook. Another common method of arranging records on microfiche is to film documents in a continuous series by rows. Because the title (heading) at the top of the fiche is easily readable by the user, fiche can easily be stored and retrieved manually, similar to index cards.

Employee Handbook (contents of)													126
Sec 1	Sec 2		Sec 3			Sec 4							
Pa 1	Pa 1	Pa 7	Pa 1	Pa 7	Pa 13	Pa 1	Pa 7						
Pa 2	Pa 2	Pa 8	Pa 2	Pa 8	Pa 14	Pa 2	Pa 8						
Pa 3	Pa 3	Pa 9	Pa 3	Pa 9	Pa 15	Pa 3	Pa 9						
Pa 4	Pa 4	Pa 10	Pa 4	Pa 10	Pa 16	Pa 4	Pa 10						
	Pa 5		Pa 5	Pa 11	Pa 17	Pa 5	Pa 11						
	Pa 6		Pa 6	Pa 12	Pa 18	Pa 6	Pa 12						index of fiche contents

FIGURE 13-3 — Layout of Images on a Microfiche

Fiche can be mailed easily and economically, just as can any 6″ × 4″ cards. With developments in color photography, fiche can be produced in colors closely resembling the colors on the original records. Color fiche can be viewed without eyestrain longer than can black and white pictures. Topographical maps filmed in color hold more information for the user. With advertising brochures and sales kits filmed on color microfiche, sales representatives do not have to carry heavy sample cases.

Jackets

A **jacket** is a plastic or card-stock carrier with single or multiple horizontal channels into which strips of 16mm or 35mm microfilm are inserted. With the use of a jacket, strips of film are protected and are easily organized into units of information similar to microfiche. The jacketed film may be duplicated without removal from the jacket. In addition, new microrecords may be inserted into the jacket, and index titles or headings identifying the jacketed strips can easily be placed at the top of the microform for easy storage and retrieval. Jackets are widely used for microrecords of personnel and medical records, as well as for correspondence, legal, customer, and policyholder files. Figure 13-4A illustrates the layout of microrecords for storage in standard card jackets approximately 6″ × 4″ in size. Figure 13-4B shows an example of a jacket that combines microrecords with identifying information about the insured client in a savings and loan institution.

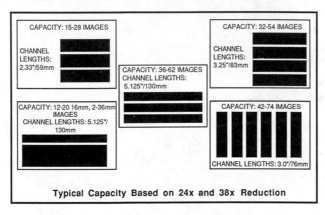

A. Standard Microfilm Jacket Layouts

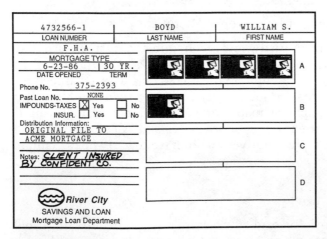

B. Card Jacket Ready for Use

FIGURE 13-4 — Microfilm Jackets

Aperture Cards

An **aperture card** is a standard data processing card (7-3/8″ × 3-1/4″) with a precut opening (aperture) for mounting microfilm. The most commonly used aperture card contains a single 35mm engineering drawing or blueprint. Aperture cards for storing 16mm film (See Figure 13-5) hold up to eight images. Four letter-size (8-1/2″ × 11″) pages can be included within the aperture at a reduction ratio of 16X; and up to 400 pages can be contained in an aperture at a reduction ratio of 160X on 16mm film.

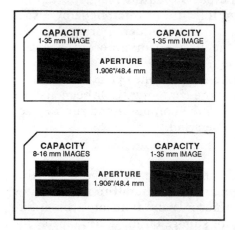

FIGURE 13-5 — Aperture Cards for 16mm and 35mm Film

Identifying information may be keypunched into an aperture card and at the same time printed along the top edge as a heading to serve as an index for storage and retrieval. Aperture cards are easy to update since they require only the removal of the obsolete card and the substitution of a new one. Interfiling new cards or replacing cards within a file of cards can be accomplished quickly.

Many large businesses and government agencies use aperture cards to store maps and other drawings, X rays, and business records. Firms have found that the principal disadvantage of using aperture cards is cost. The expense of card supplies, mounting, and the fact that fewer images can be stored on each aperture card than on microfiche, makes the costs of using aperture cards higher than the costs of other microforms. Filing space requirements for aperture cards are estimated to be at least five times greater than those of a file of records maintained on roll film.[1]

---

[1]Katherine Aschner, ed., *Taking Control of Your Office Records* (White Plains, NY: Knowledge Industry Publications, Inc., 1983), p. 75.

Computer-Related Microrecords

Two processes enable the computer to assist in the production and use of microrecords. They are: computer output microfilm and computer input microfilm.

Computer Output Microfilm. **Computer output microfilm (COM)** eliminates the need to print hard copies of paper records before filming the records. With COM, computer output stored on magnetic tape is converted to visual images on 105mm roll film or microfiche by a special tape-to-film photographic device, called a **recorder**. During this process, the computer output record is reduced to microrecord size and indexed for use in retrieval.

Figure 13-6 shows the steps involved in an **offline** operation in which the filming is not directly connected to the computer. COM can also be performed **online** — directly connected to the computer and run as a sequential automatically photographed operation.

Computer Input Microfilm. The computer can also be used with records already on microfilm. **Computer input microfilm (CIM)** takes plain language (uncoded) data on microrecords and translates this information into computer-language code for storage on magnetic tape as input to a computer. This new application of computer power to the field of microrecords holds great promise for firms with large numbers of records requiring automated input to the computer.

PROCEDURES AND EQUIPMENT FOR MICRORECORD SYSTEMS

A **microrecord system** refers to a combination of key elements that form an efficient unit for using records in microform. Of special importance in this system are the several levels of personnel, discussed in Chapter 2, who are responsible for developing and operating the procedures and equipment needed in the microrecord system. Basic procedures and equipment required for this system are discussed in this section and shown in Figure 13-7.

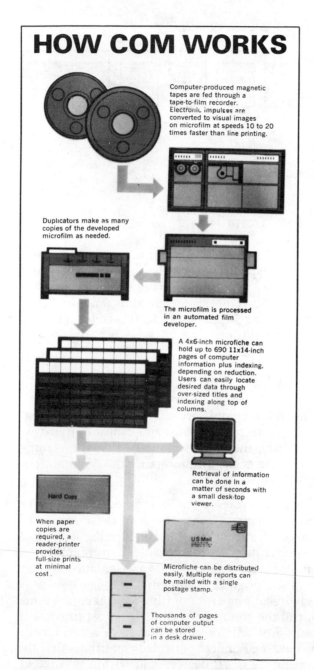

HOW COM WORKS

Computer-produced magnetic tapes are fed through a tape-to-film recorder. Electronic impulses are converted to visual images on microfilm at speeds 10 to 20 times faster than line printing.

Duplicators make as many copies of the developed microfilm as needed.

The microfilm is processed in an automated film developer.

A 4x6-inch microfiche can hold up to 690 11x14-inch pages of computer information plus indexing, depending on reduction. Users can easily locate desired data through over-sized titles and indexing along top of columns.

Retrieval of information can be done in a matter of seconds with a small desk-top viewer.

Hard Copy

When paper copies are required, a reader-printer provides full-size prints at minimal cost.

US Mail

Microfiche can be distributed easily. Multiple reports can be mailed with a single postage stamp.

Thousands of pages of computer output can be stored in a desk drawer.

FIGURE 13-6 — An Offline COM Operation
DATACORP

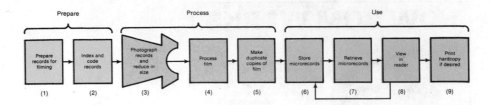

FIGURE 13-7 — A Microrecord System

Preparing Documents for Microfilming

Documents must be carefully checked before filming to ensure that the camera will function properly. This means that all paper clips and staples must be removed. Records to be filmed may need mending; and attachments to records, such as envelopes, routing slips, and duplicate copies of records should be removed. Records should also be batched and placed in sequential order before filming.

Maintaining a Controlled Environment

With constant handling, microrecords are subject to dirt, abrasion, fingerprints, contamination by foreign materials, and exposure to excessive light and temperatures. It is, therefore, important that the records manager be alert to the following needs for protecting the environment in which microrecords are stored:

1. Microrecords require the same preservation and protection measures observed for other types of records. A discussion of these measures appears in Chapter 2, page 43, "Preserving and Protecting Records." The term **file security** is often used in this regard when microfilm is relied upon for duplicating irreplaceable records as assurance against the loss or destruction of the original documents.
2. Because of the unique chemical properties of film, special precautions need to be taken to control the storage environment. Most important are temperature and humidity. Microrecords that have a permanent retention period should be stored under controlled conditions that include a maximum temperature of 70 degrees and within a range of 30 to 40 percent relative humidity.

3. Film reels and paper enclosures or attachments to the film should be constructed from special materials that are free from acids and other contaminants that can cause destructive chemical reactions on film.
4. If possible, film should be stored in sealed containers. If this is not possible, then the air in the storage room should be carefully controlled by an air-filtration system to remove abrasive particles and gaseous impurities that can harm the records.

Service bureaus specializing in the storage and preservation of microrecords are available in most large cities, in case the business organization cannot, or does not wish to, provide such controlled environmental conditions.

Providing Efficient Equipment and Procedures

It is important to understand the basic equipment required and the main functions that micrographic equipment performs. Figure 13-7 identifies the main phases in the microrecord cycle—filming, indexing and coding, processing, duplicating, reading, storing, and retrieving—and for each of these phases, equipment is needed to operate the microrecord system.

Filming Equipment.   For filming large-volume records, such as checks and invoices, a **rotary camera** is frequently used, primarily because it is the least expensive method of filming records. Rotary cameras use rotating belts to carry documents through the camera and make images on 16mm film at speeds exceeding 500 documents per minute.

A **planetary camera** uses 35mm film to microfilm oversize engineering drawings, hardbound books, and other large documents placed upon a plane (flat) surface. Filming with this type of camera is much slower than with a rotary camera since the original documents must remain stationary during filming and are photographed one by one. Hence, filming is more expensive than with the rotary camera, but a higher quality image is produced.

The **step and repeat camera** is used to film microfiche. This camera films images directly onto a 4"-wide film, which, when cut into 6" lengths, produces a standard-size master microfiche of 6" × 4" each.

In systems requiring frequent changes in the records— as in maintaining spare parts inventory records—an **updatable microfiche camera** (a modification of the step and repeat camera) is available. With such a camera, additional images can be added to a microfiche at any time if unexposed space exists on the fiche. Also, such a camera can alter existing images by overprinting such words as VOID and PAID.

Indexing and Coding Microrecords. The indexing process takes on an additional meaning in microfilming as well as in automated record systems discussed in Chapter 14. In such nonpaper record systems, indexing refers to the process of assigning some type of identification, such as an address, to each microimage. The film address may also include the film roll number, the microrecord frame number, or other type of identification for locating the microimage. Microrecord indexing is accomplished either at the time of filming when a terminal operator, stationed adjacent to the microfilm camera, assigns identifiers during the filming process. Or, the index may be prepared after filming. In this case an operator places a roll of microfilm into a retrieval terminal, views each image, and assigns an identifier by keying into the computer memory the identifier and the sequential number assigned to the microimage.

The term *index* may also refer to the list of microrecords on roll film, on a microfiche, or in an aperture card file. In this sense, an index operates like a telephone directory, which can be considered an index (list) of all telephone subscribers in the community.

Finding a microimage is rather easy if its address, as provided by the location index, is known. Several common methods of indexing are discussed in the following paragraphs.

Flash Indexing. **Flash indexing,** sometimes called *flash target coding,* is used on roll film (See Figure 13-8). Each 100-foot length of film is divided into sections or batches of information in the same way that divider tabs are used to separate the sections of information in a notebook or that guides are used with folders in a file drawer. Usually the arrangement of records is predetermined, that is, based on the original order of paper records in the file. An example is employee records in a personnel office arranged consecutively by employee number. Prior to filming the records, a **flash card** (a kind of tab or guide for a microfilm record file) with identifying information is placed in front of the batch. In a personnel office employee record file, a batch of information might

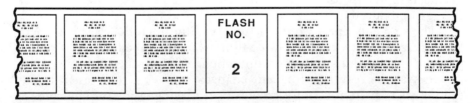

FIGURE 13-8 — Flash Indexing
Introduction to Micrographics (*National Micrographics Assoc., 1974*)

be the records for 50 employees. The records of 1,200 employees would have 24 batches requiring 24 flash cards in the file. The container in which the film is housed is then marked to show the batch position and the contents of each batch.

Image-Count Indexing.   The fully automated system for retrieving microrecords discussed later in this chapter uses **image-count indexing** to retrieve microrecords from roll film. At the time the film is recorded, a rectangular mark (blip) is placed below or above each microimage. When a specific document is requested, its image number is located in the index, and the retrieval device counts the "blipped" frames at a rate of up to 700 frames per second until it reaches the correct image. For example, a document filmed for a 16mm cartridge can be indexed in six to seven seconds and later retrieved in about thirty seconds. The original filming takes about three seconds, and a copy can be made in ten seconds. Thus, the whole process can be completed in less than one minute (See Figure 13-9).[2]

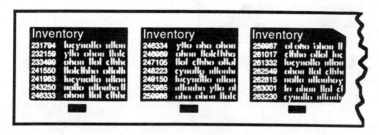

FIGURE 13-9 — Image-Count Indexing
Source: See footnote, p. 314.

Unitized Microform Indexing.   For indexing unitized microforms— microfiche, jackets, and aperture cards—an easily readable title at the top of the microform can be created by the camera or added manually. The title usually includes the name of the document and the microrecord sequence number.

Unitized microforms are coded in various ways to speed up the retrieval process. Color coding of microfiche, jackets, and aperture cards is accomplished by adding a band of color to the title or heading area of the microform. Such a color code is attached to a batch of records or to an entire file to identify a selected type of record. Misfiled microrecords can be readily identified if they are placed in the wrong batch.

---

[2]David Pomerantz, "Computer-Assisted Retrieval," *Today's Office* (April, 1983), p. 48.

Unitized microforms may also be coded in other ways. **Notching** involves cutting a small piece out of the top or bottom edge of the microform after it has been created. Each notch can be assigned a subject, range of numbers, or names. When a notch is used in conjunction with color coding, each notch position may represent a subject category within a major category represented by the color. Tabs can also be attached to microforms, usually along the upper edge, to represent coded information. When each tab in a file is assigned a specific major category similar to the tabs used in paper systems, retrieval of microforms that are filed within each tabbed category is facilitated.

Figure 13-10 shows several methods of indexing and coding unitized microforms.[3] Other methods of coding unitized microforms are discussed in advanced records management and microfilm publications.

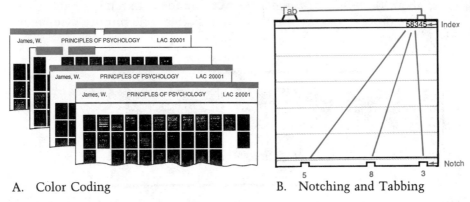

A. Color Coding   B. Notching and Tabbing

FIGURE 13-10 — Indexing and Coding Unitized Microforms
Source: See footnote below.

Processing Equipment.   After the images of the original document have been recorded on film, the film must be processed in a darkroom. Some film can be developed in regular light and therefore requires no special processing room or equipment. Inexpensive processors are available for in-house processing. More complex film processing is usually performed by commercial microfilming companies.

Duplicating Equipment.   Frequently several copies of microforms are needed. Small organizations send original microforms to commercial mi-

---

[3]The fundamentals of indexing are well covered in *An Introduction to Microform Indexing and Retrieval Systems* (Silver Spring, MD: National Micrographics Association, now called the Association for Information and Image Management, 1980).

crographic service agencies for duplication; larger firms may produce duplicate copies within the firm on special duplicating equipment.

Duplicators that are simple to operate are available. For example, a fiche-to-fiche duplicator may be placed beside a fiche file where employees can make duplicate copies for their own use. Such a practice permits several employees to use one microrecord file at the same time.

Reading Equipment. To read information stored on a microrecord, special equipment is needed. A **reader** is a device that displays the enlarged microimage on a screen so that the record can be read. Two types of readers are available: stationary (or desktop) readers and portable readers.

A **stationary reader** provides a larger screen for viewing and a wider choice of optional features (such as a hood for reducing glare) than portable readers. Some desktop readers permit the simultaneous viewing of two pages. Some readers accept only one kind of microform while others allow a number of different microforms (film, fiche, aperture cards) to be used. An example of a typical stationary reader is shown in Figure 13-11.

FIGURE 13-11 — Stationary Reader
Micro Design, Bell & Howell Company

A **portable reader** is lighter in weight than a stationary reader, usually weighing less than 10 pounds. One version of portable reader, the **lap reader,** is often used with microfiche in cars, on outdoor job sites, or in service vans. Such a reader can be powered by dry cells, by automobile battery, or operated off the cigarette lighter of a vehicle. Small hand-held viewers are also available for browsing microfiche rather than for intensive reading (See Figure 13-12).

FIGURE 13-12 — Portable Reader
Micro Design, Bell & Howell Company

Some readers, called **reader-printers**, serve dual purposes—for reading and for printing a hard copy. With such equipment, users can make a hard copy of the microrecord seen on the viewing screen. The hard copies generally range in size from 8-1/2″ × 11″ to as large as 18″ × 24″. When larger sizes are desired, an **enlarger-printer** must be used.

Storage Equipment.   For each type of microform, various storage containers are available. Typical examples of such storage equipment are shown in Figure 13-13.

Records photographed on 16mm or 35mm film are stored on reels or in cartridges or cassettes, as shown in Figure 13-2. In turn, these containers are stored in boxes on shelves or in cabinets partitioned to fit the boxes. Carousel arrangements of partitioned shelves are also common, and there are small desktop units or floor units from which to choose. Figures 13-13A and 13-13B show a conventional microfilm drawer cabinet and a carousel-type unit, respectively, for the storage of roll film, cartridges, and cassettes.

A. Microfilm Cabinet
Wright Line Inc., Worcester, MA

B. Cartridge Carousel Unit
Business Efficiency Aids, Inc.

FIGURE 13-13 — Microrecord Storage Equipment

An even wider variety of equipment is available for storing microfiche. Common examples of such equipment, as shown in Figures 13-14 and 13-15, are desktop trays and rotating stands for the use of fiche records at the workstation. In addition, fiche are frequently stored in three-ring binders and in drawer cabinets.

FIGURE 13-14 — Microfiche Desktop Storage Tray
Fellowes Manufacturing Co.

FIGURE 13-15 — Microfiche Rotating Desktop Stand
DEMCO, INC.

Since aperture cards are stored vertically, the equipment to house them is the same as for other vertical cards discussed in Chapter 11. Usually aperture cards are stored in drawers the size of the cards, as shown in Figure 13-16.

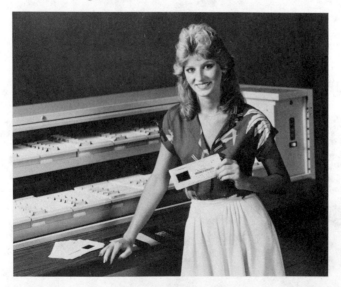

FIGURE 13-16 — Aperture Card Drawer Storage
Kardex Systems, Inc.

Plastic jackets and card jackets can be stored in the same type of housing equipment as microfiche. Desktop trays or visible filing equipment similar to the equipment discussed on page 278, Chapter 11, are commonly used.

Retrieval Equipment. In the manual systems for handling microforms, the main piece of equipment is the reader. Thus, for finding microrecords on reels, cartridges, or cassettes, no extra equipment is required. Nor is any special equipment required for retrieving fiche and jackets in the manual system. Aperture cards, on the other hand, may be retrieved by hand, or more quickly by a mechanical sorter that reads (decodes) the record-storage information that is punched into the cards.

In addition to manual methods of retrieval, the computer is also used to retrieve microrecords. **Computer-assisted retrieval (CAR)** is the process of merging the computer (for great speed in storing and searching data) with microrecord storage. It has been estimated that such storage is 500 times less expensive than the storage of data on computerized magnetic tape. Using CAR, incoming paper records are microfilmed, usually in random sequence since precise sorting of records is not required. During filming each paper record is assigned a sequential location number (address) that corresponds to the location of its microfilmed image. The microrecord address and other key information, such as record title or subject, are entered into the computer. This information becomes the computer index to the microfilmed records.

Two types of CAR systems are in use. **Basic CAR** systems store microrecords in regular storage equipment according to the location code index stored in the computer. To retrieve a microrecord from this basic CAR system, the user inputs the appropriate record identification into the computer terminal. Next, the computer searches its memory to find the location code of the microrecord. The computer terminal screen then displays the location number (page and frame numbers of microfiche, for example) or the frame number and cartridge or roll number of the microfilm record. With this information available, the user manually retrieves the microrecord container from the file for use in the reader.

In contrast to the basic CAR system with its *online* index for *offline* retrieval, an **advanced CAR** system maintains the index, record storage, and retrieval processes online. Using advanced CAR, the user registers the appropriate retrieval-request information in the terminal. The computer then searches its index and directs its micrographic retrieval device to locate and display the proper internally stored microimage on the terminal screen. COM-prepared microrecords may also be retrieved in this way. Figure 13-17 shows an advanced CAR system using a mini-computer.

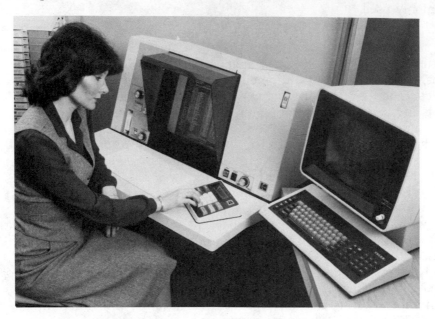

FIGURE 13-17 — Computer-Assisted Retrieval Using a Minicomputer
Eastman Kodak Company

MANAGEMENT CONSIDERATIONS

Three critical questions must be answered by managers who are considering the use of microfilmed records:

1. When should microfilm be used?
2. Are microrecords legal instruments in courts of law?
3. How can a microrecord system be evaluated?

In this section, answers to these questions are briefly discussed.

When to Use Microrecords

Experienced users of microrecords suggest that paper documents be microfilmed whenever most or all of several conditions are found. Paper documents should be converted to microrecords when:

1. *Considerable space can be saved.* Great savings in space can be achieved when microfilming is used, with the actual amount depending upon the reduction ratio used. As many as 3,000 standard-size 8 $\frac{1}{2}$" × 11" letters or 40,000 bank checks can be placed on 100 feet of 16mm film with obvious savings in storage and floor space.
2. *The records system can be made more efficient.* Microfilming large bulky materials, such as engineering or architectural drawings, eliminates serious storage and mailing problems. And with greater use of the computer in microrecord systems, much faster retrieval of microrecords can be achieved compared with the retrieval of paper documents.
3. *Microfilmed records can be preserved as long as paper records.* In a carefully controlled environment, records stored on microfilm can be protected and preserved for decades with estimates extending to hundreds of years. When the other advantages of microrecords over paper records are considered, this additional fact strengthens the case for film.
4. *The costs of microfilming, storing, and using microrecords are lower than the costs of using paper records.* The main microfilming costs include cameras to film the original records or similar costs of having the records filmed by an outside service agency; processors, duplicators, and necessary supplies; readers; storage and retrieval equipment; space for the preparation, storage, retrieval, transportation, and use of microrecords; overhead costs, such as climate control, telephone, and insurance; labor costs for performing the operating, supervisory, and managerial level responsibilities.
   Rules of thumb suggest the following:
   a. If a record is to be retained 3 years or less, it costs less to keep the record than to film it.
   b. If a record is to be retained from 4 to 7 years, it *may* be less expensive to keep the record than to film it.
   c. Records kept from 7 to 15 years should be considered for microfilming if the records are accessible and there is a cost benefit of saved storage space.
   d. Records kept on a permanent basis need to be microfilmed. Typical paper records yellow and show other signs of deterioration after a number of years.
5. *The document can be microfilmed successfully.* Remember that:
   a. Blurred copies do not microfilm well.
   b. Colors on original documents may not microfilm.
   c. Defects on the original documents may be magnified on the microrecord.

Even though microrecords have many advantages over paper documents, users find several disadvantages that need to be studied. For example, continuous or prolonged use of microrecords requiring a reader is difficult for groups or conferences; and only one person at a time can view the record on the reader. Comparing microrecords with related paper documents (such as purchase requisitions with related purchase orders) is difficult as problems often arise in getting the related records together. Indexing of microrecords presents another problem as the indexing may not be accurate or understood by a user trying to locate a record. Under such conditions, finding specific microrecords is time consuming. Often, too, the fixed location of readers is a problem since the user must go to the reader, which wastes time.

Legality of Microrecords

The most important piece of legislation on whether microrecords are fully admissible as evidence in a court of law is the Uniform Photographic Copies of Business and Public Records as Evidence Act of 1951. As passed by the Congress, this act allows microfilmed business documents to be admitted as evidence in courts of law if the following conditions are met: (1) if the microrecord was made from an original document in the regular course of business; (2) if the microrecord was photographed from an entire record to make identification of the original document easy; and (3) if the microrecord is legible enough to constitute an accurate representation of the original record.

In order to ensure the legality of microrecords, micrographics specialists recommend that records managers maintain logs to verify the accuracy of the microfilming process. Also, they recommend completing certificates of authenticity and statements about the identity of the records for each set of microrecords. A form available from the American National Standards Institute (ANSI) can be filmed and added to the beginning or other designated place in each set of microrecords. In addition, specific state legislation should also be checked. Many states consider microrecords inadmissible in court when the record involved is a negotiable instrument, such as a stock or bond.

Evaluation of Microrecord Systems

In all types of organizations, managers are responsible for evaluating how well their systems are performing. In an evaluation, the specific performance of the employees as well as the effectiveness of the equipment, the procedures, and the space used are compared with the objectives set for each of these elements in the system.

Adequate records are needed to confirm how much money is spent on the program as well as on the volume of records created, maintained, and destroyed. Records managers also need information from all departments on how frequently they have used microrecord files and how much they plan to use such files in the future. Procedures, too, must be studied. For example, it is important to know how well the procedures for converting paper records to microform are functioning; how well the equipment meets the needs of the office; and how efficient is the space devoted to the microrecords operations.

The general guidelines for evaluating records management programs, discussed in Chapter 2, page 36, can help lay the groundwork for evaluating a microrecord system. And in offices where the physical facilities and specialized staff do not permit in-house filming or storage of microrecords, a service bureau needs to be considered. The choice of such a facility can best be made by considering its reputation for service, its turnaround time, the safety (security) of the storage facilities, the ease of storing and retrieving the records, and the cost of using these services.

MICRORECORD APPLICATIONS

A large organization requires more paperwork to send information within its home office, to its branches throughout the country, and to its customers, than does the small firm. To manage more effectively their paperwork problems, both large and small firms take advantage of microrecords.

Microrecords in Large Firms

Microrecords have proved to be valuable tools for managing information in all business fields. Applications common to most industries are accounts receivable, accounts payable, and personnel records. In addition, each industry has developed applications to fit its own special needs, as discussed briefly in the following paragraphs.

1. *Government Applications.* The Social Security Administration handles several hundred million earnings items a year on 100-foot film

cartridges, each containing the complete files of 1,000 individuals. The U. S. Patent Office has converted 20 million patent records to microfilm which it uses to process the 25,000 daily requests for paper copies of the patent records.

2. *Insurance Applications.* Applications in the insurance industry range from indexing of policy numbers on CAR systems for immediate retrieval of microrecords to payment histories and policy status records.

3. *Consumer Services Applications.* Many retail stores maintain inventory records on microfiche. Oil and credit card companies keep their customer accounts on microfilm with retrieval time for providing customer service information at 20 seconds.

4. *Scientific Applications.* Hospitals place patients' histories on microfilm to provide reductions in space requirements and savings in retrieval time. The engineering profession finds many applications for large engineering drawings on aperture cards.

Microrecords in Small Firms

Many examples of the use of microfilm are found in small firms and also in small towns. In each courthouse, the county clerk searches microrecords for titles of properties owned; and when the records are found, hard copies can be quickly printed. More and more, libraries purchase microfiche that index important items of information. With such microrecords available, students can quickly locate the names of books, trade papers, abstracts, and similar publications. The only equipment needed in these cases is the inexpensive reader.

IMPORTANT TERMS AND CONCEPTS

advanced CAR
aperture card
basic CAR
cartridges
computer-assisted retrieval (CAR)
computer input microfilm (CIM)
computer output microfilm (COM)
densitometer
density
enlarger-printer
file integrity
file security

flash card
flash indexing
image-count indexing
jacket
lap reader
magnification ratio
microfiche
microfilm
microfilm cassettes
microforms
micrographics
microrecord system

microrecords
notching
offline
online
planetary camera
portable reader
reader
reader-printers
recorder

reduction ratio
resolution
rotary camera
step and repeat camera
stationary reader
unitized microforms
updatable microfiche
updatable microfiche camera

REVIEW AND DISCUSSION

1. How are micrographics, microrecords, and microforms related? (Obj. 1)

2. What four factors are required to ensure that a microrecord is of high quality? Explain the role that each plays in achieving quality. (Obj. 2)

3. List the most common microforms and the principal uses and advantages of each. (Obj. 3)

4. Describe how computer output microfilm (COM) and computer input microfilm (CIM) are produced. Explain how each saves paper in the office. (Obj. 4)

5. In nontechnical words, explain how paper records are filmed. Once filmed, how are copies of the filmed records processed and duplicated? (Obj. 5)

6. Describe several common conditions in an office that may prove hazardous to microrecords. What control practices may be considered to overcome these conditions? (Obj. 6)

7. Explain the purpose of indexing microrecords. How do indexing methods vary from one type of microform to another? (Obj. 7)

8. Explain the various types of equipment required to store and retrieve microrecords. (Obj. 7)

9. How does the computer "assist" in finding microrecords? (Obj. 8)

10. If you were responsible for deciding whether to continue using paper records or to convert them to microfilm instead, what points would you consider and why? (Obj. 9)

11. Can microrecords of business documents be used as legal evidence? Discuss. (Obj. 9)

12. Assume you were assigned to evaluate your firm's microrecord system. How would you proceed? (Obj. 9)

13. Cite three uses of microrecords in large businesses and industries in the United States. Can you think of any types of firms that would not use microrecords? Explain. (Obj. 10)

14. What role, if any, does microfilm play in the operation of small offices? (Obj. 10)

DECISION-MAKING OPPORTUNITIES (DMO)

DMO 13-1: Converting to Microrecords

Six years ago you joined the Gillette Computer Services Company as its first records manager. Since that time you have set up the records management program but have not considered the use of microfilm, thinking that such applications would come "in time."

Now, it appears that the time has arrived. Yesterday, you spoke with Bette Brant, the Vice-President of Administration, about the rapid growth of the firm that has been responsible for overcrowded offices and bulging paper files. In particular, Brant wonders about the need to consider microfilm, especially in three high-volume records areas: (1) payroll, (2) engineering, and (3) publications (the firm prints many new technical manuals and product catalogs and updates many older publications on a regular basis).

Before finishing your conversation with Brant, she asks you to provide answers to the following questions on microfilming:

1. What basic ideas should the management of the firm discuss before making a decision about the use of microrecords?
2. What steps are necessary to convert the records from these three areas to microfilm?
3. What general types of equipment and procedures would be required to put such a system into operation?
4. What sources of reliable information are available to assist the Gillette firm in converting to microrecords?

Provide answers to Brant's questions as directed by your instructor. (Objs. 5, 6, and 9)

DMO 13-2: Answering the Question, "Should I Microfilm?"

Five years ago your neighbor, Ron Stiers, opened a small craft shop. Through hard work and good management his business prospered and expanded into many new lines (most recently quilting, woodworking, and metal crafts), each requiring hundreds of small merchandise items. Thus, his inventory numbers in the thousands, which seems to Stiers impossible to control, even though he has five full-time employees and six students who work part-time for him.

During a recent backyard barbecue, Stiers discussed his concerns about maintaining good inventory records. He also asked you about the possibility of considering, in his words, "some kind of microfilm." His questions to you were very straightforward:

1. Would a microfilm system help me in my business?
2. If so, how would I go about converting my records?
3. What types of equipment and training would be needed?

Assume you wish to be a good neighbor and provide answers to Stiers' questions. In order to answer such practical questions, it is necessary to review systems concepts in records management (Chapter 1), basic principles of managing records (Chapter 2), and special records storage (Part 4). If this assignment is subdivided into major topics as suggested by your review, you should be able to answer the questions asked in a concise manner, such as in outline form.

Specific instructions for completing this DMO will be provided by your instructor, either as a group or individual project. (Objs. 5, 7, 9, and 10)

14 MECHANIZED AND AUTOMATED RECORDS SYSTEMS

Objectives

After you have completed this chapter, you will be able to:

1. Identify the essential elements of a successful technology-based records system.
2. Define mechanized records system and describe the process by which records are stored in mechanized systems.
3. Outline the steps required in retrieving records from mobile shelving and motorized rotary storage systems.
4. Explain the equation, $IP = DP + WP$.
5. List the main features of computers and the purpose of each in the processing of information.
6. Describe the main phases in a computer system and the equipment needed for operating each phase in the system.
7. Discuss the role of indexing and coding in a computer system.
8. Describe the various magnetic media used by computers to store electronic records.
9. Explain how records are retrieved from sequential files and direct-access files in a computer system.
10. Define optical data disk and describe the main advantages of its use in a records system.
11. Summarize the methods used to retain and protect magnetic records.
12. Define word processing system and explain how records are created, stored, and retrieved in a word processing system.
13. Discuss the office automation network and the role each of its components plays in records automation.

The main emphasis in this textbook so far has been on manual systems, which still comprise the most commonly used means of records storage.

As discussed in Chapter 1, in manual systems records are created, indexed, coded, sorted, and stored by hand; and when needed for use, retrieved by hand. These manual operations are slow, expensive, and inefficient—three reasons why modern businesses turn more and more often to higher-level technology to solve their records systems problems.

Chapter 13 introduced the basic concepts of microrecords including computer-assisted retrieval. This chapter discusses how well-qualified personnel create, process, store, and retrieve records in mechanized and automated systems.

TECHNOLOGY AND RECORDS SYSTEMS

Technology refers to the machines (hardware) and procedures and programs (software) needed to operate records systems. As a rule, hardware used in mechanized and automated systems is much more expensive and complex than is the equipment used in manual systems. However, technology-based systems are much faster and more accurate than are manual systems, although technology-based systems are more difficult to set up and operate. For these reasons, the records manager or office manager must study carefully the essential elements required for a successful machine records system. Such a study will reveal information on the:

1. *Volume* of records at present and expected in the future.
2. *Uses* of records and by what departments.
3. *Equipment available* and the *equipment required*.
4. *Physical form* of records entering the system, and the form of records desired as output of the system.
5. *Activity* of records (how often used and how often the information on records changes).
6. *Speed* and *accuracy* expected for records retrieval.
7. *Cost* of the machine system compared with benefits expected from its use.

Of all these elements, the most important is the ability of the system to provide the *right information* at the *right time* (the purpose of item 6 above) as desired by the users. If the requested information is not available when needed, managers will be forced to wait for information and delay their operations, which adds to operating costs.

The systems discussed in this chapter use various types of media for storing and retrieving records. Mechanized systems use paper and microfilm; automated systems also use microfilm, as discussed in Chapter 13, as well as magnetic, optical, and paper media as explained later in this chapter.

MECHANIZED RECORDS SYSTEMS

A **mechanized records system** uses some form of machinery in the storage and retrieval of records. In addition, mechanical equipment physically moves records to a location convenient for the user. Mechanized devices speed storage and retrieval by reducing the time normally required for walking to and from the files. Two types of mechanized systems are discussed in this section: (1) mobile shelving and (2) motorized (or power-driven) rotary storage.

Mobile Shelving

In **mobile shelving**, record containers (folders and boxes, as a rule) or cards are stored on shelves that move on tracks attached to the floor. In some cases, these shelving units are not motorized and thus must be physically moved by the operator. More often, the units are electrically powered, which saves time and energy for the operator. One type of mobile shelving is the **mobile aisle system** which is electrically powered so that shelves can be moved to create an aisle between any two shelf units. The mobile aisle system shown in Figure 14-1A occupies 139 square feet as compared with 758 square feet of space required for storing the same number of records (10,000 filing inches) in vertical file cabinets. The result is a saving of 619 square feet, or about 81 percent.

In some movable shelving equipment, the shelves slide from side to side. The records on shelves behind the moved shelves are then exposed for use.

Another version of mobile shelving eliminates walking in the records room. This equipment is called No-Walk, a trademark of the White Power Files Corporation, and is constructed of short shelving sections that travel in circular tracks until the desired section is found and instructed to stop in front of the workstation operator. This type of electrically powered system operates in the same manner as the equipment used for moving garments in cleaning establishments. Figure 14-1B shows an example of the No-Walk system in which the files are brought to the workstation, which reduces travel time and worker fatigue.

To store and retrieve a record, the filer must first locate the shelf code usually found on a shelf index, in a central records file, or on guides or folders housed in the shelves. Then the shelf units are moved, either

FIGURE 14-1A — Mobile Aisle System
Kardex Systems, Inc.

electrically, mechanically, or manually, to find the desired shelf. If a second record is needed from another section of the file, the rows of shelves can once again be moved to locate the desired record.

FIGURE 14-1B — Mobile Shelf Storage System
White Power Files, Inc.

Motorized Rotary Storage

Motorized rotary storage was discussed in Chapter 11 in the section "Motorized Card Records Equipment," page 276. In such equipment a motorized file unit rotates horizontally around a central hub much like the movement of seats on a Ferris wheel. Shelves that house documents in folders, cards, or microforms are available in sideways positions found in lateral files or more commonly in the regular forward position.

To retrieve records from motorized rotary storage, as shown in Figure 14-2, the operator consults a register for the number of the shelf holding the requested record. (This register is maintained and kept up-to-date by the files operator.) Next, the operator presses a button on the keypad of the storage unit for the number of the shelf to be retrieved. The desired shelf then rotates to a position directly in front of the operator. More recent innovations in motorized rotary storage include optical scanners that electronically search a file and deliver the record to the operator. In some systems the motorized rotary storage equipment is connected to a computer in which a list of all motorized records storage locations is stored. By keying in the number of the requested record, the computer identifies the location of the record from its file, activates the operation of the motorized storage unit, and automatically rotates the desired file shelf to the operator's workstation.

FIGURE 14-2 — Motorized Rotary Storage Equipment
Kardex Systems, Inc.

Refiling follows the same procedure. Also, the same procedures for controlling records (especially cross-referencing and charging out in manual systems) apply to mechanized records systems.

AUTOMATED RECORDS SYSTEMS

The field of records management is growing more and more dependent on automated records systems that use the computer. Two types of systems have evolved in which the computer is used to handle the information needs of business firms: data processing systems and word processing systems. **Data processing (DP)** refers to the transformation of numbers by computers into meaningful information; and **word processing (WP)** refers to the manipulation of words into desired form (letters, reports, and so on) by automated devices. Together the two systems comprise **information processing (IP)** as the overall system responsible for operating automated records systems (IP = DP + WP).

To understand how automated records systems are able to create, store, and retrieve records requires careful study of the roles of data processing and word processing. The remaining pages of this chapter are devoted to a nontechnical discussion of these two important systems.

Data Processing Systems

A **data processing system**, like all systems, is composed of inputs, processes, outputs, and controls to regulate the system. Also, like all systems, a DP system requires people, equipment, procedures, space, supplies, and information. Emphasis in this section centers on the computer—the heart of the DP system—and on how the computer assists in storing and retrieving records.

Main Characteristics of Computers.   Computers are often classified by *size*. The largest is a **mainframe** that controls hundreds of terminals and storage devices and is commonly used in large organizations throughout the world. Smaller in size is the **minicomputer** that provides less processing and operating power than a mainframe and is used in smaller firms or within departments of large organizations. Most recently, the **microcomputer**, the smallest in size and capability—known widely as the **personal computer**—has appeared. Personal computers are used in homes as well as in offices and by administrative support personnel as well as by management.

All computers share these common features:

1. **Electronic circuits,** the electronic channels for moving data as electronic pulses into, within, and out of the computer.
2. **Internal memory** for storing the instructions (the computer program) and the data to be processed. With a program stored in memory, the computer remembers the details of the program and follows automatically one instruction after another to completion.
3. Very fast internal operating speeds for computing, storing, and retrieving data in nanoseconds (billionths of a second) or picoseconds (trillionths of a second) in large computers and at somewhat slower speeds in smaller computers.
4. Ability to perform arithmetic operations (addition, subtraction, multiplication, and division) and to make comparisons between two or more data items. On the basis of such comparisons, the computer can sort, store, or retrieve information. (This comparing ability of the computer is discussed in more detail in the section on computer retrieval of information, page 340.)
5. Automated control of input, processing, and output activities. The computer regulates the flow of instructions in its internally stored program and performs many other operations, such as storing or printing the results of its processing operations.

Computer Systems Phases.   As the center of power in a data processing system, the computer directs the carrying out of a set of sequential steps or phases that ensures that the system meets its goals. Figure 14-3 outlines the four main phases of the system, all of which have important roles to play in an automated records system.

   Input.   Both the data (words, numbers, and other symbols) and the program (software) for processing the data must be entered into the computer. The most common method of entering input into the system is by using a *terminal* for manually keyboarding data and giving instructions to the computer. For information already in computer-coded form, on magnetic tape or magnetic disks, special tape and disk equipment (tape drives and disk drives, respectively) is available for re-entering the stored information into the computer for further processing.
   Information preprinted on documents, such as the account number and check amounts printed at the bottom of your bank checks, can be entered into a computer through the use of **scanning devices** or **optical-character recognition (OCR) equipment**. OCR readers eliminate the need

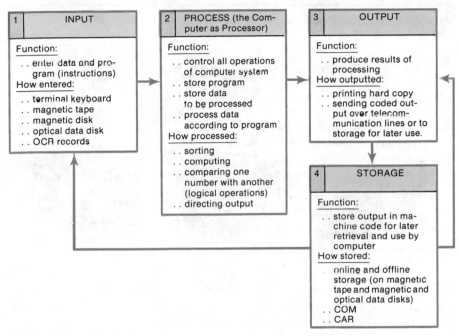

FIGURE 14-3 — Computer Systems Phases

for human operators to manually keyboard data on a terminal. The keypunching of punched cards, once the mainstay of data entry, is now obsolete and hence not covered in this textbook.

Processing. Once entered (inputted) into the system, the data are ready for the computer operations required by the program. Examples of such operations are performing arithmetic computations, sorting of numbers and alphabetic lists, and logical operations discussed earlier in this section. Figure 14-4 shows the computer file names for four major customers of a manufacturing plant randomly created when the accounts were opened. The four files can be rapidly sorted by the computer into new sequences—by ZIP code, by customer name, and by customer number—as needed in a sales manager's office. A sort command to the computer results in the files being placed in a desired order according to the data item (ZIP Code, customer name, etc.) specified.

Output. As the end result of processing, output involves making printouts of decoded information, in readable form; or the output may be stored for long periods of time in computer-coded form on magnetic

A. Random (Unsorted) Order of Files as Files Were Created:

Cust No.	Cust Name	Address	ZIP	Credit Rating
1234	Janes Soc Serv	Box 126, Perkinsville, NY	14990-2486	1
3652	Chairtown Lumber	Box 845, Gardner, MA	01440-3879	2
0078	Farmers Sav Bk	Box 125, Richmond, IA	52247-1019	1
2691	Bertas Sew Supp	40 E Lee, Tempe, AZ	85001-9105	3

B. Terminal Displays of Customer File Sorts:

(1) Sorted by ZIP Code	(2) Sorted by customer name	(3) Sorted by customer number
01440-3879 Chairtown Lumber 14990-2486 Janes Soc Serv 52247-1019 Farmers Sav Bk 85001-9105 Bertas Sew Supp	Bertas Sew Supp Chairtown Lumber Farmers Sav Bk Janes Soc Serv	0078 Farmers Sav Bk 1234 Janes Soc Serv 2691 Bertas Sew Supp 3652 Chairtown Lumber

FIGURE 14-4 — Customer File Computer Sorted into Three Categories

tape, magnetic disks, and microfilm (computer output microfilm). Temporarily, computer output is stored in the internal memory of the computer and can be displayed on the terminal screen.

Storage. The computer does not store internally the results of its processing because this space is limited and must be used for storing the program and the data to be processed. Therefore, a data processing system needs storage for output outside the computer. **Offline storage** refers to the storage equipment that is not directly connected to the computer, and **online storage** refers to the storage equipment directly connected to the computer. As shown in Figure 14-3, tape drives and disk drives are used to store output on magnetic tape and magnetic disk, respectively. Because of the extreme importance of the storage function to an understanding of automated records systems, a later section of this chapter is devoted to explaining computer storage concepts.

Creating Computer Records.   Within the computer system, records may be created in several ways. Usually this is done at the input phase of the system, as explained earlier in the section "Computer Systems Phases." In order to control a company-wide records system, the records manager must understand the reasons why records are created in the automated system just as much as the creation of records must be understood in the manual system.

Indexing and Coding Computer Records. Indexing and coding processes are needed to prepare records for computer systems. The following types of codes are most commonly used: Alphabetic (Class AAA), numeric (50-99), and alphanumeric (1A, 4F, 5EEE).

Figure 14-4 shows three examples of numeric codes, the most frequently used codes in business computer applications: customer number, ZIP Code, and credit rating. The instructions in the computer program determine how the coded information is to be arranged in the printout.

Indexing and coding have been given additional meanings in automated records systems. In computer systems, as in microrecord systems discussed on page 312, **indexing** refers to the process of assigning some type of identification or address to each storage location in the computer's record files. Computer systems also use the term *index* to describe a list or table of computer files. Therefore, within computer storage as well as in a hard-copy file available to the computer operator, an index may be created to show the complete list of accounts receivable for a business firm arranged alphabetically by customer name. For example, the short list of accounts shown in Figure 14-4 could be expanded as a full-fledged alphabetic index to show the entire file of 4,000 accounts. A portion of such a computer index is shown in Figure 14-5 with the printout appearing in typically concise (abbreviated) computer form.

Customer Name	Customer Number	Record Address
Adams Realty	0402	0001
Berta's Sew Supp	2691	0002
Chairtown Lumber	3652	0003
Dave's Crafts	0222	0004
Farmers Sav Bk	0078	0005
Garner's Jewelry	0402	0006
Jane's Soc Serv	1234	0007
. . . .	. . . .	. . . .
Zale & Yoder	0328	4000

FIGURE 14-5 — A Portion of a Computer Index of Accounts Receivable Files

Coding in computer systems is usually restricted to programming operations in which the steps for solving a problem on the computer are converted into a programming language. The coded program then consists of a set of commands or instructions that the computer recognizes and follows.

Storing and Retrieving Computer Records.   The most common types of computer storage are (1) magnetic media and (2) paper media, each of which is discussed in this section. In addition, a third type of automated record—the optical data disk—recently developed, is discussed briefly.

Magnetic Media.   The term **magnetic media** refers to the various types of records on which the computer has electronically stored its output. Examples of such storage media are magnetic tapes, disks, and diskettes.

Magnetic Tapes.   Information is stored on magnetic tape in the form of magnetized spots. The actual records are stored *sequentially* by an identifying code number, such as employee number, customer number, or stock number, that accompanies each record on the tape; such records can be updated on tape. Since many records can be stored in a small amount of space, magnetic tape provides low-cost record storage. However, in a tape file it is impossible to access individual records without reading all preceding records on the tape. The sequential nature of magnetic tape records is shown in Figure 14-6.

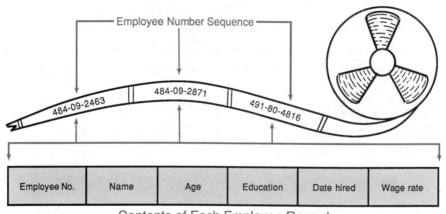

FIGURE 14-6 — Organization of Records on Magnetic Tape

Magnetic tape is stored on reels in round metal boxes that rest either on a backward-slanting shelf, in a holder attached to the bottom of a shelf, or are inserted into slotted hangers attached to the tops of shelving (See Figure 14-7). Tape reel containers are usually assigned numbers and filed in numeric sequence (See Figure 14-7). These numbers are often color coded to speed storage and retrieval of the containers, both of which are done manually.

FIGURE 14-7 — Magnetic Tape Storage

To locate a record stored on magnetic tape, files in which records are stored in sequential order (usually numeric) must be searched. As a rule, the search is made according to some **key** or code by which the records have been filed (employee number, part number, college course number, or auto license plate number). Retrieval from such a file may follow these steps:

1. The appropriate magnetic tape is obtained from the tape library and mounted on the tape drive unit, the equipment for storing and retrieving information from magnetic tape. This action is similar to placing a reel of movie film on a projector prior to viewing.
2. The operator inputs the record identification into the terminal with the appropriate instruction to search and find the desired record in the online magnetic tape file. The computer then scans the contents of the magnetic tape file to locate a record (perhaps the year-to-date earnings of employee #013782).

Assuming that each consecutive employee's number is stored sequentially on the tape along with the remainder of the contents of each employee record, a special program can find record #013782 and be instructed to display the desired information on the terminal screen; if hard copy is desired, the printer can print it out.

This process of retrieval may be slow because the entire file may have to be scanned in order to retrieve information. If the payroll file included in consecutive order employees #000001 through #014000, almost all of the tape would have to be scanned before the desired record for employee #013782 would be found. When this type of problem occurs, magnetic disk storage, described in the next section, should be considered.

Magnetic Disks.   Magnetic disks are similar in appearance to phonograph records. Large computers use disks arranged in groups or packs (See Figure 14-8). Magnetic disks rotate on a shaft that enables the mechanical arm (the device that reads the information into and out of a disk storage location) to move in and out between the disks. Each track on the disk has an address that can serve as the key for locating information immediately, even though the records may not be stored in sequential order.

FIGURE 14-8 — Magnetic Disk Packs
BASF Systems Corporation

Because the mechanical arm can go directly to the location of a specific record, disk records are often stored *randomly* with an address or code number. For this reason, disk records are often called **random-access** or **direct-access** records. An index or directory is maintained for all records stored on disks.

To find the record requested from the disk file, the computer searches its file by comparing the address (or other identification) of each record on file with the address or identification of the desired record. The simplest example of retrieving information from a disk file makes use of a **menu**, a term borrowed from restaurants. The computer program displays on the terminal screen a menu or index, usually numbered, of all files on the disk. All that is required of the operator is to select the number of the menu item (the file number) desired, and the first record in the file is displayed. This instant retrieval occurs because of the computer's speed in matching the address location or number of the requested file with the corresponding number of the file stored in the computer. The retrieved information still remains stored on the tape or disk device.

Disk storage systems have definite advantages over tape storage systems under certain conditions. For example, in a personnel office, frequent and *random* requests for information on individual employees would be serviced more efficiently through the use of a disk file. To locate data on Maria Olivera, for example, the disk drive arm would go directly to the track reserved for names beginning with O. And within the track as the disk rotates on its shaft, the reading arm would locate the specific record for Olivera. Such random-access disk file procedures are commonly followed for locating numbers in an automated telephone call-in directory service or for obtaining current registration information for individual students in your school's automated records system.

Diskettes.   Most microcomputers store information on small disks called **diskettes**. They are often called *floppies* because of the thin, fragile quality of the disk itself (See Figure 14-9). *Minidiskette* and *minidisk* are interchangeable terms for magnetic media used in word processing. Minidisks are smaller than floppy disks, but are filed in the same manner.

Standard-size diskettes vary in size from 2-1/2" to 8", although the most common size is 5-1/4" used in microcomputers. Diskettes provide storage capacity ranging from 40K-350K characters, or about 100 pages of text per side. (K is an abbreviation for **kilo**, or 1,000; in computer circles, K equals 1,024 storage locations in computer memory.)

FIGURE 14-9 — Microcomputer Diskette

Each diskette is assigned a file name that reflects the contents of the record. The file name is used for both storage and retrieval. A label with identification and any special instructions for manually retrieving a record may be attached to each disk, as shown in Figure 14-9. Diskettes are filed according to the label: (1) alphabetically by subject or name; (2) chronologically by date of creation; or (3) numerically by sequential numbers, or by a decimal system keyed to departments within an organization.

Diskettes are stored in various types of containers, depending on the intended use of the record. Figure 14-10 shows three types of diskette storage equipment. Information is retrieved from diskettes using the same general procedures as are used for locating records on magnetic disks, since both represent random-access storage systems.

A. Tray
Fellowes Manufacturing Co.

B. Rotary Stand
Ring King Visibles, Inc.

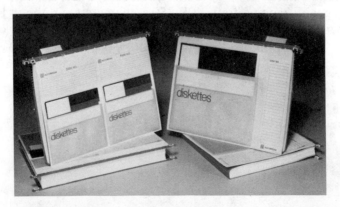

C. Hanging File
Photo courtesy of Acco

FIGURE 14-10 — Diskette Storage Equipment

Paper Media. Frequently the output of the computer is stored on paper and in a variety of arrangements including business forms. Your college transcript and grade reports are examples. Most often, however, the output appears on printout sheets that are kept in binders. These binders may be labeled by subject, by date, or by a combination of the two. Computer printouts are usually stored in binders on printout carts and on shelves or cabinets as shown in Figure 14-11, or in file drawers.

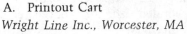

A. Printout Cart   B. Printout Shelves
Wright Line Inc., Worcester, MA   *Acme Visible Records*

FIGURE 14-11 — Computer Printout Storage Equipment

Optical Data Disks. An **optical data disk** is an automated storage device with a special heat-sensitive coating on glass or plastic for storing information. In an optical data disk system, a laser beam is used to burn or etch holes 1/120th the thickness of a human hair by which information is coded and stored (similar to the principle of storing information by means of the holes in punched cards). Or, by using the same equipment, the laser beam can raise bubbles or blisters on the thin-film surface of the disk for the storage of information. Information is retrieved or read back from the disk by using the same laser device. Optical data disks can store alphanumeric data, pictures, graphs, and drawings in a very compact manner. It is estimated that their storage capacity is 30 times that of magnetic tape, 2,000 times that of double-sided floppy disks, and 3,000 times that of microfiche. In addition, the cost of storing information on optical disks is incredibly low. For example, the cost of storing one million characters in a magnetic disk pack is $4; on a floppy disk, $2; but less than 2 cents on an optical data disk. Once data are stored on the optical data disk, they cannot be changed or rerecorded as magnetic media allow. Since optical disks are similar in shape to magnetic disks, both types of disks can be stored in the same manner.

Several methods are available for entering information on optical disks: (1) using a special terminal designed for this type of technology; (2) using a computer or word processing terminal; or (3) using scanners or optical readers that can activate the information-recording code in the optical data disk. For providing hard-copy output of images (such as charts and pictures) and text from one disk, laser printers are available that produce output at extremely high speeds.

Retaining and Protecting Automated Records.   Magnetic and optical disk records, like paper records, must be stored as specified by the records retention schedule and in a well-controlled physical environment. However, automation specialists recommend that additional measures be taken to protect automated records. The essential elements of such a protection plan are considered to be:

1. A security policy to ensure the safe, reliable operation of the records system. Such a policy is based on a detailed study of equipment used, records functions performed, data contained in the principal records, employees having access to the records, and current security devices.
2. Personnel using the hardware and software in the system who are given security checks and, if necessary, bonded. The automated records security policy should include close supervision of the work plus holding employees personally accountable for the proper maintenance of company equipment and information.
3. Special protective measures for the hardware and software. These measures range from physically locking up computer files and equipment to segregating computer equipment and personnel from other employees. Visible security controls should be provided to serve as a major deterrent to crime. Some firms have a security warning programmed into the computer for display on the terminal screen.

   Hardware should be regularly inventoried and tested and personal computers attached to furniture. An effective method of controlling access to a computer room is a card reader/combination lock system into which employees must insert their cards and punch in a personal code. Also, the magnetic records should be carefully protected. For example, envelopes should be placed over diskettes used in personal computers to protect against damage from dust, scratches, and fingerprints during handling and storage.

4. Protection for the data stored on the automated record. Safeguards to protect company data from unauthorized use include:
   a. Passwords that employees must use to retrieve data.
   b. **Encryption systems** that scramble data in a predetermined manner at the sending point in order to protect confidential records. The scrambled data must then be decoded at the destination.
   c. Call-back, a records protection procedure that requires the individual requesting data from the computer system to hang up after the telephone request is made and wait for the computer to call back. In call-back systems, telephone numbers can be checked by the computer before information is released to the requesting party to be sure that only authorized persons have access to the requested information.
   d. The records stored on magnetic and optical disks should regularly be converted to hard copy if the records are to be kept for long periods of time. This suggestion is made because some automated records may have a limited shelf life, depending on storage conditions.
   e. To protect against loss of files, most firms have a policy of copying computer files for use as backup in case of systems problems and storing the copies in fireproof cabinets or in an offsite location. Duplicating automated records is done quickly and inexpensively and provides good insurance that the records will always be available when needed.

Word Processing Systems

Although their main use has been in processing numbers, computers have proved to be highly efficient processors of words as well. For example, computers are used to input, sort, store, retrieve, output, and transmit words; and because of the success of these operations, a new automated records concept—word processing systems—has emerged. Word processing systems are directly involved in the operation of records systems in the office. For this reason, an understanding of word processing concepts is important for records management personnel. However, technical skills and information relating to hardware and software remain the responsibility of automation systems specialists.

A **word processing system** is a combination of people, equipment, and procedures for transforming the words originated by a person into a final product—a final communication or *text*—and forwarding it to a user. While this definition applies to the traditional office system—a handwritten letter recorded on a yellow pad and transcribed into mailable form by using a typewriter is also word processing—the main use of the term *word processing* is to describe an automated way of creating, producing, editing, storing, retrieving, and distributing such communications. This section reviews the creation of records in an automated word processing system and discusses briefly how such records are stored and retrieved.

Creating Word Processing Records.   Word processing systems, like data processing systems, require hardware and software for creating records. The hardware needed includes **stand-alone word processing equipment** (electronic typewriters and word processors that operate as independent units) and computers. Since the coming of microcomputers, word processing has become a common application of this type of computer. The software needed includes special programs designed for **text-editing**, such as WORDSTAR® and VOLKSWRITER™. The main function of this type of software is to record, add, delete, change, correct, and relocate copy (sentences, paragraphs, and tables) at electronic speeds. Figure 14-12 outlines the main equipment required to operate a word processing system that is based on a microcomputer.

The records management staff must understand records-creation methods and assist the office employees in choosing the most efficient, least-cost methods. The subject of cost control is discussed at length in Chapter 15.

Storing Word Processing Records.   In the microcomputer, records are stored temporarily in computer memory during the period of time the machine is in operation. To keep the record in its present form or for updating, the information is stored on the diskette. Usually hard copy is printed; however, even if hard copy is not desired, a careful operator usually makes a printout of the copy stored on the diskette in case of some failure of the equipment. Figure 14-12 shows a typical method of storing text or words in a word processing system.

Retrieving Word Processing Records.   In order to find anything—from wearing apparel at home to records at the office—memory or an index of items stored must be consulted. To retrieve information from a word processing file, the same general steps are required as are needed

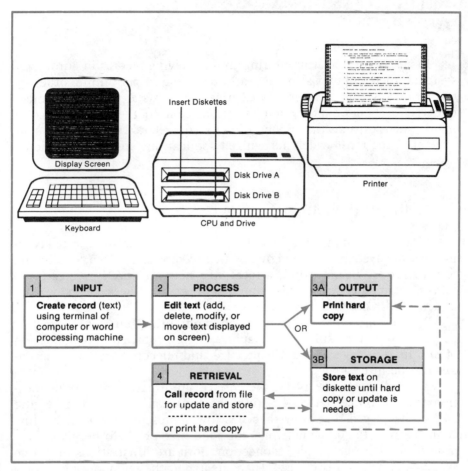

FIGURE 14-12 — Automated Word Processing System

in a data processing system. With an index of each of the files or contents of a diskette shown on a terminal screen, the operator can quickly select the desired records for display on the screen for updating, re-storing, or printing hard copy.

Many types of word processing systems are available, each having its own set of procedures for use. The procedures explained in this section include the basic concepts needed to understand records automation in the modern office. More detailed information is readily available— in school and community libraries, on the magazine racks of retail stores, and from equipment and supplies manufacturers.

APPLICATIONS OF RECORDS AUTOMATION

In addition to creating, storing, and retrieving records in automated systems, the computer also plays a leading role in performing other information systems activities. In each case, records are involved; consequently, each new application of automation to the field of records management expands the responsibilities of the records management staff. Several of the most widely recognized applications are explained here.

The Office Automation Network

When the computer is linked to the telephone system, a **telecommunication system** is created over which records can be sent to all parts of the world. Within a firm, a **local area network (LAN)** is created to transmit computerized records of business operations over telephone lines under the direction of the computer.

By combining the transmitting and computing functions, data processing, word processing, micrographics, reprographics (the reproduction of information discussed in Chapter 15), and telecommunication activities can be integrated.

By studying Figure 14-13, the entry of information at various locations in the office network within the firm can be traced. In Figure 14-13, the jagged, lightning-shaped arrow represents a telephone line connection in the office network; the solid line, on the other hand, represents an electrical (cable) connection. Both are illustrations of online systems. New automated records are created at the telephone, at a computer console keyboard, and at various computer and word processing terminals. Also, optical character recognition (OCR) machines scan documents and convert the contents into computer code and thereby create computer records; therefore, the keyboarding operation is not required to enter data into the automated system.

Electronic mail transmits records—words and images, such as drawings and blueprints—over telephone lines or relays them via satellite network. This kind of system permits many types and large numbers of records to be swiftly and inexpensively transmitted worldwide. At the same time, the system may reduce the amount of paperwork, including internal and external mail, that is required in the office.

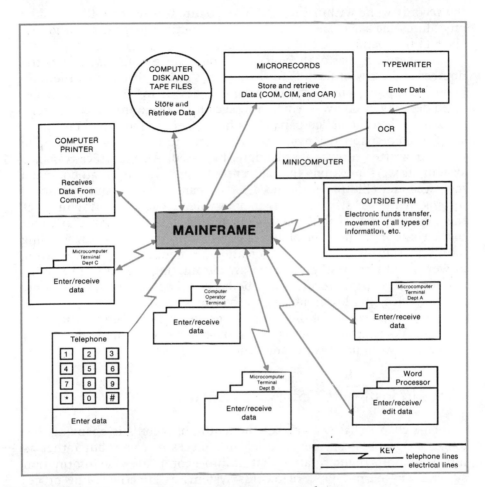

FIGURE 14-13 — Office Automation Network
Adapted from B: Lewis Keeling and Norman F. Kallaus, Administrative Office Management, *8th ed. (Cincinnati: South-Western Publishing Co., 1983), p. 665.*

In the banking industry, **electronic funds transfer systems (EFTS)** allow customers to request information about their checking and savings accounts as well as withdraw money and make deposits. And computer terminals located in convenient places, such as supermarkets and shopping malls, permit banking transactions without the inconvenience of physically going to the bank. Little paperwork is performed by the customer although the customer receives a statement of the EFTS activity at the end of each reporting period. However, a large reduction in the records work within the bank has resulted in fewer teller-window procedures and a decrease in bookkeeping functions (deposits, withdrawals, and file maintenance of accounts).

An increasing use of the voice in automated systems also affects the number and types of records in the office. **Voice mail** requires the telephone, computer, and a special recording device for immediate or delayed delivery of one-way voice messages for storage in the computer's mailbox. When the called party dials his or her mailbox to obtain messages, the computer reconverts each message to the caller's voice. The need for written records is, therefore, bypassed. Also, a **voice-response system** answers questions that alert people more rapidly than do visual messages and eliminates the need for human operators and additional records. Although still in its infancy, a **voice-recognition system** gives the computer the capability of understanding the human voice as input to the computer. This type of device eliminates the need for keyboarding of information and other records-creation problems, such as misspelling of words and transposing numbers. By automating the voice in records systems, fewer paper records may be needed; and faster response time, better service, and lower administrative costs result.

Other applications of the computer to the everyday information processing tasks continue to grow. Such topics are covered in detail in data processing, word processing, and general systems references.

Implications for Records Management

This chapter has shown that the nature of records is changing. No longer are records considered as isolated pieces of paper, but rather as integrated units of information that fit into a company-wide information system. The narrow view of records systems as effective filing procedures, discussed in Chapter 1, has given way to a broader picture of records management that includes the entire firm.

In the modern office, with the press of a button, an electronic record can be created, stored in one central location (the **database**), and made accessible to authorized persons with terminals who need the information on the record. To achieve this type of records automation requires a uniform system of indexing and coding documents and the use of standardized rules for accessing and searching records in computer storage. As emphasized in Chapters 1 and 2, *a solid understanding of these rules can best be achieved by mastering the principles of storage and retrieval in manual systems.*

The control of records discussed in Chapter 15 will be needed more than ever as the automation of records increases. Still, records will continue to exist in various forms—hard copy, microforms, and in electronic form in computer files—but more and more, records creation, storage, and retrieval will be computer-based.

IMPORTANT TERMS AND CONCEPTS

data processing (DP)

data processing system

database

direct access

diskettes

electronic circuits

electronic funds transfer systems (EFTS)

electronic mail

encryption systems

indexing

information processing (IP)

internal memory

key

kilo

local area network (LAN)

magnetic media

mainframe

mechanized records system

menu

microcomputer

minicomputer

mobile aisle system

mobile shelving

motorized rotary storage

offline storage

online storage

optical-character recognition (OCR) equipment

optical data disk

personal computer

random access

scanning devices

stand-alone word processing equipment

technology

telecommunication system

text-editing

voice mail

voice-recognition system

voice-response system

word processing (WP)

word processing system

REVIEW AND DISCUSSION

1. If you were responsible for deciding whether to change from a manual to an automated system, what elements would you consider? (Obj. 1)

2. Cite two common types of mechanized storage systems. Explain how records are stored in such systems. (Obj. 2)

3. What steps must be followed in order to retrieve records from mobile shelving and motorized rotary storage equipment? (Obj. 3)

4. Explain the importance of the equation IP = DP + WP to an understanding of automated record systems. (Obj. 4)

5. A recent guest speaker at your school stated, "Actually all computers are alike." To what common features of all computers did this speaker refer? (Obj. 5)

6. Identify the three principal sizes of computers. Which size has been experiencing the most growth in terms of usage? Why? (Obj. 5)

7. Identify each of the main phases in a computer system and the role that each plays in the operation of such a system. (Obj. 6)

8. How does offline storage differ from online storage? What types of equipment are used for these types of storage? (Obj. 6)

9. Since business computers are digital computers, does this mean that they are unable to process alphabetic data? Explain. (Obj. 6)

10. What is the function of indexing and coding in a computer system? Is their use similar to indexing and coding in a manual system? Explain. (Obj. 7)

11. What are the principal types of magnetic media used to store records in a computer system? (Obj. 8)

12. Define the terms *sequential file* and *direct-access file*. How are records retrieved from each type of file? (Obj. 9)

13. What is an optical data disk? What advantages does an optical data disk have over other more traditional computer records? (Obj. 10)

14. Briefly review the methods available for protecting computer records. (Obj. 11)

15. Identify the methods of creating, storing, and retrieving records in a word processing system. How do these methods compare with the methods for creating, storing, and retrieving records in a data processing system? (Obj. 12)

16. Identify the main information cycle functions in the office automation network. What effect does each function have on the automation of records? (Obj. 13)

DECISION-MAKING OPPORTUNITIES (DMO)

DMO 14-1: Computerizing a College Grading System

In your study of automated records systems including computers, your instructor has emphasized systems concepts throughout. Now, as you approach the completion of the records management course, you are asked to bring together systems, computer, and information concepts in order to understand *why* and *how* automated records systems are created and used. In order to integrate these concepts, you are asked to consider the problem of computerizing the grading system in your school. (Even though your present grading system is probably computerized, the mental exercise of computerizing will aid a great deal in understanding automated records systems.)

To assist you in completing this DMO, you are encouraged to consider the role of each of the systems phases discussed in this chapter in solving your problem. In addition, you will have to review the grading system, its purposes, and the major users of this system. Present your solution to this DMO stated in nontechnical, user terms in which you answer these two questions:

1. What are the main phases of the present grading system?
2. What portions of this grading system can be converted to automated records and why? (Objs. 1, 6, 8, 10, and 11)

DMO 14-2: Protecting Automated Records

In the United Credit Bureau (UCB) office, automated records of many types are kept on file. Magnetic tape and magnetic disk records are retained for the following large volume needs:

1. Clients' credit rating checks.
2. Confidential legal histories of clients' customers.
3. UCB employee payroll.
4. Accounts receivable record summaries.

In addition, some microrecords are maintained. However, there is no protection plan for these valuable records other than steel filing cabinets.

In order to understand the comprehensive nature of records protection, you are asked to (1) identify the main phases of a total records program after reviewing Chapters 2 and 14; and (2) suggest special protective measures for the types of automated records maintained by UCB. (Objs. 1 and 11)

5 – Records Control Systems

15 – Controlling the Records Management Program

Part 5 offers a comprehensive view of the most essential phase of the records system—control. Coverage in this Part includes the role of standards in achieving records systems control and practical procedures for controlling paperwork problems in large and small offices.

15 CONTROLLING THE RECORDS MANAGEMENT PROGRAM

Objectives

After you have completed this chapter, you will be able to:

1. Define control as a process in records management and give examples of two types of control.
2. Describe the purpose of control in a records system.
3. Explain how the periodic audit and the records management manual help to provide control in a records system.
4. Discuss the two main types of standards in a records system and provide two specific examples of each.
5. List the principal efficiency guidelines used in a records system, and describe how each guideline assists in the control of records.
6. Describe how an activity ratio differs from an accuracy ratio in controlling records.
7. Identify the major costs involved in a paperwork system and ways of controlling these costs.
8. State the objectives of a forms control program.
9. Understand the main objective in forms design and how each design rule helps to achieve this objective.
10. Identify principal costs involved in producing correspondence and suggest methods of reducing such costs.
11. Explain the main reprographic processes for making record copies and how costs of copymaking are successfully controlled.
12. Describe how a small office can control its records system.

The word *control* is often used in society as well as in business firms where it has important implications for management. The need for control in establishing and operating a records management program—introduced briefly in Chapter 2—is expanded further in this chapter.

THE CONTROL PROCESS IN RECORDS SYSTEMS

Systems experts refer to **control**—a key phase in all systems, as outlined in Figure 1-4, page 13—as a *process of regulating the behavior of all other phases in the system.* The control process in both general and specific terms is discussed in this section as it functions in records systems.

Types of Control

For control reasons, society tells each of us what we can and cannot do. For example, we are not allowed to steal the property of others, harm another person, or avoid paying our bills. To make sure that these controls are maintained, the court system has been developed, a long and growing body of laws has been enacted, and enforcement agencies have been set up. The Internal Revenue Service controls our income tax "behavior"; the Federal Communication Commission, our telephone system operations; and the Interstate Commerce Commission, many of our business operations. The state departments of education help to regulate the public school systems in each state. Figure 15-1 outlines in broad terms the regulatory function of control in any system.

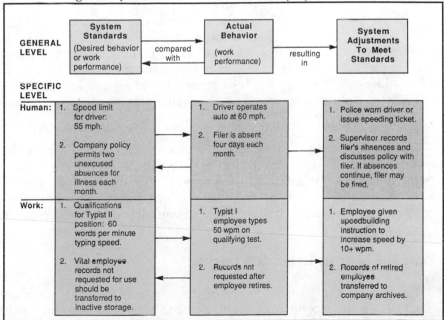

FIGURE 15-1 — Process of Control in a System

In effective records systems, controls are widely found. Records managers develop policies or broad guidelines for operating their programs. Procedures are set up to make sure that all records are indexed, coded, stored, and retrieved in an efficient manner. (Cross-references and charge-out procedures are common examples of controls in the records system). Broader examples of control include records retention schedules, budgeting, paperwork management programs, and personnel evaluation (often called performance appraisal).

Purposes of Control

The broad purpose of control in a records system is to ensure that all the goals of a records management program are achieved. In order to make this general statement of purpose "come alive," some practical control examples are needed. In the following list, all of the main elements in the records system are shown with everyday examples of controls that regulate the use of those elements:

Systems Element	Controls
1. Personnel	Attendance records and a plant security force
2. Space	Janitorial services and office space assignment guidelines
3. Equipment	Machine maintenance inspections and operator training programs
4. Procedures	Rules for access to files and use of control numbers and passwords in automated systems

These specific controls are designed to keep the system within reasonable bounds. In turn, the records manager must make sure that efficient procedures are consistently followed, that duplication of work and of information stored in the system is minimized, and that information in the system is made available in complete and low-cost form.

Control Tools in Records Systems

As discussed in Chapter 1, one of the four management functions is control. To the records manager this means waging a constant battle against human nature—resistance to change, lax employee attitudes about work, refusal to recognize the need to keep costs at a minimum, and a whole host of "I-couldn't-care-less" viewpoints. The techniques discussed in this section are useful tools to help maintain control in the records system.

Periodic Audit.   An effective practice to measure the status of the records system is the **periodic audit.** An audit is a regular examination of the records management program to determine how well the program is functioning as well as to find ways of improving its performance. The programs of large organizations may use their own technically trained staff to undertake such an audit or hire outside consultants (usually having more objectivity) for this purpose. Small firms commonly use the services of outside auditors because of the lack of qualified persons within the organization.

The audit provides three kinds of information on the records management program:

1. Information about the present operations, such as how well the objectives of the program are being achieved; whether written policies and procedures are available and followed by all personnel; and the extent of records management activities as well as the main problems associated with them.
2. Analysis of the present system and its needs, such as the layout of the files; the effectiveness of the procedures; the qualifications of the staff; the uses of the available equipment; active and inactive storage systems; security measures taken for preserving and protecting records; and so on.
3. Recommended solutions for improving the records management program and estimates of the cost of putting the recommendations into practice.

Records Management Manual.   The most important control reference for a records management staff is the **records management manual.** Such a manual serves as an official handbook of approved policies and procedures for operating the records management program. Also, it establishes responsibility for the various phases of the program, standardizes operating procedures, and aids in training employees.[1]

---

[1] For excellent, detailed coverage of manuals, see Betty R. Ricks and Kay F. Gow, *Information Resource Management* (Cincinnati: South-Western Publishing Co., 1984), Chapter 8, pp. 170-188.

The contents of a typical records management manual established by a large firm are listed as follows:[2]

Main Sections	Section Contents
1. The records system	Purpose, policies, personnel responsibilities
2. Components of the records system	Records classifications, alphabetic index, records retention schedules
3. The coding system	Records classification codes, retention and disposition codes
4. Types of files in the records system	Subject and case files, special files
5. Files cutoff	Subject file cutoff, case or project file cutoff
6. Preparation of records location plans	List of all records maintained at each storage location
7. Annual program reviews	Description of the requirements of each review
8. Storage procedures	Preparation of records to be stored; what to store and when; classification and coding; preparing cross-references; sorting records; placing records in file; restricted access to records; retrieval suggestions; charge-out system; folders and drawer maintenance
9. Records disposition	Disposition functions; how to implement retention schedules; packing records and labeling boxes; retrieval of inactive records from storage; destruction of records in inactive storage
10. Records manual maintenance and auditing	General procedures; maintenance of records classifications and records retention schedules

STANDARDS IN THE CONTROL PROCESS

Much of our everyday life is built around standards that have a direct bearing on the ways our world is controlled. In the office, there are

[2]Adapted from Katherine Aschner, ed., *Taking Control of Your Office Records* (White Plains: Knowledge Industry Publications, Inc., 1983), pp. 223-234.

standard sizes of desks, chairs, and paper records as well as typewriter ribbons. In this section, standards are explained and illustrated, with special attention given to the use of standards in records systems.

Types of Standards

A **standard** is a measure or yardstick by which the performance of a system is rated. Such measures have long been used by industrial engineers to evaluate the *quantity* and *quality* of factory and office work. Professional organizations, such as the Association of Records Managers and Administrators, Inc., the Association for Systems Management, the American National Standards Institute, and the manufacturers of office equipment and supplies have developed a large number of standards, many of which have considerable value for controlling records systems.

Quantity Standards.   A **quantity standard** is a common measure that involves simply counting *how many* products, sales, or hours of labor time have been used in factory and office operations. The Consumer Price Index is a quantitative standard for measuring economic conditions; miles per gallon, a measure of automobile performance; amount of turnover, an evaluation of a firm's new hires and fires or quitting employees; and par 72, a golfer's performance measure. In the office, the *number* of letters filed, words per minute typed or invoice totals verified—all are examples of quantity standards. Although the development of quantity standards is a complex process, basically it involves selecting a typical (average) worker with the experience needed for performing the task to be standardized. Next, the worker's performance is observed and the amount of work accomplished is measured. After the observations have been repeated a reasonable number of times and a typical work pattern is clearly discernible, a quantity standard is created. This standard is then used to evaluate the work of similar employees under the same type of conditions.

Quality Standards.   A **quality standard** measures *how good* or *how bad* the work or the worker's performance is. Developing quality standards requires the use of subjective judgment about intangible characteristics of people and their work. Under such conditions, human bias may enter into the control process, a situation that can be held in check by free and open discussions between managers and workers who share the common goals of performing to the best of their ability for the good of their employers.

Quality standards are found in all areas of work and society. Examples include courteous behavior to customers, good taste in dress, the persuasiveness of a sales letter, the neatness of a business report, and the qualities of dependability and cooperation of an employee. Clearly these qualities are not measurable in themselves but are nevertheless important factors to consider in measuring a worker's productivity.

In order to be sure that fairness is maintained in developing standards, office systems analysts frequently measure the time and motions of office workers and develop tables of standard times for basic tasks to be performed in the office. Standard times have been developed for typing standard-size letters, for the number of keystrokes produced per hour, for line or page counts used in word processing systems, and for record storage and retrieval operations. Computer users often make decisions about what computer to buy based on the standard of access time (how long a time is required to locate a record in the computer file). However, few standards are set for supervisors or managers because their work combines quality and quantity standards. In fact, relatively few standards have been developed for offices compared with factories because factory work comprises a greater number of countable operations and the office is composed of a wider variety of tasks, many of which are management oriented.

Benefits of Standards

Standards provide many specific benefits to employers and employees. These benefits include:

1. Evaluating employees' performance since the employees know the goals expected of them in terms of volume, quality, and time.
2. Enabling the immediate supervisor to measure the effectiveness of a new employee and the rate of learning that takes place.
3. Evaluating the need for improving office systems and procedures and determining the practicality of installing new machines and equipment.
4. Installing wage-incentive systems in which the earnings of employees are based upon how much the employees produce.
5. Measuring the effectiveness of departmental operations by comparing the work completed with the applicable standards.
6. Identifying high and low performers.

A review of the benefits of using standards leads to one conclusion: As a result of properly using standards in the office, better control is exercised over the scheduling, performance, and completion of office work;

and costs of office systems can be more specifically controlled. This further results in improved service to customers or clients by reducing the time needed for processing office work. A discussion of specific standards in the records system follows.

Standards in the Records System

Even though automation has continued to take over more and more office operations, a vast number of records tasks are manual. In offices where terminals and other automated equipment such as word processors are used, the speed and accuracy of operators are measured and standards developed from such measurements. More information on such automated systems standards can be found in textbooks on office systems, office management, data processing, and word processing.

Storage and Retrieval Standards.   In order to develop practical standards for storing and retrieving records, three main questions must be answered: (1) How long does it take to store a record from the time such storage is authorized; (2) how long does it take to retrieve a record from storage; and (3) what is the expected **turnaround time** (the amount of time that is required to find and deliver a record to the requester after the request for the record has been made)? Turnaround time standards are largely the concern of automated records systems depending on the speeds of computer storage systems. The other two questions can be more directly related to the published standards for manual storage and retrieval systems.

The most common standards in manual records systems focus on the activities required to store and retrieve records. Over a period of years large firms and standards associations have developed many records systems standards, some of which are outlined in Figure 15-2.[3]

Efficiency Guidelines.   In addition to measuring the work of records personnel using the standards similar to those shown in Figure 15-2, office managers and records managers should find out how well their records systems are performing. Usually this involves using two simple concepts: determining (1) the effectiveness and (2) the efficiency of the files.

---

[3]More information on setting standards and evaluating records systems can be found in specialized publications on the subject, such as Wilmer O. Maedke, Mary F. Robek, and Gerald F. Brown, *Information and Records Management*, 2d ed., (Encino, CA: Glencoe Publishing Co., Inc., 1981) pp. 164-5; and references from the U. S. National Archives and Records Service, especially "Checklist for Appraising Files Operations in Your Office," (Washington: U. S. Government Printing Office, 1968).

Task	Time Unit (h = hour; m = minute)
Code typical one-page letter	200/h
Type folder labels	100/h
Sort 5" × 3" cards	300/h
Sort invoices into 3-digit numeric sequence	1,500/h
Sort coded letters	250/h
Place cards in alphabetic file	300/h
Place papers in subject file	150/h
Place vouchers in numeric file	250/h
Retrieve record from color-coded file	2.5/m
Retrieve daily reports	.5/m
Retrieve 5" × 3" cards	180/h
Retrieve correspondence and prepare charge-out records	70/h

FIGURE 15-2 — Work Standards for Records Systems

Effectiveness Measures. The most important test of any records system is the speed with which the stored information can be located. The following items are used to measure the ability of a records system to provide such information along with effectiveness standards:

1. *The number of misfiles*, usually about 3 percent of the total records filed.
2. *The number of "can't find" items*, which one authority suggests is excessive at a 1 percent level.
3. *The time required to find items*, which should never exceed two to three minutes.

At least once a year an office or records manager should check the effectiveness of the records system. Other topics to be included in such a check are the number of records received (in number of records or in cubic feet of space occupied); the amount of space being used and how much unused space is available; how often records are requested from the files; how much equipment is (or is not) being used; and how many records have been destroyed or transferred from active to inactive storage.

Efficiency Ratios. An **efficiency ratio** is a guideline for measuring several types of records operations that furnish additional information for controlling the records system. Although such ratios have been developed for costs, space, and personnel, the most useful ratios relate to the frequency of use of the records (the **activity ratio**) and the ability of the records personnel to find the requested records (the **accuracy ratio**). Both are shown and explained in Figure 15-3.

Type of Ratio	How Ratio is Computed
1. Activity ratio (measures how often the records are used)	Divide the number of records requested by the number of records filed. Example: 500 records requested, 5,000 records filed or a 10% activity ratio. (When the ratio is below 5%, all records in the file that fall below 5% should be transferred to inactive storage or destroyed.)
2. Accuracy ratio (measures efficiency of personnel in finding the stored records)	Divide the number of records found by the number of records requested. Example: 5,950 records found, 6,000 records requested, or a 99.17% accuracy ratio. (When the ratio falls below 97%, the records system needs immediate attention.)

FIGURE 15-3 — Standards for Evaluating a Records System's Efficiency

Evaluating Costs

The size of the paperwork problem pointed out in Chapter 1 carries with it tremendous costs. These costs are estimated as follows:[4]

70%   Salaries of managers, supervisors, and operating personnel working directly with records

---

[4]Ron Monaco, "Mechanized Filing: Cost Versus Expense," *ARMA Records Management Quarterly* (April, 1984), pp. 11-12.

15%   Space occupied by records systems, including personnel

10%   Equipment used in the records system

5%   Supplies

Since labor costs represent almost three fourths of each records dollar, the greatest potential for controlling costs is in human resource areas. This cost category includes managerial, supervisory, and operating personnel salaries along with the employee benefits—pensions, social security contributions, and insurance, to name a few.

The space and equipment costs of a major records system are outlined in Figure 15-4. This information compares the costs of storing 10,000 lineal filing inches (LFI) of records using seven different types of storage equipment. From a study of this table, it is obvious that the seven-shelf movable aisle file requires the least space expenditure (at $20 per square foot of storage space). However, Figure 15-5 brings out an even more important point—the savings in labor time realized by using a 10-foot mechanized file. With such a file, only three (statistically shown as 2.97) file clerks are required to operate a records system of 50,000 folders as compared to more than ten files persons for the standard four-drawer vertical storage cabinet. However, the mechanized equipment is almost twice as expensive ($1.27 vs. $.67) in terms of the cost of storing 10,000 LFI of records.

COST COMPARISON 10,000 FILING INCHES

(1) Type of Equipment	(2) Cost of Equipment	Cost per LFI*	(3) Sq. Ft. Needed	LFI/ Sq. Ft.	(4) Cost of Space	Total Cost 1st Year	Total Cost 10 Years	Annual Cost/LFI
4-Drawer Vertical	$21,280	$2.13	833	12	$16,660	$37,940	$187,880	$1.88
5-Drawer Vertical	$19,600	$1.96	714	14	$14,280	$33,880	$162,400	$1.62
4-Drawer Lateral	$39,200	$3.92	476	21	$ 9,520	$46,720	$134,400	$1.34
5-Drawer Lateral	$36,400	$3.64	417	24	$ 8,340	$44,740	$119,800	$1.20
8-Hi Open Shelf	$10,080	$1.00	285	35	$ 5,700	$15,780	$ 67,080	$ .67
7-Hi Movable Aisle Mechanical Assist	$19,600	$1.96	192	52	$ 3,840	$23,440	$ 58,000	$ .58
10 Ft. Mech. File	$60,480	$6.05	333	30	$ 6,660	$67,140	$127,080	$1.27

(1) Letter Size Material
(2) Equipment costs have been averaged and may vary depending on quality and grade of manufacturer
(3) Figures have allowed for 36" aisles
(4) Figures based on $20.00 per square foot/annually
*LFI = Lineal Filing Inch

FIGURE 15-4 — Comparison of Equipment and Space Costs

From the information appearing in these tables, a cost of $1,203 was computed for maintaining a five-drawer file cabinet each year. This figure was based upon the square foot cost noted above and an average clerical salary of $195 per week.

LABEL/EQUIPMENT COST COMPARISON			
Equipment	File Clerks Necessary	Ten (10) Year Labor Cost	Annual Cost per LFI*
4-Drawer Vertical	10.41	$1,041,000	$12.29
5-Drawer Vertical	10.41	$1,041,000	$12.03
4-Drawer Lateral	8.06	$ 806,000	$ 9.40
5-Drawer Lateral	8.06	$ 806,000	$ 9.26
8-Hi Open Shelf	8.06	$ 806,000	$ 8.73
7-Hi Movable Aisle Mechanical Assist	8.06	$ 806,000	$ 8.64
10 Ft. Mechanized File	2.97	$ 297,000	$ 4.24

*Includes cost of equipment, space, and labor

Large Midwestern State Study
        Vertical Drawer Files — 240 file actions/day
        Lateral Filing — 310 file actions/day
        Movable Aisle — 310 file actions/day
Standard Mechanized File — 840 file actions/day

Assumptions
- 50,000 folders (10,000 filing inches) letter size materials
- 2,500 file actions per day
- $10,000 cost per file clerk
- Equipment costs have been averaged and may vary depending on quality and grade of manufacturer.
- Floor space costs are based on $20.00 per square foot/annually

*LFI = Lineal Filing Inch

FIGURE 15-5 — Comparison of Labor and Equipment Costs

Costs of equipment, space, and supplies can be controlled by eliminating unnecessary records, carefully supervising the use of equipment and supplies, and by selecting equipment that requires smaller amounts of space. The greatest opportunity for reducing costs of labor can be realized by putting performance standards into operation. The performance of employees can then be measured against these standards.

Evaluating Performance

The attitudes that each records employee brings to the job also affect control. In addition to the time standards discussed earlier, each of the following aspects of human behavior needs to be controlled in the records system:

1. Poor attendance records of workers (frequent tardiness and absences)
2. Excessive overtime work
3. Numbers and patterns of errors in work
4. Slow response to work assignments
5. Low morale and lack of interest in the work assigned
6. Lack of concern for, or inability to follow, budget limits
7. Failure to meet performance standards

Supervisors should discuss these performance problems with their employees. By working together in this way, solutions can be developed for increasing productivity in the records system.

METHODS OF CONTROLLING PAPERWORK

From your study of records management up to this time, one point should stand out—all work in the office centers around records, most of which are paper. Even though automation experts discuss the coming of the "paperless" office, what is actually found is an increasing number of automated records systems in which paper records play a very important role. The main point then is that *records control systems must be based on methods of controlling paperwork*, the subject of this section.

At this point, it is important to review the causes of paperwork problems as well as to consider suggestions for solving such problems. (Both topics are discussed in Chapter 2.) With this information in mind, you can better understand why the records manager selects "first things first"—forms, correspondence, and copymaking—in order to control paper records in the office. These areas of paperwork are chosen for discussion since they represent the largest volume and most expensive systems in the records management program.

Controlling Business Forms

The **business form** is a paper record used to record and transmit information in a standardized manner within or among departments or between organizations. The records manager's responsibilities include controlling business forms since forms are the most common type of record.

Two types of data are found on a form: (1) **constant data** (such as the word "date" and the phrase "Pay to the order of" on a bank check) that is fixed on the form and thus does not require rewriting each time by the person filling in the form; and (2) **variable data** that changes each time the form is filled in. An example of variable data is the filled-in date and the name of the person to whom the sum of money stipulated on the check is to be paid.

Objectives of Forms Control Programs.   In large firms thousands of forms are used for recording information. To ensure that these forms are efficiently and economically used, company-wide programs to control all phases of forms work are developed. The goals of such programs are:

1. To determine the number of forms in each department and how each form is used.
2. To eliminate as many forms as possible. This goal includes locating forms that overlap or duplicate each other which often makes it possible to combine forms or copies of forms.
3. To standardize form size and paper quality, which results in lower form costs.
4. To ensure efficient design of forms in all types of systems. Note that forms designed in manual as well as automated systems must be designed by people who apply sound design principles as discussed in the following paragraphs.
5. To establish efficient, economical procedures for printing, storing, and distributing forms to users. These procedures should include charging costs to those departments using the forms.
6. To set up both numeric and functional controls over forms (discussed later in this chapter in the section "Analyzing the Use of Forms").

Kinds of Forms.   Forms come in many sizes and colors and are used for many purposes. *Single-copy forms,* such as telephone message blanks, are used within one department for its own needs. *Multiple-copy forms,* such as a four-copy purchase order set, are used to transmit information outside the "creating" department. *Specialty forms* (such as the continuous forms with punched holes in their left and right margins for use in computer printers) require special equipment for their use. **Unit-set forms** are preassembled packages of multiple-copy forms perforated for easy removal of each copy. Some unit sets have inexpensive one-time-use carbon paper while others have more expensive carbonless paper.

Design of Forms.   Efficiency in the design of forms is just as important as the efficient design of a house, an office building, or an automobile. In each case, well-tested design rules must be applied. In the case of a business form, the designer must understand how the form is to be used; the items to be filled in on the form along with their sequence; the size, color, and paper weight of the form; and the amount of space for each item of "fill-in." This information is obtained from a thorough study of the purpose and use of the form in the office system.

The main objectives in forms design are to make the form *easy to fill in, easy to read and understand, and easy to store and retrieve.* These objectives can be met by applying the following design rules:

Rule 1. Study the intended purpose of a proposed form or the real purpose of an existing form, and design the form with the user in mind.

Application: Use heavy card stock for forms to be used out of doors or subject to large-volume indoor use.

Use a different color for each department receiving its own copy of the form.

Rule 2. Keep the design simple, eliminating unnecessary or unlawful information and ruled lines.

Application: Do not ask for "age" *and* "date of birth."

Place instructions for filling in the form at the top and instructions for distributing the form at the bottom.

Do not request information that may be personal or used for illegal purposes (religion, ethnic background, etc.).

Do not use horizontal ruled lines when the fill-in is to be typewritten.

Rule 3. For proper identification, give each form a name (that designates its function) and a number (that designates its sequence within the creating department). Date of form's printing may also be included in the number.

Application: Name: Sales Invoice (*not* Sales Invoice *Form*)
Number: S-15 (11/85)—to identify the 15th form in the Sales Department last printed 11/85.

Rule 4. Use standard paper stock size and standard typefaces.

Application: Use card/paper sizes that may be cut from standard 17″ × 22″ mill-size stock without waste. Such standard sizes as 5″ × 3″, 6″ × 4″, 8″ × 5″, 8-1/2″ × 11″ are economical to buy, use, and store.

Rule 5. Arrange items on the form in the same order in which data will be filled in or extracted from the form.

Application: Information on purchase orders is usually copied directly from approved purchase requisitions. In designing purchase order forms, maintain the same order of data as the order shown on the purchase requisition form.

Rule 6. Preprint constant data to keep fill-in (variable data) to a minimum and allow fill-in to stand out clearly.

Application: Brown or blue printing on a form to be filled in with black typewriting will cause the fill-in to be emphasized. Also, print size smaller than elite spacing on a standard typewriter will draw the reader's attention to the fill-in, making the form easier to read.

Rule 7. Adapt spacing to the method of fill-in (handwritten or machine) allowing sufficient space.

Application: For handwriting, use 1/4″ spacing.
                    For typewriting, allow double spacing (2/6″).
                    For handwriting or typewriting, use double spacing.

On typewritten forms only:

Know the *pitch* (12 spaces to the horizontal inch on elite typewriters; 10 spaces for pica).

Know the *throw* (6 line spaces to vertical inch on standard typewriters).

Be sure that each line begins directly below the previous line to reduce number of tabular stops.

Omit ruled horizontal lines to increase legibility and permit single-spaced typing.

On computer forms only:

Maximum space for each item of data on forms is built into the program for running the computer system; form must be designed to fit these specifications. See Figure 15-7A for examples of data-entry form appearing on terminal screen and form used to output information on a computer printer.

Rule 8. Use the box design for filling in variable data, if possible; and do not require writing if a check mark can be used.

Application: Poor design: Married?   <u>yes</u>   Sex?   <u>male</u>

Good design: Marital Status   Sex

☐ Single   ☑ Married   ☐ Female

☐ Widowed   ☐ Divorced   ☑ Male

Rule 9. Locate filing or routing information properly to speed retrieval of the form.

Application: For visible files, place filing or routing information on the bottom of the form. For vertical files storing purchase order forms, locate file number in upper right corner.

Most of these rules are applied in the example shown in Figure 15-6. In Figure 15-6A, an inefficient forms design violates most of the design rules just discussed, while Figure 15-6B shows how the design rules have been effectively applied. Note that the circled numbers appearing in both figures refer to corresponding design rules discussed in this section. The redesigned form is much easier to fill in and read, as well as much easier to store in and retrieve from a standard records storage cabinet.

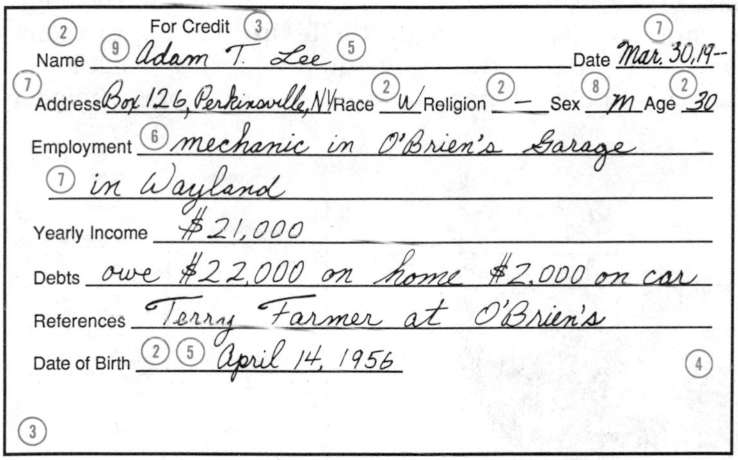
For Credit (3)
(2) Name (9) Adam T. Lee (5) Date (7) Mar. 30, 19--
(7) Address Box 126, Perkinsville, NY Race (2) W Religion (2) — Sex (8) M Age (2) 30
Employment (6) mechanic in O'Brien's Garage
(7) in Wayland
Yearly Income $21,000
Debts owe $22,000 on home $2,000 on car
References Terry Farmer at O'Brien's
Date of Birth (2) (5) April 14, 1956 (4)
(3)

A. Old Form Violating the Design Rules

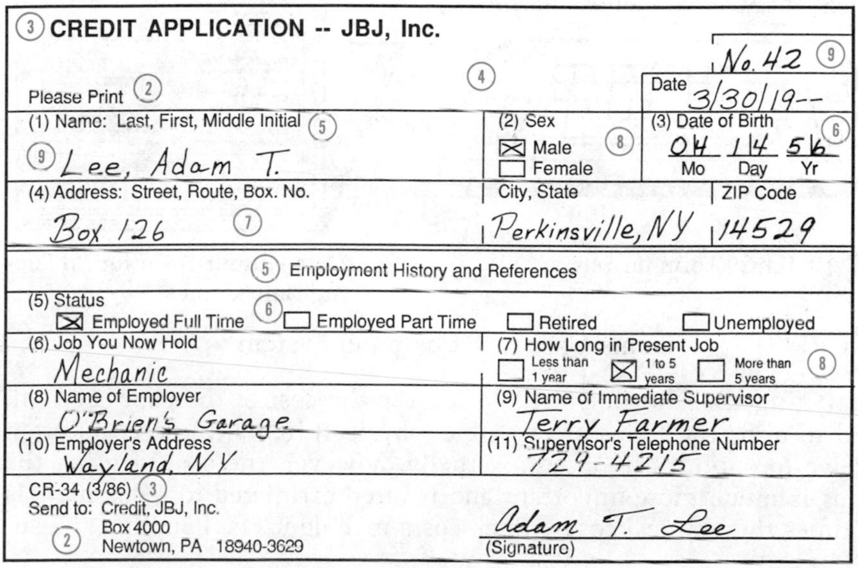
(3) CREDIT APPLICATION -- JBJ, Inc.
No. 42 (9)
Please Print (2) (4)
Date 3/30/19--
(1) Name: Last, First, Middle Initial (5) (9) Lee, Adam T.
(2) Sex ☒ Male ☐ Female (8)
(3) Date of Birth 04 14 56 (6) Mo Day Yr
(4) Address: Street, Route, Box. No. Box 126 (7)
City, State Perkinsville, NY
ZIP Code 14529
(5) Employment History and References
(5) Status ☒ Employed Full Time (6) ☐ Employed Part Time ☐ Retired ☐ Unemployed
(6) Job You Now Hold Mechanic
(7) How Long in Present Job ☐ Less than 1 year ☒ 1 to 5 years ☐ More than 5 years (8)
(8) Name of Employer O'Brien's Garage
(9) Name of Immediate Supervisor Terry Farmer
(10) Employer's Address Wayland, NY
(11) Supervisor's Telephone Number 729-4215
CR-34 (3/86) (3)
Send to: Credit, JBJ, Inc.
Box 4000
(2) Newtown, PA 18940-3629
Adam T. Lee
(Signature)

B. New Form Applying the Design Rules

FIGURE 15-6 — Comparison of Two Credit Application Forms

Although most forms are designed by hand, more and more computers are being programmed to design and use forms. For example, with a computer program, the computer can draw the design of a form, shown in Figure 15-7A, on a terminal display screen. With the blank form appearing on the screen, the operator can fill in (keyboard) information, check its accuracy, make corrections, and give a command to the computer to print out a hard copy (See Figure 15-7B). In addition, the computer is widely used in forms control to keep an inventory of blank forms being stored and also to order forms that have reached a preset reorder point.

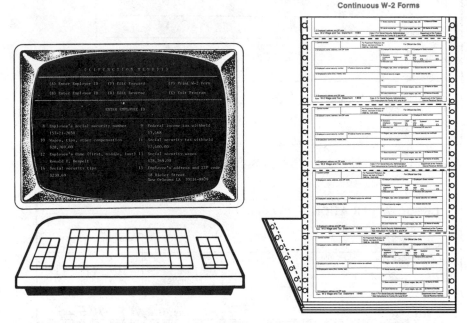

A. Data-Entry Form on Screen

B. Data-Output Form for Producing Hard Copies

FIGURE 15-7 — Forms Used in a Computer System

Analyzing the Use of Forms.   Because the cost of the paper and ink used to print the forms are tangible (physical) items, these costs often receive top priority in offices. Actually, however, the cost of *using* the forms is much more important and is often estimated to be as high as *40* times the physical costs.[5] Such costs include users' handling and su-

---

[5]Max T. Traub, "Efficient Business Forms for Managing Information," *The Office* (January, 1983), p. 159.

pervisory costs, and costs of acquiring, storing, retrieving, and distributing the form. Each of these costs is mainly the cost of various types of labor.

Since labor costs involved in processing or using the form comprise the largest portion of forms costs, this is obviously the area in which the greatest savings can be found. An example of such savings is furnished by a corporation that combined into one form four sets of forms previously written separately as a mailing label, an invoice, an acknowledgment of an order, and a production record. Hundreds of dollars in processing time were saved each year, even though the one newly designed form set cost more than the four individual forms. The new set also required a slight change in office procedures but permitted a reduction of three workers on the office staff.

Controlling Correspondence

Correspondence represents an important portion of office records, second only in volume to business forms. Usually *correspondence* refers to two types of records—*letters* that are written to persons outside the organization and *memorandums* or *interoffice memos* that convey written messages between departments within the firm. The total system of producing correspondence includes composing the message (dictating or handwriting), transcribing, and transmitting or mailing the correspondence.

Since labor costs of dictating and transcribing correspondence comprise a major portion of correspondence costs, the cost of producing letters can be expected to steadily increase as inflationary conditions, including higher salaries, continue. To illustrate this steady trend, the Dartnell Corporation of Chicago provides annual reports of business-letter costs showing that the cost of producing a letter, dictated face to face in 1960 was $1.83. By 1970 this cost had risen to $3.05; and due to continuous inflation, to $8.52 in 1985.[6] A recent Dartnell Report shows this cost breakdown:

Cost Factor	Average Cost	Percentage of Total Cost
Salary and time of dictator	$2.32	27.23%
Salary and time of secretary taking dictation and transcribing letter	2.40	28.17
Nonproductive labor (waiting time, interruptions, etc.)	.68	7.98

[6]Dartnell Target Survey, 1985. Dartnell Institute of Business Research, Chicago, IL.

Cost Factor	Average Cost	Percentage of Total Cost
Fixed costs (rent, taxes, overhead, fringe benefits, etc.)	2.46	28.87
Materials cost (stationery, envelopes, ribbons)	.26	3.05
Mailing costs (postage, gathering, sealing, stamping, sorting)	.40	4.70
Total Costs....................	$8.52	100.00%

In this breakdown, labor costs play the major part as the first three cost factors represent over 60 percent of total cost alone. However, when the same letter is dictated to a machine, thus reducing the amount of labor time, the total cost is reduced to $6.22.[7] Additional labor time and fringe benefits are partially "hidden" in the costs of mailing and sorting.

Reducing Correspondence Costs in the Manual System.   The cost breakdown outlined above refers to an average letter, typically 185 to 190 words in length and dictated to a secretary. However, there are many other ways of composing and producing letters, each of which will affect the cost of letter production. With such a wide variety of alternatives, it is important to find the most economical methods of producing correspondence such as the six effective methods outlined below:

1. Reduce writing time by using fewer handwritten letters, more form letters, greater use of dictating machines, greater use of telephones and informal replies that are handwritten in the margin of a letter received and returned to the sender, and more use of routing slips.
2. Reduce typing time by using electronic typewriters; by using simple letter styles (the Administrative Management Society states that its simplified-style letter saves 10.7 percent of typing time on a 96-word letter); using window envelopes which eliminate addressing, editing and proofreading, and retyping; and eliminating retyping of letters requiring corrections by making neatly typed or handwritten insertions.
3. Reduce rough drafting and reviewing time for all routine correspondence by devoting more care to preparing the original copy to be typed.
4. Reduce delivery time by keeping accurate address lists, including the 9-digit ZIP Code, having routine letters composed by administrative assistants or executive secretaries rather than by their supervisors, and having efficient messenger routes for delivery of mail within and outside the firm.

_____

[7]Ibid.

5. Reduce reading time by ensuring that letters are clearly written (to write or call the author asking for clarification means delay and extra costs).
6. Reduce storage time by limiting the number of copies of correspondence prepared and later thrown away. Costs are also reduced by eliminating file copies of routine correspondence, transmittal letters, and information-only copies that are seldom required. One study of stored correspondence over a six-month period showed that over 30 percent of incoming correspondence was so routine that it could have been thrown away after it was answered.

Reducing Correspondence Costs in the Word Processing System.   Many of the automatic features of word processing equipment save valuable time for the office staff. Word processing machines perform automatic centering, decimal alignment, and indentation. New software permits the detection and correction of spelling errors. Another efficient feature permits the substitution of one word for another throughout the entire stored message.

Word processing systems offer many advantages to cost-conscious managers. First, they save the time of dictators or word originators by storing form letters. Rather than compose a new letter each time, these managers can dictate a letter, revise it, store it, and then have it typed. These form letters can be produced quickly by citing key paragraph numbers stored on the magnetic media and listed by number on an index available to each employee. Most important, perhaps, is the cost savings that can result from word processing because it represents a more efficient way of employing labor. Word originators can concentrate on producing the ideas while the word processing machines can specialize in producing fast, accurate correspondence stored in memory.

Controlling Copying of Records

A leading reason why there are so many records in the office is that records are so easy to make. Easy-to-use copiers turn out records by the millions, many of which are unnecessary, adding to the ever-growing cost of running the office.

Reprographics is a term that describes the various elements in copymaking. A copy of a record is a duplicate of the original record that is made by one of two common reprographic processes—duplicating and copying. Another method of making copies is printing, a highly specialized, technical process that is not covered in this textbook.

The earliest form of copymaking—using carbon copies—is the least expensive method of duplication. Later methods of duplication using specialized machines include the **fluid** or **spirit process** (often referred to as "ditto"), the **stencil process** (often referred to as "mimeographing"), and the **offset process**. Each of these methods of duplicating requires that a master copy be prepared (usually on a typewriter, drawn by hand or by photographing an original image), which is placed on the duplicating machine in order to make a desired number of copies.

Copying machines, or copiers, on the other hand, reproduce records by a photographic process. This process, illustrated by the xerographic method of copying (now commonly referred to as "xerox") is often more expensive than duplicating processes; however, the ease and speed of office copier operations make the task of using carbon paper and preassembled carbon form sets less attractive.

Decisions on which type of reprographic process to use are based on the following needs of the user:

1. The number of copies needed
2. The need for various colors of copies
3. The ease of making master copies
4. The speed of copymaking required
5. Per-copy costs
6. The availability of trained operators

To control the costs of copymaking, records managers stress the need to be aware of one overriding point: *For every cost originated in the office, there should be an equal or greater benefit.* This means that records employees need to identify all costs of making records (personnel, equipment, supplies, space, and so on) already mentioned. In addition, there are many hidden costs, including the costs of ordering supplies and equipment, costs of shelving for storing records, mailing costs, and so on.

Many simple ideas have been developed to control copymaking costs. Examples include selecting the most suitable—and least expensive— method for the copymaking job to be done; standardizing equipment, methods and supplies so as to eliminate an unnecessary variety of machine models, which adds to maintenance costs; regularly computing per-copy cost; and charging all copymaking costs to the department involved. Tighter controls over copiers include securing the approval of a supervisor prior to making copies and installing copiers that require the use of a key to activate the machine. Such a machine may also record the job number, the number of copies made, and a reference for charging the copy costs to the using department.

CONTROLLING RECORDS IN THE SMALL OFFICE

To some students of records management it may appear that most of the emphasis in records management programs is on the large office. In many cases this emphasis is to be expected, for such programs were developed by large organizations, including the government, where the specialization required to operate such programs was available.

As you complete your introductory study of records management, it should be emphasized again—it was emphasized earlier in Chapter 2, pages 49–51, in the section "Managing Records in the Small Office,"— that the same principles of management apply to all sizes and types of offices. The number of small business firms in the United States totals 10.5 million, or 95 percent of all private businesses in the country.[8] If we assume that each of these small businesses has one or more offices, then the size of the office group whose records need to be controlled is an important responsibility of records management as a profession.

A person working in a small office has always been a "jack of all trades," a situation that is likely to continue. With little or no specialization possible, however, the small office can still be operated efficiently if many of the large office controls discussed in this book are adapted to suit its specific needs.

Basically, control in the small office starts with the manager who must have a sound understanding of good management practices, of which control is an integral part. Such a manager will apply the principles of records management and systems thinking discussed in Chapters 1 and 2, and choose one of the employees, who by temperament, experience, and interest seems well suited to some "specialization" in the records area.

Such an employee can function as a part-time records manager and ensure control over the office records by following these guidelines:

1. Building in the minds of all other office workers a basic understanding of the role of information and the part that records play in providing that information.
2. Understanding good records management practices that include:
   a. Setting up an efficient records system, deciding who has access to

---

[8] For an interesting, comprehensive review of the importance of filing and records management for the small office, see Ann Hennick, "Filing and Records Management for the Small Business: An Overview," *ARMA Records Management Quarterly* (July, 1983), pp. 14-18, 20-22, 24.

records and who does not, and training other office workers in good storage and retrieval techniques.

b. Designing, approving, and ordering all forms. Copies of such forms and all other records, along with other records control information, should be centrally located in a notebook that will function as an office manual.

c. Standardizing the format of all letters, memorandums, and reports and providing instructions to all personnel for composing and producing letters.

3. Using technology, especially the computer and word processing systems, to the fullest. The microcomputer has proved to be a powerful and inexpensive tool with great value to the small office in regard to the creation, storage, and retrieval of records.

Further assistance in controlling records in the small office is available from representatives of forms and office equipment manufacturers, usually at little or no cost. The resourceful small-office manager can also benefit from working with fellow members of professional organizations, such as the Association of Records Managers and Administrators, Inc., and by reading its publications. With this great wealth of information available, records problems can be kept under control. An effective records system should result.

IMPORTANT TERMS AND CONCEPTS

accuracy ratio	quality standard
activity ratio	quantity standard
business form	records management manual
constant data	reprographics
control	standard
efficiency ratio	stencil process
fluid (spirit) process	turnaround time
offset process	unit-set forms
periodic audit	variable data

REVIEW AND DISCUSSION

1. What is the purpose of control in a records system? Cite two examples of records management control and lack of control in your personal and business lives. (Objs. 1 and 2)

2. What is an audit? How does an audit serve as a control tool in a records management program? (Obj. 3)

3. Identify the main types of content in a records management manual. How does a manual help a records manager to control records? (Obj. 3)

4. What are two basic types of standards used to control a records system? Give two common examples of each type of standard and describe how it "controls" records work. (Obj. 4)

5. List five work standards that have been developed for controlling records storage and retrieval. How would you, as a records manager, use these standards to bring about control over records? (Obj. 5)

6. What part does time (minutes or hours of work) play in measuring the effectiveness of storage and retrieval systems? (Obj. 5)

7. Of what value are the two efficiency ratios (activity and accuracy)? How is each ratio computed? (Obj. 6)

8. What are the major costs involved in paperwork systems? How does each cost compare with the other costs in terms of its proportionate share of total costs? (Obj. 7)

9. How are paperwork systems costs controlled? (Obj. 7)

10. Why is forms control a necessary part of a records management program? What specific purposes does such a control program have? (Obj. 8)

11. Why is forms design so important in achieving control in a records system? How have computers affected forms design? (Obj. 9)

12. What are the principal costs involved in producing correspondence? What methods are available for reducing such costs? (Obj. 10)

13. How do the duplicating and copying processes differ as methods of reproducing records? What suggestions do you have for holding copymaking costs in line? (Obj. 11)

14. "Even though a small office does not have the specialization needed to bring about strong control over its records, control can still be

maintained." Comment on this statement by a well-known records analyst. (Obj. 12)

DECISION-MAKING OPPORTUNITIES (DMO)

DMO 15-1: Evaluating a Small-Office Records System

As assistant office manager in a small insurance office, you have noticed an increasing number of problems in your records system. Over the past month you have carefully observed the records operations, noting especially the following typical conditions:

1. Each of the three typists uses a different style of letter when correspondence is typed.
2. Resorting an alphabetized customer card file of 500 cards into numeric order by ZIP Code required five hours of clerical time.
3. Over a one-week period, 20 of the last 75 records requested could not be quickly found or were not found at all.
4. Two of the 25 four-drawer file cabinets have not been "consulted" for retrieval purposes for the past two weeks.
5. Each of the six office employees designs his or her own forms and orders them from outside firms on an individual basis.
6. Each employee has free access to the office copier at all times.

Analyze the problem areas cited. What broad management principles seem to be violated? What specific control problems do you see? What can be done in this small office to eliminate, or at least improve on, these conditions? (Obj. 12)

DMO 15-2: Designing a New Receipt Form

As a part-time employee of your city's recreation department, you have been asked to design a new form that will serve as a record of all moneys received by the recreation center. The office manager tells you the form will be filled in by hand and should include the following information: (1) name, (2) date, (3) address, (4) telephone number, (5) group using the center's facilities, (6) revenue code—a three-digit number to be filled in by the accounting office, (7) amount paid to the center, (8) receptionist's initials, (9) receipt number, and (10) amount of refund, if applicable.

Applying the forms design rules presented in this chapter, design a form that meets the needs of the center staff. Be prepared to defend your design as directed by your instructor. (Objs. 3, 5, 6, 8, 9, and 11)

Glossary

accession book — A book of numbered lines (used with the numeric filing method) showing the next number available for assignment.

accuracy ratio — A measure of the ability of records personnel to find requested records.

active records — Records that are used three or more times in a month and stored in very accessible equipment in the office.

activity ratio — A measure of the frequency of records use.

advanced CAR — The micrographic system in which a computer maintains the index to microrecords and stores and retrieves them online.

alphabetic card file — An alphabetically arranged card file containing names of correspondents and any subjects used in a numeric file with their assigned numbers indicated.

alphabetic storage method — A method by which records are stored in A-to-Z order.

alphanumeric storage method — A method by which subjects bear assigned numbers indicating main divisions and subdivisions, but the subjects are arranged alphabetically.

aperture card — A standard data processing card with a precut opening for mounting microfilm.

archives — The final storage place for records to be kept permanently.

as-written order — All names are considered in the order written.

basic CAR — A micrographic system in which a computer stores microrecords in regular storage equipment according to the location code index stored in the computer; includes online indexing with offline retrieval.

bellows (expansion) folder — A folder that is made with creases along its bottom and sides so that it can expand like an accordion.

block codes — A form of skip numbering used to classify records by categories.

business form — A paper record used to record and transmit information in a standardized manner within or among departments or between organizations.

card record — A small piece of card stock used for storing information, with the durability to withstand large-volume use.

card tickler file — A series of 12 monthly and 31 daily card guides arranged chronologically for reminder purposes.

card visible equipment — Filing cabinets for cards that allow one edge of each card to be visible at all times.

carrier folder — A temporary bright-colored folder containing records that have been borrowed from the original folder.

cartridges — Packages for rolls of microfilm.

charge-out — A term used to signify that a record has been taken by a borrower who is held responsible for its return to storage.

chronologic storage method — A method of storing records by calendar date.

closed (double) notation — A label showing the beginning and end of the alphabetic section contained in the storage unit.

coding — The physical act of marking a record to indicate by what name, number, or subject it is to be stored.

color accenting — A method by which different colors are used for the supplies in the storage system—one color for guides, various colors for folders, another color for OUT indicators.

color coding — A method by which different colors are used to divide the alphabetic sections in the storage system.

computer-assisted retrieval (CAR) — The process that merges the computer with microrecord storage by use of an index to provide great speed in storing and retrieving data.

computer input microfilm (CIM) — A computer input method by which plain language data on microrecords are translated into computer-language code for storage on magnetic tape.

computer output microfilm (COM) — Computer output stored on magnetic tape that is directly converted to microimages on roll film or microfiche.

computer printout files — Cabinets on wheels or open-shelf files designed to hold binders containing computer printouts.

consecutive numbering method — Numeric storage by sequential numbers.

constant data — Data on a form that do not require rewriting each time the form is filled in.

control — That function of a system that regulates the behavior of all other phases of the system in line with desired outcomes or goals.

cross-reference — An aid to finding a record stored by a filing segment other than the one selected for coding.

cycle — A set of sequential steps that are repeated on a regular basis.

data — Raw material (information) used in an office.

data processing — The transformation of numbers into meaningful information by a computer.

data processing system — The inputs, processes, outputs, and controls requiring people, equipment, procedures, space, supplies, and information to operate the system.

database — A centrally located library of files or records that are accessible to all authorized personnel.

decimal arrangement — A storage arrangement made up of ten main divisions.

densitometer — A device that determines the density of microfilm.

density — A numeric measure of the contrast between the dark and light areas of film.

direct access — A method of retrieving records that requires no index.

direct reference — Reference to a record made by going directly to the file—no intermediate step is necessary.

diskettes — Small disks (often called floppies) on which microcomputers store information.

drawer cabinet — A file cabinet with drawers within which records rest, usually on their longest edge.

duplex numeric arrangement — A storage arrangement consisting of subjects to which numbers have been assigned: Subject subdivisions are set off by the assigned number plus a second number that shows the place of each one in the classification.

efficiency ratio — A guideline for measuring several types of records operations that furnishes information for controlling the records system.

electronic circuits — Channels for moving data as electric impulses into, within, and out of the computer.

electronic funds transfer system (EFTS) — The application of computer terminals to conducting banking transactions from points outside the bank.

electronic mail — The transmittal of records over telephone lines or via satellite networks to all parts of the world.

elements — Systems resources that work together to achieve the systems goal.

encryption systems — An information-protection method that scrambles data at the sending point to protect the confidentiality of records in all phases of the system.

encyclopedic arrangement — Main subjects arranged in alphabetic order with their subdivisions also arranged alphabetically.

enlarger-printer — A microform printer that will make copies larger than 18″ × 24″.

environment — Conditions surrounding the system that influence the system's operations.

external record — A record created for use outside the firm.

Family Educational Rights and Privacy Act of 1974 — (The Buckley Amendment) An act (1) granting individuals access to personal information collected and maintained by federal agencies for nonroutine use, plus the right to be informed if others have gained access to this information and, (2) preventing the gaining of such access by others.

Federal Records Management Amendments of 1976 — Amendments that updated the Federal Records Act of 1950 by defining records management procedures for reducing paperwork in federal agencies.

feedback — That phase of the system in which the output of the system is measured against the expected output standards.

file — A collection of related records.

file integrity — The assurance that none of a set of documents microfilmed in sequence is lost or misfiled.

file security — An information-protection procedure in which irreplaceable records are duplicated as assurance against loss or destruction of the original documents.

filing segment — The name, subject, number, or geographic location by which a record is to be stored.

fine sorting — Arranging records in exact sequence prior to final storage.

flash card — A kind of tab or guide with identifying information placed in front of a batch of records to be microfilmed.

flash indexing — A method of coding roll film by assigning some type of identification to each microimage.

fluid (spirit) process — A method of making copies (often referred to as "ditto") using specialized fluid.

folder tickler file — A set of 12 monthly and 31 daily folders used for follow-up purposes.

folders — Containers used to hold stored records in an orderly manner.

follower block (compressor) — A device placed behind guides and folders in a file drawer to allow contraction or expansion of the drawer contents.

follow-up — Checking on the return of borrowed records within a reasonable (or specified) time.

forms analyst — One who studies systems for creating, processing, and distributing forms throughout a firm with the objective of making the forms more efficient and less expensive.

forms manager — A staff member who works directly with individual departments to develop forms control programs.

forms supervisor — The person who coordinates the work of the forms analysts and works directly with all departments in providing technical advice on forms.

Freedom of Information Act of 1966 with Amendments — An act giving citizens the right of access to information collected and maintained by government agencies.

general folder — A folder containing records for which an individual folder or folders is not warranted.

geographic storage method — An alphabetic records storage system arranged by the locations or addresses of the correspondents, followed by their names.

group coding — A form of skip numbering whereby subjects are assigned specific round numbers; subdivisions of subjects are assigned numbers within their main subject number.

guides — Rigid dividers in the storage equipment that guide the eye to the location of the folder being sought.

hard copy — Records that are printed on paper.

hinged pocket books — Books containing cards filed in hanging pockets.

image-count indexing — An indexing method by which a rectangular mark (blip) is placed below or above each microimage at the time of filming and counted when retrieving a specific microimage.

inactive records — Records that are referred to less than 15 times a year and stored in a less expensive storage area outside the office.

index records — Records containing information used for reference only.

indexing (classifying) — Mentally determining the name, subject, or number by which a specific record is to be stored. The process of assigning one specific type of identification or address to each storage location in the computer's record files.

indexing order — The order in which units in the filing segment are considered when filing.

indirect storage method — A storage method in which additional steps are needed for storage and retrieval.

individual folders — Folders containing records that have accumulated for one designated individual or firm.

information — The raw material (data) that is processed or changed in some way.

information cycle — The following series of sequential steps: collecting, retaining, storing, retrieving, transporting, using, returning, and destroying.

information processing (IP) — Data and word processing making up the operation of automated records systems.

input-output approach — A method by which each of the elements in a system as well as each of the phases of the system are examined to solve information-related problems.

inputs — The starting phase of the systems cycle.

inspecting — Checking a record for its readiness to be filed.

internal memory — That area of the computer that stores the instructions and the data to be processed.

internal record — A record (whether created inside or outside the organization) containing information needed to operate the organization.

jacket — A plastic or card-stock carrier with single or multiple horizontal channels into which strips of microfilm are inserted.

key — The code by which records have been filed in sequential order on magnetic tape.

kilo — A computer memory capacity of 1,024 storage locations.

labels (captions) — Information placed on the tabs of guides and folders and on storage equipment to identify their contents.

lap reader — A portable microform reader often used in vehicles or on outdoor job sites.

lateral file cabinets — Cabinets with drawers that open from the long side and look like a chest of drawers or a set of bookshelves with doors.

lettered guide plan — A geographic storage method using guides with alphabetic letters printed on them as main divisions.

library — A collection of files.

local area network (LAN) — A system of telephone lines used for the transmittal of computerized records of business operations within a firm.

location name guide plan — A geographic storage method using location names as main divisions.

magnetic media — Various types of records (tapes, disks, diskettes) on which the computer may electronically store its output.

magnetic tape cassettes — Small containers in which magnetic tape is stored.

magnification ratio — The relationship between the size of the microrecord and the enlarged record on a microfilm reader screen.

mainframe — A large computer that controls many terminals and storage devices.

management by exception — A practice by which managers are responsible for developing and controlling policy problems of special importance to management rather than for giving constant attention to routine activities.

master index — A typed alphabetic listing or a card file of all subjects used as categories for storage.

mechanized records system — A records system that uses some form of machinery in the storage and retrieval of records.

menu — An index of all files on a disk, displayed on the terminal screen.

microcomputer — The smallest computer in size and capability—also known as the personal computer.

microfiche — A series of microrecords arranged in rows and columns.

microfilm — A roll of film containing a series of pictures or images much like a movie film.

microfilm cassette — A container with two film reels—the feed reel and the take-up reel — for handling a continuous roll of microfilm.

microforms — Microrecords packaged in a variety of convenient and easily usable forms (roll film, microfiche, jackets, and aperture cards).

micrographics — The full range of services for creating, storing, retrieving, using, and protecting microrecords.

micrographics services supervisor — A technical level person who works with all departments in microfilming applications and in the training of micrographics technicians.

micrographics technician — A person who operates various types of cameras, film processors, and microfilm preparation equipment.

microrecords — Miniature or very small images of records.

microrecords system — A combination of key elements that constitutes an efficient unit for using microform records.

middle digit storage — A numeric storage method in which the middle numbers are considered first.

minicomputer — A computer smaller than a mainframe that provides less processing and operating power.

mobile aisle system — Electrically powered mobile shelving that can be moved to create an aisle between any two shelf units.

mobile shelving — Records storage shelves that move on tracks attached to the floor.

motorized/power-driven card records equipment — Card records storage equipment with shallow trays on movable shelves that operate similarly to a Ferris wheel.

motorized rotary storage — A motorized file unit rotating horizontally around a central hub.

multiple-closed notation — A label showing not only the alphabetic range of the material contained in the storage unit but also the most frequent combinations within that range.

name index — A special listing of correspondents' names used with subject filing.

nonconsecutive numbering — A system of numbers that either has no logical sequence or that has logical sequence but from which blocks of numbers have been omitted.

notching — A coding method by which a small piece is cut out of the top or bottom edge of a microform.

numeric storage method — A storage method wherein records are assigned numbers and then stored in one of various numeric sequences.

offline — Not directly connected to the computer.

offline storage — Storage equipment that is not directly connected to the computer.

offset process — A type of copy making using a specialized machine, special ink, and a master copy that offsets print to a drum before reprinting a hard copy.

on-call (wanted) card — A written request for a record that is out of the file.

one-period transfer method — A method of transferring records at the end of one period of time, usually once or twice a year.

online — A direct connection to the computer.

online storage — Storage equipment directly connected to the computer.

open (single) notation — A label showing only the beginning letter of the alphabetic section contained in the storage unit.

optical data disk — An automated storage device with a special heat-sensitive coating on which a laser beam stores and retrieves information.

optical-character recognition (OCR) equipment — A device that scans printed documents and enters the information into a computer without keyboarding on a terminal.

organizing — The process of bringing together all resources—personnel, available funds, equipment—to form a workable unit so as to achieve the objectives of the records management program.

OUT folders — Special folders that replace complete folders that have been removed from storage.

OUT guides — Special guides that replace records that have been removed from storage.

OUT sheets — Forms that are inserted in place of records removed from storage.

outputs — The goals of the system that result when raw material or data are changed into a finished product.

Paperwork Reduction Act of 1980 — An act calling for federal agencies to consider information as an organizational resource to be managed and included in their budgets, and likewise seeking to minimize the federal paperwork burden on individuals, small businesses, and state and local governments.

period folders — Folders with dates showing on their tabs.

periodic audit — A regular examination of the records management program to determine how well the program is functioning and to find ways of improving its performance.

periodic transfer method — A method of transferring records at the end of a stated period, usually one year, to inactive storage.

permanent cross-reference — A guide that is put in place of an individual folder to direct the filer to the correct storage place.

perpetual transfer method — A method of transferring records continuously from active to semiactive or inactive storage areas whenever they are no longer needed for reference.

phonetic storage — A storage method using sound and spelling combined with a numeric code.

planetary camera — A camera with a flat surface on which drawings, books, and other large documents are placed for microfilming.

planning — The basic managerial function which determines the course of action that will enable the program to meet its stated goals.

pocket folder — A folder with more expansion along its bottom edge than that of an ordinary folder.

pocket holders — Trays containing hanging pockets or slots into which cards are inserted.

portable reader — A microfilm reader usually weighing less than ten pounds that can be transported easily.

position — The location of the tab on the edge of a guide or folder.

posted record/secondary record — A card record containing information that is continually updated in some way.

posting visible equipment — A form of card equipment within which filed cards can be exposed and information entered on them with no need to remove them from the file.

primary guides — The main guides that precede all other materials in a given section of a file.

processes — The second phase of the systems cycle—human- and machine-based methods for changing inputs into the desired product or service.

Project ELF — An ARMA project to eliminate legal-size files that resulted in the adoption of standard letter-size paper by the Judicial Conference of the United States.

quality standard — A measure of the quality of the work or the worker's performance.

quantity standard — A measure that involves counting the number of resources used in factory and office operations and comparing them with standards of resource use.

random access — The method of searching for information stored on disk records in nonsequential order.

reader — A device that displays the enlarged microimage on a screen so that the record can be read.

reader-printers — Microfilm readers that also print hard copies.

reading file — A chronologic arrangement of copies of all daily correspondence.

record — Written or oral evidence of related fields of information that have been collected for use by people or machines.

record cycle — The life span of a record from creation to final disposition.

recorder — A special tape-to-film photographic device used with computer output microfilm.

records analyst — A person responsible for the creation, maintenance, and disposition of active and inactive records.

records center supervisor — A staff member who is responsible for people-related tasks in the records center.

records clerk — A person primarily responsible for daily records processing (file clerk, general clerk, files operator, filer).

records disposition — The final phase of the records cycle usually meaning the destruction of records that have no further value.

records inventory — A survey used to find the types and volume of records on file as well as their location and frequency of use.

records maintenance — The set of service activities needed to operate the main storage and retrieval systems; includes records retention, preservation, and protection activities.

records management — The process of planning, organizing, staffing, directing, and controlling all the steps involved in the life of a record.

records management manual — An official handbook of approved policies and procedures for operating the records management program.

records manager — The top position in the records management program; the one responsible for developing policies and setting objectives for the firm's records systems.

records retention schedule — A listing of each general records category with the length of time each category is to be stored.

records system — A set of related elements required to produce all phases of the records function (or records area) in the organization; includes inputs, processes, outputs, feedback, and controls.

records transfer — The physical movement of active records from the office to semiactive or inactive storage areas.

reduction ratio — The size of the microimage as compared to the original document.

reference documents — A collection of records containing information needed to carry on the operations of an organization over extended periods of time.

reference visible equipment — Panels, trays, or frames containing holders with strips of information inserted into them and used for reference only.

relative index — A typed list or card file of all main subjects and subject subdivisions and all likely variations of each.

release mark — A mark placed on a record showing that the record is ready for storage.

reports manager — A staff member who works directly with individual departments to develop reports control programs.

reports supervisors — The persons who coordinate the work of the reports analysts and work directly with all departments in providing technical advice on reports.

reprographics — The set of activities involved in copymaking.

requisition — A written request for a record or for information from a record.

resolution — Sharpness of lines or fine detail on a microimage.

rotary camera — A camera with a rotating belt for moving large numbers of documents through it so that each can be photographed rapidly.

rotary file cabinets — Wheel file equipment composed of cabinets that rotate horizontally around a hub.

rough sorting — Arranging records according to sections but in random order within the sections.

scanning devices — Input devices also called optical-character recognition equipment.

score marks — Indented or raised lines or marks along the bottom edge of a folder to show where it can be refolded to allow for expansion.

semiactive records — Records that are used about twice a month and stored in the less accessible cabinets or shelves in the active storage area in the office.

shelf files — Shelves arranged horizontally for storing records.

signals — Special add-on or clip-on movable markers attached to the top of cards or folders to show different types of information.

simple numeric-subject arrangement — The assignment of a number in random order to each subject, with storage within each subject category by sequential order.

single-tier rotary equipment — A panel containing strips of information attached to a revolving center post.

skip numbering — A numeric method retaining alphabetic sequence by assigning numbers spaced far apart to allow for file expansion between them.

sorter — A holding mechanism for records awaiting storage which serves to separate them into alphabetic or numeric categories.

sorting — The act of arranging records in a predetermined sequence, according to the storage method used, as an aid to final filing.

Soundex — A numeric system that groups together names that are pronounced similarly but that would be widely separated if they were arranged in alphabetic order.

span of control — The number of persons reporting to one person.

special (auxiliary) guides — Guides that lead the eye to a specific place in the file.

special folders — Folders that follow special or auxiliary guides in an alphabetic arrangement.

special records — Records of unconventional size, shape, or weight commonly used in business and professional offices.

special subject index — A special list showing the recurrence of subjects over a period of time, such as in books of minutes of meetings.

stand-alone word processing equipment — Electronic typewriters and word processors that operate as independent units.

standard — A measure or yardstick by which the performance of a system is rated.

stationary reader — A microform reader that is not portable.

stencil process — A method of making copies using a specialized machine—often referred to as a mimeograph—that forces ink through openings cut in a pattern, usually by a typewriter.

step and repeat camera — A camera used to film microimages onto microfiche.

storage — The actual placement of records into a folder, on a section of a magnetic disk, or on a shelf according to a plan.

storage method — A systematic way of storing records according to an alphabetic, subject, numeric, geographic, or chronologic arrangement.

storage procedures — A series of steps for the orderly arrangement of records as required by a specific storage method.

storing — The actual placement of records in containers.

straight dictionary arrangement — A method of storing subject folders in correct A to Z order.

straight order — The order in which the units of a filing segment are considered for filing, also called the "as-written order."

subject records storage method — A method of storing records by subject matter or by topic.

suspension (hanging) folder — A folder that hangs from parallel bars on the sides of the storage equipment.

system — A set of related elements that are combined to achieve a planned goal.

systems approach — A new way of thinking about problem solving—seeing the whole picture.

tab — The portion of a folder that extends above the regular height or beyond the regular width of a folder.

technology — The machines (hardware) and software (procedures and programs) needed to operate mechanized and automated records systems.

telecommunication system — A computer linked to a telephone system whereby records can be sent to all parts of the world.

terminal digit storage — A numeric storage method in which groups of numbers are read from right to left.

text-editing — The capacity of computers or related equipment to record, add, delete, change, correct, or relocate copy at electronic speeds.

tickler file — A tool used to check on borrowed records or as a reminder that a specific action must be taken on a specific date.

transaction documents — Paper records of day-to-day operations of an organization.

turnaround time — The amount of time required to find and deliver a record to the requester after the request for the record has been made.

two-period transfer method — Transfer of records from active to semiactive to inactive storage.

unit — The name, initial, or other word used in determining the correct order of records.

unitized microforms — A microfilming format that allows a single unit or file of records to be stored on one microform.

unit record — A record on which one main item or unit of information is stored.

unit-set forms — Preassembled packages of multiple-copy forms perforated for easy removal of each copy.

updatable microfiche — Microfiche on which records may be added, deleted, or overprinted.

updatable microfiche camera — The camera used to add images to microfiche or to alter existing images by overprinting.

variable data — Data that change each time a form is filled in.

vertical card file — A card file containing cards filed on edge or in an upright position.

vertical file cabinets — Conventional storage cabinets in one- to five-drawer sizes.

visible card file — A card file containing cards stored horizontally with one edge of each card overlapping the next so that one margin of each card is visible.

voice mail — One-way voice messages stored in the computer and reconverted to the caller's voice when messages are delivered by means of the computer.

voice-recognition system — The capability of the computer to recognize the human voice as input to the computer.

voice-response system — A computer-based technology that answers questions asked from data stored in the system in a voice response.

vouchers — Documents used in business to confirm that a business transaction has occurred.

wheel file — A rotary file for cards on which the records are attached directly to the equipment frame.

word processing system — A combination of people, equipment, and procedures for transforming words originated by a person into a final product and forwarding it to a user.

word processing (WP) — The manipulation of words into desired form by automated devices.

work simplification approach — A logical combination of common sense, intuition, and good judgment applied to solving problems.

Index

A